T0294817

BUSINESS DRIVEN PMO SETUP

Practical Insights, Techniques, and Case Examples for Ensuring Success

MARK PRICE PERRY

Copyright ©2009 by Mark Price Perry

ISBN-13: 978-1-60427-013-6

Printed and bound in the U.S.A. Printed on acid-free paper
10 9 8 7 6 5 4 3

Library of Congress Cataloging-in-Publication Data

Business driven PMO setup : practical insights, techniques and case examples for ensuring success / edited by Mark Price Perry.
    p. cm.
    Includes index.
    ISBN 978-1-60427-013-6 (hbk. : alk. paper) 1. Project management. I. Perry, Mark Price,
1959-
    HD69.P75B88 2009
    658.4'04--dc22
                                                                              2009008104

Phone: (954) 727-9333
Fax: (561) 892-0700
Web: www.jrosspub.com

Dedication

This book is dedicated to my two sons.

Matthew Ruud Perry, U.S. Navy

and

Paul Leonard Perry, U.S. Army

Contents

Acknowledgments

Master Kong, given the name Confucius by a Western missionary, which has no meaning to the Chinese, believed that there were three ways to acquire wisdom: reflection, which is the noblest; imitation, which is the easiest; and experience, which is the bitterest. This book seeks to provide a reflective wisdom on the subject of project management offices (PMOs) garnered and tempered by a collection of perspectives, reasoned approaches, and years of practical application and experience.

Friends and business associates often have a greater ongoing impact on our lives than they could have ever imagined at the time. From a high school friend that you might never see again to a business associate whose acquaintance you have just made, it is our relationships and interactions with others that give us insights and wisdom. More times than not, it is these shared experiences that, like seedlings, grow and mature into fruit-bearing trees.

I would like to acknowledge the many customers and partners of IBM and BOT International that have seeded my professional perspectives, curiosities, and passions for nearly three decades. I would like to especially thank the many PMOs of all shapes and sizes that I have had the opportunity to work with and learn from over the last ten years. For all that I have received from you, I am very grateful.

To the contributors that participated in this book, I respect your wisdom and honor your friendship. In order of appearance in this book, I would like to thank you personally for your contribution.

To John Maloch, CEO of Catalyst Project Solutions, Singapore, I commend your leadership in providing project management and PMO services throughout the region. As fellow expats with a passion for project management and fondness for the region, I look forward to your continued success.

To Gary Popovich, Process Engineer, Royal Caribbean Cruise Lines, your business acumen, technical skills, and process-oriented approach to project management sets an example for any PMO. Project portfolio management (PPM) applications, collaboration platforms, and enterprise project management best practices are complex and you have a bridle on them.

To Terry Doerscher, Chief Process Architect, Planview, your visionary thinking about the modern PMO guides us to new frontiers and possibilities. I truly appreciate your wisdom, perspectives, and friendship.

To Richard Eichen, PMO Practice Manager and entrepreneur, I can't think of anyone better to effectively institutionalize project management best practices throughout a large, complex organization. Scale and organizational complexity can challenge even the best of practitioners; where others come to the table with problems, you bring solutions.

To Erhardt Zingg, PMO Manager of PartnerRe, Zurich, your deep technical skills and mastery of project management is impressive, but it is your ability to strike an organizational balance between structure and flexibility that is an uncommon valor. I appreciate the opportunity to have worked with and learned from you, your hospitality in Zurich, and your friendship.

To Michael Wood, Process Improvement Guru and CEO, The Natural Intelligence Group. Where do I start? You are a gifted individual and to say thank you is not enough. Where excellence and passion intersect, you find Michael Wood. I look forward to learning more from you and your continued friendship.

To Rakan Saraiji, VP of Project Management, SHUAA Capital, Dubai, UAE, you bring comfort to complexity and keep the focus on the needs of the business, not technology for technology's sake and not project management for project management's sake. I am thankful that my first trip to the region was to be with you and your team. I look forward to your continued success and our continued friendship.

To Osama Bakir, PMO expert and CEO, PMCT Quest, Oman, Saudi Arabia, for all that you have taught me about the unique challenges and opportunities for project management in the region, I am truly thankful. To have you as a business partner is a pleasure; to have you as a friend is far more.

To Brian Rabon, PMO Director, teacher, and entrepreneurial CEO, I am truly appreciative with the recent crossing of our paths. We share a common vision about the value and importance of effective project management. Thank you for sharing with me a bit of your wisdom.

To John Chrystal, former IBM executive, Yale University director, enterprise systems expert, and Brit, I can't think of anyone who understands and has met the worldwide challenges of business and technology more successfully than you have. The opportunity to work with and learn from you in Singapore, and then in London, and then again in New York is only bested by the opportunity to have become your friend.

To Jennifer Arndt, PMO Manager, American Chemical Society, you possess not only a compendium of technical skills and knowledge about organizational project management, but a wide and refreshing perspective of both the "Ivory Towers" and the "Team on the Ground." I look forward to our continued friendship and learning more from you.

To Michelle LaBrosse, international expert on accelerated learning, founder and CEO of Cheetah Learning, former officer in the United States Air Force, and Harley bike-rider, I can't think of a more capable person to perform any task or to achieve any goal. Your contributions to the project management community have been tremendous. From the first Cheetah Learning class I attended, which was the best learning experience I have ever had, to meeting you personally and to working with you and your team, I am very grateful. Thank you, my friend.

To Ben Lichtenwalner, enterprise technology servant-leader, you recognize the disturbing trend of increasingly narcissistic leadership among today's business leaders and you offer a practical alternative birthed in servant-leadership. I am so very appreciative that we have crossed paths; I only regret that we did not meet years ago. Thank you for your help and friendship.

To Tom Boyce, Program Manager, Nuclear Regulatory Agency, you possess the unique quality of brightening the room when entering. Your business management, technology, and project management skills are enviable, but it is your results-oriented, positive attitude that I admire most. I appreciate the time, wisdom, and friendship that you have shared with me.

To Steve Romero, IT Governance Evangelist at Computer Associates (CA), your contributions to IT Governance have been of value to the project management community. CA is wise to have an advocate like you; your customers and the information technology and project management communities at large have benefitted greatly. I thank you for your help on the book and appreciate your friendship.

To Jimmy Char, CEO, Skills Group, Bulgaria, it has been a pleasure to work with and learn from you. The many years of experience and insights in implementing project management offices and developing project management capabilities is evident in your perspectives and insights. I am very thankful for your contribution to this book and your friendship.

To Dave Larson, enterprise software expert, go-to-market strategist, and scratch handicap golfer, it has been a pleasure to have worked with and known you over the years. From our competitive golfing days in high school and college to our friendly matches of today, I cherish your friendship on and off the course.

To John Schlichter, Mark Scott, and Abdullah Tamimi, I truly appreciate your leadership, expertise, and insights in a very challenging project management domain, the Organizational Project Management Maturity Model (OPM3®) of the Project Management Institute. Your knowledge of the model and practical insights and implementation experiences are second to none.

To Cornelius Fichtner, PMO enthusiast, former PMI chapter president, and project management podcaster extraordinaire, your passion for project management and excellence in all that you do is a source of great, personal inspiration to me. For the wisdom and insights that you have given to me, I am grateful.

To Drew Gierman, my publisher at J. Ross Publishing, I can't thank you enough for the help that you have given me with this book. Your insights into project management office challenges and how to convey them and your editorial advice and support helped me achieve the intended results for this book.

In addition to the contributors to this book, I would like to thank my dear neighbors and golfing friends, Greg and Cindy Register, without whose companionship and time on the golf course, this book would have been finished much earlier.

In speaking of golf, an avocation that provides me a break from an unrelenting work schedule, it would be remiss of me not to acknowledge and thank Carolyn McKenzie Andrews, Director of Golf and head golf professional at Tuscawilla Country Club in Winter Springs, Florida. As an avid golfer, past my prime physically, and seeking a game commiserate with that of my youth, I am overjoyed that you have given me one.

And lastly to my loving wife, for your results-oriented, conditional affection based upon the achievement of nonnegotiable and overly stretched objectives, I must admit that I am thankful.

About the Author

Mark Price Perry
Founder, BOT International

In 1999, Mr. Perry founded BOT International, a boutique project management firm now celebrating its 10-year anniversary. As the head of operations Mr. Perry manages product marketing, research and development (R&D), technology integration, and foreign language enablement for Processes On Demand (POD), a productized offering for the project management office (PMO) setup.

Mr. Perry has been with BOT International since its inception and has led over twenty Japan/China market entry engagements and has implemented POD in more than one hundred PMOs in North America, Asia Pacific, Europe, and Latin America, including recognized brand named companies and organizations, such as Advo, American Chemical Society, Amtrak, Austin Energy, AZ-EM, Biovail, Black Entertainment Television, Black & Veatch, Boart Longyear, Cheniere Energy, Citizen's Gas and Coke, Enbridge, GAF Materials, Gallatin Steel, Group Health Inc, GW Bakeries, Hawaiian Airlines, Hub Distributing, ING Romania, Intuit Software, Kos Pharmaceuticals, KV Pharmaceuticals, La-Z-boy, Life Touch Portrait Studios, Meggitt Electronics, National Institutes of Health, Open Solutions Inc, Partner Re, PBS&J, Port of Houston, Precision

Drilling, Purdue University, Quiksilver, Royal Caribbean Cruise Lines, Santa Fe Natural Tobacco, SHUAA Capital, Siveco Romania, Stanley Works, Stiefel Labs, Texas Association of School Boards, Toyota Motor Corporation of Australia, United States Geological Society, and Yale University.

Largely as a result of years of experience in PMO setup work with companies and organizations and with talented project management practitioners of all disciplines, Mr. Perry is a subject matter expert in the practical application of project portfolio management (PPM) applications, collaboration platforms, and PMO content assets.

Mr. Perry is the host of the "The PMO Podcast," the leading podcast for PMOs of all shapes and sizes with over 150 PMO podcast episodes to date. Mr. Perry is the author of the Gantthead blog, "PMO Setup T3—Tips, Tools, and Techniques." He is the author of BOT International PMO "Tips of the Week," a column that has provided PMO and project management tips for seven years.

In addition to formal project managers and members of the PMO, Mr. Perry has helped tens of thousands of *informal* and *accidental* project managers apply the knowledge and techniques of the Project Management Body of Knowledge (PMBOK®) Guide.

Prior to BOT International, Mr. Perry had a 17-year career with IBM, including positions as the IBM AS/400 Division telecommunications industry manager based in New York, the IBM Asia Pacific AS/400 channels manager based in Tokyo, and the IBM Asia Pacific AS/400 general manager for Southeast Asia and South Asia based in Singapore. Following IBM, Mr. Perry was the vice president and managing director of Singapore-based Saville Systems Asia Pacific, a leading provider of billing and customer care solutions, and vice president of Hong Kong-based Entrust Greater China, a leading provider of identity management and digital security solutions.

Mr. Perry is from the United States and attended the American College in Paris in 1978/1979 and graduated Beta Gamma Sigma from Virginia Tech in 1981. Mr. Perry speaks English and is conversant in Japanese, German, French, and Spanish.

Seminars by the author on PMO Setup using this book, as well as other training and consulting programs on various PMO topics are available by contacting BOT International via the internet at *www.botinternational.com* or toll-free at 1-877-239-3430.

Contributors

Jennifer Arndt, PMP, PgMP, is the PMO manager at the American Chemical Society (ACS) in Washington, D.C. She began her career as a chemical engineer, but within a few years transitioned into information technology (IT). Jennifer has more than 10 years of IT experience, specializing in the project, program, and portfolio management areas, as well as operations and process management. Since 2001, Jennifer has been honing her skills at the American Chemical Society and has led organizational improvements in project and portfolio management, knowledge management (KM), enterprise architecture planning (EAP), and business process management (BPM). Jennifer holds PMP and PgMP certifications from the Project Management Institute (PMI) and volunteers with PMI as an item writer for the PgMP exam. She is an editor on the upcoming revision to the "Portfolio Management Standard". She is in the process of earning her MBA through the University of Baltimore/Towson University program and was featured as a subject matter expert in Joseph Phillip's book *IT Project Management: On Track From Start to Finish*.

Osama Bakir, PMP, is the president and chief executive officer (CEO) of the PMCTQuest, a Canadian-based project management consulting and training group, serving the Arabian Gulf countries. Mr. Bakir has more than twenty years experience in implementing best practices of project management while assuming senior positions in project management working for Claymore Consulting, Toronto, Canada; PROJACS Middle East, AT&T, and Lucent Technologies, in the United States; and Oman Telecom, Sultanate of Oman. As a subject matter expert Mr. Bakir worked for a large telecom company. He developed, setup, and deployed the project management office (PMO). Mr. Bakir contributed in the structure and design of project management processes and procedures, trained and coached project managers and engineers, established project management information systems (PMIS) using primavera products, managed and supported megaprojects from inspection, planning, and implementation to closure. Mr. Bakir is an experienced program management consultant, certified PMP, and highly accomplished IT professional with an extensive background in project management. Mr. Bakir skills and experience include supporting organizational strategic plans, goals, and objectives; business processes engineering; policies development; and the ability to liaison between technical and nontechnical managerial persons to achieve the overall organizational vision, goals, and objectives. Mr. Bakir holds a BSc. in civil engineering, MASc. in engineering transportation planning, University of Waterloo, Canada, and an MSc. in computer systems and IT management, University of Washington. Additionally Mr. Bakir is a certified professional engineering (CPE) in Ontario, Canada. Mr. Bakir resides in Toronto, Canada with his wife, Lina, and two daughters, Dana and Noor, and enjoys travelling, reading, tennis, squash, and volleyball.

Thomas (Tom) Boyce, PMP, is the deputy chief information officer (CIO) and director, Office of Information Systems, at the U.S. Nuclear Regulatory Commission (NRC). In this position he has oversight responsibilities of an IT program with a $60+ million/yr budget, and the agency's PMO. Tom began his career in private industry as a computer system engineer. Since joining the federal government in 1986 he has held a series of IT management positions in the federal government and has established PMOs in several different federal agencies. Immediately prior to joining the NRC Tom managed one of the largest grants management systems in the federal government for the Electronic Research Administration Program at the National Institutes of Health (NIH), which manages $30 billion a year in grant payments. From 2002 to 2005, he was the CIO for the Agency for Healthcare Research and Quality. Tom has written about practical applications of project management practices for trade journals and speaks frequently on IT governance and program management. Tom received his Bachelor of Science in information systems management from the University of Maryland, University College in College Park, Maryland and is a Senior Fellow of the Council for Excellence in Government.

Jimmy Char, PMP, is the CEO of SKILLS Group and the managing director of SKILLS LTD., Bulgaria. He began his career in 1977 in Lebanon as a project team leader and became development manager after he graduated as a computer science engineer from Ecole Supérieure d'Informatique, Paris, France. During more than thirty years working experience worldwide, he was leading, mentoring, and coaching professionally many local—client and partner teams—involved in the development and implementation of large scale systems integration projects, assuring successful projects delivery. Having extensive experience in program/portfolio and project management in many countries in Europe, Africa, and the Middle East (Lebanon, Cyprus, Jordan, Dubai and Abu Dhabi in the United Arab Emirates, Russia, Djibouti, Libya, Romania, and Bulgaria) mainly as a solution provider for Harbor Activities, customs, and tax collection systems, health insurance, ERP, banking, utilities, service management, and custom project-based consultancy services. Jimmy held critical positions in Bull Middle East Ltd. and was for a period of 10 years supporting all Bull subsidiaries in the Middle East. He then was assigned a mission from Bull SA, as systems integration manager in Bull Romania for 6 years in which he delivered many successful complex projects in the country. In

2004, he was assigned the mission to open a Bull affiliate in Bulgaria where for a period of three years he held the executive director position and managed to lead the teams in successful project delivery culture and profession. During this time he also lectured at several field seminars in Europe and the Middle East. Apart from his extensive experience and professionalism, he has a strong understanding of the cultural differences and managed to transfer them to the differentiators that helped the succeed in the projects and brought high-level client satisfaction. Jimmy has held the Project Management Institute (PMI) certification PMP® since July 2000 and was actively involved in PMI Romania Chapter as a member of the board and as the vice-president for training and education. He was also the founder and president of the PMI Lebanon Chapter and is currently in the process of chartering the PMI Bulgaria Chapter.

John Chrystal is the managing partner of Intrepid Diverse Services, a company he founded in 2002. He is currently consulting on project management and PMO disciplines in the health insurance industry. Mr. Chrystal also served as the senior director of Enterprise Systems at Yale University and to whom the PMO reported. Mr. Chrystal had a successful global career with IBM where he held several senior management positions, including IT infrastructure and operations executive for IBM's Direct Marketing Channel [Ibm.Com], National E-Finance Services executive for the Americas, portfolio risk management executive for IBM Global Services EMEA, telco and media services executive for IBM EMEA North, and director of independent software vendor (ISV) relations and services for IBM Asia Pacific. He has global experience as an IBM keynote speaker in these sectors and disciplines and his leadership and quality assurance responsibilities have encompassed the classical Systems Integration, Outsourcing, and Business Process Outsourcing delivery models. Mr. Chrystal conceived and established the 1990s IBM business model for ERP Solutions Delivery and, subsequently, from Singapore and Tokyo led the establishment of the IBM regional business units for system analysis and program (SAP) project implementations across Asia. In the cross industry sector space, Mr. Chrystal is deeply experienced in the business foundation, collaborative computing, communications/command/control and Internet/Intranet/Extranet/E-commerce domains. Mr. Chrystal is an enthusiastic leader and strong mentor of colleagues in the IT Industry. He was formally recruited, trained, and certified as an assessor for IBM's Management Assessment Program and he is Chairman Emeritus of the NYC Chapter of the Technology Executives Networking Group. He sits on the advisory board of IT companies in New York State and Massachusetts, and was recently elected to the BOT International Advisory Board where he currently focuses on service delivery issues. He is a full member of the British Institute of Professional Sales, and also served as a Director of Strathmore Management Real Estate in Richmond, England until his recent return to the United States. He was born and educated in the United Kingdom and currently holds dual citizenship in the United Kingdom and the United

States. Mr. Chrystal graduated from London University where he majored in the sciences, and the theory and practice of education. His formal business development training has been at the London School of Economics, Cornell University's Graduate School of Management, the University of Virginia's Darden Graduate School of Business Administration, and IBM's Business Management Institute.

Terry Doerscher has over twenty-five years of experience as practitioner and consultant in the areas of strategic portfolio, project, work and workforce management, and PMO development and process improvement. Terry's focus is on innovating world-class business management techniques to address the unique challenges facing today's technology-driven, knowledge worker environments. Mr. Doerscher is the primary author of *PlanView PRISMS® Business Processes and Best Practices*, a companion product to Planview Enterprise portfolio management software. He also drives the acclaimed "PMO 2.0" series of whitepapers, presentations, studies, leadership forums and his *Enterprise Navigator* blog—which are a recognized catalyst for redefining the role of the PMO in integrating business management functions for the enterprise. Terry offers a unique combination of engineering discipline, passion for process integration, a deep understanding of organizational dynamics and practical experience. Since joining Planview in 1999, he has become a trusted advisor to over a hundred organizations around the world and influential in positioning Planview as a leading innovator within the industry. An enthusiastic evangelist of cutting-edge management methods, Terry is a frequently cited expert in publications, while his dynamic and candid presentation style makes him a popular speaker at industry seminars and events. He received his formal engineering education in the elite U.S. Navy Nuclear Power Program. Terry has been a member of PMI since 1997, a member of the PMI PMO SIG, Information Technology Infrastructure Library (ITIL) v.3 Foundation certified, and a Certified Process Design Engineer (CPDE).

Richard Eichen has extensive hands-on experience in creating PMOs, leading Enterprise level initiatives and turning around distressed companies as well as initiatives and programs. For over a decade, Rich had led Return on Efficiency, LLC, a specialty firm in turnarounds, re-starts, and IT and operational improvement. He has extensive large scale systems integrator leadership experience. Rich has a deep and varied range of business experiences, ranging from leading a NASDAQ listed company's overseas unit during war, revolution, and hyperinflation to stabilizing a PE portfolio company so it could both cut the burn rate and attract a Series C round of investment. He led the revival of a global technology firm's professional services unit and led multiple new product development and rollout processes, enterprise level projects, and systems implementations. Having led companies and projects during severe economic downturns and instability, Rich is adept at structuring projects so they will achieve strategic business goals and align an entire project portfolio in line with recession-based realities. Rich's view of PMOs, project management, and business turnarounds is based on real-world operating considerations as well as visionary thinking.

Cornelius Fichtner, PMP, is a senior member of the BOT International management team and leads in the PMO practice. Mr Fichtner is a Swiss National and recognized expert in project management with over two decades of international business experience and over seventeen years of PMO and project management experience in such diverse industries as paper mills, management consulting, retail industry, internet software development, and the financial industry. He has worked in Switzerland, Germany, and the United States where he led projects on overhead value analysis, process improvement in logistics and electronic data interchange, development of a project management center of excellence, established internal project management methodologies for PMOs and rewrote overly complex corporate system development life cycle (SDLC) processes to be implemented in small divisions. He holds a degree as a certified organizational planner issued by the Swiss Government as well as the PMI's Project Management Professional Certification. In 2005, he founded ScopeCreep Project Management Consultants and is known around the world as the host of The Project Management Podcast™ and The Project Management PrepCast™. Mr. Fichtner speaks Swiss German, German, English, French, and he is conversant in Italian.

Michelle LaBrosse, PMP, is the founder of Cheetah Learning and author of *Cheetah Negotiations* and *Cheetah Project Management*. The Project Management Institute, www.pmi.org, selected Michelle as one of the 25 most influential women in project management in the world. She is a graduate of the Harvard Business School's Owner President Managers program and also holds engineering degrees from Syracuse University and the University of Dayton. As an Air Force officer in the mid-1980s, Michelle created the origins of the Cheetah Project Management Methodology. Cheetah Learning is a virtual company and has 100 employees, contractors, and licensees worldwide. To date, more than 30,000 people have become "Cheetahs" using Cheetah Learning's innovative project management and accelerated learning techniques. Michelle has been running her company virtually for the past 20 years. She has grown the company one hundred fold in the past twenty years, and she credits her success to using the Cheetah Project Management Method to better manage both people and technology. Michelle's mission is to help people achieve great results, FAST, by making it fast, easy, and fun to learn and practice project management. Her articles have appeared in over one hundred publications around the world. Her monthly column, the Know How Network, is carried by four hundred publications, and her monthly newsletter subscription list includes more than fifty thousand people. Michelle lives in Nevada with her family and likes to rejuvenate in Alaska where you'll often find her kayaking, golfing, or hiking.

Dave Larson is a senior member of the BOT International management team and leads the sales & marketing go-to-market (GTM) PMO practice. Prior to BOT International, Mr. Larson held business development, project management, and executive positions at U.S. Steel Corporation, JDEdwards, SSA, Manugistics, Entrust Technologies, and NuMoon Technologies, and has worked with leading corporations and technology firms. Mr. Larson has twenty-five years of experience in financial controls and information technology management. Mr. Larson began his career as a professional accountant with the U.S. Steel Corporation where he worked for eight years in accounting, business planning, and management. In his position as the controller, he led the U.S. Steel Corporation in business planning, financial management, audit and internal controls, and in the implementation and use of enterprise financial planning and management software. Due to his success at U.S. Steel, Mr. Larson was recruited by JDEdwards, a leading provider of enterprise financial planning and management software, to develop and execute GTM plans and territory sales strategies for the JDEdwards enterprise software products and service offerings. In addition to JDEdwards, in the last seventeen years Mr. Larson's skills and experiences have spanned from manufacturing industry systems, shop floor control, enterprise resource planning (ERP), supply chain, financial value chain, procurement, electronic invoice presentment and payment (EIPP), and enterprise IT and security infrastructure. As the leader of the BOT International sales and marketing GTM practice, Mr. Larson helps sales organizations bring products to market more effectively, improve lead generation, and increase sales conversions. Mr. Larson graduated from the Florida Atlantic University in 1979, with a BS degree in business administration and accounting and is a professional accountant, accomplished golfer, and avid snow skier.

Benjamin S. Lichtenwalner specializes in technology servant-leadership. Throughout his career Benjamin has implemented technology solutions and overseen the expansion of IT services at companies, including Inc. 500, Fortune 500 and Non-Profit Organizations. Across these organizations, Benjamin has held senior leadership roles, managed infrastructure, E-Commerce, web 2.0, ERP and social media teams. He also has extensive experience establishing project management teams and best practices. In addition to his for-profit work, Benjamin also consults with many nonprofit and philanthropic organizations. Mr. Lichtenwalner holds a BS in management science and information systems from the Smeal College of Business at the Pennsylvania State University and an MBA with a concentration in corporate entrepreneurship from Lehigh University. Regardless of his professional success, Mr. Lichtenwalner understands that it is not about him. He has been blessed with incredible teams and a wonderful network of colleagues, family, and friends who have been essential to his continued success. Beyond his professional interests, Benjamin enjoys spending time with his family, reading, and riding his motorcycle. Along with his wife and son, Benjamin currently spends most of his time between Westchester County, New York and Southwest Michigan.

John Maloch is the senior partner and managing director of Catalyst Project Solutions, a Singapore-based organization focused on the provision of project services across Asia, Australasia, and the Middle East. John possesses more than thirty years of IT-related experience, including significant experience in large systems computing and telecommunications. Previously John held senior management responsibility for the Asian division of Getronics, a large technology services firm, where he held full budget responsibility for an operation exceeding 1500 employees throughout the pan Asian region. John has extensive experience in project management and business development and has led a number of large, cross-border outsourcing engagements. John holds a business degree from the UHDC in Houston, Texas, and completed the Asia International Executive Program from Insead in Singapore.

Gary Popovich is the PMO process engineer for Royal Caribbean Cruise Lines, LTD in Miramar, Florida. Gary is a 1977 graduate of Fayette Technology Institute in Pennsylvania and has over thrity years of IT experience in various industries. Gary started his career in the banking industry as an application developer in 1977 but quickly moved into the role of project manager/analyst for a worldwide manufacturer of aluminum products where he was successful in implementing process improvement methods and structured analysis techniques. Gary received his Six Sigma certification in 2000 while working as a project manager for General Electric and received his MBA in Information Technology in 2006. Over the years Gary has been a contributing member of several user groups such as Mid Atlantic SUG and Virginia EDI users group. Gary's career has spanned four decades of IT and has been instrumental in implementing requirements gathering, systems analysis, and structured design techniques, improving the quality of products delivered to the end user community. Gary is passionate about using techniques such as Six Sigma DMAIC and DMADV along with DSSD for system design to deliver quality products and process improvements that are long-lasting. Gary also believes that PMO governance goes well beyond the IT organization and is critical to bridging the chasm between IT and the business.

Brian Rabon, MSEE, PMP is an IT professional with over twelve years of industry experience. Brian holds a BS degree in computer science from Auburn University and a MS degree in electrical engineering from the University of Alabama-Birmingham. Brian is director of project management at XSP, a financial software company specializing in corporate actions processing. In this role Brian leads the company's PMO. Brian is responsible for driving IT project management, governance, and standards while ensuring that XSP's business and technology goals are achieved. Brian is also the owner of Braintrust Software, LLC, a software engineering and project management consulting company and author of Braintrust's cutting-edge blog covering contemporary topics in the world of project management. Brian is passionate about teaching and is an adjunct instructor at the University of Alabama-Birmingham where he leads clients of the information engineering and management masters degree program on an exciting journey through the world of technical project management. When not in the classroom Brian can be found around town evangelizing the benefits of project management to the likes of the Internet Professionals Society of Alabama and the Birmingham chapter of the PMI. Brian is an avid author, writing for organizations, including the Alabama Information Technology Association, Birmingham Business Journal, and the University of Alabama-Birmingham. Brian gives back to the community by serving as the event chairman for TechMixer University, a free educational event hosted by TechBirmingham that attracts more than 400 attendees annually.

Steve Romero is the vice president, IT governance evangelist, at Computer Associates, Inc. In this capacity he acts as a strong advocate for the customer, speaking around the world to users, prospective clients, industry organizations, and IT luminaries to identify and communicate IT governance best practices. His mission is to help enterprises realize the full potential of their IT organizations for strategic and competitive advantage. Steve is an innovative, passionate IT professional with over 30 years experience working in nearly every area of IT. For the past fifteen years his career has focused on helping large enterprises transform their IT organizations from cost centers to strategic assets. Steve is a recognized expert in IT governance, IT program and project management, and BPM. He is a certified PMP, a certified Information Systems Security Professional, ITIL Foundation certified, a ertified process master, and a certified computer professional. Steve's extensive technical and IT leadership background started in the U.S. Navy before joining Pacific Bell where he founded numerous groundbreaking governance processes. He then joined Pacific Technology Consulting to lead their IT project management consulting practice. Steve worked at Charles Schwab and the California State Automobile Association as an IT director where he resumed leading the establishment of formal process management and IT governance processes. Steve is a member of the Information Systems Security Association (ISSA) and the PMI. He is a San Francisco Chapter committee member of the Information Systems Audit and Control Association (ISACA), and the President of the Information Technology Service Management Forum (ITSMF) San Francisco Local Interest Group.

Rakan Saraiji, PMP, is the vice president of project management at SHUAA Capital in Dubai, UAE. He has more than eighteen years of experience in the IT and project management fields. He has a computer science degree and started out working with a nonprofit organization in Washington, D.C., where he spent more than four years working as the director of computer services. He then focused on Oracle database administration and worked for four years with a major law firm in Washington, D.C., and for two years as an independent consultant contracting with various organizations. He then started focusing on project management and earned a graduate certificate in project management and got his PMP. He worked for six years with Computer Science Corporation in Washington, D.C., working on various projects. Recently he moved to Dubai, UAE where he works as director of strategy and product development for a real estate software company and then moved to SHUAA Capital to establish and manage their PMO office.

John Schlichter is CEO of OPM Experts an organization development and project management consultancy specializing in organizational project management (OPM) based in Atlanta, Georgia. A certified PMI OPM3 Product-Suite Assessor and PMI certified consultant, John is a management consultant specializing in strategy development and implementation. In 1998, John was asked by PMI, the global project management advocate, to lead the largest standards development initiative ever undertaken by PMI. His charter was to develop a standard in OPM for industry and government designed to help organizations assess and develop the capabilities necessary to execute their strategies through projects. In that capacity John led a team of 800 people across 35 countries for nearly 5 years. Later John was contracted by PMI to help develop the PMI OPM3 ProductSuite Assessor/Consultant Certifications beyond the PMI PMP certification. John is widely credited with being the world's foremost expert in the OPM3 standard's content and application and has implemented OPM3 in many name-brand companies, including ADP, Battelle Memorial Institute, Harris Corporation, Panasonic-Mobile, Popular Financial Holdings, Northrop Grumman, T-Mobile, among others. He was also a member of the PMI sStandards Committee, the PMI Standards MAG, and a co-founder of the PMI Metrics Special Interest Group. John began his career as an analyst for a management consulting firm, serving Fortune 100 companies. He worked in positions from PMO director to EVP Business Development, and has implemented PMO's for many companies, led large-scale organizational change, managed multimillion dollar technology projects, and mentored all levels of management. He is invited to speak to audiences about project management across the globe. John holds an MBA from the Goizueta Business School of Emory University in Atlanta, Georgia.

Abdullah Tamimi is assistant planning manager at the Saudi Arabian Ministry of Interior's National Information Center (NIC). The NIC entrusted him to setup and manage their PMO, which consists of eighty complex IT projects and fifteen programs. He plays a pivotal role in envisioning and planning IT strategy as well as IT systems management processes & procedures at his organization. Establishing portfolio management capability at the NIC is one of his recent achievements. He is involved with NIC's main committees, for example, IT, technical direction, planning and projects, training, and IT portfolio steering committees. For four years Abdullah was editor-in-chief for PMO's monthly e-newsletter. In acknowledgement for his outstanding service, he has been awarded special recognition certificates from the Minister of Interior and the director general of the National Information Center. He holds a master's degree in computer science from Florida Institute of Technology.

Michael Wood is an educator, author, and currently the president of The Natural Intelligence Group (www.tnigroup.com) a strategic planning and process improvement consultancy. He has published *The Helix Factor*—The Key to Streamlining Your Business Processes, which is a series of books on The Helix Methodology© (an integrated business process improvement (BPI) and SDLC method) specifically focused on business process improvement. Over his more than twenty years in the field, Michael has conducted numerous workshops and seminars on BPI, cross-functional facilitation, stakeholder value-driven business, business application design and project management. Michael is currently the subject matter expert on process improvement and IT Strategy for http://www.gantthead.com, the leading online community for project management in the world. Over 60 of his articles on BPI and other relevant topics can be found at gantthead.com. As an educator Michael served as an adjunct professor in Pepperdine University's MBA program and as an associate professor at California Lutheran University. He has conducted workshops and seminars on a national and international basis for organizations like Penton Learning Systems, the California Society of CPAs, and Ascend Media. His broad industry background and experience has positioned Michael as an expert in the field of BPI and reengineering.

Erhard Zingg, PMP, is a senior project manager at Partner Reinsurance Ltd. in Zurich, Switzerland. He started in the airline industry as an air freight specialist and joined the IT industry as a consultant and programmer in the mid-1980s. He has over eighteen years of experience as a project manager and consultant in finance, insurance, automotive, and manufacturing. Erhard worked for several companies, including AT&T, NCR, Cap Gemini Ernst & Young or Credit Suisse where he acquired a proven track record as project manager in many national and international projects. His experience includes mergers, start-ups, infrastructure, and software development projects as well as strategic and operational consulting in the domains of project portfolio management (PPM), project management, and the PMO. Erhard holds a PMP certification from the PMI and a master's certificate from George Washington University. He was a founder of the PMI Switzerland Chapter where he served as chapter president and VP members.

Preface

For decades project management offices (PMOs) have had difficulties getting started and staying on the right track. Some critics place the blame with the executive team for not taking on the right projects, taking on too many projects, allowing business areas to continue with their pet projects, and abdicating to the PMO the management and coordination of the resulting mess. As someone who has set up PMOs in over one hundred organizations around the world, I'd have to agree that there is some merit to this premise.

Other critics blame the PMO and project managers for having an overly inward mindset on theoretical PMO models, rigid and too detailed project management methodologies, and a focus on project documentation as the primary measure of progress as opposed to more contemporary agile views. In my humble opinion, blindly pursuing and adopting academic and theoretical approaches and models as opposed to practical business strategies tempered with good business, technology, and financial judgment is perhaps the greatest single reason for the poor track record of PMOs.

What many of the critics and pratitioners too often overlook is the simple fact that when PMOs are driven by the needs of the business for which they exist to serve, they succeed. When PMOs are driven by any other motivations or rationale, they fail. While the concept of being business driven might seem easy and intuitive to grasp and execute, regrettably for many PMOs it is not.

Most PMO books are written by academics, trainers, and consultants from the project management community. The knowledge they provide is important, but the majority of these books tend to be a reincantation of standards, bodies of knowledge, and theoretical models. For most organizations planning to set up or refresh a PMO, this limited set of theoretical cookie-cutter PMO models that for decades have failed all too often will continue to fail today and in the future. There are a few books that break away from this mold, including Craig Letavec's book *The Program Management Office*, which provides real-world guidance for a few general categories of PMOs. Additionally there is the *Advanced Portfolio Management and the PMO* by thought-leading gurus Gerald Kendall and Steven Rollins, which is targeted in application to the larger or more advanced PMO. However, there is still a lack of books applicable to PMOs of all shapes and sizes with a focus on practical business application, effective strategies, useful techniques, and streamlined approaches that can be applied and sustained.

This book seeks to fill this void in the current literature by shedding light on how to create and maintain a business driven PMO. It boldly challenges many of the so-called experts in the field by providing examples of the many errors in thinking and ineffective advice that has been espoused for far too long. To thrive, not just survive, PMOs of all shapes and sizes must have a relentless focus on the needs of the business and a wide focus on where project management and the PMO can meet those needs and deliver tangible results.

Business Driven PMO Setup was written by and with over 20 contributing authors from all over the world; veteran line executives who directly manage PMOs, have PMOs reporting to them, or are subject matter experts that service them. The thirteen chapters of this book present a set of topics, issues, and practical considerations that every PMO will face. Each chapter includes a variety of practical tips, tools and techniques, and concludes with a discussion, study questions, and one or more real-world case examples. Contributed by distinguished executives and project management experts, these case examples referred to as Executive Insights provide more than just concepts and knowledge of what PMOs are and do. They provide the judgment and wisdom required to achieve success.

Business Driven PMO Setup: Practical Insights, Techniques, and Case Examples for Ensuring Success offers executives, managers, and practitioners information that they must know to establish a successful business driven PMO that is tailored to the needs of their organization. In a few hours of reading you will gain insights from the author and contributors' combined 500+ years of PMO-related experience. For those seeking to set up or revitalize a PMO, this book will facilitate an effective dialogue in your organization and spare you countless and immeasurable time, cost, execution difficulties, and organizational frustration.

Mark Perry
Orlando, Florida

Introduction

Recently I was asked to comment on the views of a leading market analyst firm that suggested that in the coming years the anticipated investments made by project management offices (PMOs) would be on the decline as a result of the complete saturation of PMOs within today's leading organizations, the purchases in project management systems already made by these organizations, and the increasing trend of business units, outside of the purview of the PMO, preferring to do their own thing rather than use the tools and best practices of the formal PMO. In essence, according to these experts, the PMO as a business construct had proven itself successful and there was little else, aside from business as usual, for it to do. Victory declared.

I, and many others, beg to differ. The traditional views on PMOs and on project management in general are regrettably far too shortsighted. There is an *inside the box* thinking about PMOs within the formal project management community that too often is limited in application to the strategic level within an organization, the enterprise level within an organization, or somewhere within the IT department. Hence, there is a resulting blind spot within the formal thinking about PMOs that is oblivious to the ubiquitous nature of project management and the needs of all those who are involved in some kind of a project effort. These are not accidental project managers, these are not accidental projects, and the needs of these workplace practitioners in the form of tools, processes, and knowledge are not accidental needs. It is not only incorrect to view these things as accidental or to overlook them altogether, but it is bad business judgment and intellectually dimwitted. Not convinced? Consider the following real life examples.

Sally, an administrative assistant to the department head of a large nonprofit organization, was tasked with managing the annual conference of the organization. In managing the many tasks of her project leading up to the event, a few items were overlooked and poorly planned. She had ordered free-flow coffee each day of the event, rather than morning and afternoon coffee breaks. As a consequence the coffee bill for the event was $50,000 instead of $35,000.

Paul, the head of worldwide sales, travels incessantly taking an average of one roundtrip flight per week. Though the flight tickets for well over half of these trips could have been planned and purchased two weeks in advance, resulting in an average cost savings of $400 per ticket, Paul nearly always waited until the last minute. As a result Paul's annual travel expense, just for airfare, was $35,000 instead of $25,000.

Ralph, a course instructor for a large company, was asked to develop a new class. Not being a project manager, Ralph went to the IT department to see if they had anything that could help him project manage his effort to develop the new class. He was given a copy of Microsoft Project, no training and no instructions, and was told he could use it if he wanted to. After two months of trying to learn and use Microsoft Project, Ralph gave up. As a consequence, two months of salary, $15,000, was squandered.

Mark, a sales manager and golfing enthusiast, was selected to manage a customer appreciation golf tournament. The enjoyment had by all was heightened greatly as news spread that on the first hole of the shotgun start tournament, one of the customers, a beginner at golf no less, had made a hole-in-one, winning a brand new, fully loaded IBM laptop computer. Regrettably Mark, at that time, had no training or exposure to project risk management and did not think to get hole-in-one insurance. As a consequence the event ran $10,000 over budget; the cost of the IBM laptop.

Still not convinced? Take a $50m company that has 500 employees and do the math. Let's start conservatively and say that a mere 10 percent of these employees have at least one accidental project a year to manage and that on average a $10,000 improvement of some kind, like in the examples above, can be realized just by managing these projects slightly more effectively. Collectively this would result in a $500,000 benefit, in this case just cost savings. Let's assume further that the net profit margin of the company is 10 percent, a number quite high for most companies. At a 10 percent net profit margin, a $500,000 cost savings would be the revenue equivalent of $5,000,000. This is a significant amount and would represent, in this case, 10 percent of the company's revenues. As a CEO in today's stressed economy, what is likely to be more easily achieved; increasing revenue 10 percent or doing a slightly better job at project management?

Now do the math with a more aggressive, and perhaps more accurate, estimate of the number of employees in the company that have some kind of accidental project to manage at least once a year. Instead of only 10 percent of the employees having an accidental project to manage, let's say that every employee has one. If not every employee has one, that's in fact okay, as some employees will, no doubt, have more than one. Collectively these five hundred accidental projects with their $10,000 benefit would result in $5,000,000 of cost savings to the company. With 10 percent net profit margin, the revenue equivalent to the company would be $50m. Now what sounds easier to achieve; doubling the revenues of the company or doing a slightly better job at project management?

Still not motivated to step outside the box? Then consider this real-life example. Scott, an enterprise software sales representative, was managing a large sales opportunity. The sales effort, which I call a project, was a temporary endeavor spanning nine months, utilizing numerous resources, guided by a project plan, seeking to achieve a unique outcome; in this case a decision by the customer to purchase and implement a two million dollar security software solution for identity and access management. Scott's company, an $80M publicly traded firm with a market capitalization of $3B, was forecasting a $20M performance for the quarter which included Scott's $2M sale as it had been forecasted by management and committed to investors. Regrettably Scott's project schedule for the sales opportunity was not very thorough. He did not allow sufficient time for the customer legal team to review the software contract and services statement of work and, as a result, the sale, and thus revenue recognition for the firm, slipped into the next quarter. When Scott's firm posted the revenue results for the quarter which fell short of the company's prior forecast to investors by $2M, the amount of Scott's slipped sale, the stock price plummeted from $84 per share to $42 per share in just one day. Scott's project management skills or lack thereof cost the firm over $1.5B in market capitalization.

I would hope that you would agree that the value of all project management to an organization, not just the formal projects of the PMO, is tremendous. Who in the organization should accept the challenge to ensure that this value is realized? Amid the executive priorities and complex challenges that a CEO must lead, should advancing project management capabilities be added to that list? Surely someone else in the organization at a different level would be a better fit. Should a talented individual such as a senior project manager be called upon to lead such a charge? Probably not, as such an undertaking would likely be beyond the scope of an individual contributor's role within the organization.

If the organization has a PMO, then the logical person to call upon to improve the project management capabilities of the company, the entire company, is the PMO manager. This is a logical middle-office responsibility from which sensible goals and objectives can be set and reasoned plans and strategies can be executed. Surprisingly few PMO managers take on this challenge and the project management community, for the most part, doesn't even recognize it. Not long ago when speaking at a project management conference, I asked the attendees if they felt improving project management throughout the entire organization should be an objective or at least an initiative of some kind for the PMO. Five in an audience of fifty said yes. To some, 90 percent responding in the negative would be viewed as a rather poor reflection on the state and mindset of the project management community. To me this was an encouraging sign, because it was the first time in ten years of asking that I had a single favorable response, not to mention five of them.

Why is this response not higher? Who better than the PMO to know the value of project management to the organization, the entire organization, and act as its ombudsman? I hope that the Project Management MUSIC Model presented in chapter one of this book begins a serious examination and discussion within the project management community of the many dimensions of project management within today's businesses and how best to serve the needs and pursue the opportunities that those dimensions present. If the project management community wants to take a pass on this challenge or to defer it to human resources or to functional management, then just say so; it would be disappointing but not surprising.

To suggest that PMOs have reached a saturation point of any kind requires a good deal of suspension of disbelief. Certainly there are those that maintain that every project within a company, enterprise, or organization should be managed via a single methodology, contained within a single project portfolio management (PPM) system, and led by a trained, if not certified, project manager. This sounds good and even possible in theory; but as a matter of practical application it is flawed thinking fraught with many oversights, assumptions, and judgmental errors. No wonder the business units are doing their own thing; the traditional PMO isn't helping them.

There is tremendous benefit in advancing systemic, organizational capabilities in project management, but it is not easy and it is not a one-shoe-fits-all-sizes proposition. There is no shortage of tools from which to choose. Project management applications are providing more functionality than ever. Collaboration platforms and nonproject management tools are providing more and more features for managing projects and project-related work. Yet to be addressed are the capabilities and features of these systems and tools required to bring about the behavioral changes needed to advance and optimize organizational, as well as individual, project management capabilities and product of the project outcomes. Again I must add, this includes not just the projects of the strategic, enterprise, or IT PMO, but all of the project efforts both formal and accidental of the entire company. This is far more a matter of processes and knowledge tempered with practical application than it is the adoption of a theoretical PMO model and selection of a best-in-class vendor offering. In this area, only the tip of the iceberg is presently in view.

PMO victory declared? Nothing of significance left to be explored? No problems left to be solved or opportunities lying in wait? Perhaps, if one's perspective emanates from the confines of an extremely small box, the answer is yes. But for the rest of us the answer is no and we see the promise of the PMO, its unlimited potential, and ubiquitous application both deep and wide as a journey just begun. Toward that PMO trek of unending possibilities and opportunities, I hope this book provides practical insights and ideas worthy of your consideration.

Mark Perry
Orlando, Florida

At J. Ross Publishing we are committed to providing today's professional with practical, hands-on tools that enhance the learning experience and give readers an opportunity to apply what they have learned. That is why we offer free ancillary materials available for download on this book and all participating Web Added Value™ publications. These online resources may include interactive versions of material that appears in the book or supplemental templates, worksheets, models, plans, case studies, proposals, spreadsheets and assessment tools, among other things. Whenever you see the WAV™ symbol in any of our publications, it means bonus materials accompany the book and are available from the Web Added Value Download Resource Center at www.jrosspub.com.

Downloads available for **Business Driven PMO Setup: Practical Insights, Techniques, and Case Examples for Ensuring Success** include free practical tips covering 20 PMO knowledge areas, a solutions manual for professors of end-of-chapter questions, and a guide to 150 episodes of The PMO Podcast™.

1

Mission, Goals, and Objectives:
Business Driven
vs
Theory-Driven

For many project management offices (PMOs), Figure 1.1 paints an all too familiar picture. Rather than focusing on mission, goals, and objectives like the other business units in the company must do, many organizations skip this important step altogether during the initial setup of the PMO, delving right into strategies and tactics. Far too often the first order of business is to evaluate and select the best-fit PMO model from the many theoretical approaches that are presented and discussed at length within the project management community. Then, based upon the PMO model selected, there is a thorough discussion and debate about what the roles and responsibilities of the PMO should be. This, of course, produces a list of requirements and needs regarding people, process, and tools. Since setting up, managing, and improving a PMO is a journey and not a destination, the final step in the PMO setup process involves laying out a roadmap of phases, activities, and tasks for the PMO to implement in order to take root, evolve, and achieve higher levels of organizational project management maturity. To the project management practitioner and PMO enthusiast, this all makes sense and the value of the PMO to the company is intuitively understood. However, to the business executive with financial and budgetary responsibility to whom the PMO reports, as well as to those throughout the company for whom the PMO exists to serve, in the absence of defined and

Figure 1.1   PMO comics–PMO goals

measurable goals and objectives, the value of the PMO is far less understood. There is no better way for the PMO to snatch defeat from the jaws of victory than to go about its initial setup without a clear focus, collaborative development, and an unambiguous declaration of its mission, goals, and objectives.

One way to succeed is to avoid traditional thinking about the mission and goals of the PMO in terms of the PMO models, roles and responsibilities, and paths of maturity. A new multi-dimensional construct needs to be presented, not to replace the existing constructs and typical ways of thinking about PMOs, but to complement them. The addition provides a wider perspective that has practical applicability to PMOs of all shapes and sizes, enabling them to be business driven and goal-oriented. This need has stimulated an ongoing discussion among chief information officers (CIOs), PMO managers, project management thought leaders, and colleagues for years. What has collectively emerged from these numerous perspectives is that there are multiple dimensions—five altogether—of project management that exist within an organization. Therefore, these dimensions need to be understood so that an organization can establish the optimal and business driven mission, goals, and objectives for the PMO.

Much like the way in which dimensions are described in classical physics—a line describes one dimension, a plane describes two dimensions, a cube describes three dimensions—time is often referred to as the fourth dimension. The fifth dimension is occasionally referred to as probability, or all of the possibilities such as alternate realities; so too the dimensions of project management can be described this way. In a project management context, the five dimensions are: (1) *myopic*, (2) *ubiquitous*, (3) *size*, (4) *intervals of time*, and (5) *chance*. These five dimensions, known as The Project Management MUSIC Model, are shown in Figure 1.2 in an organizational project management context.

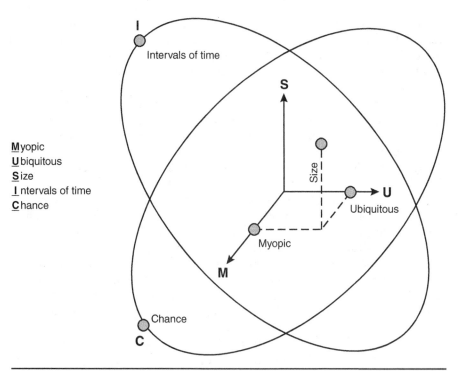

Figure 1.2 Project management MUSIC model

Myopic Dimension

There are numerous factors that contribute to a myopic view of project management. In many cases the manner in which these factors come about is similar to the chicken or the egg causality dilemma. For example, standards organizations, including the Project Management Institute (PMI®) with nearly 300,000 members in virtually every country, advocate the profession of project management. In the last four decades PMI has advanced project management from a skill set to a valued profession, and companies of all shapes and sizes have benefitted from more effective techniques and approaches to project management. Additionally, an unintended consequence of the formal establishment of project management as a profession has occurred. The informal development of "The Project Management Community" consists of not only the practitioners of project management but also the consultants, vendors, trainers, educators, and pundits, who, in one way or another, weigh-in, shape, and influence the profession. For the most part this is beneficial because these organizations have tremendous value to provide in terms of knowledge, products, and services. However, a noted problem of this community is the tendency to think from inside its own box in terms of project management—especially PMO models and strategy—with a perspective and bias that is often more theoretical than practical and in some cases self-serving. The result of this kind of thinking spans from the undoable to the outrageous.

Myopic project management, inside-the-box thinking, is not difficult to recognize. Thomas R. Block and J. Davidson Frame (1998, p. 7) suggest, "If an organization carries out projects only occasionally, there is no need to develop systematic capabilities to engage in project efforts. In this case, establishing a project office would be analogous to killing mosquitoes with a shotgun." For many organizations, especially smaller companies and information technology (IT) departments, nothing could be less advantageous. These firms do not regularly carry out projects; therefore, it is important that the project managers have a supporting project office or PMO from which they can access advice. These project managers are frequently *informal* or *accidental* project managers. That is, they have a full-time job and occasionally manage projects. These workplace professionals are not project managers by title and probably have not had, nor do they have the time to attend, project management training. Therefore, useful direction and helpful guidance with respect to project management tips, tools, and techniques is welcome. There are several options for setting up a PMO. A PMO doesn't have to be a large organization with a dedicated staff, a formal portfolio of programs and projects, a complex and expensive project portfolio management system, nor an overly detailed and bureaucratic methodology and set of procedures that is all too often the conventional thinking typically espoused by those in the project management community. To these people, project management is extremely one dimensional and it is only formally recognized at a few levels, such as within an IT department or a strategic project management organization. Even the PMO, as an organization model, is viewed to have only a limited number of constructs and styles. But even in the smallest of organizations, the decision to have a PMO or virtual PMO can offer tremendous benefits. Such a PMO or virtual PMO can be setup and managed as one of many duties by a manager or even a non-manager, such as a subject matter expert within any part or at any level of an organization. To categorically dismiss the value of a PMO or to suggest that only a large organization that routinely manages projects can benefit from establishing a PMO is an example of the myopic dimension of project management. At best this is a theoretical perspective limited to a narrow view and, at worst, it is bad business judgment that lends itself to missed opportunities for achieving business results through better and more effective approaches to managing projects.

In another example of the myopic dimension of project management, Kerzner (2001, p. 72) advises, "Develop an ongoing, all-employee project management curriculum such that the project management benefits can be sustained and improved upon for the long term." In his book about strategic planning for project management, Kerzner does not suggest that *some or even many* employees get trained in project management, rather he states that *all employees* should be trained in project management. For most organizations this is simply not possible. The financial impact to an organization as well as the time required to train every employee in any skill, not to mention project management, is simply prohibitive with the possible exception of mandatory equal opportunity, employee harassment, and organizational safety and health training programs. In theory, training all employees in project management might sound like a good idea to those who are strong and outspoken advocates of project management, but for most companies and organizations it is neither a practical nor a viable option.

The myopic dimension of project management is the conviction that certain techniques always be applied in the management of projects. Earned value management (EVM) is an example. EVM is a project management technique for measuring the accurate progress of a project, and its value for some projects is not debatable. However, there are those in the project management community that suggest if earned value management or some kind of earned value analysis is not used, then the project performance is not accurately reported nor is the project managed properly. While this might be technically correct in theory, the practical reality is that many projects, especially smaller, short-term projects often do not require overly complex approaches or techniques for project reporting and, in many cases, such techniques cannot be effectively applied. For example, minor projects, including the installation of a test server for an application, efforts to conduct competitive market research, or the development of management reports all serve as examples of projects that usually have a limited number of tasks and are quickly completed. For such projects, effective earned value management analysis might not be possible because the duration of the project is too brief. Additionally, such projects might be managed using simple tools like Microsoft Word or Excel or even a visual mapping tool like MindMapper. Hence, there is no ability to perform earned value analysis native to the tool used. Minor projects that do not require earned value management represent a large percent of the projects that most PMOs have in their active projects mix. Thus, there needs to be practical guidelines, as a matter of PMO policy, for when such techniques as earned value management can or should be used as opposed to the theoretical mindset that all projects, regardless of shape and size, should employ the technique.

Kendall and Rollins (2003, p. 316) state that the PMO should increase the number of projects (throughput) that it completes year-over-year and that the completion-of-projects percentage should be a key measurement of the PMO. Although their book, *Advanced Project Portfolio Management and the PMO*, is arguably one of the best books on the PMO, a personal favorite and one I recommend, the perspective of the book is often myopic and one-dimensional. Much of this can be attributed to the fact that the book is written for the advanced PMO audience. It provides well thought-out insights and strategies for achieving high levels of value and measurable return on investment for an organization's (strategic) PMO. For a number of PMOs, especially strategic PMOs within an enterprise, this book has an exciting, practical value. But for many PMOs it is a theoretical read. The idea that the number of projects completed by the PMO year-over-year should be a key measurement for the PMO sounds reasonable in theory; however, in an actual business setting it is not practical. For example, most PMOs, especially at the time of setup, seek to reduce the number of projects that the organization is attempting. Too many organizations take on more projects than they can successfully deliver and oftentimes there is significant duplication. The first order of business for most PMOs is to inventory the project mix, both formal and informal, and to cut away at the number of duplicate, failing, and unnecessary projects. In this case, a measurement that suggests a PMO is doing poorly unless it increases the year-over-year number of projects that it completes might not be the most beneficial. Additionally, many PMOs search for ways to perform fewer projects overall by selecting potentially effective projects and removing ineffective projects from the project pipeline and active projects portfolio. Moreover, most PMOs are not immune to the natural business cycles that companies face and if a firm is in a troubled industry or business segment—the current U. S. financial services mortgage sector—the needs of the business might dictate an immediate reduction in the number of projects of the PMO. Likewise, if a PMO is in a high-growth, high-profit industry or business segment—the U. S. energy industry presently—the needs of the business might dictate and provide for significant increases in project investment and the overall number of projects of the PMO. Project count as a PMO measurement could easily lead to gamesmanship in which large projects are broken down and reported as multiple smaller projects, or, worse, a situation in which a number of small projects are selected over a large project motivated by the desire to achieve the project count measurement for the PMO. Even with value and resource-based weightings and adjustments, for most PMOs the measurement of projects completed year-over-year is likely to be one of those approaches that sounds good in theory in terms of a key business measurement but in practice cannot be effectively applied or might not be sensible to attempt.

Should PMOs be measured? Absolutely. But the measurement should be based on the needs of the business for which the PMO exists to serve, not an inwardly focused, game-like, manufactured measurement.

Ubiquitous Dimension

Simply put, project management is ubiquitous. Projects exist in every corner of today's business organizations and project management is an activity undertaken by all kinds of business professionals and in organizations, divisions, and departments of all shapes and sizes. Examples of these projects are plentiful, including:

♦ A product manager's project to conduct a market segmentation analysis for a new offering
♦ A sales executive's project to hire and train a regional sales team
♦ A business development executive's project to recruit and enable an international business partner
♦ A customer service executive's project to design and perform a customer satisfaction survey
♦ A financial executive's project to perform due diligence for a potential acquisition
♦ A human resources executive's project to develop a performance planning, compensation, and evaluation program
♦ An administration manager's project to streamline the accounting process
♦ A manufacturing engineer's project to perform shop-floor maintenance
♦ A marketing staff person's project to manage the annual customer conference
♦ A sales operations manager's project to conduct strategic account reviews
♦ A trainer's project to improve or develop a new curriculum
♦ A security officer's project to test existing systems and policies

As illustrated in Figure 1.3, these ubiquitous projects are invisible to the formal PMO much like the part of the iceberg that is below the water is invisible to an ocean liner.

Regrettably, the project management community at large, and many PMOs, do not recognize such invisible projects as "real" projects. These ubiquitous projects rarely show up on the list of formal projects that the PMO is undertaking, nor should they. However, the PMO should be aware of the ubiquitous dimension of project management. Deliberate action and care should be undertaken to ensure that those in the organization who have projects to manage have the ability to access support and guidance. That support might be in the form of right-sized and intuitive project management processes, tips, tools, and techniques for the project efforts. Otherwise these business professionals can be left out of the project management club altogether thus denying them the project management goodies. In fact there are those that would argue that the collective estimated monetary value of these ubiquitous projects throughout an organization might be as substantial as both the formal project portfolio of the strategic PMO and the projects of the IT PMO. Therefore, business driven PMOs should have specific goals and objectives in their mission to meet these ubiquitous project management needs.

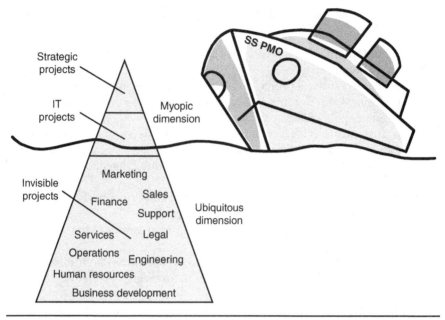

Figure 1.3   Project iceberg

Those who are passionate about the need for today's PMOs to recognize the ubiquitous dimension of project management usually have deeply rooted convictions based on past experiences in managing departmental projects or belonging to departmental project offices. In my case the first of many ubiquitous PMO and project management experiences occurred in 1982. I had just finished the eighteen-month IBM field marketing training program and was a rookie salesman in the Dallas branch office of the IBM Data Processing Division—known simply as DPD by customers and IBM employees. We were the mainframe guys. We sold, installed, and serviced the data center hardware and software that companies needed to run their business operations. The technology products of DPD included: large, water-cooled mainframes (CPUs); channel systems and control units; direct access storage devices (DASD); magnetic tape subsystems; mainframe terminals display devices; operating systems; databases; applications and application development tools; and a wide variety of industry-specific devices. In 1982 we had two mottos; "if it don't drink, it don't think" (a barb intended to discredit the new air-cooled mainframes coming from Japan), and "if God thought distributed computing was a good idea, then He would have put brains in our wrists" (another barb intended to dismiss the growing interest in mini-computers and the newly announced personal computer).

As a newly qualified marketing representative, I was waiting to be assigned to one of the six industry marketing units within the branch office. The entire management team was in an all day, closed-door meeting and, when they dispersed, my manager, Bill Paulk, came to my desk and told me that the branch manager, Doug Potter, wanted to see me. I went to Mr. Potter's office immediately and was ushered in by his personal secretary and told to have a seat and wait for Mr. Potter to return. After a few minutes Mr. Potter came in, motioned for me to keep my seat, and asked me what the most important thing I learned in the IBM training program was. As Mr. Potter was reclining back into his deluxe executive chair, I tried to think of what the correct answer could be and it quickly dawned on me that I really didn't understand the question. I replied that the most important thing that I learned was that there are no such things as problems, only opportunities. With that Mr. Potter grinned and told me that he had an "opportunity" for me.

He proceeded to explain a problem that IBM had. The 1982 IBM business model was primarily a rental business. A customer could not purchase an IBM mainframe, but rather rented it. If the customer wanted an IBM mainframe, he/she had to order early as there was typically a two-year backlog and waiting period for delivery. This model had served IBM well. Eighty percent of the next fiscal year's revenue was under contract and ensured. Furthermore, a two-year backlog of orders for new mainframe computers and associated equipment provided a complete and comfortable view of expected year-on-year revenue growth. In 1982, IBM was a cash cow with profit margins that were the envy of the industry. So what was the problem?

The market analysts, experts, and pundits in the information technology field saw a number of early warning signals indicating troubled waters ahead for IBM. For one, increasing competition from Japan was offering mainframe computers with significant price-performance improvements over the existing IBM mainframes as well as delivery schedules and customer availability measured in months rather than in years. Additionally, the anticipated growth rate in the consumption of information technology was increasing significantly and well beyond IBM's raw plant manufacturing capability. How could IBM meet the "new" and "unplanned" needs of its customers in this high-growth technology adoption life cycle if customers had to wait two years for a computer system? Furthermore, if information technology continued its rapid change and growth pace, how could IBM ensure that after the two years that their mainframe computer would still be a viable and compelling technology choice for the customer amidst ever-increasing competitors and alternatives. It couldn't. Additionally, another irritant to the analysts and IBM watchers was its rental business model. The market analysts wanted IBM to move to a customer purchase-oriented business model fueled by the introduction of new products with much shorter delivery times as opposed to that ongoing recurring rental revenue.

In response to the market conditions and the advice from the experts, IBM made a number of transformation decisions and adjustments to their business model and strategy, including the decision to move away from its equipment rental model to a purchase-only model. Wall Street immediately approved IBM's changes, announcements, and actions and it's stock price enjoyed substantial and sustained gains. To ensure that IBM's new financial strategy and goals would be achieved, specific measurements, in the form of quotas, were established for the purchase of new (PON) and the purchase of installed (POI) and currently rented equipment and machines; these quotas were passed down to all of the IBM branch managers and became the control measurement. This left the more than two hundred IBM DPD branch managers with a number of problems or, as I have learned to view it, *opportunities*. The opportunities included:

◆ How to inform customers about the new pricing structures and financial offerings?
◆ How to educate the field marketing teams in how to analyze and present to the customer the new purchase and leasing programs?
◆ How to prepare, analyze, and provide to their many customers the purchase of install (POI) quotes for the thousands of machines on rent?
◆ How to quickly learn the total cost of ownership analysis skills required for selling the new, more expensive IBM mainframes over lower initial cost alternatives, mainly Japanese and after-market used IBM mainframes?
◆ How to get their fair share of IBM's internal staff resources to help with all the work that needs to be done?

It was the belief of Doug Potter and his management team that the best way for the IBM Dallas branch office to address all of the required work was to form a "revenue" PMO, and I was the fortunate individual available and named to lead it. The mission of this revenue PMO was simple: to support the new IBM financial strategy through the identification and execution of revenue-enabling projects. The goals and objectives were also clear: $250,000,000 of revenue had to be attained in a prescribed mix of PON and POI equipment. As Figure 1.4 displays, the revenue PMO was placed low in the Dallas branch office organization and was far beyond the visibility of IBM's executive ranks.

The PMO was staffed with only one full-time-equivalent dedicated resource. All other resources were made available on a shared, as-needed basis. By the end of the year this low-level departmental PMO had performed over seventy-five revenue-enabling projects, ranging from customer events, executive fly ins, implementation of new tools and systems, internal training events, strategic account analysis workshops, and a wide variety of process improvement activities. In addition they established and provided control reporting regularly, showing year-to-date progress against the PMO revenue goals, status

Figure 1.4   IBM Dallas branch office revenue PMO

of projects underway, resource requirements, and critical issues. Most importantly, the PMO exceeded its $250,000,000 goal by 8 percent contributing a $20,000,000 surplus in revenue. As a result the Dallas branch office achieved the number one ranking in both total revenue and percent of revenue plan. The revenue PMO was recognized as a key driver of revenue performance and a key differentiator between the Dallas branch office and its many peers who had the same set of business conditions but did not arrive at the same strategic decision to establish a departmental PMO.

It is important to note that the focus of the visionary branch manager, who suggested the PMO and the management team that used and benefited from the PMO, had little to do with project management as a discipline or even a skill set. Rather, the focus was solely on achieving the branch office's revenue goals and objectives. Of course, schedules, activities, and tasks were reviewed and issues were discussed and resolved; however, the success of the PMO was measured not by how well we managed projects or how well we used and improved upon our tools and processes, but rather by the degree to which we met and, hopefully, exceeded the business objective for which the PMO was created. This is a common characteristic of ubiquitous project management and ubiquitous PMOs. Regardless of where they exist in the organization, the value of these PMOs lies in their relentless focus on achieving the business objective at hand. All other areas of capability, influences, and interests are secondary. In a large company the collective achievements of these ubiquitous PMOs are vast and make a significant contribution to the bottom line. In a small company, just one of these PMOs can make a tremendous difference and contribution to the goals of the company.

Regrettably, too often project management and PMOs as an organizational construct are confined to a role and location within the organization. For example, J. Kent Crawford (2002, p. 56) suggests that there are three levels of a PMO (see Figure 1.5):

◆ Level 1: The project control office reports to a functional area within IT.
◆ Level 2: The business unit project office is an IT PMO that reports to the head of IT.
◆ Level 3: The strategic project office is an enterprise project office that reports to the CEO.

This view of PMOs results in two behaviors. First, it limits the imagination and innovation for PMOs to the traditional inside-the-box view of project management and the PMO. The PMO is placed in the organization either as a strategic PMO or some kind of PMO located within the IT department. Second, opportunities for line of business, departmental, and functional PMOs are missed altogether by not understanding the ubiquitous nature of project management and the value that PMOs of all shapes and sizes throughout the organization can provide.

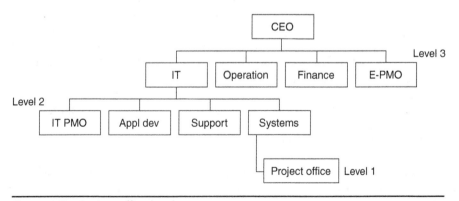

Figure 1.5 Project office levels

Size Dimension

Size matters. In a project management context, the size dimension is extremely important and it provides economies of scale opportunities for the PMO to take advantage of and realize. Project management size can be measured in a number of ways:

- ◆ Number of projects the organization performs
- ◆ Complexity of projects in terms of tasks and activities
- ◆ Resources to complete the projects
- ◆ Investment to fund the projects
- ◆ Time to deliver the projects
- ◆ Level of tooling to manage the projects
- ◆ Risk inherent in the project mix
- ◆ Level of project management processes to manage the projects
- ◆ Level of governance to select, optimize, and deliver the specific project portfolio

Far too often organizations go about setting up their PMO without giving any serious consideration to the characteristics of the project management size dimension. Typically the formation of a PMO is based on one of the popular theoretical models. This is followed by decisions to implement complex and costly project management systems and to develop and conduct a project management training curriculum. Surprisingly, the development of effective processes for project management and governance of the project portfolio, as well as the goals and measurements for the PMO as a business unit are addressed last if at all. All organizations have these project management size dimensions (see Figure 1.6).

Let's look briefly at each of these size dimension characteristics. The number of projects that the organization performs likely impacts the amount of tools and training the organization needs. The complexity of the projects, in terms of phases, activities, and tasks, is a significant driver in the selection and usage of tools for project scheduling. The amount of resources involved in the project mix and the degree to which these resources are sharable plays an important part in determining what kinds of PMO staffing models would best serve the organization as well as the degree to which project and resource management tools can be effectively used within the organization. The level of planned project investment serves as a good barometer of the importance of project management to the organization and the degree to which the organization can benefit by establishing a project management culture. The time involved or project duration that is typically required for the project mix can be a major driver of project management tools and time-recording systems. The existing tools that the organization has deployed to its workplace professionals, including desktop

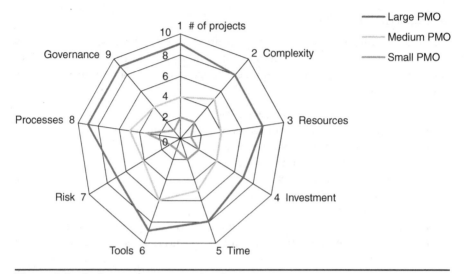

Figure 1.6   Project management size dimensions

tools, collaboration platforms, and enterprise applications can be a key consideration in developing the toolkit and systems architecture for the PMO. The risk represented in the project mix can influence the degree to which both tools and project management risk mitigation processes and PMO oversight policies are required. The number of project management and PMO processes that an organization has can impact the degree to which the PMO requires a manageable framework for PMO content assets. The extent of existing governance and what is required is a determining factor in how the PMO interfaces with management and the leadership team.

Collectively these characteristics of the project management size dimensions play a key role in determining the type of PMO and PMO goals best suited for the organization it serves as well as the degree to which specific tools, processes, and policies can be implemented effectively. There is not one, categorically correct answer. Organizations with a large number of projects, planned project investments, sharable resources, high degrees of project complexity and risk, and so on are likely to benefit from the establishment of a formal PMO, dedicated staffing of the PMO, and the implementation of tools and processes for project management as well as governance of the project portfolio. Likewise, organizations with a small number of projects, a lesser amount of planned project investments, few if any sharable resources, and minimal amounts of project complexity and risk, and so on are likely to be better served by a less formal, minimally staffed PMO. For both, the project management size dimension is an integral consideration that offers opportunities and economies of scale and directly influences the mission, goals, and objectives of the PMO.

Intervals of Time Dimension

Intervals of time as a dimension impact nearly every system, and project management is no exception. When it comes to PMOs, many people frequently refer to the establishment of a PMO and the project management culture as a journey, not a destination. Nothing could be more applicable to a journey than the marked and measured segments of that journey and for many PMOs this is where the project management intervals of time dimension comes into view. Three models that naturally fall within this dimension are the Project Management Maturity Model, the Business Cycle Model, and the Technology Adoption Life Cycle Model. Collectively these models provide valuable insights and direction to an organization and can help the management team ensure that the mission, goals, and objectives of the PMO are optimized and aligned to the needs of the business.

According to Kerzner (2001, p. 41), "All companies desire to achieve maturity and excellence in project management. Unfortunately, not all companies recognize that the timeframe can be shortened by performing strategic planning for project management." The Project Management Maturity Model (see Figure 1.7) is comprised of five levels representing different degrees of maturity:

◆ Level 1: *Common language.* Organizations speak a common language and have a good working knowledge of the project management fundamentals.
◆ Level 2: *Common process.* Organizations have common processes for project management that are defined and adhered to.
◆ Level 3: *Singular methodology.* Organizations combine various corporate methodologies into one singular methodology or framework.
◆ Level 4: *Benchmarking.* Organizations measure level of adherence to the process.
◆ Level 5: *Continuous improvement.* Organizations implement appropriate improvement strategies based upon benchmarking measurements and information.

The Project Management Maturity Model serves as an excellent roadmap to improve on the project management capabilities of the organization. No two organizations progress through the various levels of maturity at the same pace and experts suggest that it can take one to two years to advance from one level of maturity to the next. Important to note, the Project Management Maturity Model has a few practical limitations that need to be taken into consideration when establishing maturity goals and objectives for the PMO to achieve as part of the PMO mission. For one, the maturity model is typically applied to the formal project management of the organization. This can and does often lead to the setting of goals and objectives within the formal

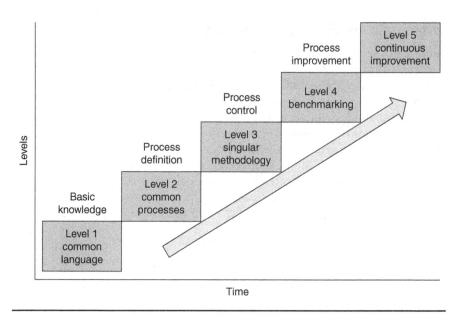

Figure 1.7   Project management maturity model levels

project organization to increase its maturity from one level to the next while at the same time other areas within the company that perform informal project management remain at their current level. Hence, an IT PMO with a Project Management Maturity Model level of 3 might be managing projects via its singular methodology while at the same time workplace professionals in the various functional departments go about managing their informal projects in an ad hoc manner that would likely be assessed at a level 1. Another practical limitation of the Project Management Maturity Model is that most organizations do not operate in a project management vacuum. The time and expense required to implement project management maturity programs often need to be tempered and balanced with the competing priorities and constraints of the organization. Windows of opportunity for project management maturity are sometimes open and at other times they are closed. Therefore, the intervals of time dimension of project management is an important dimension to understand and leverage. Whether narrowly focused on the formal projects of the PMO or widely focused on project management as it is applied throughout the enterprise, project management maturity models, along with the intervals of time they require, provide roadmaps, guidelines, and objectives to help the PMO continuously improve.

In addition to the traditional Project Management Maturity Model, a Business Cycle Model is a practical and useful constructs to help the PMO stay

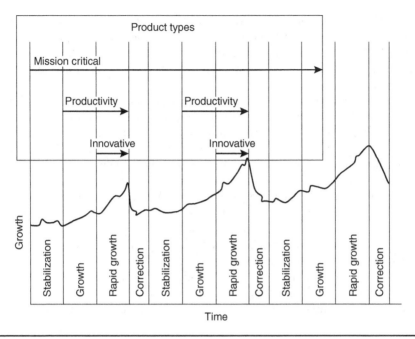

Figure 1.8 Business cycle model

aligned to the needs of the business. As shown in Figure 1.8, business cycles can impact the priorities of nearly any company.

Most companies seek to align and optimize their goals, objectives, and strategies to the business cycle phase (stabilization, growth, rapid growth, correction) for the industry that their company belongs to because the marketability of their products or services are greatly impacted by the current and next-expected business cycle. Typically, mission critical products and services can be marketed within any phase of the business cycle. Even in a period of correction, mission critical products and services are needed. Similarly, productivity products and services are marketable in most of the business cycle phases. In market correction business cycle phases, there is frequently a slowdown in sales for productivity products, but as the business cycle progresses to the growth and rapid growth phases, the demand for productivity products increases. Innovative products and services sell best during high-growth business cycle phases and it is not uncommon to find that expenditures for innovative products during correction and stabilization phases are often postponed if not cut from the budget. This alignment and optimization of goals and objectives to the phase demand of the industry business cycle directly impacts the lines of businesses, departments, and functional units that comprise the organization entities of the company. Forward thinking PMOs continually seek to ensure that their goals for the PMO best reflect the needs of the business with respect to its business cycle phase and that the project mix is appropriate and optimized for that business cycle phase as well. For many PMOs, this is a natural extension of their portfolio management and strategic project alignment processes.

In a similar fashion, the Technology Adoption Life Cycle Model provides another useful and practical construct within the project management intervals of time dimension. The Technology Adoption Life Cycle (see Figure 1.9) describes the likely adoption of new technology products and services according to the psychological characteristics of the defined market segment adopter.

The process of adoption is typically represented by a normal distribution or bell curve. As Geoffrey Moore (1991, p. 11) explains it, "The model describes the market penetration of any new technology product in terms of a progression in the types of consumers it attracts through its useful life."

The Technology Adoption Life Cycle Model is useful to PMOs in two ways. First, as a purchaser and user of technology products, the PMO is able to best align its tooling strategies to its own adopter psychographics. PMOs that are part of innovative and early adopter organizations are more likely

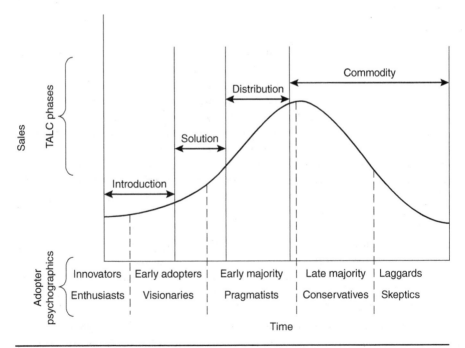

Figure 1.9 Technology adoption life cycle (TALC) model

to implement the latest in vendor products and services offerings, including new entrant vendors and vendors with alternative delivery models such as Software-as-a-Service offerings. Conversely, PMOs that are part of conservative organizations with a strong tendency to implement new technology and approaches only after acceptance in the mainstream are more likely to be late majority adopters. Second, as a provider organization in terms of the product of the project, the PMO is able to align its ability to deliver projects to the acceptance psychographics of its customers and stakeholders. For example, if the customers of the PMO are technology enthusiasts and visionaries, then the PMO has an opportunity to deliver their project product that best meets their customers' usage expectations. Take the case of a leisure industry PMO that is working with its internal customer, an upscale, trendy restaurant chain that features an extraordinary dining experience and is seeking to improve on its customer table-wait that on average is more than an hour. Instead of providing patrons with a low-tech device that flashes and vibrates when a table is ready, the restaurants of this trendy chain are seeking to provide patrons with an intelligent device, a PocketPC, that provides patrons entertainment in the form of games, songs, contests, and trivia as well as the restaurant's menu and chef specials of the day. The return on investment of this approach is not only measured in terms of the quantifiable estimate of hard-dollar benefits due to increased patron retention, but also the non-quantifiable estimate of soft-dollar benefits due to enhancing the trendy and innovative brand image of the restaurant. Being mindful of the Technology Adoption Life Cycle from the perspectives of both user and provider enables the PMO to more effectively select and implement tools and applications used within the PMO, as well as to more effectively serve and protect its customers from their technology adoption proclivities.

The project management intervals of time dimension are not as obvious or easily understood as its predecessor dimensions. But without too much difficulty, it is seen that many of the time- and phase-based behavior models are applicable to the PMO. Collectively, the three models presented, the Project Management Maturity Model, the Business Cycle Model, and the Technology Adoption Life Cycle Model, provide yet another dimension of project management that can help the management team keep the focus of the PMO on track.

Chance Dimension

Classical mathematics presents three physical dimensions: a line describes one dimension, a plane describes two dimensions, and a cube describes three dimensions. These three dimensions are referred to as spatial dimensions. Time is often referred to as the fourth dimension and it has been occasionally stated that the fifth dimension is chance or probability, meaning that the fifth dimension is the entire range of possibilities or alternate realities that can happen. In the context of the project management MUSIC model, the fifth dimension of project management, the chance dimension, is a construct that helps us anticipate, understand, and mitigate unplanned events and behaviors.

Chance events are characterized as unknown events. They are rare but when they occur they present a significant potential for decision making. In the context of a PMO, the project management chance dimension serves to remind us that no matter how thoroughly we plan and strategize there is always the likelihood that an unplanned event or behavior can happen. It may well serve the organization for the PMO to test these plans with respect to chance dimension considerations in order to uncover potential areas of improvement and benefit delivery.

Project management chance dimension considerations exist in a number of forms. Consider the following adages:

- Murphy's Law: If anything can go wrong, it will
- Parkinson's Law: Work will expand to fill the time available for its completion
- Student Syndrome: People will only start to fully apply themselves to a task just before its deadline
- Entropy: It is a natural tendency to move from order to disorder
- Game Theory: An individual's success in making choices depends on the choices of others (i.e., Nash Equilibrium, Prisoner's Dilemma)
- Pyrrhic Victory: A victory with a devastating and perilous cost to the victor
- Winner's Curse: In an auction, the winner will tend to overpay
- Mexican Stand-off: Multiple opponents with weapons aimed at each other will not fire the first shot
- Pavlov's Law: Repetitive event conditioning can trigger automatic pre-event responses
- The Peter Principle: In a hierarchical organization, employees will tend to rise to their own level of incompetence
- Peter's Corollary: In time, every position tends to be occupied by an employee who is incompetent to do the job
- The Dilbert Principle: Ineffective workers are moved to the place where they can do the least amount of damage
- Goodhart's Law: When a measure becomes a target, it ceases to be a good measure
- Pareto Principle (the 80/20 rule): 80 percent of the effects come from 20 percent of the causes
- Hanlon's Razor: Never attribute to intentional malice that which can be explained by sheer stupidity

Take the case of the student syndrome adage as it relates to project management and the PMO. Basically, the student syndrome suggests that those with tasks to perform procrastinate starting the task until the last possible minute. They begin only when they think they have just enough time to complete the task before its deadline. Now think of all of the tasks in the work breakdown structures in the various projects of the PMO. How many of these tasks are immediately worked on by the performing resource and how many are put off until the last minute? Assuming all tasks can be worked on without procrastination and unnecessary delay from time to time, how much improvement can be made in the project schedule? Additionally, if the product of the project is delivered early, how much benefit can the organization realize and how might this impact the mission, goals, and objectives of the PMO?

Consider the two simplified project schedules in Figure 1.10. Both of these projects were started and completed as indicated by the tracking Gantt chart. The first project ran its course without incident as evidenced by the "good" status symbol, because all tasks started and finished on time according to the planned schedule. It seems that the second project, however, did not go smoothly. Several of the tasks started late, took more time to finish than originally planned, and the project completed ten days late. As summarized by the status symbols, the second project did not go as well as the first and drew the attention of management along the way. From the perspective of the PMO manager or the executive to whom the PMO manager reports, which of these two projects is more problematic for the organization? What action should be taken?

At first glance, most PMO managers and their bosses conclude that the first project went quite well and the second project did not. Won't it be great if the project manager for that second project can plan and manage the next project with less difficulties and having nothing but "good" status indicators for every task of the project. Oddly enough, both of these projects were the exact same project. In Project 1, the project manager allowed the student syndrome to take effect. Tasks were scheduled and managed according to plan. All tasks completed on time, the project completed on time, and all involved thought that a good job was done. In Project 2, however, the project manager did not allow for the student syndrome to take effect. The project manager for Project 2 set aggressive durations for each of the tasks, twenty days as opposed to twenty-five days as planned by the project manager in Project 1. With these more aggressive task deadlines, the student syndrome was squeezed out of the schedule. Some of the Project 2 tasks finished on time, many finished late, and though Project 2 completed late by 10 days compared to its initial schedule baseline of 100 days, overall Project 2 finished earlier than Project 1 by 15 man-days and by 21 calendar days.

Let's add a little more color to the picture. The benefit stream of the product of the project is on average $1,000,000 a month. Hence, Project 2, by finishing 21 calendar days earlier than Project 1, produced an additional $700,000 of

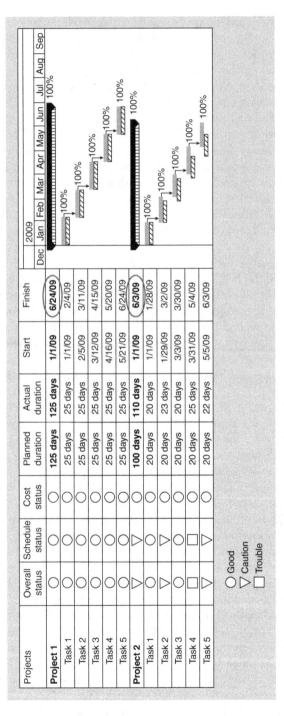

Projects	Overall status	Schedule status	Cost status	Planned duration	Actual duration	Start	Finish
Project 1	○	○	○	**125 days**	**125 days**	**1/1/09**	**6/24/09**
Task 1	○	○	○	25 days	25 days	1/1/09	2/4/09
Task 2	○	○	○	25 days	25 days	2/5/09	3/11/09
Task 3	○	○	○	25 days	25 days	3/12/09	4/15/09
Task 4	○	○	○	25 days	25 days	4/16/09	5/20/09
Task 5	▽	▽	○	25 days	25 days	5/21/09	6/24/09
Project 2	▽	○	○	**100 days**	**110 days**	**1/1/09**	**6/3/09**
Task 1	▽	▽	○	20 days	20 days	1/1/09	1/28/09
Task 2	○	□	○	20 days	23 days	1/29/09	3/2/09
Task 3	□	□	○	20 days	20 days	3/3/09	3/30/09
Task 4	▽	▽	○	20 days	25 days	3/31/09	5/4/09
Task 5			○	20 days	22 days	5/5/09	6/3/09

○ Good
▽ Caution
□ Trouble

Figure 1.10 Project schedule comparison–student syndrome effect

hard-dollar benefit to the organization. Which project, Project 1 or Project 2, best served the company? Without a doubt Project 2 best served the company as measured by real dollars as opposed to project status indicators. What action should the PMO manager and the executive to whom the PMO manager reports take? Should they reward the project manager for Project 1 because the project ran so smoothly not once having anything but a "good" status indicator for every task? Should they encourage the project manager for Project 2 to more effectively manage future projects so that task schedules are met as planned? In this particular example, the project manager for Project 2 should be rewarded for reducing the project cycle time, enabling the company to realize even more benefits of the product of the project. The PMO manager and leadership team should be mindful that while every project in the portfolio displaying nothing but "good" status indicators might give the appearance that all is well with respect to the cost and schedule status of the project, in reality, tremendous missed opportunities for reduced project cycle time, reduced project costs, and earlier realization of benefit streams are likely to be behind those "good" status indicators. One could easily argue that if the project portfolio status is "good" for all of the schedule and budget estimates, then there is likely to be too much cost and budget in the plan. Rather than being averse to "caution" and "trouble" status indicators, management should expect to see a healthy balance of all status indicators. This will likely help ensure that both the project budget and status estimates are not artificially inflated and that those carrying out project tasks will have sufficient pressure to minimize, if not alleviate, the opportunity for project management chance dimension events such as the student syndrome, Parkinson's Law, and others to set in.

Kendall and Rollins (2003, p. 281) believe that "To improve project management results, the PMO must be able to permanently and positively change human behavior." The project management chance dimension addresses the many forms of uncertainty—human behavior, organizational and market—and unplanned/unforeseeable events. For some PMOs, this will present an opportunity to optimize their mission with respect to their true status of current and desired capabilities and to set goals and objectives that result in the fulfillment of that mission.

Summary

To achieve the purpose for which it was created, an organization must have a mission, defined goals, and measurable objectives. Despite this universally accepted premise, many PMOs are created to be patterned after theoretical models and left to run as mid-office staff organizations with no real mission, goals, and objectives other than to manage the projects that come its way as effectively as they possibly can and to report the progress to management. In determining the mission for the PMO (or multiple PMOs) within an organization, it is helpful to consider first and foremost for whom the PMO exists to serve. Is the PMO needed to be a strategic PMO with a myopic focus on just the formal projects of the organization? Is the PMO needed to be an IT PMO focused on the delivery of infrastructure and applications projects in support of both strategic and operational initiatives? Is the PMO needed to be an enterprise PMO focused on strategic projects, IT projects, and establishing project management as a core skill set to be utilized by both formal and informal project managers in the management of all project within, as well as outside of, the PMO? Is the PMO needed to implement the tools, processes, and training required to get started with the basic organizational project management? Is the PMO needed to strategically align the goals of the company to the best possible project portfolio mix? Is the PMO needed to drive systemic process improvement within the organization? Is the PMO needed to avert an impending disaster?

All of these considerations are valid drivers of the PMO and in many instances organizations have multiples of these drivers to contend with. The issue never is what is the right PMO model or approach, but rather what is the right PMO model or approach for your specific organization at this point in time. There is some value in the traditional PMO models espoused by the project management community; however, most of these models are simple, one-dimensional constructs that serve a singular purpose rather than the full set of needs that an organization currently has and will face in the future. The project management MUSIC model provides a multi-dimensional view of project management that enables the PMO to expand its focus, vis-a-vis its mission, goals, and objectives, from the traditional myopic dimension of project management to the other dimensions of project management that exist within every organization thus achieving the fullest extent of its potential.

Questions

1. What is the relationship between mission, goals, and objectives?
2. What are the five dimensions of the project management MUSIC model?
3. What is myopic project management and what factors lead to it?
4. What are three examples of theoretical project management approaches or techniques that typically have limited practical applicability to an organization?
5. What are three practical challenges likely to be encountered when measuring a PMO on the number of projects that it completes year-over-year?
6. Why is project management considered to be a ubiquitous activity?

7. What is the difference between formal projects and informal projects?
8. What are invisible projects and do they exist where within an organization?
9. What are three examples of the project management size dimension?
10. How does the project management size dimension impact the PMO?
11. What is an example of the project management intervals of time dimension?
12. How does the project management intervals of time dimension impact the PMO?
13. In which business cycles are innovative products most marketable?
14. What are the four Technology Adoption Life Cycle phases?
15. What are the five adopter psychographics of the Technology Adoption Life Cycle?
16. What are three examples of the project management chance dimension?
17. How does the project management chance dimension impact the PMO?
18. Using the student syndrome, describe how project management status indicators can be misleading?
19. In determining the mission, goals, and objectives of the PMO, what is most helpful to consider first?

References

Block, Thomas R., and J. Davidson Frame. 1998. *The Project Office*. California: Crisp Publications.

Crawford, J. Kent. 2002. *The Strategic Project Office*. New York: Marcel Dekker.

Kendall, Gerald I., and Steven C. Rollins. 2003. *Advanced Project Portfolio Management and the PMO*. Florida: J. Ross Publishing.

Kerzner, Harold. 2001. *Strategic Planning for Project Management Using a Project Management Maturity Model*. New York: John Wiley and Sons.

Moore, Geoffrey A. 1991. *Crossing the Chasm*. Harper Collins Publishers.

Executive Insights

The Importance Of Clarity

John Maloch

CEO of Catalyst Project Solutions, Singapore

Introduction

Our business is focused on providing project-related professional services across Asia, Australasia, and the Middle East. As part of our services offerings we design, build, and manage PMOs for clients in a number of business verticals. Like many of our competitors, during the performance of these PMO engagements, we have experienced results ranging from highly successful to what can only be described as dismal failures. We have learned that the more successful PMO engagements all expended significant time and effort upfront in exploring and clarifying important aspects with the client's sponsor.

This clarification is not the same as simply understanding and agreeing to deliver what the client originally requests. Properly implemented, the PMO becomes an integral support group for the entire organization. If the design and implementation of the PMO results in an awkward fit with the other business units, it can quickly become an expensive and useless impediment to the client. This fact alone makes it important for the supplier and client to understand that the design of the PMO is a good fit with the overall business.

In the following sections, I want to address the two areas that I believe are critical aspects of any PMO—organizational fit and resourcing of the projects to be executed within the PMO. While clarity is important for all facets of a PMO, I selected these two points for discussion because they continually arise in these types of engagements. In describing these issues I also provide actual experiences we have encountered, both successful and unsuccessful, to demonstrate the points.

Organizational Fit

When approached by clients to build a PMO for their companies, we find that many of them do not have a clear view as to how the new entity fits into their organization. Many see the PMO as some sort of "black box" that fixes the problems that impact their IT organizations. Many times our clients are responsible for managing large IT departments that are under stress. The stress arises for any number of reasons: project skills within the department are inadequate;

expenditures on project budgets have risen to a point that the business is questioning the department's effectiveness; projects are started but never seem to be properly completed; or the project portfolio is simply unmanageable with the available skills.

These are indeed problems, however, before introducing a PMO to resolve these issues, I think it is important to address how the new PMO fits into and operates within the larger organization. Three important points to clarify concerning the organizational fit of the proposed PMO include:

◆ Business value provided
◆ Organizational culture in which the PMO must operate
◆ PMO interface with the various operating units

Business Value

It is important that the client is able to clearly articulate the business value expected from setting up, funding, and managing a PMO. While this appears to be a simple thing to ask, most of our clients have not considered the issue from the view of their core business. When asked to articulate the expected business value from the proposed PMO, many sponsors responsible for our engagements initially provide comments such as:

◆ Project expenses always overrun the budgets. We need better control of costs.
◆ We need better communications. I never know what is really happening with our projects.
◆ Our projects take too long to complete. I want projects to meet their schedules.

While issues around control, communications, and scheduling are all commonly encountered in projects, these are far from clear statements as to how the PMO is going to add value to the business.

In our experience, ignoring the concept of business value in the early stages of a PMO nearly always results in significant problems within a year of initiation. For example, a PMO is generally going to add costs to the organization. Eventually these costs are reflected in the budgets of the operating units and need to be justified. Another example of a business unit impact is when the PMO stops or delays a project that is an emotional favorite of one of the business unit leaders. Operating unit managers generally try to purge costs they do not understand or that they have no control over and external interference of any type is met with obstructionist behavior. Without a clear linkage between the value provided by the PMO and the success of the business units, the existence of the PMO cannot be guaranteed.

The PMO's value to the business must be clear and must be communicated in the language of the business. The following examples are clear statements of business value to be provided by the PMO:

◆ Over the past three years IT costs have been rising and now stand at 8 percent of revenue. The PMO will ensure IT costs are maintained at less than 5 percent of projected revenue.

◆ Over the past two years we have acquired six companies. During the post-acquisition transition of information and communication technology (ICT) infrastructure and services we discovered, on average, $10,000,000 of costs that we could have passed to the selling company had we only known about them in advance. The PMO intends to work with the merger and acquisition (M&A) teams in an effort to reduce these "unknown" ICT transition costs by 70 percent per deal.

◆ For each dollar of costs the PMO adds to operational budgets throughout the organization, the projects it oversees should add one thousand dollars of revenue or one hundred dollars of cost reduction.

Business leaders can understand statements such as these because they present clear business targets and directly impact their operations. But such value-targets need to be identified, measured, and communicated before they are used.

When working with a potential client to articulate the expected business value that is provided by the PMO, I find it takes several meetings to complete the task. The first meeting might produce some acceptable results, but this is generally the period in which the sponsor is coming to terms with what you are requesting. Once developed and documented, the PMO executive should distribute the business value statements with both the core business units and other supporting organizations. This process not only reveals additional or more concise ways in which the PMO can add value to the business, but initiates the "buy-in" process that is so important to successful PMO engagements. By your second meeting the client has fully considered the PMO-core business relationship and is able to provide a number of business value links to the PMO. If required, this information is further simplified into a clear and articulate value proposition for the PMO.

If the client cannot provide any links between the PMO and direct value to the core business, several factors are considered. Can the business support the additional costs of building and operating a PMO? Does the executive who is building the PMO have the required support of the core business and other support organizations? The worst situation in which you can find yourself is attempting to build a PMO that the organization neither values nor can afford to operate upon completion.

In 2007, we were engaged by a Malaysian telecommunication organization to design and build a PMO to manage all of their project activities. The sponsor insisted there was no need to expend any effort in identifying or discussing the business value of the PMO. After implementing the tools and content portion of the PMO, we initiated the transition of the ongoing projects into the control of the PMO. This transition included ongoing training for project managers (new tools, processes, and templates) and, as requested by the client, assisting them in obtaining professional certifications. Additionally we supported the organization in identifying, hiring, and training the staff responsible for running the PMO.

The end of this engagement happened to coincide with the start of the client's annual budget cycle. Since we had delivered a projected annual operating budget for the PMO, these numbers were included in the IT budget submitted to the company's senior management. In this particular organization, 100 percent of the costs associated with the support services were charged back to the various operating units of the company. During the budget process, these increased costs came under intense scrutiny and the executive in charge of the PMO was asked for detailed justifications for the increased costs. Because he had not performed a value linkage between the PMO and the core business of the organization, he found himself behind the curve in defending his expenditures. In this particular case, the PMO was retained, but man-months of effort could have been avoided by building the business value linkage upfront and obtaining business unit approval through the statement distribution process.

Organizational Culture

When discussing the development of a PMO with a potential customer, a full understanding of the organizational culture within which the PMO will operate is necessary. The client might be hoping that the implementation of a certain type of PMO will introduce organizational changes, but our experience is that the existing culture of the organization rarely can be changed. To be effective, a PMO must be built to complement the culture.

To understand the organizational culture you need to interview a number of people both inside and outside of the client organization. We find it most effective to include discussions with management and staff from both the revenue-producing business units and from one or two of the supporting cost centers. After gaining what we believe to be a common perspective, we normally test our assumptions by speaking with one or two of the organization's major suppliers. In my experience, suppliers generally have a clear view of their clients' organizational culture because they must negotiate it on a regular basis to be successful.

Pay particular attention to understanding how the organization accepts and digests change programs because an effective PMO will certainly introduce changes. Many businesses today are run with a constrained number of staff who might be responsible for an operational role plus one or two special project roles. It is not uncommon for these special projects to be some kind of organizational change program that was designed and initiated from a remote headquarters unit and is now being rolled out through the organization. Employees have become good at "checking all the boxes" of these types of programs, sending the reports back to headquarters, and calling the program a success. They fully understand that before anyone has time to audit the program and calculate the true benefits, another program is being implemented and attention on the first program diminishes to the point of irrelevance. If the organization in which you are implementing a PMO has experienced a large number of these change programs, you must be diligent to keep your program from receiving similar attention.

Another aspect of organizational culture that is important to understand is how the organization makes decisions and controls the delivery of projects. Some companies, such as ICT equipment manufacturers, might be highly centralized in both their decision making and their control of internal projects. Others, such as a globally integrated chemical company with many joint venture operations might make high-level centralized financing decisions and then leave all other operational decisions to the remotely located business units. It is likely that rolling out a severely structured PMO in this latter type of culture will result in an expensive failure. Figure 1.11 depicts how different types of PMOs might work within various organizational cultures.

This does not mean that a PMO cannot add value in an organization that has remotely dispersed decision making and operating responsibility. It does mean that you have a responsibility to your client to steer them toward a PMO design that, while it might not offer the promise of organizational change, it offers value to those who elect to utilize the services offered.

Two examples can best illustrate the importance of matching PMO design with organizational culture. One of our clients is a large, global energy company that runs all projects through a highly structured PMO. The PMO is organized in a manner that project funding has a direct correlation to processes under control of the PMO. Any projects started outside of PMO control simply die from lack of funding. The organizational culture, already comfortable with annual centralized funding decisions, was quickly accepting of the PMO, and the operating units across the organization view it as a valuable support organization.

A second example points out what happens when the requested design does not match the culture of the organization. One of our clients, an ICT Systems Integrator, contracted us to build a structured PMO for their cross-border organization. Besides adding a missing level of control to their cross-border engagements, the client wanted to use the PMO to force the various country organizations to work more closely. Within the company each country was managed by a director who was wholly responsible for their annual revenue

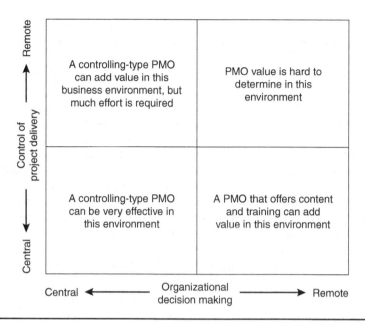

Figure 1.11   Organizational culture and the PMO

and profit targets. Any costs or controls introduced from external sources were viewed as unnecessary at best and generally considered to be intrusive enough to negatively impact their ability to reach their financial targets.

Building a highly structured PMO in this culture would have been expensive and potentially a failure. Eventually we convinced the client to build a PMO that provided project content, tools, and staff training which was then made available to the country directors at no cost for the remainder of the fiscal year. For the following fiscal year, the cost of the PMO was the responsibility of the country directors, but they were sold on the value of the service by that time.

PMO and Operating Units

This last point concerns clarity around project to operational transition. In implementing projects and programs across all industries, we occasionally find a built-in reluctance from the operational staff to take responsibility when the programs are completed. This reluctance arises from many sources—some valid and some no more than avoidance of any change to the current environment. Our experience shows that if you do not address this issue early in the program you might find your project team pushed into quasi-operational roles at a time when you planned to move the resources on to other tasks.

We ensure our PMO uses a process that guarantees the operating units become involved in the program early in the planning stage. The advantages of early involvement are two-fold. First, we ensure the communication process includes the people who are actually responsible for operating the new systems. In many of our engagements we find that some level of information concerning the new program has been provided to the management of the operating units, but the information does not reach the people who will be required to work with the new system once it is in place. I suspect the reason for this communication bottleneck is due to a number of factors. For example, the operations management might not be comfortable with their level of understanding of the new program at this early stage; there might be some concern the information will cause uncertainty and a corresponding decline in productivity within the operations staff; or they might simply see no value in the effort required of staff communications at this stage of the program. Whatever the reason, we find that early communications with the operating staff is advantageous in gaining the important "buy in" required for program success. The second advantage of early operating unit engagement is the ability to raise operational issues that can be barriers to a successful transition. The early identification of these issues provides ample time to address the problems and formulate the solutions required to ensure success. While there are a number of ways to ensure PMO clarity with the operating units, the diagram in Figure 1.12 describes the PMO process we have found to be the most successful.

During the planning phase of the program, we identify key operational staff to include in the engagement process. We have found, especially in large multi-national organizations, it is important that you do not utilize an operations representative for this task, because you leave yourself open to too many opportunities for excuse making when it comes time to put the system in operation.

Instead, set up a workshop that includes both key program staff and key operational staff and perform a walkthrough of the entire program. List the concerns of the operations staff and, most importantly, document the steps required for them to assume responsibility of the new system. The workshop should also be used to ensure the operations staff understands the PMO requirements for formally transferring the new system to their control. Both groups should exchange the documents that are used to communicate the handover process. Finally, formalize a process for communication between the two groups that will ensure no surprises await you during the transition period of the program. When the new program enters the delivery phase, ensure that all operational requirements are provided as promised. Get the PMO comple-

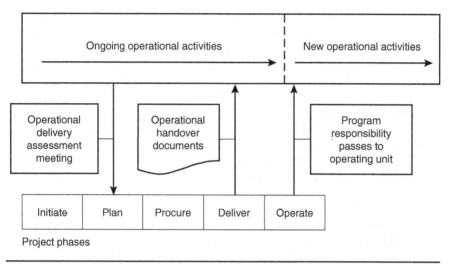

Figure 1.12   PMO process

tion documents approved and signed and disengage the project staff as quickly as possible. Do not allow them to become semi-operations support resources.

As an example of how the handover process can go wrong, consider our experiences with a large multi-national energy client. The program was a multi-project stream to expand an existing data center combined with a large server migration effort. Because we had used a single point of contact with the operating units, we immediately ran into issues as the new servers were migrated into the data center. The operations team took various positions to keep from assuming responsibility for these new servers: configuration management information from the project teams was not properly formatted, the amount of work had not been accurately communicated, and they were not properly staffed for the increased workload. One could make the point that the project teams had not performed well or the operations interface had not properly communicated the requirements, but the effect was that project staff was still supporting the new servers three months after they should have been working on other projects.

Project Resources

The last point regarding clarity that I want to discuss is project resources. Almost without fail our clients want to provide as many of the project resources as possible. The reasons given are numerous: possession of domain knowledge, reduced project costs, the wish to build project skills within the existing organization, to name a few. However, my experience is that this type of resourcing is a bad idea because, in general, the client-provided resources come from existing operational staff.

My desire to avoid using the client's operational staff as project resources is due to their lack of accountability to the project. This lack of accountability arises from a number of issues. First, in many cases, the client's operational staff is expected to work on the project while continuing to oversee their daily operations responsibilities. In the event of an operational problem, these staffs quickly become unavailable to the project. This is an understandable issue from the organizational point of view, but it can quickly lead to missed deadlines and scheduling problems within the project.

Second, I find the client's operational staffs do not demonstrate the same sense of concern toward schedules and budgets as do project-specific resources such as contractors or third-party suppliers. In many cases these project-specific staff can lose their job or incur financial penalties for poor or slow performance. However, I find it a rare situation when one of the client's operational staff loses his/her job over poor project performance.

Lastly, the existing relationship between the client's operational staff and the client management team generally results in heavier communication efforts for the PMO. While the PMO and project manager see the entirety of the project and are using the agreed communication process with the client, operational staff often bypass this process and communicate directly with the client's project sponsor. In many instances the operational staff does not fully understand the issues being discussed and perceive problems where none exist. Or, they might simply be the type of person who habitually raises issues to their managers in an unconscious effort for recognition. Whatever the reason, their actions often cause the PMO and project manager to devote extra efforts to out-of-cycle client communications and continual restatement of previously reported status situations.

An example of these types of project resourcing issues can be illustrated with an engagement we completed with a large Asian-based healthcare organization. The program included the simultaneous execution of multiple project streams and the client insisted on providing a significant amount of the required resources out of their existing operational staff. For the medical-related projects, doctors on the hospital staff were assigned to the project teams. Although highly intelligent individuals, the doctors had busy operational schedules to attend, were unable to dedicate adequate blocks of time to the project, and tended toward separating into factions for the purpose of disagreeing with each other. The planning cycle ended up taking three times longer than expected and the plans were then submitted to a medical approval board that knew nothing about the issues. It was easily the least efficient project team with which we have had to work.

The nonmedical projects were staffed by equally bright people—nurses and administrative personnel. The fact that the same people were assigned to multiple projects was completely lost on the project sponsors. Most of these projects immediately ran into scheduling problems due to this constrained set of resources. In addition, due to the amount of "back channel" discussions between the operational staff and the project sponsors, the PMO had to add resources simply to manage the increased reporting requirements. The program was eventually completed, at a significantly higher cost than originally planned, but could have been delivered much more effectively by using specialized third-party vendors as opposed to in-house staff.

To ensure program or project success, I think it is important to clarify expectations with the sponsor concerning the time commitment and control of the operational staff assigned to any project plus the acceptable communication process to be utilized. The sponsor must agree to push back on out-of-process communications concerning any aspect of the project and to support the project manager in his request for staff members to adhere to schedule and budget commitments.

Conclusion

Our experience shows that clarity around the PMO should be front-end loaded. While it is important to understand what the sponsor is requesting, it is probably more important to understand and communicate what type of PMO can be most effective within the client's organization. The sponsor must be able to clearly articulate and map the value of the PMO to the overall business goals of the organization. The interface between the PMO and the operational units must be clear and easily understood to ensure successful transition of products and services. To ensure project success, it is important that responsibilities and expectations are in agreement regarding project staffing.

2

Organization:
Constituent-Oriented
vs
Inwardly Focused

For many executives considering the implementation of a new project management office (PMO), Figure 2.1 depicts a familiar dilemma. In many instances, no sooner is the potential for a PMO mentioned than a runaway train leaves the station—fully loaded with ideas and opinions for what the PMO ought to be. Regrettably, these ideas are not focused on the constituent for whom the PMO exists to serve; instead these ideas are inwardly focused on the PMO itself as if it were a stand-alone business entity, unbridled and free to pursue whatever objectives and course it chooses. Rather than first taking the time required to fully understand the business need for the PMO, enthusiasts hastily advance proposals and commence lobbying for their interests.

Immediately lost in the debate is the definition and understanding of the business needs for the PMO, the customers of the PMO, the specific goals that need to be reached, and the problems that the PMO needs to solve. Although common sense would seem to demand a relentless focus on the customer, few organizations can escape the tendency to focus inwardly during the establishment of the PMO.

What could be so wrong with wanting to have the best PMO on the block? Who wouldn't want to be the envy of the project management community— fully staffed, equipped with the latest and greatest in tooling, and funded with a herculean-sized budget for training and development. To the extent that such things are actually driven by business needs, there isn't a problem. But

Figure 2.1 PMO comics—needs of the business

when the tail begins to wag the dog, the considerations for the PMO transcend, if not totally dismiss, the constituent. The result is a PMO that likely fails to meet the needs of the organization and that has difficulty obtaining its buy-in and support. For many PMOs this is a significant problem; one that might come back to haunt them and potentially lead to their abandonment.

How PMOs Become Inwardly Focused

No matter how good the intentions are for the PMO, there are many contributing factors that ultimately lead to an inward focus. The inescapable notion that the PMO, as a business proposition, must be sold to the executives of the organization is a gross fallacy that has caused untold damage. Nonetheless, as evidenced in many books, white papers, and articles, there is a belief and unwavering mindset in the project management community that the PMO must be sold to management. According to Block and Frame (1998, pp. 71–72), "The establishment of a project office should be carried out in two broad phases; selling the idea of creating a project office, and actually creating it." This mindset (see Figure 2.2) nearly always creates a *the-answer-is* justification effort in which the proposer's desired outcome is known in advance.

In addition to the obvious problems with having a desired outcome that is known in advance is the accompanying bias that often exists by those performing the analysis. Such bias exists in many forms, for example, the individual who wants to be the PMO manager or the external consultant who wants to perform consulting services to help establish the PMO. The combination of the desired outcome known in advance and the justification of that outcome performed by a biased individual create the least desirable form of analysis.

Block and Frame (1998) add that "It is important at the outset that project office planners take well-defined steps to educate their colleagues about the need for a project office, and that they describe clearly how it will function."

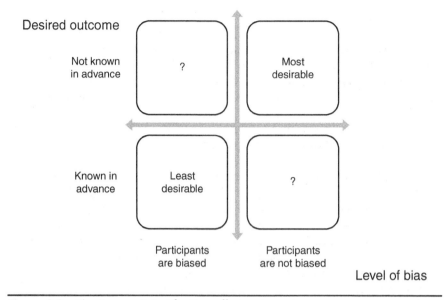

Figure 2.2   *The-Answer-Is* justification effort

At the outset it is far more important to establish an unbiased approach and a team that first listens to colleagues, discovers their needs, and then determines potential solution alternatives than it is to educate colleagues about the proposed solution.

Noted PMO expert, Mark Mullaly (2003) suggests that even when you believe in your soul what the academically perfect PMO is, you can't go further until you've sold your idea to someone. Mullaly's remedy is actually quite endemic to the problem. Not only is the idea of selling the PMO the wrong approach, but the thought process of believing in your soul what the answer should be and defining an academically perfect solution is simply the wrong approach. That approach loses sight of the customer, who is the entity for whom the PMO exists to serve. What the customer believes in the foundation of their soul is that which is important, not the other way around.

Regrettably, for many organizations this looking-through-the-wrong-end-of-a-telescope mindset describes all too well what frequently happens. An individual—often the PMO manager candidate—envisions ways to make it happen. Based upon past PMO experiences and knowledge, which can range from significant to minimal, this individual goes about constructing the solution well in advance of any real discussions about the needs of the business and the set of goals to be achieved that constitute the *raison d'être* (reason for being) for the PMO. This does not even include business timings, organizational constraints, and other executive priorities and synergies, or lack thereof, that always exist and can influence, positively or negatively, the PMO decision.

Another noted PMO expert, Craig Levatec (2006, p. 17) writes, "Without a clear vision of the purpose and goals for the PMO, the ability to sell the PMO concept to management will be severely limited." Levatec is correct when it comes to the need to first clearly understand the needs of the organization and to have those needs as the basis for the purpose and goals of the PMO. But where Levatec and so many PMO enthusiasts go astray is in their misguided belief that it is the PMO as a concept that needs to be sold to management. It doesn't.

First, it is not the PMO concept that requires the focus but rather the benefits and value to the organization of having met the defined, agreed to, and prioritized set of needs. This is what should be placed in center view. The PMO as a concept, in whatever form envisioned for the organization, is merely a vehicle to achieve the desired results. In the scheme of the business proposition, the PMO as a concept is subordinate to the needs of the business. Though the PMO exists to meet the needs of the business, to many PMO enthusiasts it can appear as if the needs of the business exist to meet the need for a PMO.

Second, the notion that the PMO needs to be sold to management is problematic. The idea of selling suggests that you have a seller and a buyer. The seller has but one goal; to make the sale. Without the sale, the seller makes no money and suffers a hardship such as the loss of a commission, the failure to make quota, or even the possibility of going out of business. The buyer, on the other hand, obviously is motivated by the desire to satisfy a need; *their* need that is, not the need of the seller. The motivation of the buyer and decision making is tempered with a *caveat emptor* (let the buyer beware) mindset. Is this seller-buyer mentality likely to produce the atmosphere that is most conducive to good decision making with respect to establishing a PMO? For most organizations, the answer is no.

The predisposition that the PMO needs to be sold to management is simply a bad idea. Management doesn't particularly enjoy being sold a bill of goods. If the effort to sell the PMO comes off as too salesy, it might risk falling on deaf ears.

An alternative approach is to view management as a group of people whose job it is to make well-informed decisions and ensure that those decisions are executed. Instead of having a selling mindset in which the goal is to sell management something, have a facilitating mindset in which the goal is to help management make the best possible decision. Ideally, the manner in which the business proposition is brought to management should be needs based, positioned in light of other options and alternatives for meeting the needs, and developed and presented by an unbiased individual who does not have a vested interest or stake in the outcome. This not only enables management to make the best decision, but it also ensures that management takes responsibility for and is committed to the implementation of the decision.

How many times have we heard that there is no buy-in to the PMO? This is often the result of the PMO being sold to management as opposed to management, with facilitation, making a decision to have a PMO and an unwavering commitment to the implementation of that decision. Without the proper approach from the beginning, the decision to have the PMO stands on a weak foundation. If the PMO is not truly aligned to the needs of the business, misalignments can quickly occur in even the best of intentioned PMOs, then the foundation quickly crumbles.

For many seasoned business professionals and experts in management consulting, such terms as *selling management* and *facilitating decision making* are used interchangeably. Those business professionals and experts in management consulting who have experience in strategic selling are keenly aware of the many fine nuances of the craft and the need to have a relentless focus on needs. When such experts go about selling an idea to management, they instinctively put needs first, perform the requisite analysis tasks, and provide management with the needed information so that they can make an informed decision.

This is a far cry from teeing up and pushing through a predetermined outcome. With no intent to discredit project management professionals, their knowledge of sales is no greater than the sales professional's knowledge of project management. Hence, the mindset for selling the concept of the PMO to management rather than facilitating management decision making is the wrong approach to take from the start and it results in an inwardly focused PMO rather than a constituent-oriented focus.

The Problem with Inwardly Focused PMOs

For many PMOs, it can be difficult to break from the factors that contribute to an inward focus. As PMO experts Kendall and Rollins (2003, p. 14) write, "Executives embrace a PMO that will dramatically increase the probability of meeting their goals." But how many PMOs are focused on the goals of the executives? Regrettably, most organizations go about setting up a PMO with a focus first placed on the PMO model.

Although PMOs that are based upon business needs can take on an unlimited variety of models, not long after the evolution of PMOs, three models emerged in the consulting community as the recognized approaches for establishing a PMO; the project repository model, the project coach model, and the enterprise PMO model. Market analysts like the Gartner Group led in the establishment of these models with research studies, white papers, and seminars. Not far behind were the project management vendors, consulting firms, and training organizations. The problem is that the resulting buzz and hype over these PMO models soon became the center of attention rather than helping those executives meet their goals. From the beginning, organizational strategies are developed and decisions are made for the wrong reasons. These are just the first of many problems that inwardly focused PMOs have.

Case Study

Take the case of a small but rapidly growing technology company. The specific name of this company and the names of the individuals involved are not important, but their story is. The CEO of this emerging company was faced with many of the common problems associated with market success. Large companies were keen to engage in pilots for their new technology, business partners were lining up to seek technology partnerships, and existing customers were adopting the technology enterprise wide. As a technology firm that engages in a wide variety of projects as a means of doing business, the CEO found himself no longer able to manage the business by instinct and good judgment. There were just too many projects and too many opportunities now underway. The ad hoc approach to project management never did work that well and with the company doubling in size and the number of projects increasing more than fourfold, the CEO presented the idea of a PMO to his leadership team.

The leadership team all responded favorably, albeit each with their own hopes for improvement and reasons for support. The head of sales wanted more resources to perform billable project engagements. The head of professional services wanted the sales teams to use more project management discipline in their approach to sizing customer requirements and proposing firm commitments for price and delivery. The head of business development wanted the ability to pursue and treat nonrevenue-producing strategic business partner projects with the same degree of priority as the revenue-producing projects. The manager of product development wanted to create a barrier to prevent the temporary assignment of his development resources to high-priority sales opportunities comprising the ability to develop new products on time. The chief financial officer (CFO) wanted timely and accurate forecasts for project delivery to manage revenue recognition and the financial plan. The chief executive officer (CEO) wanted all of these things as well as the ability to double the size of the business over the next year.

The CEO and the leadership team interviewed a number of candidates for PMO manager. All of the candidates possessed excellent credentials and interviewed well. After a second round of interviews for the short-listed candidates, the selection of the new PMO manager came down to two well-qualified candidates. One candidate had been a PMO manager with three different companies and had a recognized certification as a project management professional. This candidate was also experienced in establishing a PMO, developing project management methodology, and in implementing project management systems.

The other candidate had never been a PMO manager nor was he certified as a project management professional, but this candidate had line management experiences in sales, marketing, business development, and professional services with a number of small, high-growth technology companies, not unlike the company now interviewing him. After careful consideration, the CEO and the leadership team decided that it would be best to hire the candidate with PMO experience and project management credentials as their PMO manager.

PMO Manager 1—Inwardly Focused

The CEO and the leadership team each met informally with the PMO manager and welcomed him to the team. At the next leadership team staff meeting a few days later, the PMO manager presented his strategy (see Figure 2.3) for the PMO.

The PMO manager's plan called for the immediate setup of a coaching model PMO. This PMO model would be staffed with a small team of project managers that would provide mentoring and project consulting. The business units would continue to own their projects and be responsible for managing them successfully. The PMO would implement a project management system that would provide project and resource management capabilities along with issues management and executive reporting. A singular management methodology aligned to the Project Management Institute (PMI) *Guide to the Project*

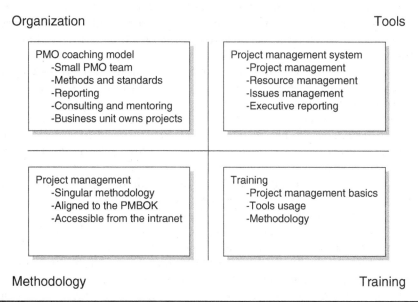

Figure 2.3   PMO strategy

Management Body of Knowledge (PMBOK®) would be developed and made accessible on the company intranet. Additionally, training in project management and the use of the project management system and methodology would be held. In his presentation, the PMO manager presented alternative PMO models and most of the discussion was centered on which of the PMO models was easiest to implement.

By the end of the first month, the PMO manager had hired a small staff of project managers; five altogether. The role of the PMO would be a coaching role and the role of the project managers in the PMO would be a mentoring, training, and assistance role; the project managers in the PMO soon took ownership of the strategic, high-priority projects as these projects were all in need of project rescue. The strategy of the coach model PMO was all but abandoned, but the CEO and leadership team enjoyed a sense of progress and confidence because the newly hired project managers had been effectively utilized.

By the end of the second month, the PMO manager had arranged demonstrations of a project management system to the leadership team. The PMO manager had experience with the vendor and application at three other companies and envisioned no particular issues or difficulties for the implementation. One subtle difference was the fact that at the three other companies the PMOs were all IT PMOs focused on managing internal IT projects better as opposed to being a PMO focused on managing external customer projects more effectively. But that difference, regrettably, did not seem to be significant at the time. The project managers of the PMO immediately started using the project management system and it soon became populated with project tasks and data for their projects which were but a small subset of the total projects underway.

By the end of the third month, the project management methodology was developed and made available and the project management system was rolled out for use throughout the company. Although the project management system was becoming populated with more and more projects and data, training had not formally started so the integrity of the project plans and application data was suspect. Also, users were having difficulties with the new tool and the project management methodology was perceived as too bureaucratic. As a broad view, the PMO manager had established with management that it takes training and at least six months for the processes and tools to come together and for the coaching and training to take effect.

For months four, five, and six, the PMO manager was relentlessly driving the training plan. Project management training sessions were provided to teach the basics of project management. The PMO manager and his team performed the project management training for the company, which was an introduction to the nine knowledge areas of the project management body of knowledge. They also performed training in how to use the project management system and in how to apply the project management methodology.

By the end of the first six months, just about everyone was unhappy with the PMO. The head of sales had nothing but complaints from his team because it took too long to get new projects underway. The services team was also unhappy because the PMO project management methodology did not effectively address the management of requirements and pricing of billable work. The business development team realized no benefit of the new PMO because their nonrevenue-processing strategic business development projects did not rank high enough to be supported. The product development manager was unhappy because his resources were still being called in to support critical sales projects and taking them away from product development tasks. The CFO was a bit disappointed that with all of the time and effort expended to implement the project management system, and information within the system was not timely, nor accurate, nor could it be used to forecast revenue recognition. While the CEO was appreciative of the efforts of the PMO manager, he was becoming concerned that the PMO manager and team were spending too much time in the minutia of project management that was perhaps better suited for an internal IT PMO within a much larger company than it was in a small, customer-facing technology firm.

In the next executive staff meeting, the PMO manager was besieged with questions. Each of the business heads had their own interests and questions, but the overall concern was that there was no visible sign of improvement. The PMO manager responded as best he could under the circumstances, suggesting that it takes time to advance the organizational project management maturity and capabilities of a company, but he was using a project management vernacular with which no one was familiar. The PMO manager also advised that many of the areas of difficulties that the company was having were outside of the scope of the PMO as the PMO was a coaching organization, not a performing organization.

The PMO continued to operate this way for another six months. The project managers within the PMO were, for the most part, deployed to high-priority projects. The project management system was never fully used within the organization. The project management methodology was accessible on the company's intranet, but no one really followed it. Attendance at the monthly project management training classes dwindled to just a few people.

Everything that worked so well for the PMO manager at his other three companies did not work at this company. It never occurred to the PMO manager that he was too inwardly focused on the PMO as a particular model and corresponding set of roles and responsibilities. Lost in his planning were the specific needs of the company for which the PMO was created to serve. After the first year mark, the PMO manager resigned. The CEO still believed in the value that a PMO could bring to his company. He tried to convince the PMO manager to stay on and head a new course for the PMO, but the PMO manager declined.

At the next staff meeting the CEO and the leadership team discussed what they should do with the PMO. Initially, a few members of the team thought that the PMO should be disbanded, but after further discussion all were in agreement that the PMO should be given a second chance. They were also in agreement that the key reason that the PMO failed the company, in their opinion, was that it did not directly or materially address any of the key needs and problems that the company faced. They also proposed to the CEO that perhaps they had hired the wrong guy and that the other short-listed candidate, the one with the small technology company and customer-facing experience, might have been a better choice.

PMO Manager 2—Constituent-Focused

As fate would have it, the CEO contacted the other candidate and after a few weeks of discussions and meetings, the company hired the second PMO manager. Unlike the previous PMO manager who quickly developed a plan to implement a coaching model PMO, the new PMO manager scheduled a working session with the leadership team to prioritize and agree upon the company's key problems that would be tackled by the PMO. In advance of the working session, the PMO manager distributed a one-page business planning template (see Figure 2.4) and asked each participant to come prepared to the meeting with a working draft of their input.

I.   Top three problems to be solved:
    1. _____
    2. _____
    3. _____

II.   Vision
    • The vision of the PMO is to _____.

III. Mission
    • The mission of the PMO is to _____.

IV.   Goals and objectives
    • The goals and measurable objectives of the PMO:

Goals	Objectives (how much by when)
1._____	1._____
2._____	2._____
3._____	3._____

Figure 2.4 Business planning template

The business planning template was simply a high-level, one-page document that contained four sections: (1) problems to be solved; (2) vision; (3) mission; and (4) goals and objectives. Prior to the planning session, the PMO manager met with each of his colleagues to discuss the purpose of the planning session and the critical need for their input and participation.

The planning session began with all participants seated at the conference room table. The PMO manager laid out the ground rules and expectations for the planning session and then he stood and made the following comments:

"Gentleman, I would like to start this meeting by first thanking you for the opportunity to join this fine company and be your PMO manager. I gladly accepted this opportunity for three reasons. First, I believe in the products and technology of this company. Second, I believe in the capabilities of this management team. And third, I believe in my abilities to work with you and help this company reach its full potential.

"Now, I would like to stress that this PMO is not my PMO; it is your PMO. I am but the steward, in whose hands you place, to plan and carry out the tasks necessary to meet your business needs for which this PMO exists to serve. And lastly, a PMO can be different things to different people. It is easy to get distracted in pursuit of good ideas and worthy causes. It is always far more difficult for a PMO to commit to, and be held accountable to achieve, specific goals and objectives. The challenge for a company is seldom a matter of selecting the approach for the PMO that is right, rather it is selecting the best possible approach and making it right.

"Toward that aim, the PMO, your PMO, must be driven by goals and objectives that you establish, not me. With your help in establishing the top problems to be solved by the PMO and the vision, mission, and goals and objectives that you need the PMO to have for the next twelve months, I am confident that I can develop and execute the PMO plans and strategies needed to achieve our objectives. As always, if we focus on every problem that we face, then we will not accomplish very much.

"So to ensure that doesn't happen I have called us together in this planning session. By the end of this session we will have accomplished the following:

◆ First, we will have an agreed to list of the top three problems that our company faces to be addressed by the PMO over the next twelve months. Of course, the PMO will seek to help in other areas of difficulty, but these other areas will be secondary.

◆ Second, we will have a shared vision for what the PMO is to be.

◆ Third, we will have a mission statement that clearly states the purpose of the PMO.

◆ And fourth, we will have three specific goals with measureable objectives for which the PMO will be held to account.

With time and success the PMO can take on more, but for now we need to tightly align and narrowly focus the PMO to your top needs. Gentleman, let's get started."

By the end of the planning session, the leadership team had arrived at a consensus position for all four components of the business planning template (see Figure 2.5).

They reached agreement on the top three problems to be addressed by the PMO. The first challenge was the need for the company to forecast and manage project-based revenue more effectively. The second challenge was the need to increase the capacity of the company so that it could take on more projects. The third challenge was the need the leadership team had for a complete and holistic view of all of the projects of the company: customer projects, business development projects, and internal product development and IT infrastructure projects.

It is important to note that the leadership team also reached agreement that the other areas of need, such as business development wanting more resources for nonrevenue-producing projects and product development wanting a policy barrier put in place to stop the borrowing of product development resources for high-priority customer projects, would be secondary in importance over

---

I.   Top three problems to be solved:
1. Poor forecasting and management of project-based revenue
2. Not enough capacity to perform more projects
3. Lack of visibility of all the projects of the company

II.   Vision
- To be an enabling and facilitating organization that is focused on, and accountable for, the project-based success of the company

III. Mission
- To develop and execute annual plans and strategies that solve the major project-related problems faced by the company

IV.   Goals and objectives

Goals	Objectives (how much by when)
1. Improve project revenue management	1. Reduce forecasting margin of error to 5 percent
2. Increase project capacity	2. Increase of 100 percent by year end
3. Provide holistic view of all projects	3. Effective reporting in place within 90 days

---

Figure 2.5 Business planning summary

the course of the next twelve months. The plans to address these and other needs would only be made after the plans to address the top three needs were well underway and demonstrating positive results.

After the business planning meeting was finished, numerous members of the leadership team privately remarked to the CEO on how different the two PMO managers had approached the business challenge at hand. The previous PMO manager had told the leadership team in their first meeting what his PMO plans were in terms of staffing, tools, methodology, and training; the new PMO manager did none of that. His focus and interest was on understanding and establishing unanimous agreement on the project-related needs faced by the leadership team and ensuring that the PMO had the right vision, mission, and goals to meet those needs.

The following day the PMO manager met with the CEO to discuss a few PMO strategy changes that he wanted to make. For the PMO organization, the PMO manager wanted to change the roles of the five project managers. Each of the five project managers in the PMO were directly managing high-priority customer-facing projects, taking direction from the account managers in the sales organization. Little, if any, transfer of skills or mentoring from the project managers to the account managers was taking place as originally intended. Rather the account managers were focused far more on lobbying management for the limited project management resources of the PMO than they were developing the skills needed to manage the customer-facing projects themselves. The new PMO manager believed, and presented to the CEO, that as a project-based technology firm, the account managers in the sales organization needed to be able to manage their own customer-facing projects independently with the possible exception of the few large and complex projects. Therefore, the PMO would allocate three of the existing five project managers to project manage these large, complex projects. Based upon the complex projects in the pipeline, this amount of project management resource was adequate. Having expert project managers on these large revenue-producing projects was critical to address the need for more accurate forecasting and management of project-based revenue and to achieve the newly set objective of reducing the revenue forecasting margin of error to five percent.

Next, to increase the project capacity, the PMO manager felt it was critical to increase the project management skills of the account managers and to streamline the overly detailed project management methodology. Collectively, if the team of account managers could manage their projects more effectively and with shorter cycle times, this would significantly increase the overall project capacity of the company. To that end, the PMO manager felt that it was critical to recast the role of one of the two remaining project managers in the PMO. The PMO manager suggested to the CEO that the PMO needed a full-time individual, a PMO officer, to be responsible and accountable for increasing the project capacity of the PMO. This would be achieved by streamlining the project management methodology that the account managers would follow and by providing training to the account managers in both the new, streamlined methodology and in the helpful tools that the account managers need to be able to use.

Lastly, the PMO manager told the CEO that to achieve effective reporting and a holistic view of all projects, a full-time, dedicated resource needed to be assigned to manage all aspects of the organization's project portfolio management system. The project portfolio management system that the previous PMO manager brought in was fine, but the laissez-faire approach toward usage was not. First, the PMO needed to modify the system a bit to meet the reporting needs of the leadership team. Second, the PMO needed to provide training in the system to all of the users, including management. Third, the PMO needed to proactively work with all required parties to ensure the integrity of the information in the project portfolio management system so that it could be used for the forecasting of project-based revenue. Otherwise, the objective of reducing the project revenue forecasting margin of error to five percent could be not achieved. Toward this important goal, the PMO manager would recast the duties of the remaining project manager, as a PMO officer, to the management of the project portfolio management system.

Rather than continuing in the project firefighting and best-effort based assignment of project managers that they had been using, the PMO manager aligned the five-person PMO team to the PMO goals as developed and agreed to in the planning session (see Figure 2.6). The CEO liked the new PMO manager's plan and, more importantly, he understood it and could see how it directly related to the needs of the company.

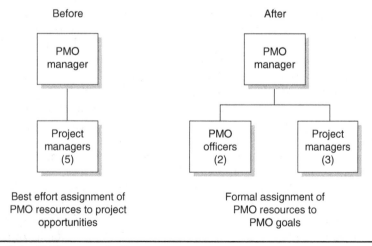

Figure 2.6 PMO reorganization

Over the course of the first six months of the new PMO manager's reign, the PMO manager worked with the three project managers assigned to the large, complex customer-facing projects and ensured that they were not stretched too thin as they had been before. This enabled the project managers to have a more reasonable project workload and to do a more efficient job. In particular, it helped the project managers to proactively drive and shorten the project schedules, rather than being in a constant state of project firefighting and issue management.

The PMO manager worked with the PMO officer who was dedicated to streamlining the project management methodology. As part of that effort, they worked with the head of sales and the top account manager to both stream-line the methodology and incorporate best practice tips and techniques for tool usage. Initially, the PMO manager envisioned that the tools tips would be centered on the use of their project scheduling tool and the project portfolio management system. However, it soon became apparent that two critical tools used by the best account managers in the management of projects with their customers were (1) a visual mind-mapping software package that helped greatly with joint customer brainstorming, idea generation, and decision making and (2) an internet-based collaboration tool that some of the account managers had been successfully using with their customers to share information and management of project tasks and communications. Working as a team, the PMO manager, the PMO officer, the head of sales, and the most effective account manager streamlined the project management methodology and incorporated all of the tool usage best practices so that all account managers could perform and manager their projects to the same level as the sales department expert. This also contributed to increasing the integrity of the project plans and reducing the forecasting margin of errors.

The PMO manager also worked with the PMO officer in charge of the project portfolio management system to ensure that the goal of providing a holistic view of all of the projects and the objective of establishing effective reporting within thirty days was accomplished. In addition to the training of the users, which was done by the PMO officer, the PMO manager and the PMO officer met regularly with the department heads to review progress made by the teams in the usage of the portfolio management system. Additionally, the PMO manager and the PMO officer met regularly with the head of sales and the head of finance to review the progress of the project portfolio and to develop best case revenue forecasts.

It didn't take long for the CEO and the leadership team to realize and acknowledge that the same five people in the PMO organization had achieved more in six months with the new PMO manager than they had in a year with the previous PMO manager. What was the difference? It wasn't the five people. It wasn't the project management skill of the new PMO manager nor his knowledge of project management methodologies or tools. Rather, it was the mindset and focus of the PMO as an organization. The first PMO manager was focused inwardly. He envisioned the PMO, his PMO, and constructed the PMO strategy without a great deal of real consideration given to the needs of the leadership team. Though the efforts were herculean, the end results achieved were minimal. Arguably, the organization was no better off with the PMO than they had been before. The second PMO manager, on the other hand, was focused on the constituent. This was made evident in the initial planning session, in the alignment of PMO resources in support of the goals of the PMO, and in the ongoing execution of the PMO strategy.

Summary

For many PMOs, the key determinant in their success is the extent to which they are focused on meeting the needs of their constituents. It is tremendously important to fully understand the reasons why an organization is establishing a PMO as well as to continually validate existing and new areas of need. Establishing a new organizational unit within the business always presents a challenge. This challenge is even greater in middle-office organizations and support organizations, like PMOs, that by design must interface and interact with other organizations in the company. Unlike a sales organization that is instinctively driven to achieve obvious goals, it can be easy for organizations like PMOs not to have defined and measurable goals in place. This can, and nearly always does, lead to a bureaucratic environment where the perception, and reality, can be that not much real work gets done.

Every organization seeks to succeed. Over the years, organizational success is researched, studied, and categorized into models. The PMO has been no exception. Though organizational models can be helpful for the purposes of conveying information and ensuring that all parties involved have a common view and understanding of things, they also can be problematic in terms of practical application. The greatest problem isn't so much that organizational models can be overly simplistic and at times theoretical, rather that they inherently bring about an inward focus on the model itself.

Of course, PMO models are based upon characteristics that are driven by need, but it is actually quite important for the needs of the business, those that the PMO exists to serve, be the center of focus for the PMO. This center of focus must be the driving force behind the vision and mission of the PMO and additionally, it must be translated into the goals and objectives of the PMO. PMO goals should never be to staff the organization in a prescribed and predetermined manner, or implement an application, or develop a methodology, or provide training in project management. These things might support a goal, but they are not the goal unto themselves.

PMOs that fall into the trap of becoming inwardly focused often do so as a result of having a *selling the PMO* mindset. A glance is no doubt given to the needs of the business and priorities of management, but it is often a cursory look. With assistance from those that might have a bias, or just a satisfying experience elsewhere, considerable amounts of time and budget can be expended prior to the train finally running off the tracks. For some organizations, following the design of a particular preconceived model has led to success. But for many other PMOs, success is not reached until specific PMO goals and objectives, which are based upon the needs of those the PMO exists to serve, are put in place and achieved.

Questions

1. What characteristics distinguish a constituent-oriented PMO from an inwardly focused PMO?
2. What contributing factors lead to an inwardly focused PMO?
3. What is a *the-answer-is* justification effort?
4. What problems are inherent with a *selling the PMO* mindset?
5. What forms of bias by those *selling the PMO* to management can potentially exist?
6. In the case of the small, rapidly growing technology company
   ◊ How did the first PMO manager determine how to establish the PMO?
   ◊ What level of involvement did the first PMO manager seek from the leadership team in developing the PMO strategy?
   ◊ How did the first PMO manager determine how to assign projects to project managers?
   ◊ How did the first PMO manager go about developing the project management methodology?
   ◊ What basis for selection did the first PMO manager use in implementing the project management system?
   ◊ While managed by the first PMO manager, how well did the PMO perform?
   ◊ How did the second PMO manager go about determining the plans and priorities for the PMO?
   ◊ To what extent did the second PMO manager involve the leadership team in the development of the PMO strategy?
   ◊ How did the second PMO manager align the members of the PMO?
   ◊ What approach did the second PMO manager take in developing the project management methodology?
   ◊ While managed by the second PMO manager, how well did the PMO perform?

7. In what ways can adopting and following a PMO model be risky for an organization?
8. How can past PMO experiences help, or hinder, the establishment of a new PMO?
9. Why might a PMO that is established following a prescribed and pre-determined model face a lack of buy-in and support?
10. Which is more important for a PMO manager to have, project management skill or business management skill?

References

Block, Thomas R., and J. Davidson Frame. 1998. *The Project Office*. California: Crisp Publications.

Kendall, Gerald I., and Steven C. Rollins. 2003. *Advanced Project Portfolio Management and the PMO*. Florida: J. Ross Publishing.

Levatec, Mark. 2006. *The Program Management Office*. Florida: J. Ross Publishing.

Mullaly, Mark. 2003. "Selling the Value of the PMO: What's In It for Me?" http://www.gantthead.com/articles. (Accessed June 2, 2008)

Executive Insights

Serving the Needs of the Business

Gary Popovich

Process Engineer, Royal Caribbean Cruise Lines

Introduction

The relevance of information technology to Royal Caribbean Cruise Line's (RCCL) long term success is more important today than at any other time in our history. Technology is in one way or another necessary to the achievement of virtually every element of the corporate strategic plan and especially in supporting our competitiveness with other cruise brands as they continue to aggressively aggregate their IT spending. As RCCL has grown in breadth and depth, so has the IT organization in response to the increased demand for business solutions throughout the company. Due to our size, diversity, and company-wide scope, the need for new solutions have led to an exponential increase in systems portfolio complexity and, in many cases, related business value.

With over 120 active projects at any given time and over 200 active technology products to manage, RCCL recognized the need for an overarching organization to manage the entire product life cycle from inception through retirement. The company realized that the basic components were in place in the form of standards, procedures, and performance measurements but there was no formal organization to manage the life-cycle activities across the various functional areas within IT and the business. It was clear that there was a need to establish a PMO charged with the duties of maintaining standards, evaluating performance, and ensuring compliance in all project-related activities. A team of executives were assembled to evaluate the company culture and the tolerance for change in relationship to tighter controls and project/product oversight. The team looked at all aspects of the life cycle, from ideas submitted by the business to product maintenance requests, to determine the best approach to establishing an oversight group who would look to improve project performance and reduce ever-increasing product maintenance costs.

Evaluation

The study revealed that the lack of a formal oversight organization increased the risk of project failure, reduced the company's ability to change as techniques advance, and increased the risk of noncompliance to standards and government regulatory requirements, such as Sarbanes-Oxley. The study also revealed that the lack of governance increased the risk of high product maintenance costs once the project delivered the product to the business. Armed with this information, the executive team evaluated two types of PMO organizations and their fit within the business.

The first type of PMO evaluated was one that performed in a support role, which encourages the PMO staff to be a driving force behind initiating new projects, and the second was a PMO model that was supervisory in nature. It was more restrictive but ensured alignment with corporate goals. The team reviewed these options and came up with a modified version that was more in line with the business model.

The study of organizations in a support role—the first type—showed that the PMO was a driving force in initiating new project opportunities. The problem with this approach was the limited controls that allowed projects to be initiated everywhere and, once in motion, could be difficult to control, each developing a life of its own. This model permitted marginal projects to continue even if they were no longer in line with business objectives, which could lead to wasted IT spending on products providing minimal payback.

The second approach was to empower the PMO to supervise and coordinate projects across the organization by tying the PMO to the office of the chief information officer (CIO) thus ensuring that the project portfolio aligns with overall business goals. This approach enables establishment of rules for approvals based on project type and estimated cost. As a result, projects were slow to start, resulting in many small projects taking longer to be approved than to carry out. The concerns with this approach were that creativity could be stifled by bureaucracy and that projects that lead to important technological advances needed to differentiate RCCL from its competitors could be delayed.

PMO Model 1—PMO in a Support Role

This model established the PMO as a consulting organization that imparts project management skills into the organization. In the model, the PMO provided a mentorship to the project managers (PMs) across the entire organization. The PMO team provided training, tools, templates, and methods needed by the project manager to perform successfully. The PMO might develop tools to improve specific tasks, as well as standard documents such as a project charter or project plan that is consistent across the organization. In addition the

PMO staff can be a back-up source for groups in need of help with project management, particularly when projects are in trouble and need experienced personnel to help correct the project's course.

Downside

The PMO in a support role acts only in an advisory manner across the organization. It's not a governance force, since it has little or no control over which projects are funded, and no authority to ensure projects align with business needs.

PMO staff typically cannot compel project managers to accept their guidance. For example, they cannot force user groups to adopt a common methodology or adhere to standards; they can only encourage them to do so. When the PMO is powerless to enforce standards, a PM or department may ignore the PMO's advice without recourse. This is especially true if the department has had past successes and believes that change to their existing operations is not necessary for them to be successful.

Another downside to this model is that the lack of a formal governance model allowed product maintenance costs to spiral out of control. As the maintenance and support budget was already in place, many small enhancements were planned through the maintenance cycle, in order to expedite deployment and eliminate the need for an additional request funding process, contributing to an ever-increasing product backlog. This allowed product changes to fly under the radar. They were also difficult to control, encouraging the business to spend the entire budget and not leave anything behind.

PMO Model 2—PMO in a Supervisory Role

This model is implemented especially when projects and budgets are out of control. In this model the PMO staff is given a supervisory role, with budgetary authority to determine project funding. Project managers, instead of being attached to departments, are part of the PMO staff and sourced to project teams as needed. The PMO might even control who gets assigned to which projects, depending on the project need and the resource's subject matter knowledge and experience.

This PMO model can overcome issues inherent in the support model. It can impose greater discipline on the choice of projects and the manner in which they are executed. Utilization of standard methodologies, processes, templates, and tools can be enforced. The PMO can decide the fate of projects that are not delivering. In short the PMO plays a strong role in project governance. This model also allows it to take tighter control of product maintenance spend, eliminating the practice of using maintenance budget for small enhancements without justification.

Tighter Alignment with Goals

In a supervisory role the PMO is enabled to ensure project alignment with business goals and to ensure project performance. For example, if the company's goal is to increase sales by 10 percent, then the PMO can decide that only projects aimed at developing enhanced sales tools are supported. In the supportive role, managers are able to ignore the implications of such a policy because they control the funding for their own projects; however, in the supervisory model, managers have no choice but to adjust to the PMO's direction. In this role all IT expenditures from project initiation through product support must be planned and justified to ensure compliance and alignment to corporate goals.

Downside

This supervisory PMO model works only within a highly structured environment, and to superimpose it upon a decentralized organization is to invite trouble. Taking away managers' authority and imposing decisions from above produces a culture clash and provokes resistance. Introduction of more bureaucracy into the approval process can slow innovation throughout the firm as people would rather focus on the deliverable than the administrative efforts and delays imposed waiting for approval. Another downside of this model is that product maintenance and support must go through an annual justification and approval process as opposed to the unmanaged approach of adding five percent to the actual expenditure of the prior year to establish the new budget.

Best of Both Worlds: PMO in a Facilitator Role

The main question that the team was faced with is "How can a project management office encourage innovation and still make it possible to recognize and shut down failing projects?" The company implemented a model that enables the PMO to take a facilitating role, working to bring business planners, portfolio managers, and IT together for joint decisions governing project investments. In order for this type of PMO to be successful, it is critical that the project managers be given a shared sense of ownership and encouraged to see the need for prioritization in terms of overall business goals.

The project managers play a significant role in providing the necessary feedback to the decision makers in the areas of scope creep, resource issues, and other risks that could cause the project to fail. The PMO, working in conjunction with IT finance and the portfolio leaders, help determine the costs and timeframes associated with new opportunities submitted by the business owners. This is accomplished by utilizing metrics and the requirements gathering techniques established by the PMO, which ensures constant and accurate information used by the executive committee to assist in the funding determination process.

Royal Caribbean Cruise Lines Implementation: The Project Management Office

The executive team realized that to have effective IT governance the PMO needed to ensure that IT delivers the required business value, supports overall IT performance management, helps establish IT credibility, and forces better alignment with business objectives. With the appropriate processes and tools in place, the business is able to measure performance, rapidly adjust to changing market conditions, and continuously improve processes and systems that deliver service to the stakeholders. The key factor to improve business agility is through partnerships between IT and the business. The focus of IT is to provide ongoing service and project delivery while working with the business to manage governance and business alignment issues, ensuring that spend is better aligned with strategic imperatives.

Royal Caribbean Cruise Lines Implementation: The PMO Directive

The executive team charged the PMO to upgrade processes to prioritize all efforts, enforce accountability by allocating product spend prioritization to the *using* departments and, ultimately, the Executive Committee members. The plan also called for an annual planning process that allows the organization to respond quickly to dynamic business needs by establishing controls, monitoring performance, managing risks, and ensuring compliance.

Additionally the Executive Committee is provided with periodic checkpoints on critical IT spend areas, supporting the ongoing monitoring and approval on major projects. As the market forces a more agile approach to business change, the Executive Committee is better prepared to evaluate project requests, manage strategic IT spend on an ongoing basis, and can quickly redirect funding as needed for mission critical efforts.

The strategy for our Project Life Cycle Management is to evolve our methodology by developing a portal that enables the enterprise to communicate, utilize, and monitor performance to standards. We want to create this learning culture that as we learn from our past projects we want to have a mechanism to store and reuse. The PMO was charged to look outside the organization and identify other companies' ideas and best practices that could be applied. The PMO must communicate new ways of thinking, introduce new tools and processes, refine evaluative metrics, and work constantly to establish a new baseline of performance.

The executive team recognized that it was critical that there be one official source for project-related information and determined that the PMO plays this crucial role in knowledge management (KM), effectively becoming the organization's memory by keeping records of projects—what works and what doesn't—including the steps through which certain processes must pass. It was apparent that different parts of the organization were unaware of what has been done by others, and new staff had no knowledge of what has gone before. Effective KM ensures that valuable lessons are retained and passed on to others.

Summary

At RCCL it is viewed that the PMO's role should be one of mentoring and supervising. The PMO is a trusted adviser, a function that the company can call on to ensure business objectives are met or to affect change. The PMO serves as an interface between the company's business units and its IT department; there to soothe the sometimes antagonistic relations between them.

The RCCL PMO supervises processes without dictating them and ensures regulatory compliance. The PMO puts controls in place and monitors them in a consultative fashion and provides training when necessary to ensure consistent delivery of products in the most efficient manner. Such activities require considerable people skills. Reason and persuasion, rather than carrots and sticks, are the tools most needed by PMO staff.

Once the RCCL executives recognized the need for a governance organization to ensure alignment to business strategy, they acted by determining the company culture and reviewing various PMO models to accommodate the organization. Once the evaluation was complete, a PMO was established using the best practice of both models. This change has enabled the organization to control the IT-related expenditures from new projects to product maintenance.

PMO 2.0—Adopting a Value-Based Approach

Terry Doerscher

Chief Process Architect, Planview

Changing Role of the Modern PMO

Corporations, private concerns, and public agencies around the world are recognizing a growing need for a business management center of excellence as a key component of the organization. We use the term *PMO 2.0* to describe this emerging trend in the next generation of business integration and how the traditional PMO is being transformed to fulfill it.

This is not a theory or presumption—the shift in the scope of functions of the PMO is tangible, widespread, and rapidly evolving. In September 2008, Planview initiated a PMO 2.0 Survey. Over 450 organizations responded, representing a diverse range of industry verticals and different sizes. Eighty-three percent of these organizations indicated that they have one or more PMOs in place (71 percent) or in development (12 percent). The results indicate a definite shift in thinking and in practice regarding the purpose of the PMO.

Almost 40 percent of respondents indicated they had a PMO operating at the enterprise level to coordinate, align, and report on the activities of different business units, departments, or divisions. Almost half (46 percent) of these respondents had multiple PMOs. Of the total respondents, 60 percent indicated they had extended their PMO services beyond support of formal projects to include other types of planned work and/or service delivery and operations. Over 65 percent of the organizations indicated their PMOs are involved in facilitating the strategic planning process, with over 30 percent indicating they are actively supporting the investment analysis process and/or providing benefit realization measures. PMOs are also becoming more involved in profit center functions with over a third of respondents indicating they were supporting new product development and managing product life cycles.

Business Drivers for PMO 2.0

This shift in the role and scope of the PMO is being driven by the compression of business operations in general and particularly with respect to faster development cycles and shorter life expectancies of products and services. Successfully managing this truncated business environment requires an essentially frictionless value stream from ideation to production and beyond. As a result historically segregated processes such as strategic planning, investment analysis, design and development, marketing, and operations no longer have the luxury of being managed as quasi-independent functions that are performed within organizational silos, using different approaches, terms, and tools.

Disconnects and misalignment in how various parts of the organization operates and interacts is a major contributor in making relatively poor project selection decisions, which reverberate with subsequent impacts on overall costs of doing business. A McKinsey Global Survey published in 2007, "How Organizations Spend Their Money," indicates that investment decisions on projects are off by approximately 40 percent, either in terms of those that should not have been approved or should have been subsequently cancelled, or in terms of the percentage of potentially beneficial projects that were incorrectly rejected. Conversely, in his book, *Optimizing Corporate Portfolio Management*, Anand Sanwal estimates that on average 30 to 40 percent of operating expenses are discretionary.

Despite the different sources and populations studied, the magnitude and similarity of these outcomes are no coincidence. Execution of the wrong projects inevitably leads to the wrong deliverables being placed into production, further wasting time, money, and resources in the operational theatre. Of course even these significant numbers do not tell the whole story by themselves; there are secondary explosions. The potential bottom line impact must also include the cost of missed opportunities, resulting from the initial and ongoing misdirection of money and resources; no doubt a staggering sum in terms of the cumulative total of these inefficiencies.

The requirement to better integrate overall operations and address the challenges of an increasingly dynamic business environment makes the need for a centralized point for coordination, collaboration, and information increasingly apparent. New and existing PMOs are evolving into full-service business management hubs, bringing their scope of operation to bear on areas such as: strategic planning facilitation and investment analysis; financial management; product, service, and asset management; process ownership and automation; and integrated work and workforce management.

Whether serving the enterprise to improve overall business alignment or functioning at a departmental level to facilitate integrated IT management, PMO 2.0 concepts are steadily becoming an established part of technology-driven, knowledge-based environments.

A highly integrated business management perspective that focuses on end-to-end business processes enable the PMO and the organization it serves to better understand and respond to total demand compared to available resources and financial capacities, manage supporting assets, and monitor and control the benefit of the product and service portfolio. Managing competing demands for limited capacity and understanding costs relative to business benefit is a necessity to maximize efficiency and deliver the most value to the organization. A dedicated center of excellence committed to seamlessly enabling these functions is a vital component to maturing business management competencies and recognizing integration objectives.

Rethinking the Role of Projects and the PMO

In *The PMO Handbook,* Gerard Hill notes, "The role of the Project Management Office (PMO) transcends multiple professional disciplines in its efforts to integrate project management practices with business performance objectives." Taking that concept one step further, can the PMO be leveraged to help to transcend the discipline of project management, integrating it with the broader aspects of overall business management? In other words, what functions do projects fulfill, and how does adopting that perspective serve the overall interests and performance of the business?

Historically the typical PMO has limited its focus to project management, either providing business controls and administrative functions for a single large project (project management office), a group of projects aligned to a common initiative (program management office), or the general population of formally managed projects (portfolio management office). See Figure 2.7.

But a project itself has no tangible business value. In fact, worse than simply being neutral, projects require an inordinate amount of managerial oversight, invite considerable risk, and greatly distract from otherwise normal operations, consuming time, money, and effort along the way.

Only a small minority of all project proposals are successful at running the long gauntlet of potential mishaps and hurdles to deliver substantially

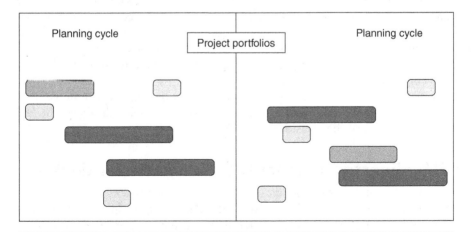

Figure 2.7   The classic project portfolio perspective

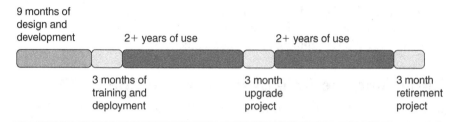

9 months of
design and
development   2+ years of use   2+ years of use

              3 months of   3 month   3 month
              training and   upgrade   retirement
              deployment   project   project

Figure 2.8   Projects and the product or service life cycle they act on

more business benefit for what they cost. Figure 2.8 shows that we should place projects into proper business context to understand why they should be undertaken.

Projects give us the vehicle for changing the status quo of products or services, either by creating new ones or modifying existing offerings. The overriding consideration for making a go-forward decision on a transformation initiative should be based on an assessment of whether the existing product or service can effectively achieve its strategic imperative. Encouraging the organization to embrace this wider view of the role that projects play (see Figure 2.9), ensures that the decision to pursue them is approached with a sharp focus on outcomes.

This linkage must be articulated and maintained throughout the life of the initiative to avoid losing sight of its purpose. Once a project or portfolio of projects becomes decoupled from its business objective and expected benefit, it invites a tolerance for failure. Attitudes about the project portfolio become complacent to the point that a certain percentage of projects delivering no discernable benefit becomes acceptable, rather than viewing each and every one as a critical investment that must be carefully managed. That's not to suggest that organizations become so conservative that they quit taking measured risks, but these should be a deliberate business decision, taking into account the overall risk-reward balance of the portfolio. An initiative must be actively and contiguously managed to *achievement of intent*—delivery of business value. Given that expected outcomes may take weeks or months to emerge, it is critical that a mechanism is in place to continue to maintain oversight and management until the transformation matures into its operational state.

PMO Functions, Constituents, and Perceptions

As part of exploring the orientation of the PMO and current trends, it is useful to put the fundamental purpose of the PMO into perspective, regardless of its size, charter, or the level of maturity and interests of the organization.

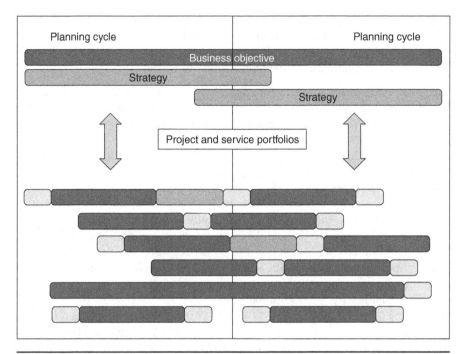

Figure 2.9 Project and service portfolios aligned to business objectives and strategies

The PMO does not make executive or engineering decisions, nor does it play a leading role in directly achieving the core objectives of the organization; it advances the collective efficiency, effectiveness, and performance of the organization it serves by providing supporting management functions (monitor-control-correct-improve) and attendant administrative responsibilities. The role of the PMO is much like that of a ship's navigator; rather than define the port of call or plan of attack, man the guns or set the sails, its duties are to read the charts, assess conditions, plot a safe and efficient route, and to always know the current position relative to the intended destination.

With these considerations in mind, we can list the primary support functions that a PMO typically provides:

◆ Defining and managing related business processes and supporting tools
◆ Work intake, processing, prioritization, backlog management, and dispatching
◆ Gathering and distributing information
◆ Facilitating communications, coordination, and collaboration

- ◆ Providing specialized expertise, knowledge, and internal consultancy
- ◆ Monitoring, analyzing, and reporting performance
- ◆ Identifying, analyzing, and communicating significant issues, roadblocks, or recommended improvements for all of the above

These general capabilities can be applied to a wide variety of different processes, levels of work, types of information, and performance measures. *The PMO inherently defines the constituency it serves based on how it chooses to scale its scope of interest.*

This is a critical point, because the community that the PMO services ultimately characterizes its benefit and sets the tone for its perceived value throughout the organization. Since the PMO is not directly involved with achieving immediate business objectives, it serves at the sole discretion of its benefactors more so than any other commonly found group within an organization. As evidenced by the significant number of corporations and agencies that still do not have a PMO, it is not generally regarded as a strategic necessity. Even in most organizations with a PMO, few have reached a point in which it is considered mission critical to ongoing business operations.

This explains why the traditional, project-centric PMO, even those that are successful, often become a target of cost-cutting whenever economic pressures emerge—the wheels do not immediately fall off the wagon if its services are scaled back or dissolved. Looking at the functions that a PMO provides, most of these are nominally performed as collateral duties of line management when a PMO is not present. For a PMO to be regarded as indispensable, it must establish itself as a significant strategic differentiator.

Accordingly, support, sponsorship, and funding for a PMO only continues based on its perceived benefit relative to its costs. How the PMO is perceived to a great extent also determines whether it can successfully influence other parts of the organization given that the PMO does not wield any direct authority over them. Because of this, perhaps the most debilitating risk for a PMO is to be generally regarded as an optional group that is limited to adding marginal value to the project management process.

Characteristics of an Inwardly Focused PMO

The trademark of an inwardly focused PMO is that it primarily adopts a tactical approach to delivering its capacities. It usually has a focus limited to some predefined project portfolio, and therefore expends much of its capabilities on improving project management processes, skills, and tools needed to track project performance against time and budget targets (see Figure 2.10).

While these functions may add some degree of benefit to general project efficiency and performance, the business value of such a PMO is inherently constrained. On the vertical plane the operational ceiling of the inwardly

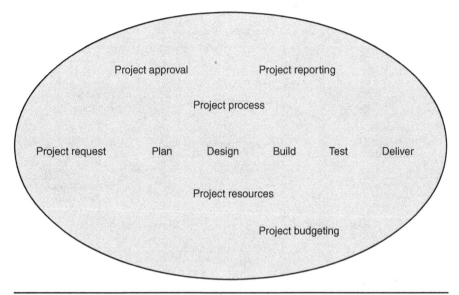

Figure 2.10 Traditional PMO span of influence

focused PMO starts with the project portfolio and drills downward to the functions and details necessary to perform project planning and execution. On the lateral axis, an inwardly focused PMO begins with the listing of proposed projects and ends with the turnover of resultant deliverables. Monitoring and control functions are generally directed toward project-level variance to plan. Corrective actions and improvement initiatives tend to focus on individual projects or the project management process itself.

By definition such positioning establishes a constituency that is comprised primarily of project managers and assigned staff from the line organizations. Only limited services of passing interest are being provided to sponsors, executives, and other stakeholders, typically in the form of lagging status reports.

Constituent-Oriented PMO

A constituent-focused PMO significantly extends its span of influence and services outward by adding *strategic* and *operational* elements to its scope. By providing supporting functions that help manage product and service portfolios throughout their life cycles, such organizations give themselves permission to focus on facilitating alignment between strategic intent, leverage projects as transformation agents, and follow through by monitoring both

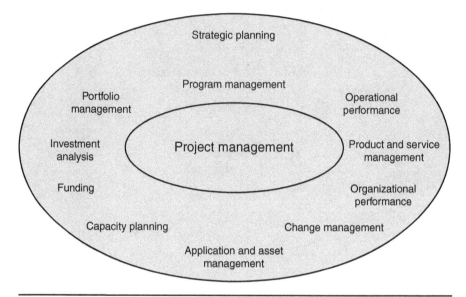

Figure 2.11   Extending the PMO span of influence to integrate business management processes

the costs incurred and benefit delivered by resulting products and services (see Figure 2.11).

Because of this elevated perspective, performance metrics tend to concentrate more on measuring business value as outcomes rather than simply reporting on project performance. *On time and budget* may reflect ability to execute projects, but they are meaningless measures when it comes to assessing whether real business value resulted.

By applying this wide-angle lens to view the business beyond the project portfolio, PMO services capture the interest of a broader constituency, now including customers, senior managers, department heads, and C-level executives—those who can employ these services to make a positive strategic impact on business operations. Stock in the PMO dramatically increases in value. To approach this degree of benefit, the PMO must first position itself and its charter to methodically extend its services into areas that deliver benefit beyond the project portfolio.

Adopting a Value-Based PMO Posture

There are a few key elements that characterize a comprehensive, value-based PMO operating in 2.0 mode. These distinct functions are in addition to the tactical necessities normally found within a typical project-centric PMO. A value-based PMO:

◆ Prompts a proactive, forward looking posture
◆ Drives organizational and strategic alignment
◆ Markets the improvements to all levels of the organization to garner buy-in
◆ Extends its capabilities and services to strategic decision support
◆ Assists in assessing the benefit delivered by products and services
◆ Actively partners with all stakeholders; program, project and line managers, executives, and customers
◆ Provides business-oriented performance information

Ultimately to achieve these results, a PMO functioning as a full-service, value-based business management center, should focus on maturing the supporting elements.

Define and Manage the Network of Core Business Processes

Define and integrate key processes that are required to manage the product and service ecosystem from inception to retirement, as they are all interdependent and form the primary mechanism for how the organization interacts. Include all of those processes that play a primary role in:

1. Managing demand: processes that affect total operational and strategic demand generated by both internal and external customers, including strategic decision making, change management, and all forms of work (both active and the pending backlog), including ongoing level-of-effort delivery functions
2. Managing capacities: processes that control how human resources, money, supporting tools, and enabling infrastructure are utilized
3. Managing benefit: processes that are associated with developing projected benefit of any change proposals, as well as measuring actual benefit delivered
4. Managing costs: processes that control risk and budgets, and measure actual expenditures for capital improvements and ongoing operational expenses

Making demand versus capacity and cost versus benefit decisions constitute the major trade-offs that occur continuously throughout the business model. Accordingly, all of these processes must form a single network that enables the unobstructed flow of work, business communications, and data to all parts of the organization. Assess each of the identified processes for their level of maturity and effectiveness and to identify constrictions and friction points. Map the supporting applications and interfaces that enable these functions. Analyze and prioritize improvement and integration opportunities. Several specific capabilities should be in place within this process network, including a common centralized mechanism for generating demand (requests) and a single quantifiable prioritization approach that can be applied to them. Similarly, the PMO should have visibility into how the most fluid capacities—people and money—are being planned and actually utilized.

Define, Organize, and Communicate Organizational Goals, Objectives, and Strategies

The PMO should be able to establish, maintain, and disseminate a view of the business plan as a structured hierarchy that clearly depicts the alignment between strategic intent and actionable work. This may be initially as simple as mapping business goals to supporting products, services, and projects, but should be steadily refined into a consistent structure with enough levels to enable executives, stakeholders, and sponsors to actively monitor and manage their respective scope of responsibility. For example, a descending hierarchy composed of top-level missions, the quantified objectives that achieve them, underlying supporting strategies, and enabling initiatives or programs provides sufficient granularity and extensibility to effectively illustrate and manage complex enterprise-level business plans across the myriad management levels, business units, and departments involved in accomplishing them.

This strategic portfolio should be actively managed as each cycle progresses from planning to execution to assessment and revision; the PMO should provide the necessary administration, support, and reporting capabilities to reinforce this critical business management function.

Identify and Manage Product and Service Portfolios

The PMO should catalog the primary deliverables provided to internal and external customers as product and service portfolios. Working with respective product or service managers, quantify each component in terms of their alignment to customer needs and related parameters, such as:

- ◆ The applicable life cycle and the stage each product/service is in
- ◆ Costs and/or benefit, either as revenue or internal business value
- ◆ Identify and map relative alignment to other key considerations such as technological architecture, preferred manufacturing methods, or targeted verticals

- Identify gaps between current products/services and strategic requirements
- Assess the key products/services that must be transformed; prioritize opportunities

Establish and Deliver a Full Spectrum of Performance Measures and Metrics

A PMO operating as a business management center must deliver information on several different planes to different consumers. In addition to the common tactical reporting associated with ongoing projects and programs, it is important that the proper performance measures also be developed and delivered for strategic elements, current products and services, and the organization itself. Organizational metrics are often the most overlooked because they do not focus on performance of an individual work entity or portfolio, but measure how well the people and processes themselves are performing in support of meeting strategic, business, and tactical objectives.

The most overt quantifiable indicator of organizational performance is overall throughput—trending the volume of deliverables that are output per unit of time. Related organizational measures that place quantity in balance include those associated with the quality of these deliverables, their unit costs, customer satisfaction, and human factors such as monitoring hours being worked, utilization, process compliance, staff morale, and attrition.

Added to these are measures of process effectiveness and efficiency. While throughput monitors the volume of work being delivered, process measures monitor indicators such as how long it is taking from point of request to delivery, and any gates in between, by type of work. The PMO is also ideally positioned to sponsor and initiate benchmarking studies or informational audits to supplement routine organizational performance metrics. Much like a traditional project-centric PMO, performance reporting also encompasses communication and collaboration elements associated with identifying opportunities, risks, and issues. In the case of the extended PMO model, the span of interest increases with the scope of its service.

PMO 2.0 Positioning

In addition to extending the services provided by a PMO operating under a 2.0 model, there are important internal considerations that must be addressed, including defining the role of the PMO relative to other management positions and functions, setting up appropriate governance, and positioning the PMO relative to other parts of organization.

As services are extended, getting consensus on (and documenting!) the new role that the PMO plays relative to other management areas in the organization is a critical element to ensuring that unstated assumptions or mixed messages do not muddy the overall management structure and degrade operational interactions.

For example, one common trap that many PMOs fall into is unwittingly becoming the 'Process Police'. That occurs when the burden of holding staff accountable to general business management expectations are placed on the PMO. Oftentimes this seems logical to some managers, particularly if new methods of conducting business are perceived to emanate from the PMO; "They're not *my* processes—if the PMO wants them followed, then it is up to them to enforce them." Unfortunately this puts the PMO in an untenable position given that the PMO leadership does not have direct authority over anyone other than their own staff. Any expectations set by the PMO are often interpreted by the general staff as being optional if they sense that their direct supervisor does not buy-in and fully support the PMO. The symptom most often exhibited by this situation is poor process compliance.

The responsibility for setting operational expectations and holding individuals accountable to them should *always* be positioned first by direct managers and then follow lines of authority upward. Certainly the PMO has a role to play in helping to codify processes or to help communicate related expectations to the management team it serves, but line managers must accept responsibility for embracing these policies and holding their staff to them. This dictates that the executive stakeholders visibly 'own' and support such changes or improvements, and make it unambiguous to their staff that any expectations for how the organization functions are those of the senior leadership team and that full compliance is expected.

Closely related to the role of the PMO relative to management decision making are governance processes and responsibilities. As the PMO extends its capabilities to provide more information to a broader population of constituents, it is important that appropriate mechanisms are in place so that the information can be properly addressed and acted upon. For example, it does little good for the PMO to undertake application portfolio management without a steering committee in place and prepared to make decisions on application retirement, consolidation, and integration opportunities. In short, whether the PMO is a traditional project office or a full-service business management center, its role in the organization is primarily to assist in providing the information, tools, analytics, and advisory support needed by line management so that they can make better decisions—not to replace direct management authority.

As the scope of responsibility and service area is revised, it is important to recognize that the PMO's position within the organization should also be assessed to ensure it is proper relative to changes in its mission. This is a common issue when PMO expectations and objectives are retooled; since the

PMO must influence, without authority, its ability to wield influence is greatest among its organizational peers. To illustrate, an IT PMO that is chartered to support both innovation and operations should be positioned such that it has parity with the department heads it serves. If such a PMO is located within application development, then its effective span of influence would likely diminish significantly outside of the directorate it reported to. A general rule of thumb is that an enterprise-level PMO supporting strategic functions should report to the C-level of the organization, while a departmental PMO should report directly to the department head. This ensures that the parts of the organization that the PMO is chartered to serve and influence recognize its role and inferred authority. Thus, the PMO leadership is positioned on the same level and reports to the same executive.

Summary

Clearly expanding PMO functions to the level of service described in this section is more of an ongoing journey than a final state. Addition of new or enhanced capabilities into an existing or newly formed PMO is generally approached in increments; each step providing a foundation for subsequent improvements. For example, a PMO might begin extending its scope of operations by first becoming more involved with facilitating the strategic planning process or the process of analyzing investments or by cataloging and performing a basic assessment of current products and services. It is important that a PMO 2.0 initiative employs an iterative approach to avoid over-functioning, to risk resistance to excessive change, or to miss opportunities for feedback, and then make adjustments before taking on additional responsibilities.

References

Hill, Gerard. 2008. *The Complete Project Management Office Handbook*. Florida: Auerbach Publications.
McKinsey and Company. 2007. "How companies spend their money: A McKinsey Global Survey." http://www.mckinseyquarterly.com.
Sanwal, Anand. 2007. *Optimizing Corporate Portfolio Management*. New York: John Wiley and Sons.

3

Managing Projects:
Think Process,
Not Methodology

The key to having a useful and usable approach for managing projects is to think process, not methodology. In fact, when it comes to words that conjure up mixed emotions, heated debates, and differences of opinions among those involved in the project efforts of a company, there is no word more capable of opening up Pandora's Box than methodology. Methodology can be, and often is, perceived differently by different people (see Figure 3.1). For many people methodology is a good thing. It presents a formalized way to manage projects and it demonstrates a level of project management capability and skill that is an order of magnitude better than the skill associated with managing projects informally and by ad hoc best efforts. For other people, however, methodology is not normally viewed positively. It represents everything that is wrong with organization and bureaucracy and, rather than being a help to project management, it is a hindrance. For some people, methodology is a four letter word.

Theoretically project management methodologies are a good thing, but in practice they can be a source of many problems and frustrations. Project management methodologies are not developed with the idea of becoming an evil or a bad thing, but it is true that they usually are or become just that. Take the case of David Cartwright (2007), a technology consultant with expertise in IT infrastructure and applications development. In his article "Why I Bloody Hate Formal Methodologies," Cartwright pens an amusing rant and rave and cites one example after another as to why he hates formal methodologies.

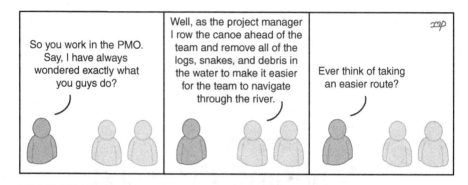

Figure 3.1 PMO comics—complex project management

Making his list are some of the inevitable byproducts of formal methodologies. One such by-product comes in the form of certification requirements for the methodology. As an example, Cartwright discusses the PRINCE2 certification and requirement for PRINCE2 practitioners to pass a three-hour, open-book, essay-type exam. As Cartwright puts it, ". . . I can just about contemplate there being a modicum of value where any idiot can be set up as a trainer, because at least you have to pass an exam—though you can take your book with you." Cartwright goes on to reveal that even the experts point out that not all aspects of the methodology, in this case PRINCE2, is applicable to every project and that one cannot take for granted that the blind application of the methodology results in a successful project. Nonetheless, according to Cartwright, qualified professionals without a certification in the methodology have missed out on job opportunities and employers seeking to hire only certified practitioners have missed out on quality candidates.

It is a mistake to think that such opinions on project management methodology as Cartwright's are lone voices in the woods. In response to Cartwright's article, Andy Reed comments, ". . . Dave is right in that once the industry loses sight of the real objectives and gets bogged down in the methodology itself then we have a recipe for disaster. I recall one project in which I gave up trying to correct the Project Initiation Document that had been put together by the Project Manager (all 97 pages of it) when it became apparent that doing so would take longer than the project itself."

And in another reply to Cartwright's article, Mark (last name withheld) comments, "I have witnessed meetings where the assorted gathering flew into a flurry of Prince2 code talk trying to one up each other with their use of the notation. Despite scarily understanding the piffle they were spouting, when asked for my input on project delivery I had to tell them all to speak bloody English and do something, anything, to actually move towards delivering results."

Ramon Padilla (2005) coined the term M&Ms to describe those folks in IT departments and project management offices (PMOs) who have decided, for whatever reasons, that the methodology is an end unto itself and drives the work. Unlike the chocolatey goodness in the form of those little candies that melt in your mouth not in your hands, this M&M refers to *mired in methodology* and it is anything but goodness. Padilla writes, "So the organization adopts a project management framework designed to launch the space shuttle and then requires all its projects to fit this framework, both large and small—failing to realize that your project management methodology needs to scale with the size of your project." What Padilla and others see firsthand is that project management methodologies such as these do not guarantee project success, only that the project takes forever to complete.

Cartwright, Padilla, and many others are all too aware of the impact, often negative, that methodology-oriented thinking has on PMOs and those managing projects. But how do we define this problem in terms that we can understand and fix as opposed to simply having one example after another as to why formal methodologies are a bad thing? As is often the case with complex problems, it is helpful to define and address key areas that contribute to the problem. In the case of project management methodology, three areas that quickly stand out are mindset, technology, and economics.

Mindset

Mindsets are often the result of past experiences such as observing, learning, or doing. Few people have a mindset for things that they have no awareness of and, conversely, most people quickly develop a mindset for things that they confront each and every day. In theory a methodology-oriented mindset is thought of by many people as a good thing to possess. But in practice a methodology-oriented mindset, even when well intended, can have a negative impact on the PMO and all those involved in projects. Some of the many differences between a methodology-oriented mindset and a process-oriented mindset are shown in Figure 3.2.

Methods-Based vs Outcomes-Based

One of the greatest differences between a methodology-oriented mindset and a process-oriented mindset is the core attitudinal basis of thinking. For those with a methodology-oriented mindset, this core basis of thinking is centered on methods to be used and rules to be followed. Merriam-Webster's online dictionary defines methodology as "a body of methods, rules, and postulates employed by a discipline" and this aptly describes a methodology-oriented PMO. The focus is placed on the methods as an end rather than as a means. In a process-oriented mindset, on the other hand, the core basis of thinking

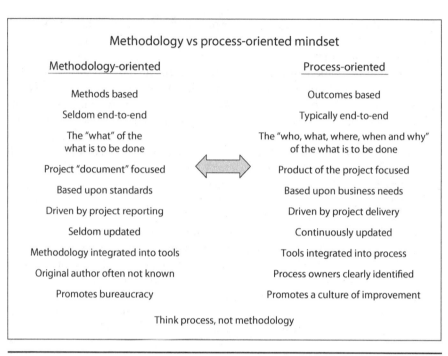

Methodology vs process-oriented mindset

Methodology-oriented	Process-oriented
Methods based	Outcomes based
Seldom end-to-end	Typically end-to-end
The "what" of the what is to be done	The "who, what, where, when and why" of the what is to be done
Project "document" focused	Product of the project focused
Based upon standards	Based upon business needs
Driven by project reporting	Driven by project delivery
Seldom updated	Continuously updated
Methodology integrated into tools	Tools integrated into process
Original author often not known	Process owners clearly identified
Promotes bureaucracy	Promotes a culture of improvement

Think process, not methodology

Figure 3.2   Methodology vs process-oriented mindset

is always centered on the outcome. As defined in Merriam-Webster's online dictionary, a process is "a series of actions or operations conducing to an end." Those with a process-oriented mindset put the achievement of the outcome first and construct the requisite processes to ensure the outcome.

Seldom End-to-End vs Typically End-to-End

Traditionally, methodologies do not address the complete end-to-end work effort that an organization such as a PMO must undertake to select a project, deliver the product of the project, and to perform the post-project activities required to ensure continued improvement. Methodologies typically address the project work, starting with the project charter document and ending with some kind of end-of-project document such as lessons learned. Depending upon the phases of the methodology, this starting point takes place in the first phase of the project methodology and the ending point occurs in the last phase of the project methodology such as the initiating and closing phases of the PMBOK® initiating, planning, executing, controlling, and closing (IPECC) processes. In theory this might sound like the correct place to start and end, but in reality the actual starting point for a project occurs well before the project charter and the ending point isn't reached just because the project work has been completed. For example, long before the project charter document is created, an event happens in the organization that compels someone to believe in and act upon a project idea. Such an event can be strategic planning, an operational assessment, a competitive win or loss review, a customer or employee satisfaction survey, a trouble ticket or a helpdesk call. Possibilities for new project ideas are endless. The starting point for a project isn't the point in time at which the project charter is created; it is the point in time at which the idea for a project is implemented (see Figure 3.3).

Likewise, at the end of the project, there is more to do than to document lessons learned. Post project activities such as classifying and archiving project artifacts for access and potential reuse by others, updating the PMO's historical estimating database with updated types and values, preparation and presentation of continuous improvement recommendations to the PMO, and other management as appropriate and, in some cases, post-project benchmarking and audit of the product of the project benefits.

Who, What, Where, When, and Why

Typically most project management methodologies document only the *what* of the what is to be done. Rarely do they address the what, where, when, and why as well. Hence, methodologies are like a cookbook that tells you how to make eggs. Processes, on the other hand, are focused on the outcome; they tell you how to make breakfast.

There is no better example to illustrate this point than to share a little story with you about my dear mother. My mother, who passed away years ago, was a perfectionist. According to her there were two ways to do any task; her way

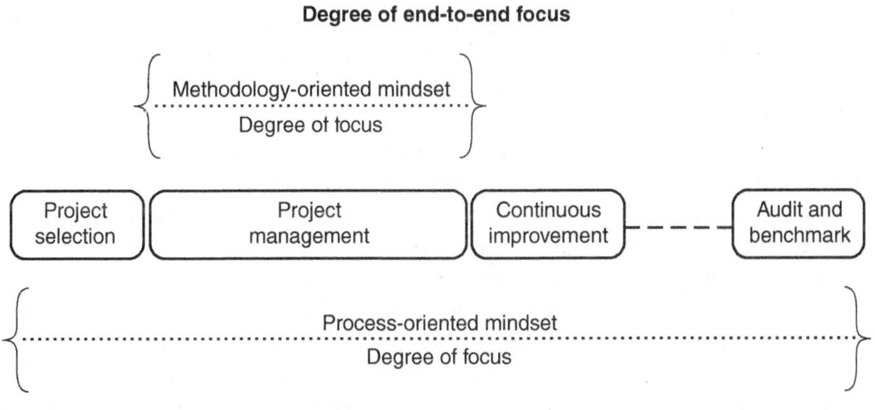

Figure 3.3 Degree of end-to-end focus

and the wrong way. As a graduate in home economics from the Mississippi State College for Women, my mother was an expert in managing all aspects of the household and especially in managing the kitchen. I would say cooking, but that would only be a part of the overall work effort in preparing a meal.

In my mom's later life when she was unable to cook, she enjoyed asking her visiting children to make the meals, especially breakfast. You see to my mom, breakfast isn't a simple matter of frying a few eggs sunny-side up; rather it is a production that must be carried out according to plan. For example, every activity must be done and, at the right time. This might seem trivial, but there is much more than meets the eye if you want to succeed.

How would you go about making bacon, eggs, toast, and coffee? If you are like me, you wouldn't give it much thought. You would just do it. But in my mom's kitchen and with her watching, this is what was expected. First you wash your hands. Then you turn the stove on high and start cooking the bacon. While it cooks you make the coffee. Once the bacon begins to fry, you turn down the heat just a bit to achieve that more than chewy but not too crisp texture. While the bacon finishes, you set the table. This involves laying the tablecloth and placing the special breakfast plates on the table with the napkin on the left side of the plate.

Next the forks go on top of the napkin, the knives are placed to the right of the plate with the cutting edge faced inward, and the spoons are placed to the right of the knives. Of course, such items as salt and pepper and jellies and jams are placed on the table. The cooked bacon is placed on paper towels on a plate to absorb the grease and, after draining some of the bacon grease from the frying pan, the eggs are cooked.

While the eggs are cooking, thin slices of butter are cut and put on the butter dish and placed on the kitchen table where the butter can soften. After the eggs are turned, the toast is placed in the toaster so that it pops out at the same time that the eggs are ready. Cold toast just won't do.

When the eggs are finished, eggs and bacon are placed on the serving platter and put on the table. Likewise the bread is placed in the breadbasket and put on the table. Breakfast is announced, coffee is served, and everyone enjoys the first meal of the day.

But don't think for one minute that breakfast is over. When it comes to making breakfast for your mom in her own kitchen, it is not over until everything that needs to be cleaned has been cleaned and everything that needs to be put away has been put away, and in the right place I might add.

Now this might sound overly detailed, bureaucratic, or even draconian, but it isn't; not by a long shot. When it comes to making breakfast for the woman who brought you into the world, who raised you, who loved you unconditionally, and who is now in her last years, you do anything to please her. No detail, if it is important to her, is too small to tend to. Anything less would be disrespectful or, as my mom would say, *déclassé*, her special euphemism for a behavior or an attitude that was not up to her standards.

The difference between cooking eggs and making breakfast for your mom in her own kitchen is the difference between methodology-oriented thinking and process-oriented thinking. As process improvement guru Michael Wood (2000) puts it, "Any methodology worth its weight in salt seeks to harvest the wealth of knowledge that exists within the minds of those who actually do the work." Those with a process-oriented mindset incorporate any and all things useful and usable that facilitates the achievement of the desired outcome.

Project Document vs Product of the Project-Focused

Many critics of project management methodology complain that they are more focused on producing documents than they are on producing the product of the project. As project management subject matter expert Andrew Makar (2008) points out in "Too Many Templates," project managers often spend more time producing and updating project documents than they do managing the day-to-day risks, issues, and schedule delays. Makar points out that there are always a critical set of documents. Hence, the issue isn't the fact that there is a need to perform administrative tasks, rather that there needs to be a mindset that is open to and focused on streamlining the process and eliminating nonvalue-added documentation.

In addition to project management subject matter experts, noted experts, including Scott Ambler in Agile software development, are quick to concede the value and importance of project documentation, but that effective documentation should be concise and focused on capturing the minimal, critical information required. However, too many templates and too much template detail are the opposite of this and prove to be ineffective. Ambler (2007) writes, "There is no solid relationship between project success and writing comprehensive documents, and in fact it is more likely that the more documentation you write the greater the chance of project failure." The wise advice of Andrew Makar and Scott Ambler, among others, is an example of process-oriented as opposed to methodology-oriented thinking.

Standards vs Business Needs-Based

When it comes to creating the project management methodology for the PMO, those with a methodology-oriented mindset are often too quick to adopt and document an out-of-the-box standard as the organization's approach for managing projects, as opposed to employing that standard to create an optimized and streamlined process for managing projects. For example, it is not uncommon to find that many PMOs have a project management methodology that is directly aligned to the Project Management Institute's *Guide to the Project*

Management Body of Knowledge (PMBOK® Guide). Such a project management methodology no doubt includes the five project management process groups (initiating, planning, executing, monitoring and controlling, and executing), the nine areas of knowledge (integration, scope, time, cost, quality, resources, communications, risk, and procurement), and the associated forty-two processes that fall into these groups and knowledge areas.

In theory this seems like a good approach. But in reality does this kind of a project management methodology meet the needs of the business? Does it work for projects of different types and sizes? Are all of these distinct processes mandatory or can some of them be combined or even omitted? Does the methodology tell you such things as what tools to use or are available for different tasks? Does it provide contextual guidance, advice, and information for carrying out the prescribed tasks? Does it tell you where you can find example project artifacts similar to your project, or task estimates applicable to your project tasks? Does it tell you how to go about project administration, frequency of producing project performance updates, which techniques such as earned-value analysis or simpler techniques can be used relative to the complexity of the project? Does it tell you where to store your project documents and when and how to update project team members and project stakeholders.

Project management approaches created with a methodology-oriented mindset typically do not answer these questions; rather their focus is primarily on aligning to standards. However, approaches for project management that are created from a process-oriented mindset do answer these questions. By design, they focus on the needs of the business and seek to employ, optimize, and streamline available standards.

Project Reporting vs Project Delivery-Driven

PMOs of all shapes and sizes, inherently, do some amount of project reporting. In many cases, larger PMOs with a greater number of projects have a business need to do more reporting and management of the portfolio than smaller PMOs with fewer projects and complexity. This can often lead to a project reporting mindset instead of a project delivery mindset.

As noted by PMO subject matter expert John Filicetti (2006) "The focus on project management lacks the urgency of inertia and 'getting it done!'" Filicetti, like many other PMO experts, recognizes that project reporting can easily become the core focus of a PMO. To no discredit of any PMO, project reporting is essential and the need for it only increases as the PMO becomes more strategic, more visible, and more in demand by its constituents.

PMO thought leaders Kendall and Rollins (2003, pp. 44, 80) take the need for the PMO to have a project delivery mindset even further suggesting a *deliver now* PMO model in which emphasis is placed on delivering measureable value to the executive team within each six month period. For some PMOs, especially strategic and advanced PMOs, the focus on project delivery can be a model unto itself. It would be a mistake, however, to suggest that a project delivery mindset is a mindset reserved and applicable to only advanced PMOs or that a PMO must align itself to a specific model to achieve a project delivery mindset.

As shown in Figure 3.4, all PMOs can take measures to increase their focus on project delivery. Two measures to consider include creating a sense of urgency to deliver the project and establishing project delivery behaviors.

The sense of urgency includes not only the focused placed on delivering the project, but also the much needed focus for the PMO to show results to management and the leadership team period by period. For large PMOs this period could be six months; for smaller PMOs this period could be quarterly. A project does not necessarily have to be long or complex to be a value to the organization.

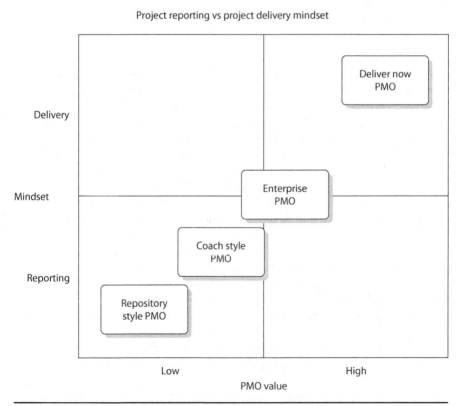

Figure 3.4   Project reporting vs project-delivery mindset

Project delivery behaviors are no doubt the same behaviors found in any sound project management approach, but a heightened importance is placed on them to ensure an understanding of their importance and overall effect on the ability to deliver a project. Such project delivery behaviors include:

◆ Ensuring that a good project plan exists
◆ Ensuring that the project participants are committed to the project plan
◆ Ensuring that the project participants have the ability to carry out their assigned tasks
◆ Ensuring that risks are considered and contingency plans are put in place
◆ Ensuring that the critical path for the project is identified and understood
◆ Ensuring that communications and progress reporting, commensurate with the needs of the project, are in place
◆ Ensuring that problem and issue tracking is performed and that escalation routes are in place
◆ Ensuring that appropriate management is involved and committed to the project

All PMOs can benefit from focusing on project delivery.

Repository model PMOs that exist to provide methods and tools to the enterprise business groups performing projects can drive a project delivery mindset. The fact that the enterprise has chosen a business-centric project ownership approach does not prohibit, or limit by policy, the PMO's ability to establish a project-driven mindset and a deliver-now sense of urgency.

Coach model PMOs are often an extension of the repository model and they too can extend their coaching to specific project delivery tactics and activities for both project managers and the functional business heads.

Enterprise model PMOs play a major role in the organization and often represent a high degree of investment made by the organization. Enterprise PMOs inherently move to a project-delivery mindset on account of the project and portfolio management processes and strategic alignment activities that is manifest in their mission. Of course with the scale and complexities of enterprise project management there can frequently be a continual *putting out forest fires* effort and effect with respect to project and resource management. This naturally can interfere with a PMO's ability to stay focused on delivering measurable value by each six month period.

Deliver-now PMO models are, of course, maniacally focused on project delivery to the point of subjugating processes and methods to maximize benefit delivery.

While some PMOs might be able to evolve from one of these PMO models to the next, for many PMOs this is not possible nor a good idea as it should be the needs of the business that drive the PMO model rather than the desire by those in the PMO to pursue personal interests and preferences. But what all PMOs, not just strategic and advanced PMOs, can and should do is to seek to establish the mindset and behaviors for project delivery as a key part of the PMO's project management process. Rather than a methodology-oriented mindset that tends to focus on reporting, a process-oriented mindset enables the PMO to instill a project delivery mindset that is focused on increasing benefit delivery, as derived from the product of the project to the customers of the PMO, as well as increasing the recognized value of the PMO.

Seldom vs Continuously Updated

Perhaps one of the least desired attributes seen in PMOs with a methodology-oriented mindset is the infrequency of updating the project management methodology of the PMO. Those with a methodology-oriented mindset go about producing a lengthy, overly detailed methodology document. Such works might be formally titled, "The Project Management Methodology (PMM)" or "The Solution Delivery Methodology (SDM)" and frequently they are posted in Print Document Format (PDF) on the IT intranet where they can be found, printed, and stuffed into large, three-ring binders. Seldom are these lengthy documents updated and if even they were updated, users would likely have no way of knowing what areas had been changed.

Additionally the effort to produce the document, though well intended, was likely an assignment that was given to the poor individual who was the least busy at the time. Therefore, there is no visible or real ownership of the methodology document or commitment to keep it updated. In fact, in many cases, the PMO or IT department might have contracted with a third-party consultant to write the project management methodology.

This can be problematic on its own as observed by Fortune 500 management consultant Allen Eskelin (2008), "Consultants will not have the experience delivering projects within the organization so the industry best practice may not be the best practice for the organization." Hence, its usefulness and longevity of purpose quickly decreases as time passes and eventually there comes a point in time in which the methodology is so out of date that it needs to be completely rewritten. Of course the rewrite is contracted out to a different consulting firm, the existing methodology is thrown out in its entirety and the new, and hopefully improved, methodology is developed from scratch.

Australian project management expert Neville Turbit (2004) advises that "A methodology is not a series of templates. It is a process that needs to be adapted to suit each situation. Feedback is also important. The methodology will not stand still. It will evolve and become more applicable to the organization. As such, there needs to be a mechanism in place to cater for 'learning from experience.'"

What Turbit and many other experts in project management understand is that a project management process is not a set of static, unchanging documents; rather it is a living and managed process resource, a best practice framework, which requires as well as enables constant care-taking and improvement. Figure 3.5 illustrates that methodology-oriented approaches such as static methodology documents only offer an initial value and are short-lived, whereas process-oriented approaches evolve with usage and offer lasting value.

Seldom updated methodologies quickly become of minimal usefulness and value. As the PMO undertakes project management training, whatever topics are presented and skills are learned do not make it into the methodology. As the PMO performs projects and makes discoveries in the form of lessons learned, these improvement opportunities are invisible to the static methodology. As the PMO implements new tools and new processes and subprocesses, the methodology becomes even more out of date and irrelevant. And as the

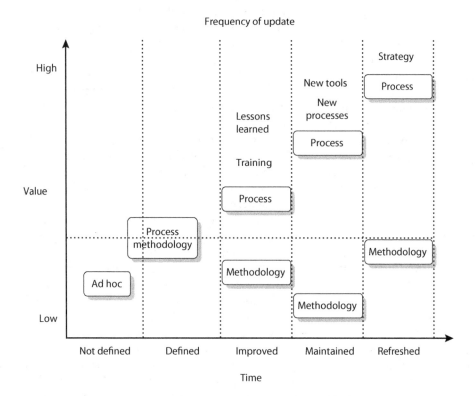

Processes are continuously improved and add value;
methodologies are seldom updated and become inconsequential

Figure 3.5   Frequency of update

PMO and leadership team make changes to strategy and policy, the static methodology is so entirely out of date that a complete refresh and rewrite is required.

Process-oriented frameworks for project management, on the other hand, do not become outdated. Unlike static methodologies that are seldom updated, process-oriented frameworks, by design, are collaborative and frequently updated. As the highly regarded CEO of PM Solutions, Kent Crawford (2002, p. 76) advises, "Building a world-class set of processes and methodologies also involves taking advantage of the lessons your own project managers learn while engaged in projects." Lessons learned documents do not get filed away and forgotten as is the case with static methodologies; rather they get acted upon and applied to the process framework.

Likewise, investments in training are applied to the process framework and institutionalized throughout the PMO, which enables skills to be retained and everyone to benefit from the training investment, not just those in attendance. While new tools are implemented, the process framework is updated to reflect both the availability of the tools and the contextual use of the tool related to the PMOs processes and policies. As the PMO and the leadership team develop and implement strategy, the process framework is refreshed with the updated and new processes, policies, and metrics.

Although methodology-oriented thinking stops at the production documents that are rarely updated, process-oriented thinking only begins its journey at that point with frequent updating points along the way. Continuous improvement is perhaps one of the most significant differences between the methodology-oriented mindset that produces static documents and the process-oriented mindset that provides a managed framework and it offers a compelling reason for PMOs to adopt a process-oriented mindset in the form of longevity of use and value.

Methodology Integrated into Tools vs Tools Integrated into Process

Most PMOs recognize that tools should be integrated into your processes and not the other way around. When tools are integrated into the process framework of the PMO, the end result is a useful project management process that provides not just the *what* of the what is to be done, but all of the details surrounding the who, what, where, when, and why of the project work to be completed. However, there are those who advocate an approach of integrating the project management methodology of the PMO into a single project management tool or system. Although this approach might sound like a good idea, nearly always it is not.

Take the case of the PMO that chose to integrate its project management methodology into a tool. In this instance the tool was Microsoft Project. Considerable thought and effort was taken to develop an all encompassing Microsoft Project template that provided a complete ready-to-use work breakdown structure for a new project. Each phase and step of the project management methodology was shown in a traditional work breakdown structure hierarchy. For each step of the methodology, project document templates were listed and hyperlinked as lower level tasks for the step and task notes were attached to each work breakdown structure to provide the guidance for the project management methodology. For months the PMO struggled with this approach:

1. The tool imbedded project management methodology was too rigid. There was no flexibility to allow for projects of different sizes and types. Whether the project effort was an IT infrastructure project—upgrading the servers, a major software development project, implementing an enterprise resource planning (ERP) system, or a minor software maintenance project, applying a new release, each project was subjected to exactly the same inflexible project management methodology.

2. Not all of the methodology phase, steps, and templates were applicable to the projects of the PMO. Hence, a first order of business for the project manager was to carefully think about and delete tasks, sometimes entire blocks, of the Microsoft Project work breakdown structure. This, in essence, resulted in each project manager creating and using his/her own version of a methodology for the project.

3. The PMO quickly discovered that all of the project work was not necessarily performed within the functional boundaries of Microsoft Project.

4. As shown in Figure 3.6, unless the project manager had Microsoft Project, he/she could not access the project management methodology. While this did not seem to be a problem because all of the project managers in the PMO used Microsoft Project, a per-user licensed and installed application, many members of the project team did not. Therefore, it was not cost effective or even a consideration to roll out Microsoft Project to every project team member or potential project team member.

5. As the PMO evolved, matured, and began to establish additional PMO processes, sub-processes, policies, and metrics, it was simply not possible to incorporate these items into the tool imbedded project management methodology or share them in any meaningful way.

6. When the project management tool changes, the tool imbedded methodology is lost and has to be rewritten and reintegrated into yet another tool.

Integration approaches

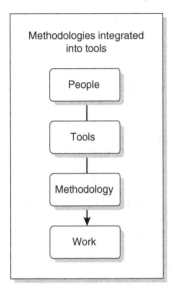
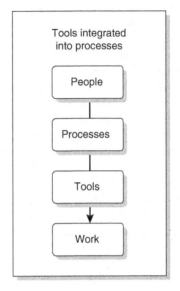

Figure 3.6 Integration approaches

Once again, where methodology-oriented mindsets are too focused on just the methods, a process-oriented mindset leads to the integration of all things useful and usable into the project management process. This includes tools and applications whether the preferred project management tool of the PMO is Microsoft Project or a high-end project portfolio management system. In fact the many disadvantages of imbedding a project management methodology only increase and become more problematic with higher-end project management applications. Additionally, complexity increases as the number of projects the PMO undertakes increases, their corresponding types and sizes vary, and the number of people who are served by and become constituents of the PMO grows.

Original Author not Known vs Processes Owners Clearly Identified

Every IT department and PMO has some kind of project management methodology or systems development life cycle (SDLC) model. Many have more than one. Years back, such documents were hand written and submitted to the word processing center where they were typed and placed in a three-ring binder. It was not uncommon to have multiple authors and contributors to the methodology document, each with their own set of pages. But rarely was there a document owner or owner of the methodology. Methodology documents were nearly always a point-in-time effort to produce the requisite number of hardcopy manuals. With the passage of time and the normal changes that all organizations experience, these cobbled together methodology documents often outlived their original authors.

The fact that these documents no longer have a known author presents two problems. First, with no known author it is unlikely that the content contained within the document, such as the project management methodology or the SDLC, will ever be updated. Second, and more problematic, is the fact that the document was likely to have been written with no appreciable consideration given to, or importance placed upon, the real need for the document to be maintained, updated, and revised over time and as necessary in anticipation of all of the component parts that make up a methodology. This is typically not in the thinking of those with a methodology-oriented mindset and is evidenced by the fact that not one major methodology has any concept or mention of owners, neither for methodology steps or phases nor for the project management methodology in general. Even the PMI Guide to the PMBOK® fails to address this in any meaningful way.

Conversely, those with a process-oriented mindset intrinsically recognize that a process without an owner does not stay a process for long. Process-centric PMO methodologies clearly identify who the owner of the process is and process ownership down to the process step level (see Figure 3.7).

Process owners are critically important. For small PMOs, the process owner is likely to be the PMO manager for the entire project management methodology. For larger PMOs, process ownership can be delegated to specific owners, perhaps a member of the PMO team, for a particular process or even one process step. For the smallest of organizations—a one person virtual PMO—ownership of the process can be the responsibility of the manager or care-taker of the virtual PMO or assigned to a subject matter expert.

Among other roles, process owners have four key duties:

1. The process owner has the responsibility for the care-taking of the process. This involves ensuring that the content of the process such as workflows, templates and checklists, guidance, and information are all documented and described at an appropriate level of detail for the PMO.

2. The process owner, in addition to content, makes available any and all tools, applications, and platforms that are used as part of the work effort. Outputs of the process need to be contextually listed and de-

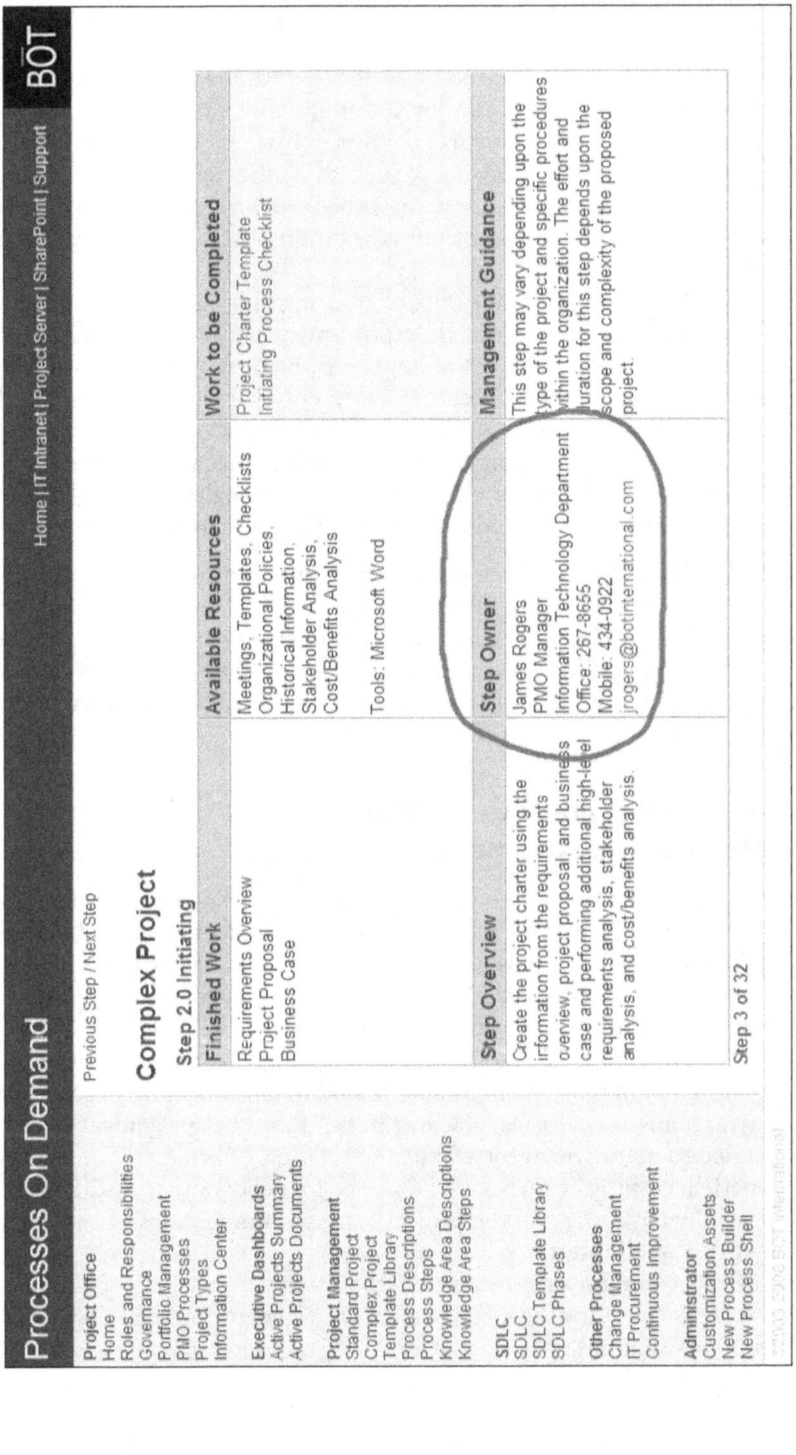

Processes On Demand

Home | IT Intranet | Project Server | SharePoint | Support

BOT

Previous Step / Next Step

Complex Project

Step 2.0 Initiating

Finished Work
Requirements Overview
Project Proposal
Business Case

Available Resources
Meetings, Templates, Checklists
Organizational Policies.
Historical Information.
Stakeholder Analysis,
Cost/Benefits Analysis

Tools: Microsoft Word

Work to be Completed
Project Charter Template
Initiating Process Checklist

Step Overview
Create the project charter using the information from the requirements overview, project proposal, and business case and performing additional high-level requirements analysis, stakeholder analysis, and cost/benefits analysis.

Step 3 of 32

Step Owner
James Rogers
PMO Manager
Information Technology Department
Office: 267-8655
Mobile: 434-0922
jrogers@botinternational.com

Management Guidance
This step may vary depending upon the type of the project and specific procedures within the organization. The effort and duration for this step depends upon the scope and complexity of the proposed project.

Project Office
Home
Roles and Responsibilities
Governance
Portfolio Management
PMO Processes
Project Types
Information Center

Executive Dashboards
Active Projects Summary
Active Projects Documents

Project Management
Standard Project
Complex Project
Template Library
Process Descriptions
Process Steps
Knowledge Area Descriptions
Knowledge Area Steps

SDLC
SDLC
SDLC Template Library
SDLC Phases

Other Processes
Change Management
IT Procurement
Continuous Improvement

Administrator
Customization Assets
New Process Builder
New Process Shell

© 2003-2008 BOT International

Figure 3.7 Project management process owner

scribed and, ideally and if possible, made accessible via hyperlink interfaces or application integration.

3. The process owner needs to be available, within a prompt and reasonable timeframe, to answer any questions that those adhering to the process might have. Of course the process owner does not do the work associated with a process step, such as completing a project charter in the initiating process, but the process owner can be of assistance and value by answering any questions that those performing the work might have.

4. The process owner has the duty of ensuring that the process is continuously updated and improved. Improvement opportunities such as lessons learned, development of new best practices, rollout of new tools, and incorporation of project management training via tips and techniques cannot resonate throughout the organization until such time as they have been incorporated into the project management process. At this point behaviors and skills can be institutionalized throughout the organization and counted upon, rather than merely hoped for.

For those PMOs with a methodology-oriented mindset, it is common to see little attention or regard, if any, for the original author of the methodology and the concept of ownership of the methodology likely does not exist. By way of comparison, for those PMOs with a process-oriented mindset, process owners are clearly identified and provide a significant value to all those involved in the projects of the PMO.

Promotes Bureaucracy vs a Culture of Continuous Improvement

To many people, a PMO can be perceived to be a bureaucratic organization. To no discredit of those not well-versed in project management as a discipline, many of the early PMO models were centered on control and documentation. In fact the once popular organizational term, project management community of practice (PMCOP), has all but been abandoned in the jargon of today's PMOs. This term is perceived to have a connotation that creates a vision of a policing organization rather than a value-providing organization. According to project management expert David Carr (2008) "Project management is a necessary service to be provided for all but the smallest of projects. The curse of the inexperienced project manager is that he/she believes that his/her goal is to bombard the customer and the project team with mountains of paperwork equivalent to a small forest."

One of the common difficulties that those with a methodology-oriented mindset have is that they view the project management methodology of the PMO to be a voluminous work that provides the definitive approach to be taken for managing a project regardless of its shape or size. Typically, such one-shoe-fits-all methodologies are written to the level of detail required for the largest and most complex of projects. Sometimes there is the ability to pick and choose areas of the methodology to use based upon project type and size guidelines, but frequently it is inflexible.

As IT and project management veteran Vernon Riley (2008) cautions, "The size and scope of some of the methods can give rise to serious issues as the project manager seeks to decide which elements from the methodology can be treated as optional and tries to downscale the approach to smaller projects." Even when there is a sympathetic understanding that the project management methodology might not be especially well-suited or fitted for smaller projects, it is up to each project manager to determine how best to make use of it. The tendency to set up a complex, overly detailed project management methodology is a bit ironic and further compounded by the fact that for most PMOs, large projects represent a small population of the project mix. As is the case with so many units of measure, Pareto's Principle, the 80/20 rule, applies to the project mix of the PMO in which the truly large, complex projects represent 20 percent, and often much less, of the total projects of the PMO.

So how does the PMO address the need for flexibility in project management? For many PMOs, the answer is that they don't. As project management expert Duncan Haughey (2008) warns, "My worst experiences have been with organizations that stick blindly to the methodology regardless of whether it adds value. This leads to many methodologies being perceived as needlessly bureaucratic . . . Organizations should ensure that project managers aren't overburdened with process that doesn't add value, just for the sake of adhering to a certain methodology."

Though all project managers who have managed more than one project recognize flexibility as a much needed good thing, surprisingly many noted experts advocate singular positions and rigid approaches that are difficult to understand. For example, in the 7th edition of his definitive text on project management Harold Kerzner (2001, p. 84) writes "When a company feels the need to have multiple methodologies, time is wasted up front arguing on which methodology to use." It is difficult to tell which is more unbelievable; that a noted expert could have such a mindset or that any organization would spend more than an ounce of time considering which methodology to employ.

For example, let's take the case of a health industry PMO located in Tampa. This is a well-known and well-managed company that most people recognize. This PMO has a generic project management methodology aligned to the PMI Guide to the PMBOK® that is used for generic projects, a Waterfall-centric SDLC for large software development projects and an Agile Scrum methodology that is used by the application development team in support of the company's online customer portal.

There is no doubt among any of the project managers, the project team members, or the functional managers of the organization as to which methodology is to be used. If any arguments take place, it is likely because someone comes in and mandates that all groups must use the same methodology.

Can you possibly imagine the ire of the Agile Scrum team, accustomed to their thirty-day sprints and Scrum process, being told that they must stop what they are doing and follow the generic PMBOK® aligned project management process?

Can you envision the consternation of the IT project manager with the assignment to the server upgrade project being told that, instead of following his generic PMBOK® aligned project management process, he must now learn and apply the Agile Scrum process to his project effort?

Can you fathom the disbelief of the ERP project manager consultant being told to abandon the application specific SDLC process in order to comply with the whimsical thinking that a PMO should have only a singular methodology. Such a prescription would be unbelievable.

Regrettably, this kind of methodology-oriented thinking doesn't stop there. In his book on project management maturity Kerzner (2001, pp. 77, 82) writes "Level 3 is the level in which the organization recognizes that synergism and process control can best be achieved through the development of a singular methodology rather than using multiple methodologies." He adds "The development of project management methodologies at level 2 are based upon rigid policies and procedures. But in level 3, with a singular methodology based more upon informal project management, methodologies are written in the format of general guidelines and checklists."

This is erroneous. First, it is bureaucratic thinking. There is no real control in having a complex, rigid methodology that, at the end of the day, no one follows. Second, without consideration for projects of different sizes and types within the PMO, optimization of the methodologies to best fit the best practice and associated domain knowledge, not to mention potential areas of required compliance, the best that a one shoe fits all sizes, singular methodology could ever be would be the lowest form of dominator of the collective, and summarily dismissed, unique methodologies.

Should an organization have an unlimited number of methodologies? Of course not. No two PMOs are the same, but somewhere between one and too many is the correct number of distinct approaches for project management that the organization needs.

Kerzner's contentions that Level 2 methodologies need to be rigid and Level 3 methodologies need to be informal are both wrong. Methodologies, whatever the level, should never be rigid. They should always embrace flexibility and enable the project manager to best meet the needs of the project on account of adhering to the methodology, not being burdened by it or having to deviate from it. And in Level 3 methodologies, the PMO and project managers do not engage in informal project management. You can call it what you want, but informal project management is ad hoc project management and nearly always reverts back to lower levels of maturity.

At higher levels of project management maturity, the PMO's project management methodology doesn't become loose and extemporaneous; instead it becomes optimized and value-based. Rather than informal guidelines and checklists, at higher levels of maturity the PMO continually improves its processes. The PMO seeks out ways to incorporate practical experience from such things as lessons-learned feedback. It seeks to incorporate knowledge acquired from training into the methodology. The PMO continually integrates into the methodology tool usage and new and special purpose processes and subprocesses. The value of the methodology increases not by a laissez-faire approach, but by a commitment to continuous improvement, which is only made possible with a process-oriented methodology framework that accommodates multiple approaches.

PMO thought leaders Kendall and Rollins (2003) advise, "What has been missing in the approach to date is the umbrella under which various methodologies can operate in harmony." In addition to housing the multiple methodologies, perhaps the greatest advantage of the *umbrella* methodology is that it promotes a culture of continuous improvement in project management.

As renowned Kaizen expert Masaaki Imai (1986, p. 16) writes "Kaizen (continuous improvement) generates process-oriented thinking, since processes must be improved before we get improved results." More and more PMOs and PMO thought leaders are advocating streamlined approaches for project management. The methodology-oriented mindset promotes bureaucracy and this mindset is on the decline. The process-oriented mindset has proven to be effective from the teachings of Deming, to the manufacturing excellence of Japanese, and to the many PMOs that are promoting a culture of continuous improvement in project management.

Technology

When it comes to establishing and maintaining the processes of the PMO, using too little or too much technology can present a problem. For some PMOs there is little to no technology involved when setting up, using, and managing their PMO processes for project management. They create or hire a project management consultant to develop a project management handbook. Frequently this handbook is in the form of a methodology document and set of project management templates; sometimes, it is simply in the form of a PowerPoint presentation. After review and acceptance by the PMO manager, a training session is scheduled and conducted for the project managers in which they receive an overview of the newly created project management methodology and their own hardcopy of the methodology neatly organized and tabbed in a three-ring binder. Some project managers refer to the handbook frequently; others might place it high on the shelf where it can be, but seldom is, reached.

At the other end of the pendulum, some PMOs are overly eager to use far too much technology. Such technology enthusiasts seek to create a functional application for the PMO's project management processes as if project management, like order entry, was a transactional application. When they see a project management template, such as a project charter document, they don't see the purpose and content of the template. Rather, they see an opportunity to design a form that populates data into a database. Whether or not the data in the database can be used for anything meaningful other than producing a report is not a consideration.

Likewise, such overly enthusiastic technologists envision ways to develop application workflow to render just the project management methodology components that they think different users should see or, perhaps, to configure the unique path of the project based upon project type and size parameters. They might develop a rigid document workflow with routing and triggers for approvals and exceptions. After all, the technology exists to do all of these things. Complex technology can be thrown at any problem, but why do this and who is asking for it?

Certainly, if there is a business case and compelling reason to apply complex technology to the project management processes of the PMO, then such an effort might be justified. But without a clear vision and compelling business case such an effort can quickly become a technical exercise that gives the appearance of solving a problem when in fact the problem that it solved didn't really exist and the problem that did exist wasn't really solved.

For most PMO project management processes there is a natural point of equilibrium relative to the technology infrastructure of the organization. This equilibrium point is neither too primitive, from a technological point of view, nor too complex. The level of technology applied has a direct impact on the degree of use and effectiveness of the project management processes of the PMO (see Figure 3.8).

No matter how good a project management process is in theory, paper-based processes don't work. Book knowledge and hardcopy project management methodology manuals and handbooks might give the illusion of having a project management process but, in reality, such notebooks and binders rarely leave their shelves. Some project managers no doubt take the time and effort to read and adhere to such playbooks, but many other project managers do not. They are too busy managing too many projects and sometimes even performing some of the tasks of the projects themselves. Outside of the immediate team of project managers, few, if any, of the project team participants, functional resources, or management take the time, or have the time, to read,

Technology supporting PMO processes

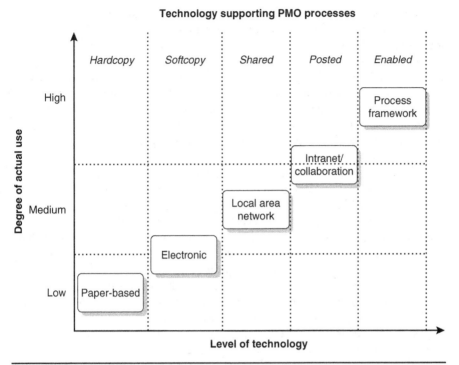

Figure 3.8   Technology supporting PMO processes

understand, and benefit from the methodology manual. They probably don't even have a hardcopy.

Electronic forms of a project management methodology are a step up from paper-based approaches. But if the electronic project management methodology is simply a Microsoft Word document or PDF file, it is emailed throughout the immediate team of project managers where it is skimmed once or twice and stored on their PC hard drive.

The next step up on the technology ladder is to use the organization's local area network (LAN) and store the methodology document on a shared drive. At least in this approach there is one form of the methodology available via shared access for the team to find and use. Of course, only those in the organization with access to the LAN file share can find the methodology document so in many cases those in the business units who have projects of their own or who are team members of the projects of the PMO do not have the accessability to use the project management methodology.

Intranet sites and collaboration platforms are a significant next step up in the application of technology to the PMO's project management processes.

Intranet sites offer wide access to all of the users who make up an organization. No longer constrained by physical network and server infrastructure, company intranets enabled wide sharing of information. Many PMOs benefit from having their own intranet site, often a subsite of the IT department intranet. The PMO intranet site can provide useful information to all those involved with projects and the PMO such as processes and templates, announcements and events, and project management training and reference materials. Intranet sites can range from HTML-based approaches to the use of vendor collaboration platforms such as IBM Lotus, Microsoft SharePoint, and the many other vendor offerings.

The next step up on the technology ladder for the PMO's project management processes is the establishment of a project management process framework. For most PMOs, the value of the process framework is tremendous for two reasons. First, it enables the PMO to properly house the content assets of the PMO. Content assets are all of the nonapplication items that PMOs have such as processes and templates, policies and guidance, executive summary dashboards, tips and techniques, and project management training and reference information. Second, and most important, the process framework enables the PMO to render the content assets of the PMO to the user in the context of the PMO project management processes being accessed and followed. In terms of adherence and effective usage, this is a significant and natural next step up in the use of intranet-based technology.

Rather than posting a methodology document on the intranet where users still have to read through a lengthy and often overly detailed document, the PMO provides users with a process framework that enables them to easily navigate through the appropriate processes and find the information that they require. Figures 3.9, 3.10, and 3.11 are examples of a PMO process framework that provide such PMO content assets as executive dashboards, project management processes, and process step guidance.

For PMOs of all shapes and sizes the process framework is far more than a methodology. It is a right-sized playbook for not only the project management processes and policies but for the executive processes as well such as governance, new project selection, and management of the portfolio. As a framework, tremendous amounts of content can be accessed with relative ease—far more than could ever be placed in a methodology document. A project management methodology document, if kept to a small and manageable file size, likely would not provide the level of detail and information required by the users. Conversely, if the methodology document does attempt to capture the full amount of detail required to stand up to a comprehensive project management process for the PMO, then it is likely to become so large, in terms of page count, that few users would have the time or desire to read through it.

From a technology perspective, if the PMO settles for applying too low of a technology to its project management process, then it is likely that the PMO

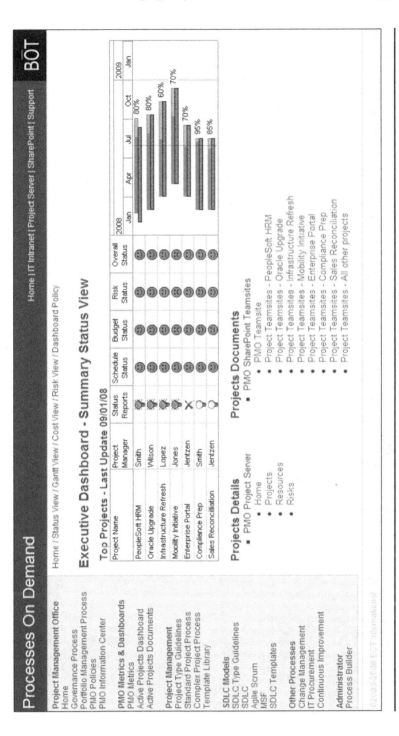

Figure 3.9 Executive dashboard

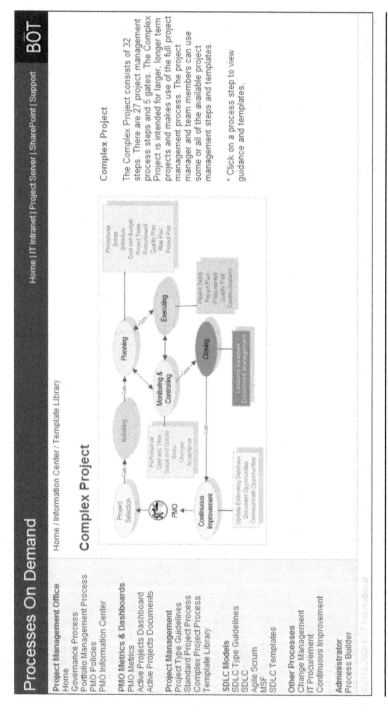

Figure 3.10 Complex project process

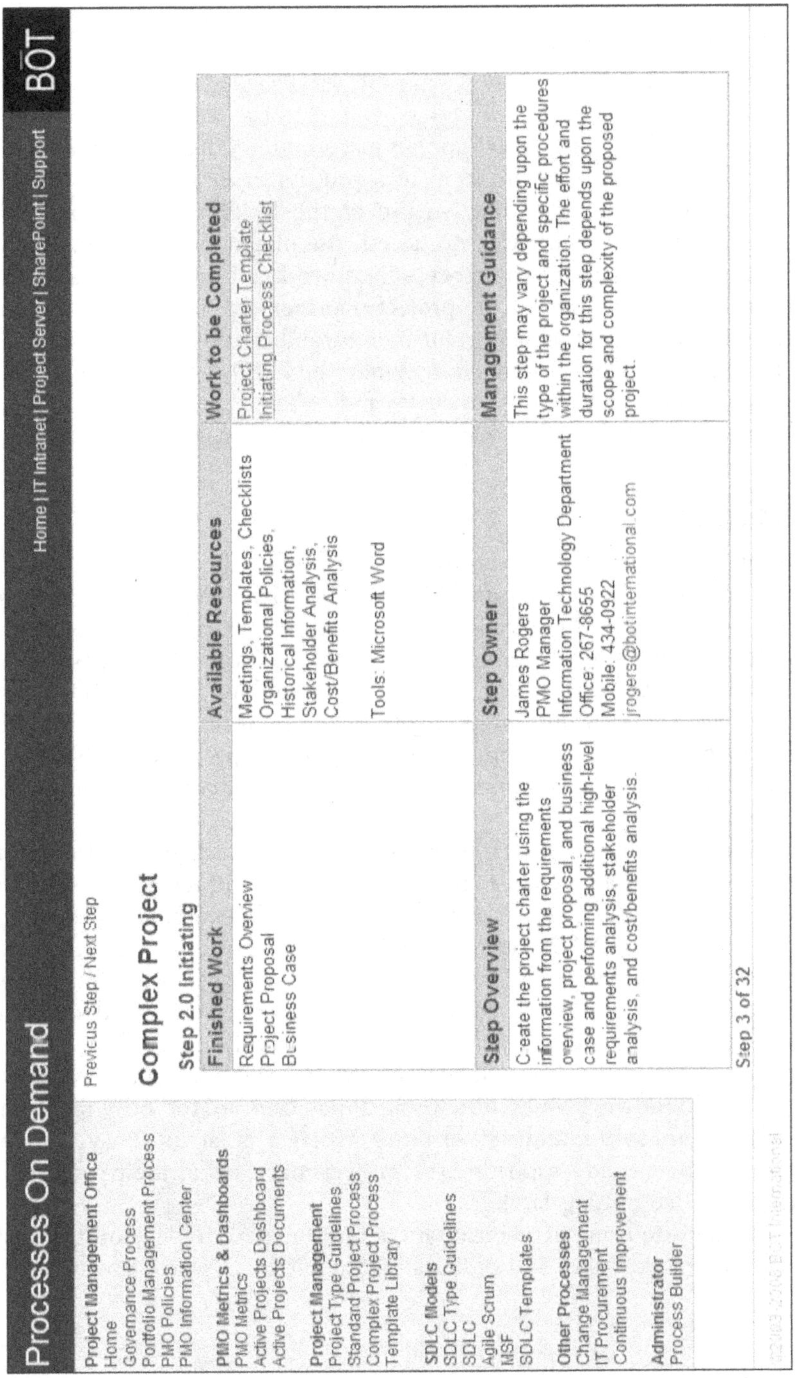

Processes On Demand

Home | IT Intranet | Project Server | SharePoint | Support

BŌT

Previous Step / Next Step

Complex Project

Step 2.0 Initiating

Project Management Office
Home
Governance Process
Portfolio Management Process
PMO Policies
PMO Information Center

PMO Metrics & Dashboards
PMO Metrics
Active Projects Dashboard
Active Projects Documents

Project Management
Project Type Guidelines
Standard Project Process
Complex Project Process
Template Library

SDLC Models
SDLC Type Guidelines
SDLC
Agile Scrum
MSF
SDLC Templates

Other Processes
Change Management
IT Procurement
Continuous Improvement

Administrator
Process Builder

Finished Work	Available Resources	Work to be Completed
Requirements Overview Project Proposal Business Case	Meetings, Templates, Checklists Organizational Policies, Historical Information, Stakeholder Analysis, Cost/Benefits Analysis	Project Charter Template Initiating Process Checklist
	Tools: Microsoft Word	

Step Overview	Step Owner	Management Guidance
Create the project charter using the information from the requirements overview, project proposal, and business case and performing additional high-level requirements analysis, stakeholder analysis, and cost/benefits analysis.	James Rogers PMO Manager Information Technology Department Office: 267-8655 Mobile: 434-0922 jrogers@botinternational.com	This step may vary depending upon the type of the project and specific procedures within the organization. The effort and duration for this step depends upon the scope and complexity of the proposed project.

Step 3 of 32

Figure 3.11   Process step guidance

ends up with a methodology-oriented mindset in the form of static methodology manuals and sets of templates. Though well intended, this does not bring about the desired level of effective usage and adherence to the PMO processes and policies.

On the other hand, if the PMO applies just a bit more technology to enable its methodology content in the form of a process framework, then a much greater level of buy-in and effective use of the PMO processes and policies occur. They are much easier to access, use, maintain, and improve on. The PMO project management process framework not only serves as an on-demand guide to execution of the project management process, but a useful resource for both project management training and continuous improvement. Using the technology of a process framework, the PMO is able to integrate all things useful and usable into its processes and policies driving higher levels of project management skill and organizational project management capabilities.

Economics

Surprisingly, economics has a subtle, negative effect on the processes and policies of many PMOs. The reason for this is simple. Many PMOs don't have the time or resources to develop their PMO project management process frameworks. Developing a process framework from scratch takes far more work and thought than most people realize unless they have done it before. First, you have all of the research, information gathering, and discussions and debates required to put forth a skeleton model of the PMO processes and policies. Though it is helpful to have standards to draw upon, a great deal of authoring needs to take place.

In addition to gathering all of the requisite process information and supporting documents, such as project management process and templates, substantial work needs to take place to determine and develop common formats for the information. Few PMOs are happy with a set of processes and templates each of different formats, styles, character sizes, and font types that have been cobbled together. Some organizations have internal standards for documents and intranet web pages along with authoring and publishing guidance, which can save a great deal of time in design and development, but many organizations do not. So for the PMO whose project managers are too busy managing projects to do this work and whose PMO manager is far too busy working with the executives and supporting the project managers in their projects to do this work, what options are left?

One option is to bring in a consultant, a PMO expert, to develop the project management processes and policies for the PMO. The problem with this approach is that most consultants who provide methodology consulting to their clients do this on a consulting engagement basis:

- ◆ Step one establishes the goals and objectives for the engagement.
- ◆ Step two involves the performance of a gap analysis through extensive interviews with management and staff.
- ◆ Step three includes the consultant's preparation and presentation of the gap analysis findings. Sometimes the gap analysis is related to the desired present and future state of how the PMO wants to operate. Other times the gap analysis is more of a report that ranks the assessed level of project management skills and capabilities of the project managers to a prescribed project management model such as the PMI Guide to the PMBOK®. In either case, nearly always the consultant is presenting information of which the PMO manager is already all too aware.
- ◆ Step four, the consultant develops the project management methodology for the client. This can take several days though much of the end product is similar from one client to the next.
- ◆ Step five, the consultant delivers and reviews the project management methodology with the PMO and changes are made if necessary.
- ◆ Step six, the consultant performs a number of workshops and training sessions to present the methodology to management and to train, in greater depth, the project managers in the methodology.

Many PMOs find this option to be too costly and time consuming. After all, they are not looking to purchase a lengthy consulting engagement, rather they are searching for a customizable project management process framework. Some PMOs might go forward with this option, but many others look for another option or accept the fact that they might have to do it themselves.

Another option is to work with the vendor that provided the project management training to the PMO. Every project management training firm has some kind of methodology offering. However, most of the methodology offerings provided by project management training firms have the look, touch, and feel of their training materials. They are structured more like an electronic version of a body of knowledge than a project management process for a PMO. Of course, their core business is performing project management training and in achieving economies of scale in the training business model so there is not a great deal of focus on, or time for, developing and implementing customizable project management methodology offerings. The economics of product development preclude most training firms from engaging in it.

Another option that the PMO might consider is the numerous internet-based products and services for project management methodology. Many of these subscription offerings and downloadable products are well-suited for individual use and they are inexpensive. In fact, without too much effort, one can search the internet and find a website or blog offering project management methodology documents and templates for free. Of course these things are of little value to a PMO. Most PMOs already have methodologies and templates. The IT infrastructure team already has their project delivery approach for IT infrastructure projects, the enterprise applications team already has their systems development methodology for major implementations of enterprise software, and the applications development organization already has their Agile software development methods for developing and maintaining software applications. What the PMO needs is not yet another approach for managing a project, but as Kendall and Rollins (2003) advise, an umbrella under which the various methodologies can operate in harmony.

For larger PMOs that have project portfolio management software applications such as those represented in the Gartner Group Project Portfolio Management (PPM) Magic Quadrant Report, another option for consideration to meet the project management process needs of the PMO is the PMO and project management best practices that are available from the PPM vendors. Some of these best practices are provided at no charge as part of the PPM application; others are modules that can be provided on a per-user licensable basis.

Many of these PPM vendor best practice frameworks are designed to work both with the vendor's PPM application as well as to be customizable to meet customer specific PMO processes and policies. These best practice frameworks cannot only save the PMO a considerable amount of time in establishing project management processes, but they are also tailored and integrated to the vendor's PPM application. Hence, they not only serve as the PMO's project management process, but also a roadmap for effective PPM tool usage.

In addition to the application and the project management processes, many of the leading PPM vendors have teams of PMO subject matter experts and project management process methodology consultants who are available to assist with PMO setup, methodology development, and, of course, PPM application usage. Of course if the PMO is not ready, or does not want, to implement a leading project portfolio management application, then the economics of cost and benefits likely preclude the PMO for acquiring the PPM vendor's application just for the sake of getting their project management process best practice framework. However, PMOs that are using these leading project portfolio management applications are well served by fully utilizing the project management process modules, workflows, and frameworks along with the methodology development and customization services provided by these vendors.

In response to the need that PMOs of all shapes and sizes have for a flexible and customizable project management process framework that can be quickly implemented and easily maintained, a number of *content-only* methodology offerings have emerged on the market. Some of these offerings are delivered as traditional out-of-the-box products, others are provided as subscription offerings, and yet others are provided as customizable solutions that come with, or require, implementation services to install and modify. Collectively these offerings offer an ability for the PMO to purchase and quickly set up and tailor their PMO processes and policies instead of the time consuming, and sometimes bothersome, task of doing it themselves from scratch.

There is no shortage of vendor solutions that address the process and policy needs of the PMO. As shown in Figure 3.12, some of these solutions are single-user offerings such as PC products and internet subscriptions that are typically used in a stand-alone manner by those managing projects; others are designed and intended to be multi-user solutions providing a complete framework for the PMO consisting of processes and policies, dashboards and metrics, and integration to the functional tools and applications of the PMO such as project portfolio management systems (Project Server, Planview, Clarity, ITG) and collaboration platforms (SharePoint, Lotus, eRoom).

Typically the PC-based products such as Method123, IT Toolkit, ProGo, offer sets of preformatted project management templates saving the PMO the

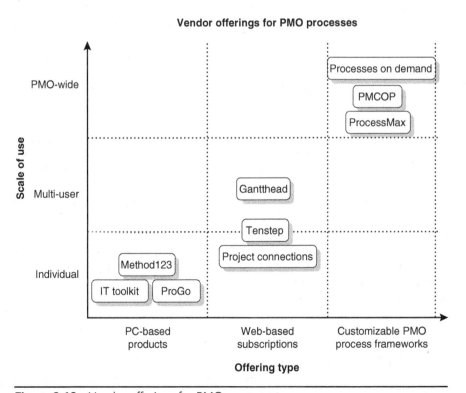

Vendor offerings for PMO processes

Figure 3.12   Vendor offerings for PMO processes

time that otherwise would be required to author project management documents. Such templates come in the form of a kit that is customarily licensed on a per user basis, which can often be problematic from a PMO expense perspective. Technically the project management templates are simply files, usually in Microsoft Word format. Most PMOs have a project manager or two who have purchased a project management template toolkit product of some kind. While there is some degree of value to template toolkits, most PMOs quickly realize that they require not just templates but a usable framework to render the templates as well as other information and guidance, and in the context of a set of scalable processes, best practices, and policies.

Web-based subscription offerings for PMO processes and policies such as Gantthead, Tenstep, and Project Connections offer not only project management templates but much more detailed information in the form of process workflows, guidance, and examples. As a subscription offering from the provider's website, PMO processes for project management are available as is on a licensed, per user basis. Though there is not an ability to customize the content, there is significant referential value to the PMO in having access to a wide range of processes, policies, and information that is maintained and updated by the provider. Such subscription information is helpful to most PMOs. A few of the PMO staff could draw upon a wide variety of project management and software development life cycle processes to review and use as input in the development of their own PMO processes. These selected processes can be used by those in the PMO with a per user subscription, or more likely, they can be tailored, implemented internally, and made available to users throughout the organization.

The effort to repurpose off-the-shelf PC-based methodology products and web-based subscription content into a useful and manageable PMO process framework requires a considerable amount of work. More and more PMOs are looking to vendor solutions for ready-to-set-up-and-use PMO process frameworks. Such solutions as Processes On Demand, PMCOP, ProcessMax, RUP, among others, provide not just the content for managing projects and managing the PMO, but also the much needed process framework. To the user the process framework is like an online playbook that not only provides all of the plays, but also the score of the game. To the PMO manager, or owner of the processes, the framework provides the ability to effectively manage the best practice content of the PMO and, more importantly, to truly achieve buy-in to the PMO, adherence to the PMO processes and policies, and institutionalization of project management knowledge and skills.

Collectively the emergence of these vendor products, subscriptions, and customizable PMO process frameworks has lessened the economic burden that, for many PMOs, has negatively impacted the development processes and policies. For PMOs that are resource- and budget-constrained, these vendor offerings can provide considerable assistance in the setup of PMO processes, policies, and supporting PMO content assets. Additionally, as productized solutions, in addition to cost and time savings, significantly higher levels of product quality are prevalent as compared to in-house developed approaches because of ongoing product development and numerous customer installations.

Summary

For many people in project management, the word methodology evokes many different visions. To some, methodology is a good thing; a way to describe that which is to be done. For others, methodology means bureaucracy and, irrespective of intent, methodologies are perceived to be too rigid, too lengthy, too detailed, and of too little actionable value. Some PMOs have intentionally moved away from using the term methodology in order to overcome resistances to standardized methods. Other PMOs have moved toward a more streamlined way of thinking about how the processes and policies of the PMO should work, how they should be provided, used, managed, and improved.

For most PMOs the key to having a useful and usable approach for managing projects as well as managing the PMO is to establish a useful and usable process framework that can be accessed by all those involved in the projects of the PMO. This requires the right kind of mindset. Rather than a methodology-oriented mindset in which the focus is limited to the *what* of the what is to be done, a process-oriented mindset keeps the focus on the results to be achieved. Process-oriented thinking has no limits and it seeks to answer, in context, not just the *what* but the *who, when, where, and why* of that which must be done.

Questions

1. What negative byproducts can be the result of formalized project management methodologies?
2. Does following a project management methodology always result in a successful project outcome?
3. In practical application, what are some of the problems that practitioners have when trying to follow a project management methodology?
4. In what three areas can methodology-oriented thinking have a negative impact on the PMO and those managing projects?
5. What are the characteristics of a methodology-oriented mindset?
6. What are the characteristics of a process-oriented mindset?
7. What is the difference between the methods-based mindset and the process-based mindset?
8. Why do project management methodologies typically fail to address the complete end-to-end work of a project that a PMO must undertake?

9. What are the limitations for project managers and the PMO of typical project management methodologies that only address the *what* of the what is to be done in the project effort?
10. Why do critics of project management methodology complain that they are focused too much on producing documents?
11. What are the key differences and limitations between project management methodologies that are solely based upon standards as opposed to project management methodologies that are based upon and driven by business needs?
12. What two measures can be taken to increase the focus on project delivery?
13. What do project delivery behaviors include?
14. What factors can interfere with an enterprise PMO's ability to focus on project delivery in terms of achieving and reporting measured PMO value each six month period?
15. How does an out-of-date project management methodology impact the PMO?
16. What kind of information in a project management methodology typically needs to be updated over time?
17. Why is integration of the project management methodology into a project management tool nearly always a bad approach for the PMO to take?
18. What problems are typically incurred by the PMO when project management methodology documents have no known or assigned owner?
19. In a process-centric PMO, what are the duties of the project management process owner?
20. What are the disadvantages of the singular project management methodology?
21. Describe the levels of technology that are typically applied to a project management methodology?
22. How does the level of technology that is applied to the project management methodology impact its usage?
23. How does economics negatively impact the project management processes and policies of the PMO?
24. As an alternative to the time and cost of creating processes and policies from scratch, what three kinds of vendor offerings for PMO processes and policies are available?

References

Ambler, Scott. 2007. "Agile/Lean Documentation: Strategies for Agile Software Development." http://www.agilemodeling.com/essays. (Accessed June 2, 2008)

Carr, David. 2008. "Minimise Your Project Management Documentation." http://www.projectsmart.co.uk. (Accessed June 2, 2008)

Cartwright, David. 2007. "Why I Bloody Hate Formal Methodologies," http://www.techworld.com. (Accessed June 2, 2008)

Crawford, Kent. 2002. *The Strategic Project Office.* New York: Marcel Decker AG.

Eskelin, Allen. 2008. "Why PMO's Fail." http://www.projectsmart.co.uk. (Accessed June 2, 2008)

Filicetti, John. 2006."The Focus Should Be Project Delivery, Not Project Management." http://www.gantthead.com/discussions. (Accessed June 2, 2008)

Haughey, Duncan. 2008. "Avoiding the Project Management Obstacle Course." http://www.projectsmart.co.uk. (Accessed June 2, 2008)

Imai, Masaaki. 1986. *Kaizen.* New York: McGraw-Hill Publishing. (Accessed June 2, 2008)

Kendall, Gerald I. and Steven C. Rollins. 2003. *Advanced Project Portfolio Management and the PMO.* Florida: J. Ross Publishing.

Kerzner, Harold. 2001. *Project Management,* New York: John Wiley and Sons.

Kerzner, Harold. *Strategic Planning for Project Management using a Project Management Maturity Model.* John Wiley and Sons.

Makar, Andrew. 2008. "Too May Templates." http://www.amakar.com. (Accessed June 2, 2008)

Padilla, Ramon. 2005. "Mired in Methodology." http://www.techrepublic.com. (Accessed June 2, 2008)

Riley, Vernon. 2008. "Project Methodologies—Not a Silver Bullet." http://www.projectsmart.co.uk. (Accessed June 2, 2008)

Turbit, Neville. 2004. "Project Management and Software Development Methodology." http://www.projectperfect.com.au. (Accessed June 2, 2008)

Wood, Michael. 2000. "What is a Process Improvement Methodology Anyway." http://www.gantthead.com/articles. (Accessed June 2, 2008)

Executive Insights

Evolving from a Traditional PMO to an Execution-Oriented PMO

Richard Eichen

Managing Principal, Return On Efficiency

Most companies have the PMO they deserve, not the one they need. In fact, the easiest way to take a snapshot view of an organization is via its PMO and project management approach.

Rules and Procedures-Driven PMOs— Reporting over Executing

Those companies that are heavily calcified or have a punitive view of mistakes tend to have rules and procedure-based PMOs (RPMOs) that act as gatekeepers and reporting agents. It adds little to the actual success of a project and often leads to neglecting to issue an early warning that the scope is too small/large and that a project will not achieve the required business goals (but all issues are well documented). Its value-add is in allowing senior managers to horse trade among themselves for resource allocations and priority or provide political cover should anything go wrong.

Consider the following real life scenarios:

- ◆ Scenario 1: A large global insurance company has a highly political systems function, employees who had been there too long to be effective and old systems (overwhelmingly 20+ year old undocumented systems). They acted like a defeated army, going through the motions. Case in point—for many years Treasury sent a file at the end of each quarter with the foreign exchange rates approved for all financial reporting across the company.

In an effort to modernize, Treasury built an intranet site with these rates posted, simultaneously shutting down the file transfer. This last move required the systems group to disconnect the existing file transfer functionality and forced clericals and two levels of management to enter and then approve these rates, simultaneously creating a Sarbanes-Oxley issue.

Bottom line, it was recommended by outside consultants that the foreign exchange rate file transfer be reinstated and a cost to turn existing code back on was estimated at just under $100K, all-in. The existing manager who supervised the manual entry of the rates felt put upon and resisted filling out the PMO required justifications and request forms, saying "I've been trying to fix this for five years, why will they do it now?"

The consultant prevailed and the manager reluctantly completed and submitted the forms for the project to the PMO who promptly let it sit and stall. It became apparent to the outside consultant that the systems culture was based on political infighting and vendetta and that the PMO was perfectly aligned with this dysfunctional organization. An analogy would be an argument on the Titanic one April evening over who had jurisdiction over lifeboats and therefore who should run that project.

- ◆ Scenario 2: One of the largest systems companies in the world had their PMO project commissars review projects and then filled in forms to show progress, earned value, and other relevant information. The good news: it relieved the operating/executing managers from having to fill out a stack of forms, online or otherwise. The bad news: the PMO added zero value and was generally seen as a hindrance.

- ◆ Scenario 3: A global financial firm forced to sell major *crown jewels* to stay alive had long been known for both a *rock and roll* culture as well as for its multiple reporting oriented PMOs. This perceived lack of PMO value by operating executives is exemplified by a C level comment to the effect of 'we can divest as required by the buyer (of each crown jewel) and don't need a PMO'. Thus the culture that got them into financial distress was manifested in their PMO approach which in turn continued even as they shrank to a fraction of their former size.

- ◆ Scenario 4: A global financial services firm had so many strategic projects in-flight that a centralized PMO function was implemented to track and report to the audit committee and senior management. The organizations' highly political culture involved presenting results in the best possible light, spinning as required without actually completely misrepresenting. Results were often reported as *completed* rather than *approved* to sidestep the lack of business management's happiness with many projects deliverables and scope. The end result? The detached PMO reported what was present to them. Again, they had little value-add that a good project reporting tool couldn't provide faster and with more colors.

The underlying common denominator of these examples is a rigid methodological view of a PMO embedded within the organizational unit it protects.

Focused on PMBOK® Guide style methodology, the PMO success is measured in timeliness of reporting, not project results. The good news is that the salary structure of reporting oriented PMOs are relatively inexpensive, but as the adage states 'you get what you pay for'. Organizationally, it sits alongside the sidelines of the organization supplying information to the project's leaders.

Execution PMO—Responsible for Execution as Well as Reporting

A newer form of PMO is rapidly gaining currency. The executing PMO (EPMO) is more in tune with the times than the centralized command and control form of RPMO related above. This new form of PMO takes on execution responsibility as well as reporting functions. It twists and turns as projects require, but always around a firm understanding that they are completely responsible for producing business-aligned results. Organizationally, it *is* the project leadership.

The EPMO structure involves an empowered matrix in which project managers are embedded into specific contributing departments and interface both with the contributors as well as with the department's senior leadership to ensure the department is not being overloaded with project demands/timelines without senior leadership input/workload balancing. Contributors thus do not feel torn between their boss' demands and those of the project.

The EPMO matrix is applicable to project portfolios in which multiple projects touch the same departments each with their own levels of demand and timelines. It is, therefore, the preferred approach to business projects such as mergers and acquisitions, divestiture and new product introduction initiatives as well as to strategic enterprise-wide IT projects, including the creation of a common financial language (for consistent and timely reporting and overall risk controls), and the required IT infrastructure such as a global SAP implementation. EPMO reporting and processes are real-world, accurate, action-oriented, and compliant to the guidelines of Sarbanes-Oxley.

A typical EPMO organization and mandate structures are illustrated in Figure 3.13, highlighting how the EPMO both synchronizes all projects with each business unit/department and also controls the entire project. Thus, it has the ability to execute not just report.

Each project manager also has to be a subject matter expert relative to the department in which they are embedded. For example, from experience implementing and observing the operation of EPMOs, the embed project manager in finance and accounting must be an accountant (preferably a CPA) who understands the financial world, such as the issues and pressures behind the periodic fiscal quarter closings and regulatory/statutory reporting (ex: 10Q and 10K). The IT embed project manager should have an application develop-

Execution PMO (EPMO) model

	Embedded project managers			
	PM Project 1 ex: New GL	PM Project 2 ex: New product	PM Project 3 ex: divestiture	EPMO SME/PMs
Finance and accounting	X		X	Embed PM
Information technology	X	X	X	Embed PM
Sales		X		Embed PM
Field operations	X		X	Embed PM
Product marketing		X	X	Embed PM
Supply chain and logistics		X	X	Embed PM
Manufacturing		X	X	Embed PM
Legal and compliance	X	X	X	Embed PM

Figure 3.13 EPMO model—embedded project managers

ment leadership background, understanding the various app dev methodologies, such as waterfall, agile, etc.

The key reason for this high level of project manager expertise is to ensure that the embed project manager knows what needs to be delivered, reviews results from the subject matter expert point of view, and manages accordingly. He/she also commands peer level respect from busy business unit leaders and direct contributors. EPMO staff is typically more expensive than the typical PMO employee, but from an enterprise perspective, the overall number is reduced and therefore the cost is the same but the results are significantly improved.

The following examples illustrate the benefits of the EPMO:

♦ A financial services firm had an urgent series of enterprise-level transformation projects to modernize their entire back office, ranging from people to systems to reporting. Even though this organization had multiple PMOs in place (the usual RPMO variety), management rightly decided to run this enterprise project through an execution-focused EPMO. The result was a tightly synchronized series of projects delivered on time and within budget with controlled disruptions in the contributing areas.

♦ A global Fortune level company had to disentangle newly divested business units quickly as part of an overall slimming down when it was decided to exit businesses rather than cut expenses across the board.

The typical PMOs were reporting results, while not pre-identifying or assisting with the entire legal, infrastructure, personnel and other real-world components of selling off businesses. Everything was done on an as-discovered basis. An EPMO was implemented which, after a brief start-up period, accomplished the disentanglements.

◆ A well-respected global company, a component of the Dow, was implementing a new and large-scale global financial system. The technical PMO was rigidly adhering to a nine-month work stream that many business leaders considered unrealistic. It came to a head during a confrontational steering committee meeting when one of the business leaders told the old-style PMO project managers 'you'll be off onto your next project and I'll be left holding the bag still unable to close the books within a reasonable timeframe'. The traditional PMO leader replied 'we're your partners', to a reply of 'when I lose my job because this isn't working, will you lose yours? If not, we're not partners'. From that point forward the project lost support and eventually failed. An EPMO, staffed by SMEs with project management experience would have avoided this.

In summary, the major differences between the EPMO and the usual RPMO are:

1. The EPMO is tasked with final delivery not just status reporting.
2. Each contributing department or business unit uses their embed project manager for overall coordination across all projects, reducing confusion, conflicts, and frustration.
3. The project manager and embedded project managers all have the businesses' strategic goals completely in mind. Projects remain aligned and sufficiently scoped.

Summary

How does an organization move from the static RPMO to the more dynamic EPMO? Each organization has its own unique culture. Some are distributed but cooperative, others are balkanized and still others hierarchical. Some are punitive toward mistakes (stifling innovation but encouraging CYA behaviors) and others embrace change. An EPMO is culture changing.

Organizations embracing change can implement an EPMO culture quickly using internal personnel. These are elite organizations with high-quality human resource (HR) models and employee tenure is often in the 4- to 7-year range, refreshing itself with quality new hires and fresh perspectives. The EPMO approach is simply the formalization of how they think and act.

Balkanized or hierarchical organizations (often called traditional) have great difficulty in evolving to an EPMO with long tenured (20 years is not unusual) employees knowing how to do things *our way*, forcing conformity on change adverse to new hires. They are comforted by using the traditional PMO approach, even if it is no longer up to the tasks at hand.

Often an undeniable cataclysmic event is required to force a rethink of business as usual and this is the best time to break with the past and implement the EPMO paradigm. These organizations have to make the decision to thrive in the new economic and global reality before they can adopt an EPMO, which can then be used to heal the organization.

New project management leadership and a non-balkanized culture are required. Assuming an entire organization did not have its toxic assets blow up and nearly kill the entire entity thus forcing immediate enterprise change, as in the current case of the financial services industry, the best approach is to start with a single strategic project, spanning business units, and a focus not mired in methodology. Rather the focus is on execution and on demonstrating, by example, the value of the EPMO. Put subject matter expert project managers in the business departments and think process, not methodology.

4

Managing the PMO:
Embracing Flexibility
vs
Mandating Conformance

In the well-intended spirit of establishing consistency in project management, many project management offices (PMOs) struggle with quickly becoming overly bureaucratic and narrowly focused. This can easily result in becoming more and more detailed over a smaller, inside-the-box, point of view. The cartoon (see Figure 4.1) shows that with experience and upon reflection the need for flexibility within the structure is likely to arrive at the doorstep of the PMO. Some PMOs recognize and act upon this need, but many others do not. Instead, they continue to exhibit bureaucratic behaviors, not so much because of a desire to be rigid, but more on account of a misplaced focus.

For example, in his project management office handbook, Gerard Hill (2008, p. 3) writes "A methodology is developed to apply adopted standards and practices to project management, such as that contained in *A Guide to the Project Management Body of Knowledge* (PMBOK®)." At first glance Hill's description of why PMOs develop a methodology seems accurate and innocuous. Who can disagree with the premise that a methodology is developed to apply adopted standards? Well, there are three significant problems with this premise that Hill and so many other PMO enthusiasts are too quick to espouse.

The first problem with this premise is that the purpose of a methodology is not to apply an adopted standard. The purpose of applying a methodology is to achieve a predictable and successful outcome. If adhering to an adopted standard, or more than one adopted standard, helps achieve that objective,

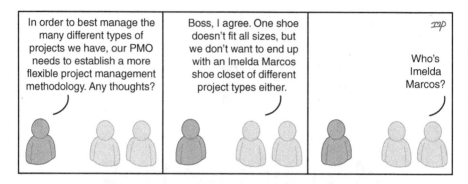

Figure 4.1   PMO comics—flexible methodology

then that is a useful strategy to consider. But the adherence to an adopted standard is a strategy to use, an approach; not the goal of the methodology.

Case in point, a large pharmaceutical PMO developed a methodology for project management (PMM). They took the approach advocated by Hill and others and went about developing their PMM to apply the latest version of the Project Management Institute (PMI) standard for project management, the Guide to the PMBOK®. They produced a detailed process workflow consisting of the 44 process steps of the PMBOK® along with a few other steps and gates of their own. The end result was a 52-step PMM complete with templates, checklists, and signoffs for every step that was utilized for every project performed by the PMO.

Almost immediately after its introduction and rollout, the PMM had to be completely overhauled. That the initial methodology was aligned to the PMBOK® was not debatable. That the methodology provided an approach for project management that would achieve consistent and successful results was not only debatable but it was quickly dismissed as even viable. Where the team that developed the PMM went astray in their effort, as do many PMO enthusiasts, was in their mindset that the goal of the methodology was to apply the accepted standard. Only after rejection of their work did they come to realize that the goal of the PMM should have been to ensure that projects could be managed in a manner that would produce consistent and successful outcomes.

The second problem of the premise is that most standards for project management, such as bodies of knowledge and popular life cycle models, by design, typically do not provide a great deal of prescribed guidance for projects of differing sizes and types. In the case of the 52-step PMBOK® Guide aligned PMM that the pharmaceutical PMO team developed, it was much too detailed for all but the largest of project efforts. For small- and medium-sized projects, the methodology was overkill.

In addition to not accommodating small- and medium-sized projects, the methodology did not accommodate projects of different types. In particular, the enterprise applications development team had already developed and had been using a software development process aligned to the Agile Scrum model. The development team was already successfully managing their enterprise applications projects and rejected the PMO's PMM outright. To the development team, the suggestion to abandon their leading edge and optimized approach in favor of a PMM just because it is based upon a standard was a large step backward.

And the third problem of the premise that a PMM is developed to apply adopted standards is the fact the most PMOs need to address work that takes place both before and after the various steps of the standard. For example, in the popular Project Management Institute (PMI) work, the Guide to the PMBOK®, this standard starts with the initiating process and ends with the closing process. For most PMOs there is a defined and repeatable amount of work that begins before the initiation of the project. Some PMOs call this work project selection; others call it project origination. The name of the process step is not important, but what is important is the understanding of all of the work that is required to take place and the documentation of this work in the project management process. Likewise, most PMOs have a post-closing process step. Some PMOs call this step continuous improvement; other PMOs have different names that describe the work to be performed after the project has completed the closing step of the process.

The difference between approaching the development of a PMM with a mindset to apply a standard instead of a mindset to achieve consistent and successful outcomes is often the difference between a PMO that is perceived to mandate conformance and a PMO that is perceived to embrace flexibility. If all projects were the same in terms of size, type, risk, complexity, technology, tools, and people, then conformance would be a good thing. But for most PMOs, projects are not homogeneous and strict conformance to an inflexible methodology only produces consistency in frustrating the project team.

In another example of approaching project management with too much of a mandatory conformance mindset, in their book on the project office, Block and Frame (1998, p.27) write "If the project management approach is to be implemented well, it is vital that everyone in the organization march to the beat of a single drummer." For most PMOs this is bad advice. The mindset of a singular methodology or path to follow for project management is a dangerous one. It can lead to the thinking that an organization can approach managing all of their projects—upgrading a server, moving a data center, implementing a vendor application, developing a software product, not to mention all of their line-of-business projects such as sales and marketing—in a consistent and successful way simply by applying a standard. Even a drum beater has more than one drum. So too, the PMO frequently needs more than just one approach for managing projects, standard or not, to meet the project challenges it no doubt faces.

Mandating Conformance

Mandating conformance within the PMO is not always a bad thing: sometimes mandating conformance is necessary (see Figure 4.2). Conformance to the processes and policies of the PMO are driven by many factors both internal and external. Some areas of compliance are non-negotiable and are easy to understand.

Conformance as driven by external compliance requirements is the easiest to grasp and it is typically mandatory. If Department of Defense contractors want to participate in a large bid, among other things, they have to demonstrate compliance to the ANSI/EIA-748 Standard for Earned Value Manage-

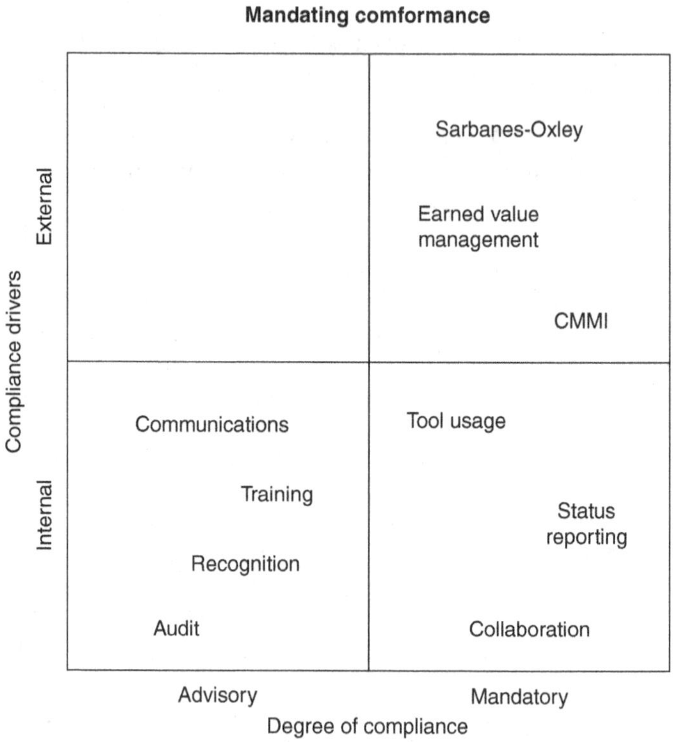

Mandating comformance

Figure 4.2   Mandating conformance

ment Systems. Likewise, CMMI certification is becoming a requirement for companies to do business in a number of industries, including the U.S. Government, the military, and in aerospace. With the passage of the Sarbanes-Oxley Act of 2002, also known as the Public Company Accounting Reform and Investor Protection Act of 2002, many companies now complying to the Sarbanes-Oxley Act have instituted processes and internal controls that are no longer just good governance, but mandatory. As espoused in the IT Control Objectives for Sarbanes-Oxley published by the IT Governance Institute (2004, p. 13), "Although the Act and supporting regulations have rewritten the rules for accountability, disclosure, and reporting, the Act's many pages of legalese support a simple premise: good corporate governance and ethical business practices are no longer optional niceties." There might be some in the organization who view processes required for such external compliance to be overly bureaucratic or taxing on their particular areas of work, but this is a price that the organization is willing to pay.

Conformance as driven by internal factors can range from advisory to mandatory. Mandatory conformance is often required as a matter of policy. For example, if a PMO implements a project portfolio management (PPM) system, then there no doubt are several areas of mandatory conformance and participation. For one, usage of the system is mandatory not optional. To the extent that a project manager, project team members or other functional departments might not want to use the new system or see the value in it and would prefer to go on using their own tools and approaches, this might be nice to know but it doesn't exempt them from mandatory participation. Since a PPM system cannot meet the needs for which it was intended unless it is used properly, as a matter of management policy the users must discard their old approaches and get on with the new.

This not only applies to tool usage, but also extends into the requisite processes and best practices supporting the tool usage and the management of the project effort. Where project processes such as monitoring and controlling might have been performed ad hoc and with a high degree of variance from one project manager to the next for such things as reporting of project status, project issues, and change requests, the implementation of a PPM system likely requires a common approach to these activities to provide management with actionable information. In this context, mandating conformance is not a bad thing at all. In fact, it is required to achieve objectives set by management.

There is also room for areas of internal compliance that are advisory in nature. Such policies as project communications might vary based upon project size, complexity, and the overall duration of the project. Weekly reporting is fine for shorter term projects, but for complex longer-term projects it is inadvisable to report weekly. Project management training and certification is advised for some and mandatory for others. And management activities related to the project such as project audit and project team recognition can vary based upon guidelines and management discretion. All projects do not warrant the same amount of recognition, nor do all projects warrant the time and effort that it takes to perform a post-project audit.

In general, mandating conformance is not necessarily bureaucratic, but it can quickly become that way especially when the reasons for conformance are not clearly stated and understood, as well as when areas of conformance that require guidelines and discretion are absent of them.

For many organizations there is a belief that project management is overhead. It requires project managers and team members to spend more time filling out forms and reports than doing, or contributing to, real work. This belief can be even more pronounced in smaller, more agile companies and departments where there is an anti-bureaucracy mindset. These devout anti-process, anti-methodology people recognize that some amount of project management is required for the really large projects, but they are adamant in their belief that project management is not required for smaller projects. This attitude can be justified easily by past experiences in smaller project initiatives in which the project manager and project team were required to follow a one-shoe-fits-all-sizes methodology. Though conformance to the methodology was mandatory, it was clear for all to see that the prescribed steps of the methodology did not fit the project effort and that many of the templates would have been helpful or were needed when managing the project. But when it comes to managing small projects, not having a methodology is not much better than an overly detailed and unusable methodology. In fact, it might be worse.

When organizations manage small projects without a methodology, they encounter untold, but small, execution difficulties. Projects run well over their initial schedules, but slippage is measured in weeks not months. The projects also run over their budgets, but again by small amounts and the overage is measured in thousands of dollars not hundreds of thousands of dollars. Usually only a handful of people such as specialists doubling as project managers and their immediate management are aware of these continual schedule slippages and budget overages that are present in so many of these small projects. But then one day, one of these small projects blows up and becomes a huge, visible problem and embarrassment for the organization. That is when the management spotlight shines on the department and such comments as 'not again guys' or 'you guys can't even manage a simple project' or 'when will you guys ever learn?'

The bottom line is that developing a PMM that does not meet the needs of all of the projects of the organization is no longer an option for most PMOs. The days of the singular PMM in which everyone marched to the same drum beat are over. Though mandating some degree of conformance is required by the PMO, the mindset of the PMO needs to be on embracing flexibility and making project management more pertinent to the project effort and easier and more effective to use for all those involved in the project initiatives of the organization. When an organization does allow for, and apply, guidelines and discretions to its processes and policies, then it is well on its way to embracing flexibility and this offers the potential to greatly improve performance and finally get project management right.

Embracing Flexibility

For the PMO there are many benefits to embracing flexibility, but there is a fine art to it all. Whereas embracing flexibility allows for the practical application of different approaches to different situations, it does not mean that there is an absence of processes and policies or that simply winging it is ever acceptable. Although it is critical to welcome new ideas and healthy debate over how to improve on or establish new methods, this does not mean that the existing approaches that the PMO has worked so diligently to put into place can be ignored or abandoned. Unlike operational work that lends itself to a steady state, optimized workflow, project managing and managing the PMO lends itself to a barrage of opportunities. While some PMOs might choose to remain static in how they apply techniques for managing projects, in how they manage the PMO, and in how they influence project management throughout the organization, most PMOs do not. Hence, for these PMOs there is a need to embrace flexibility while at the same time establishing an environment conducive to achieving success through consistent and repeatable methods not just earnest work and hope.

For PMOs of all shapes and sizes there are three key challenges to embracing flexibility while at the same time establishing consistency throughout the organization (see Figure 4.3). The first challenge is framed around how project management is viewed as an organizational discipline. The second challenge is centered on how projects, as an opportunity to deliver value or satisfy a customer, are perceived. The third challenge to embracing flexibility is directly related to how the organization institutionalizes, encourages, and rewards the behaviors that produce good results and eradicates those behaviors that are undesired and produce ineffective results.

How Project Management Is Viewed

The way in which project management is viewed throughout the organization can sometimes be a significant challenge that the PMO must overcome. And it is not so much that one organization views project management favorably and another does not, it is rather that within every organization there are pockets of opinions about project management that span a gamut of beliefs and convictions. Fortunately, most people that have been exposed to project management quickly become converts. As Kim Heldman (2005, p. 14) writes, "Utilizing good project management techniques puts you in the driver's seat.

Keys to embracing flexibility

	Discourage	Encourage
View of project management	Time consuming Tedious Bureaucratic	Reduces errors Streamlined to fit Enables decisions
View of projects	Time and cost based Formal and complex IT centric	Value based Collaborative Organizational wide
Organizational behaviors	Singular approach Rigid methods Spotlights failures	Multiple approaches Open to improvement Rewards success

Figure 4.3   Keys to embracing flexibility

Instead of your project running wildly out of control and bumping into every obstacle in its path, you'll steer it to successful completion by applying the tools and techniques of an established project management process." Those that have had training in project management and that have had experience in managing well-defined, formal projects that fit the PMM well are among the greatest enthusiasts for project management as a discipline. However, not everyone in the organization fits this mold.

On the other hand, many people view project management as bureaucratic and rigid. The initiating process can be overly demanding and call for information that is not known and analysis that cannot easily be provided. The planning process can be overly detailed and tedious as well as complex with respect to the use of project scheduling tools. It is not too difficult to find ways to spend an inordinate amount of time before any real project work even gets started. These are all valid concerns and it is important to recognize that those that are objectionable to traditional project management have their opinions and biases not because they are unskilled and want to take shortcuts. Sure, there are people who no doubt fit that mold, but they should not be lumped in with the folks that have well-reasoned arguments against traditional project management.

For most organizations there are some useful points of contrast that shed light on the fundamental differences between advocates of project management and those who believe project management can, and often does, get in the way. Four key points of contrast are planning, controlling, completion, and quality.

When it comes to project planning, proponents of project management put considerable time and effort into building the project plan. It is assumed that with enough preparation all project requirements can be identified, defined, and planned with precision and accuracy. Opponents of this project planning mindset question the assumption that enough can be known in advance. The project plan will most likely change, therefore, it should not be viewed as a fixed roadmap. This sets expectations that can't be met. No doubt, in a fixed project environment where requirements are known in advance, the detailed project plan can be of use. However, in a change-ridden project environment in which many requirements are not known and cannot be known in advance, the overly detailed plan can be counterproductive.

Another area of contrast is project controlling. Proponents of project management engage in project monitoring and control and make use of status reports, project performance reports, and logs for issues and change requests. It takes considerable time and effort to document these details and hold meetings to resolve issues, but these controlling activities provide the basis for understanding the true performance of the project relative to the project plan baseline. Opponents of this project controlling mindset view their role in project controlling to be one of developing relationships and taking action. As the project is inherently faced with change and uncertainty, the focus for project controlling should be placed on managing by walking around (MBWA) and removing any obstacles that the project team faces, rather than producing documentation, reports, and calling for meetings. Such MBWA provides a forward view of problems and opportunities as opposed to an after-the-fact view that comes with spending large amounts of time updating the project documentation.

Project completion is another area of contrast between proponents of project management and those less convinced. Proponents of project management typically measure project success as a function of how well the project performed in terms of schedule and budget. If the project ran significantly behind schedule or over budget, it would be deemed an unsuccessful project. Opponents of this mindset measure project success, not by budget and schedule, but by the delivery of value as established by the customer. Rather than a plan-driven approach that leads to producing the planned result, opponents of project management simply focus on producing the desired result. If the desired result was what was originally planned, that's all the better. But in an environment of uncertainty and rapid change, it is anticipated and even welcomed that the intended deliverable might evolve over time based upon real or perceived value to the customer. This shifts the mindset from one of checking off a list of planned deliverables completed to ensuring customer satisfaction and acceptance of the deliverables.

There is one more area of contrast in project quality. Oftentimes, proponents of project management view project quality as a means to assess how well the project followed the plan. In such circumstances, quality assurance activities might be concerned with the inspection project documentation. Hence, if the project plan does not change and the project follows the plan and all of the documents are completed, then the quality of the project would likely be assessed to be on the high side. Opponents of this mindset view quality differently. They anticipate that the project plan will not be followed. So rather than measuring conformance to the project plan, they seek to measure the degree to which the customer is satisfied with the deliverables.

For many organizations the way in which project management as a discipline is viewed all comes down to tolerance for uncertainty and change. Traditional project management does not like uncertainty and change. Of course there are processes and controlling mechanisms for the mitigation of risks and the management of project changes, but the assumed premise is that enough can be known in advance to build an accurate project plan. Those less sold on traditional project management have a different view of project management. They would like to see a more flexible mindset for project management along with a set of less rigid, change-tolerant project management practices. The PMO must provide leadership in the way project management is viewed by both camps by providing flexibility within structure to best meet the needs of the project. If the PMO provides overly detailed methodologies and rigid approaches for project management, then many in the organization find ways to skirt around the processes performing the bare minimum amount of work required to conform to the methodology. This heightens the view that project management is time consuming and stands in the way of real work getting done. On the other hand, if the PMO embraces flexibility so that practitioners can follow best-fit approaches for the needs of the project at hand, then the view of project management by all involved is a positive one and project results achieved are likely to be better.

How Projects Are Viewed

Just as different people can have a different view of what project management is, so too can different people have a different view of what a project is. The word project is increasingly used these days in a wide variety of ways from traditional business settings such as an IT department or PMO to television shows such as "The Apprentice" made famous by Donald Trump and his end-of-show pronouncement *You're Fired!* And, not long ago in a meeting that I had with the PMO manager of a leading university, an individual who the PMO manager was mentoring and grooming for further responsibility and advancement was even referred to as a project.

So what exactly is a project? The official definition in the PMI's third edition of *A Guide to the Project Management Body of Knowledge* (PMBOK® Guide 2004, p. 5) reads "A project is a temporary endeavor undertaken to create a unique product, service, or result." While most organizations are happy to abide by this definition, there are some organizations that are not. Glen Alleman (2004), the Vice President of the Program Planning and Controls consulting practice for a Denver professional services firm, comments in his Herding Cats blog, ". . . the definition of a project as given in the PMBOK® Guide and the like is actually too narrow." Alleman points out that these definitions assume that a project has a finite duration, a specific deliverable, and a start and an end. While such a definition of a project might be useful in a discrete project, for modern firms and especially the IT department, it limits the management of a project effort.

Randy Englund, noted author and project management consultant, provides another view on what a project is. Englund (2008) writes "Because you apply this approach [project management] to more activities and improve your overall return on investment by treating everything as a project, you find yourself asking yourself the same question, 'What is not a project?'" When asked by a participant in a project management workshop what is a project the response Englund gave was "Not much."

But getting back to the formal definition of a project, some folks such as Agile enthusiasts challenge the premise that a project is temporary as defined by having a defined start date and end date. The issue isn't that the project effort is temporary, rather that the project start and end date might not necessarily be defined. In theory it would seem that all projects would have a start and end date, but in reality things are not always so neat and tidy. For many organizations, there are many initiatives that are referred to as projects that have a general start date and timeframe for completion. It is not so much that these organizations are immature with respect to project management. To the contrary, these organizations might be skilled in project management yet prefer to view project completion as a measure of customer satisfaction instead of the delivery of deliverables by a certain date. Even though we, as project managers, seek to establish control and manage the chaos, the organization might not be focused nor operate that way. So while it is desired to view the project as a temporary endeavor with a known start and end date, this might not necessarily be the case.

In addition to the notion of the project being a temporary endeavor that might or might not be universally agreed to, there are those that struggle with the concept that a project produces a unique result. This does not mean that a project can't be similar or even exactly identical to another project. To the contrary, you can have projects that are virtually identical to each other such as upgrading the servers in the New York data center and upgrading the servers in the Los Angeles data center. The unique outcome isn't a function of the type of project or the characteristics of the project, rather the specific outcome at a given point in time.

As in the server upgrade example, there can be many server upgrade projects, but there is only one unique project to upgrade the servers for a specific location at a point in time. A useful way to think about the uniqueness of the project outcome is to compare and contrast the outcome of an assembly line to that of a project. The outcome of the assembly line, from machine bearings to automobiles, is ostensibly the same. The project outcome, however, from one project to the next is not.

Another useful way to think about the uniqueness of a project is to compare and contrast operational work from project work. Operational work such as the IT helpdesk involves the performance of tasks usually in a support capacity. A user might need a password reset, calls the helpdesk, and the attending service specialist performs the appropriate tasks. Such work that can be performed with minimal or no planning is viewed by most people as operational work, not project work.

For most organizations the real challenge is not so much what constitutes the definition of a project. Most teams can work within the traditional definition of a project, though contemporary approaches toward project management such as the many forms of Agile principles and concepts are adding new, and welcomed, points of view. A far greater problem for organizations in terms of how projects are viewed is the lack of, and the need for, a well-defined view of the many different categories of projects. The root of this problem lies in the fact that different project types require different project management approaches and this leads to competitive schools of thought that prefer to bicker with one another and find shortcomings in each other's approaches rather than admit that there is, and needs to be, room for multiple approaches.

Take the case of Kent, the new chief information officer (CIO) at a banking institution. Upon his arrival, one of the many challenges Kent faced was what to do with the PMO. The PMO had been started two years previously to provide support and gain better control over all of the projects within the IT department. The infrastructure team had one approach for managing projects and the applications team had an altogether different approach for managing projects. The infrastructure team followed a legacy project life cycle model and the applications team had developed an Agile approach for software development. Neither approach was aligned to nor embodied the project management processes and knowledge areas of the leading standard for project management, the Guide to the PMBOK®. The PMO team developed and rolled out a singular PMM document complete with process steps, detailed instructions in the methodology, and a large set of project management templates, forms, and checklists to be filled out for every project effort.

Kent met individually with the PMO team, the infrastructure team, and the applications team and heard their complaints regarding the new PMM document. Kent's solution to the problem was to take one member from each of these groups to form a team and to have this team come back to management with an updated singular PMM approach that would be adhered to by all. Several weeks went by with minimal result. The small, three person team could not agree on an approach for managing projects. The team member representing the PMO was a certified project management professional (PMP) and insisted upon a PMM that was rooted in the Guide to the PMBOK®. The team member representing the IT infrastructure team had a strong preference for their legacy project life cycle approach as it had been streamlined greatly and had served them well over the years. The team member representing the applications group was equally as firm in his resolve not to deviate from the Agile approach to managing software development projects that the applications group developed and had been using successfully.

After a few months the issue of what project management approach to take had not been resolved, so Kent decided that he, along with the PMO manager, would develop their singular methodology. The end result was similar to that which the PMO had developed together in the first place. Whereas the infrastructure team reluctantly accepted the new PMM, the applications team steadfastly objected to it. Soon they found ways to take shortcuts and circumvent the PMM and many of the methodology steps and templates were only followed to the barest extent necessary. On the side and out of the view of the PMO, the applications team continued to employ their Agile approach and methods.

Even when the various project performing organizations and teams try to cooperate in the development of best practices for project management or a PMM, the exercise can be fraught with difficulties. More times than not, these difficulties are not related to the project management skill and expertise of the organization. In fact the differing skills levels from seasoned experts to newly certified professionals to skilled and knowledgeable contributors can make for differences of opinions as well as annoyances and distractions. The real problem is how best to deal with the various categories of projects that make up the project mix, or portfolio, of the organization. Robert Youker (1999) writes "As the Project Management profession moves into the 21st century we are going to have to move to a new level in the project management body of knowledge and develop extensions that define the differences in requirements and approach for different kinds of projects . . ." Figure 4.4, based on Youker's work "The Difference Between Different Types of Projects," identifies nine different project types along with their characteristics and the required approaches.

Despite the seemingly obvious need to treat various kinds of projects differently, there has been minimal progress in this area as standards organizations and consortiums steadfastly promote and defend their own approaches rather than providing a leadership view of how best to apply different kinds of approaches to different kinds of projects. Commenting on the need for PMO methodologies to treat projects in terms of their classification, Jolyon Hallows (2002, p. 157) writes "One of the disadvantages of most project management

Major types of projects

Type of project	Example	Required approached
Administrative	Installing an accounting system	Team building and refinement of objectives
Construction	A building or a road	Control of cost and labor hours
Software	A new computer program	Project control and change management
Design or plans	Architectural or engineering plans	Detailed project management system
System installation	An IT or telecom system	Contingency planning
Event or relocation	The Olympics or an office move	Detailed planning and good teamwork
Maintenance	Plant maintenance	Detailed planning and tight control
New Product	A new drug or aerospace product	Quality planning and time management
Research	An analysis or feasibility study	Relaxed project management

Figure 4.4   Major project types

methodologies is that they do not allow project managers to differentiate between a project that requires a high degree of control and one that does not." The desire to mandate conformance to a singular PMM force fits the view of projects into a singular view even though they have considerable differences and are best managed with different approaches. Embracing flexibility enables the PMO to provide not just one but multiple approaches in response to the needs of the project effort. While proponents of one approach might stand resolute in the use of that approach and in their conviction that their method is the best over all other alternatives, the PMO needs to maintain a neutral position and provide stewardship over the selected, best fit, methods and approaches. The mindset should not be PMBOK® *or* Agile, rather PMBOK® *and* Agile.

Organizational Behaviors

The third challenge to embracing flexibility is directly related to the behaviors of the organization. The culture of an organization can, and often does, vary from one workplace to another. Where one organization actively promotes a culture of innovation, risk taking, and questioning of authority, another organization might seek and be better served by a different culture. These cultures, of course, manifest themselves into organizational behaviors.

Perhaps no better example of this is provided than by Steve Yegge (2006) in his blog post "Bad Agile." Yegge provides a colorful commentary on what he believes to be shortcomings of the Agile movement as well as an insightful look into how Google manages projects and develops software. Yegge writes "The project management techniques that Google does use are more like oil than fuel: things to let the project keep running smoothly, as opposed to things that force the project to move forward." Yegge goes on to describe the many ways that Google behaves in an agile-centric manner, while at the same time being critical of the Agile movement at large. He refers to *little a* agile as good and the actual behavior of an organization behaving in an agile manner.

In Google's case, their approach to software development is neither an Agile Methodology, nor a Waterfall Software Development Life Cycle, nor Cowboy programming. They move fast and react fast, but they don't have an all-consuming focus on one particular method over another. In contrast to Google's good *little a* agile, Yegge cites *big A* Agile as bad and the act of layering methodology on top of good software development. Yegge also likens the Agile movement to a fad-diet style marketing scam brilliantly devised to sell seminars and books and to provide a tour ground for Agile consultants.

No surprise, Yegge's blog post critical of Agile set the internet blogospere abuzz and was met with immediate responses from Agile enthusiasts all over the world. Many Agile defenders were quick to criticize Yegge and cite the fact that Google is no ordinary company. Nonetheless, a few responders offered additional insight and cautionary advice that nearly any PMO would be wise to follow. For example, in response to Yegge's blog post on "Bad Agile," Ryan Cooper (2006) writes "There are people in the Agile community so excited about their chosen methodology or approach that they start treating it like a Golden Hammer." Cooper goes on to suggest that there are many practitioners that operate in an agile way though they might not necessarily be practicing a given Agile methodology. Though there needs to be not just tolerance for, but acceptance of, different approaches such as methodologies for project management and software development, far too often there isn't. As Cooper observes "I've noticed a pattern in the high-profile bloggers/developers who have a poor opinion of Agile: it seems that someone has tried to push a particular Agile methodology on them even though they had no pain for it to solve." Mandating conformance instead of embracing flexibility for any one approach or method, even Agile, can and likely will result in execution difficulties for the project team and frustrations for the organization.

Many PMOs are caught in the middle of competing methodologies, bodies of knowledge, and approaches such as PMBOK®, CMMI, PRINCE2, Waterfall, RUP, MSF, and of course the many forms of Agile. This can result in an unnecessary focus and debate on which approach is categorically the best and should therefore be implemented and used in all projects as opposed to which few approaches provide the organization with the ideal balance of flexibility within its structure. As an alternative to having some groups abide by the approved PMM of the PMO for standard project types and other groups doing their own thing to best manage their different kinds of projects, more and more PMOs are seeking to establish a small set of approved approaches for managing projects of different classes.

Classes of projects can be useful in both understanding the project and in selecting the best approach for managing the project. Simply put, not all projects are the same. Different projects require differing amounts of project management as well as different approaches. Larger projects require more project management than do smaller projects simply as a matter of size. Project complexity and risk are also factors that require more project management as are cost and the amount of coordination that is required to deliver the product of the project. Since all organizations have these project characteristics from projects of differing types and projects with varying degrees of known requirements, developing a project classification guideline is critical to establishing project management as a practical and effective discipline for the entire organization.

Figure 4.5 illustrates that perhaps two of the most important factors to consider when developing project classes are the degree to which the project requirements are known, or can be known up front, and the degree to which the approach to managing the project is based upon a general purpose standard or a special purpose model.

Traditional project management has served organizations of all shapes and sizes well. It is disciplined and involves deliberate planning and control methods and activities. Project life cycle phases are intuitive and easily recognizable and tasks are planned in advance and completed according to schedule. For example, in a data center move project, the project manager determines the full requirements and develops the plan for the entire data center, not just one or two servers. Traditional project management assumes that requirements are known, or can be known, and planned in detail as part of the planning process. Typically, approaches to project management that are aligned to general purpose project management standards such as the Guide to the PMBOK® and PRINCE2 are well suited to projects of all shapes and sizes in which the project requirements are known.

However, not all project requirements are known in advance. In particular, projects that involve the development of software lend themselves to an environment in which many requirements are simply not known, and can't be known, in advance. For example, the development of an Order-to-Cash collaborative application in which the full requirements, both transactional and collaborative, of the customers and trading partners are not known is a good example of a project with many unknown requirements. For these projects

Project class factors

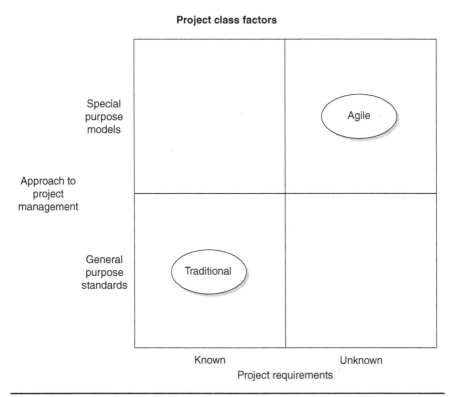

Figure 4.5   Project class factors

in which many requirements are unknown, traditional project management has proven to be less effective. Because of the poor track record in software development and the grass roots movement known as the Agile Manifesto, an alternative approach to traditional project management known as Agile Project Management has emerged.

Agile Project Management is characteristically different from traditional project management. Where traditional project management assumes requirements are known, Agile Project Management assumes that many requirements are not known. Whereas traditional project management places considerable time and focus on planning, Agile Project Management seeks to avoid the Big Design Up Front (BDUF) that slows real work on the project and prevents features from discovery ever becoming part of the product of the project. Naturally the approach to project documentation and communications are quite different between traditional and Agile Project Management. With traditional project management, documentation is extensive and communications are formal and periodically held. In an Agile Project Management environment, there is minimal project documentation and project communications are informal and typically held everyday.

In the context of project classes, Agile Project Management serves software development projects quite well. Important to note, such software development projects would be the actual application development of a solution or product, not projects to install commercial off-the-shelf software or projects to implement IT infrastructure such as upgrading a server. This distinction is important to make on account of the runaway enthusiasm and tendency of pundits and practitioners to jump on the latest bandwagon and summarily dismiss all other approaches. In terms of a negative impact to the organization, jumping on the latest method to project management and applying that method as the only approach to be used can be just as detrimental and ineffective as maintaining a traditional project management method as the only approach.

If every project were the same, project classes would not be necessary; a PMO could have one singular methodology that is embraced by the entire organization and meets the needs of every kind of project effort. But since projects and their characteristics can be extremely different, project classes are critical to both enable the application of different methodologies, both traditional and Agile, and to provide the project teams with what they need to achieve success. Those that suggest Agile Project Management is really just winging it are mistaken. Likewise, those that contend Agile Project Management is suitable for any and all projects of the PMO are clearly misguided, though perhaps well-intentioned. It would be a huge mistake to categorically dismiss one approach over the other and it would foster undesired organizational behaviors as project teams find ways to work around the mandated approach.

Summary

Frequently managing the PMO can be a balancing act. The need for structure in the form of policies and procedures needs to be tempered with the need for flexibility. In some areas, mandating a high degree of conformance is required and tremendously beneficial. For example, implementing a PPM application without the requisite conformance of use can seriously jeopardize the overall value and benefit realization to the organization of the application. In other areas there is a need to not only allow for flexibility, but to embrace it. An inflexible methodology for managing projects that forces all projects to be managed in a rigid, singular approach might not only frustrate project teams with projects of different types and sizes, but it might thwart and interfere with software development teams or line-of-business functional departments that have adopted, or need to adopt, Agile or special-purpose project management approaches.

Practitioners and functional departments can take a narrow view and be experts, using their preferred approaches with little care or concern for others throughout the organization who have projects to manage better suited by other approaches. The PMO must take a wide view and seek to position the organization to be a proponent and steward of all of the needed approaches for managing projects. The concept of a singular methodology for managing projects is outdated and not in tune with the project management best practices of today and tomorrow. To meet the diverse project management needs of all those in the organization, the PMO is best served by a common framework for project management, not a singular methodology, which provides all of the needed approaches for managing projects along with their specific positioning for selection and context of use. The PMO and leadership team must both select these project management approaches to be used throughout the organization as well as continually keep abreast of new approaches and techniques that would be of benefit to adopt and apply. In this way the PMO can provide the overall structure and flexibility for project management to be applied throughout the organization.

Questions

1. What is the purpose of applying a PMM?
2. What problems can arise when the purpose of developing a methodology is to apply an adopted standard?
3. In what ways does mandating conformance benefit a PMO?
4. What kinds of conformance are mandated by external guidelines for compliance?
5. What kinds of conformance are mandated by internal company policies?
6. What kinds of conformance to internal policies are advisory, but not necessarily mandatory?
7. How do proponents of traditional project management and those opposed to traditional project management differ in their approach to project planning?
8. How do proponents of traditional project management and those opposed to traditional project management differ in their approach to project control?
9. How do proponents of traditional project management and those opposed to traditional project management differ in their approach to project completion?

10. How do proponents of traditional project management and those opposed to traditional project management differ in their approach to project quality?
11. What are project classes?
12. What two factors are important to consider when establishing project classes?
13. What kind of approach to project management assumes that the project requirements are known and can be planned with a high degree of accuracy?
14. What kind of approach to project management assumes that the project requirements are not all known and cannot be planned with a high degree of accuracy?
15. What are the kinds of projects that are well suited to traditional project management?
16. What kinds of projects are well suited to Agile Project Management?
17. What are the risks to the organization of a singular PMM?
18. What are the benefits to the organization of a PMO framework for project management that provides multiple approaches for managing projects?
19. What kinds of PMOs are likely to benefit from having a singular PMM that everyone must conform to?
20. What kinds of PMOs are likely to benefit from having a PMO framework that provides multiple approaches for managing projects?

References

Alleman, Glen. 2004. "Everything is a Project." http://www.herdingcats .typepad.com. (Accessed June 4, 2008)

Block, Thomas R. and J. Davidson Frame. 1998. *The Project Office.* California: Crisp Publications.

Cooper, Ryan. 2006. "On Stevey on Agile." http://www.on-agile.blogspot.com. (Accessed June 4, 2008)

Englund, Randy. 2008. "What is Not a Project." http://www.maxwideman. com. (Accessed June 4, 2008)

Hallows, Jolyon. 2002. *The Project Management Office Toolkit.* New York: AMACOM.

Heldman, Kim. 2005. *Project Management Jumpstart.* California: Sybex.

Hill, Gerard. 2008. *The Complete Project Management Office Handbook.* Florida: Auerbach Publications.

IT Governance Institute. 2004. "IT Control Objectives for Sarbanes-Oxley," Illinois: ITGI. (Accessed June 4, 2008)

Project Management Institute. 2004. *A Guide to the Project Management Body of Knowledge*. Pennsylvania: PMI.

Yegge, Steve. 2006. "Bad Agile." http://www.steve-yegge.blogspot.com. (Accessed June 4, 2008)

Youker, Robert. 1999. "The Difference Between Different Types of Projects." http://www.maxwideman.com. (Accessed June 4, 2008)

Executive Insights

Establishing Flexibility within Structure

Erhard Zingg

PMO Manager, PartnerRe, Switzerland

Introduction

> *"Start by doing what is necessary, then do what is possible, and suddenly you are doing the impossible."* St. Francis of Assisi

The facts are simple: companies invest money and other resources into product development, marketing, organization, or people to ensure further existence. This is not only to secure the status quo but also to make progress and be competitive. Investing money wisely and getting the expected value back is therefore an imperative and a priority for any well-run company that wants to stay in the marketplace. Projects are a means to invest resources and to get the desired result.

Investing wisely means that you want some assurance that the money goes into the right projects and that you have some control that resources are spent reasonably and yield the results expected. It is tempting to establish a rigorous framework of rules and policies to keep things under control. People are expected to adhere to the rules and policies in order to do things correctly and in a consistent and predictable way. But sometimes people have trouble following strict rules and policies, and they challenge their significance or adaptability to certain projects or project situations. Frequently the PMO falls into the trap of applying a straitjacket to the discipline of project management and consequently to the project managers. Undoubtedly it is with the good intention to support the project managers in their project work and at the same time to satisfy the justified needs of the senior management and to receive a return on investment. All too often that does not pay off: management claims that overhead costs become too high and project managers complain that a bureaucratic and overly regulated approach keeps them from doing the *real* project work. What can we do about it? How can we ensure a consistent and predictable delivery of projects without exaggerating our control needs usually resulting in detailed policies and the demand for strict conformance to them? What can the PMO do to have structure and flexibility in place? What are the benefits?

Flexibility within Structure

Flexibility within structure became an important aspect to us when the PMO was mandated with the initiative to implement a new PMM[1]. One of the PMO's targets was to elevate from a project management maturity Level 2 (structured process and standards), in many areas even from Level 1 (initial process), to Level 3 (Organizational Standards and Institutionalized Process) according to the Project Management Maturity Model (PMMM^{SM}) as proposed by J. Kent Crawford (2002, pp. 279–286). The PMMM^{SM} is precise and comprehensive in what needs to be accomplished to gradually obtain maturity Level 3. Such a model serves as an adequate benchmark as to where your project management maturity is currently standing. The challenge we faced was to design a methodology that fit our organization's need but, above all, respected the diverse proficiency of our project management community.

While talking to our project managers about the new initiative we were confronted with requirements like the methodology has to be *global, lite, lean, transparent, flexible, supportive, based on recognized standards* just to name a few. Soon it became clear that they wanted something comprehensive but yet flexible enough not to be perceived as a straitjacket—and by no means should it be too bureaucratic. On the other hand there were expectations from management that the application of a new PMM would result in decreased cycle times and better results. The challenge is obvious: only a structured approach promises a consistent, predictable, and repeatable application of the methodology and only flexibility allows for self-dependent project management and appropriate use of the methodology. That sounded much like flexibility within structure! (See Figure 4.6.)

Based on our own experience as both project managers and PMO staff, we were aware that we had to observe a couple of things upfront and during the development phase to raise our chances of success with the new methodology in general and to minimize the risks around the concept of flexibility in particular. Looking back we consider the following premises as critical to our success.

Project Management Office

The PMO must be in the position not only to lead the initiative but as Rad and Levin (2002, pp. 6–7) conclude "The PMO is the organizational entity with the facility to provide services and organizational focus in core and supporting

---

[1]This article concentrates on flexibility and its implications and deliberately omits other important aspects to be considered when introducing a new methodology.

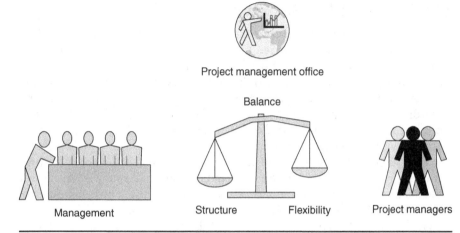

Project management office

Balance

Management   Structure   Flexibility   Project managers

Figure 4.6   Flexibility within structure

areas of project management." This means that skilled and credible staff are needed and appropriate service offerings need to be in place to support the project management community when applying the methodology. This is important in promoting flexibility and as long as the PMO enforces regular project health checks, offers in-house training, or provides mentoring and consulting. In fact, this is true for the proper application of any PMM, whether flexible in approach or not.

People

As mentioned earlier, we soon realized during our interviews with the project management community and other project stakeholders that people expected certain flexibility in the actual application of the methodology. The reason is that mature employees draw some of their self-esteem from working independently and with an attitude of responsibility. That's exactly how we wanted our project managers to behave. That was motivation for us to put as much flexibility into the methodology as possible. On the other hand we knew that there had to be some measures in place to avoid things slipping out of control. In other words we had to balance flexibility versus structure.

Balance

When talking about flexibility we had the following definition of the term in mind, "The ability to adapt to a given situation or event and its characteristics to achieve the desired outcome in the most effective and efficient way possible." Though flexibility can basically be applied to any area in which the PMO is active, it is important to understand when, where, and to what degree it is reasonable. This is particularly important when your project management community is heterogeneous and consists of full-time project managers whose maturity ranges from junior to senior levels as well as employees who are infrequently doing project management assignments. We learned that when you grant flexibility in one area you must apply more structure in another. When the project manager has flexibility in the actual application of the PMM then the PMO must have structures in place to compensate for it. One measure to apply directly to the methodology is a sound project governance standard as discussed later. Processes like the PPM Process support the balancing of flexibility and structure with clearly defined interfaces to the project management process, i.e., monthly project progress reporting, which require predefined process interactions from the project manager.

Credibility

Personal credibility is an important asset when developing and implementing a new PMM. Credibility means that you must be an expert in project management and project management methodologies. It is only with good practical and theoretical knowledge in these areas that you are in the position to judge where flexibility can be granted and where structure has to be applied. Besides the fact that some of the project managers might be knowledgeable in the topic as well, speaking their language, understanding where they come from, and facilitating the discussions helps to introduce structures needed to make the methodology useful and applicable.

Contribution

While it is you who sets the agenda, you must actively seek for the contribution of the key project players in your organization. In our case key project players included project management leads (persons responsible for a team of project managers), seasoned project managers, and representatives of senior management. For instance during the development of the methodology we scheduled monthly review meetings with the project management leads reviewing and discussing the material until we reached mutual agreement. Applying that approach turned contribution into commitment because the results were not the results of the PMO but became the results of the project management community.

Project Management Methodology
Vision and Structure

You need a strong vision on what your end product—the PMM—will look like and how it will be used. This is important because along the way of developing the methodology you will have to make compromises. That is ok but you should never lose track of your final target. Only when you know what you want to achieve are you able to judge whether a compromise is still reasonable or when you have to demonstrate perseverance to avoid things getting misdirected. One of the cornerstones of our vision was that the methodology had to be online: available at the fingertip of the project manager and intuitive to use. We did not want to produce just a piece of shelf ware, which was archived and forgotten, but a product that would come as close as possible to how people work today. That meant that we had to look for a structure that would host the methodology on our intranet. Once we implemented the organizational framework we started to develop the content of the methodology, upload it, and structure the framework as it fit our needs. Having the methodology online not only gives flexibility to the project manager when using it—anytime, anywhere—but also to the PMO: updates and additions can be uploaded and made available to all users immediately.

Methodology and Structure

We decided that the new PMM would be based on the PMBOK® Guide and industry best practices. We defined a generic project life cycle comprising of the five phases: initiation, planning, execution, monitoring and control, and closure. Whatever size and content a project might have, it always runs through the five phases. Only the level of detail when using the PMM differs as the complexity of projects varies because, as the PMBOK® Guide (2004) states, "This does not mean that the processes and related activities or work products described should always be applied uniformly on all projects. The project manager, in collaboration with the project team, is always responsible for determining what processes are appropriate, and the appropriate degree of rigor for each process, for any given project."

We adapted the generic project life cycle to serve the two project types: standard and complex[2] and defined the process steps for each of them. The

---

[2]The Standard Project Life Cycle is intended for medium, mid-term projects and consists of nine project management process steps and five gates that provide guidance and templates. If additional guidance is needed the project manager refers to the Complex Project Life Cycle.

rigor of application should be commensurate with the size and complexity of the project. Finally, as conceptually shown in Figure 4.7, we developed what we called the *guardrails*: process step descriptions, guidelines, procedures, (governance) standards, templates, and other supporting material.

All of this was set to determine that the work be completed in a specific way. The structure of the life cycle remains the same for every project: initiation, planning, execution, monitoring and control, and closure. The ingredients remain the same, for example the project management plan, the project team meetings, the steering committee, the project progress reports, the scheduling and so on. In short, the structure remains fixed but the activities are not.

Two Kinds of Flexibility

The flexibility offered by the methodology is twofold: flexibility of application and flexibility of use. Flexibility of application is the kind of flexibility warranted in the degree of adherence to a given process. For instance, the project process requires that all projects have to plan the project and produce a project management plan, which serves as a reference document for all project members in regard to the delivery of the project. The project management plan covers the project management approach including the project management plans, the project scope, deliverables, schedule, organization, roles and responsibilities, operating procedures, control mechanisms, reporting guidelines, and tools for the entire project. While a large, complex project requires a thorough and formal plan to define how the project is executed, monitored, and controlled, a much smaller project might only require a plan that broadly frames the most important project management aspects like scope control,

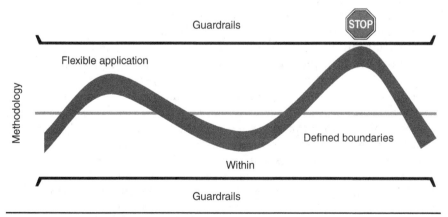

Figure 4.7　Methodology guardrails

budget control, resource allocation, or project organization. This brings us to the flexibility of use, which is the kind of flexibility offered in the choice and application of available tools or templates. All projects require communication but not all projects need to have a detailed communication plan. The methodology offers a communication plan template that covers all relevant aspects of a communication concept. Depending on the complexity and prominence of formal communication required by a particular project, the project manager decides whether to implement a full-blown communication plan or if it is sufficient to outline the communication measures in summary.

Flexibility Means Responsibility

Although most project managers want to have flexibility at hand in the actual application of the project management process, they have to be aware that it puts increased responsibility on their shoulders. It becomes a key element of the project manager's job to select the appropriate portions of the process for managing a specific project. They are accountable to tailoring the methodology to the needs of their projects. Some project managers have difficulty dealing with it because they are not experienced enough to make the appropriate decisions consistently either because they are new to the project management job or are assigned to lead a project only occasionally. That is where the PMO has to step in and offer appropriate training, mentorship, initiation support, and project assessments.

Project Governance

Another area we emphasized was project governance. We defined project governance as providing the structure and process by which a project is directed, controlled, and held to account. Based on this principle we developed a project governance standard that outlines the roles and responsibilities of the project sponsor and the steering committee. The project manager now has a clearly established board to which he/she reports project status and from which to get approvals on key project documents, project change requests, and project critical decisions. Additionally the document proposes the composition of the steering committee, frequency and agenda of meetings, as well as project tolerance levels. Project tolerance levels are another means to span the level of authority of the project manager and at the same time relieve the governing bodies from minor project issues and decisions. Well-defined thresholds provide a simple and effective escalation path for projects. The important task for the PMOs at this point is to make project sponsors and steering committee members familiar with project governance principles and the responsibilities associated with it and to support them in their assignment.

Summary

Establishing flexibility into the application of our PMM was a rewarding goal for good reason: promoting self-dependent project managers and ensuring an appropriate use of the methodology delivering the desired results are good means to create a sustainable project culture within the organization. While pursuing this goal, all our measures are in proportion to the needs and capacity of the organization and the project management community. The goal cannot be to create and implement the *perfect solution* right from the start but to mature the methodology while the project managers' community makes progress in the adherence of it.

References

Crawford, Kent. 2002. *The Strategic Project Office—A Guide to Improving Organizational Performance*. New York: Marcel Dekker.

Project Management Institute. 2004. *A Guide to the Project Management Body of Knowledge. (PMBOK® Guide) Third Edition*, Newton Square, PA: Project Management Institute.

Rad, Parviz, and Ginger Levin 2002. *The Advanced Project Management Office: A Comprehensive Look at Function and Implementation*. Boca Raton, FL: St. Lucie Press.

Executive Insights

Using Process Improvement to Drive PMO Flexibility

Michael Wood

CEO, The Natural Intelligence Group

Introduction

With today's immense focus on IT PPM, you would think that the state of the Project/Portfolio Management Office (PMO) would be alive, well and thriving. Sadly, however, the PMO is still not a household word in the majority of organizations. If not for Sarbanes-Oxley, the PMO might be just another idea reserved for only the largest and most complex of organizations. Even in the face of organizations comprised of hundreds of thousands of members, the PMO is still a source of controversy and great debate. Consider the following facts:

- Googling Project Portfolio Management yields 756,000 hits
- PMI boasts over 265,000 members
- Gantthead.com (the world's largest site dedicated to project management) has over 400,000 members
- Wikipedia lists approximately 50 different project management software offerings

So why isn't the PMO flourishing in corporate America? Perhaps the problem is one of practicality. When looking over the literature on PMOs it seems to be conspicuously lacking the voice of *real world* practitioners; those who know what works and what doesn't because they have lived it.

Being somewhat of an expert in business process improvement, I have trained my sights on the PMO with an eye toward streamlining the process and rethinking its value proposition. Before leaping into the rethinking of PMO processes it is beneficial to have some basic information:

- Definition of a PMO
- Issues/perceptions that cause resistance to PMOs
- Major challenges facing PMOs
- When to formalize the PMO function
- PMO's roles and responsibilities

Next the processes of the PMO are addressed in the following sections:

◆ Typical PMO processes
◆ Typical PMO paperwork
◆ Streamlining the PMO for value and effectiveness

Finally the launching of a streamlined PMO are presented with:

◆ Getting started (the PMO project)
◆ Developing a project prioritization methodology
◆ Developing PMO compliance policies and procedures
◆ Developing standards
◆ Developing reusable project templates
◆ Launching the PMO
◆ Conducting pilot projects using a streamlined PMO approach
◆ Evaluating results

When completed, you have a comprehensive mini-guide to creating a PMO that enhances the success rate of projects while improving governance over the process. Let's get started.

Definition of a PMO

In its simplest form a PMO is an organization that vets projects for their value, monitors and provides oversight for approved projects, and assesses the effectiveness of the projects once completed and deployed. A mature PMO also monitors and reviews project documentation to ensure that it complies with agreed-to standards. It also provides project managers with resources such as standardized forms, templates, project plans, and expert guidance. Ideally the PMO also serves as a roadblock remover, assisting the project manager in anyway practical to cut through red tape, resolve loggerheads, and other barriers.

Unfortunately, PMOs become a source of angst. Frequently the bureaucracy of the PMO causes frustration with projects, project managers, and stakeholders. It is essential that those leading a PMO remember that the PMO is there to ensure that projects get done quickly and efficiently, using processes, tools, and protocols that are repeatable.

Issues/Perceptions that Cause Resistance to PMOs

When looking at the issues and perceptions that cause resistance to the PMO, it is important to realize that a new PMO, no matter how well-organized, represents change and therefore should expect pushback from project managers and their teams. That said, there are other issues that inhibit the effectiveness of PMOs; issues that are not without foundation. In the absence of improved project throughput and success, a PMO is just another layer of cost and therefore often deemed cost prohibitive. The justification for the PMO lies in its ability to provide better governance over projects. Good governance protects the interests that stakeholders have in projects, not the least of which is the expectation for superior returns on investments (ROI). The ROI goes well beyond mere returns on dollar investments made. When it comes to projects, the ROI is also a function of the time invested and the other projects that were not pursued in favor of the ones being implemented. Therefore the PMO should establish and maintain metrics as to its effectiveness in improving the success rate of projects lest it become part of the problem and not part of the solution.

Another common downfall of PMOs is the paperwork and procedural bureaucracies they create. Usually this is due to the leadership mindlessly following a set of standards for PMOs that look good in theory but fail miserably in practice. In addition, the body of knowledge for PMOs has embedded terminologies that are not common in business and thus increase resistance and mistrust among constituents.

For example the project charter is often a boilerplate form that is confusing and more like a legal document than a roadmap for project success. In essence it sets forth the rules of engagement and defines the risks, benefits, stakeholder expectations among other things. The term itself is foreign to most. Where else in the organizations are charters used? Are there marketing campaign charters or asset acquisition charters? And why must the charter be so overbearing and sterile?

I submit that instead of project charters, the PMO opt for project proposals. Proposals are a common tool used in business to present an idea that, if approved, becomes the agreement between two parties toward a common goal. While it contains much of what a charter might contain, it is a readable document that is tailored to the specifics and interests at hand. Later, we take a more in-depth look at processes and paperwork.

Major Challenges Facing PMOs

Beyond the already mentioned issues facing the PMO, there are external systemic problems that can hinder the PMOs effectiveness. Often the resistance of project managers to buy into the PMOs standards, rules, and processes is anything but subtle. As a general rule IT folks have an innate aversion to documenting their work. Many see documentation as a sign of management distrust. This is fueled in part by the nonconformist attitudes found in those with a bent toward engineering and technology. Whether a defense mechanism or arrogance, it is far too often a road block to PMO success.

For project managers with little formal training but with years of success, the resistance can be extreme as they persist in wanting to *do it the way they always have done it*. For young project managers lacking field experience, they don't appreciate the need for the level of diligence needed to ensure quality project governance. In either case, the result is a level of reluctant compliance that misses the mark. Forms get filled out inaccurately, project updates are painful to obtain, passive and sometimes active resistance is a continuous drain on the PMO, project managers and project teams.

Leading the PMO requires an approach that draws people into the process in a way that allows them to shape the standards and compliance rules. Buy-in can't be forced, it must be allowed to evolve; something often missed by PMO leadership. To be sustainably effective the PMO must be agile and nimble. The paperwork surrounding the project process needs to be kept to a bare minimum and should be scaled to reflect different levels of project complexity and risk.

The leadership of the PMO needs to reach out to the project managers and the community in a way that demonstrates the importance of keeping the project moving forward. This means proactively stepping up to help expedite process and procedures and continuously finding ways to work around resistance.

One area that PMOs can add tremendous value in this regard is through providing project managers with project administration assistance. Instead of beating on project managers for their team's progress reports, the PMO can assign project analysts and administrators to teams whose sole purpose in life is to leverage the team's ability to perform core project tasks and to stay focused. Doing this makes the PMO an ally in the project process not a perceived entity that exacerbates progress. In addition, helping the project managers identify scope creep and adding the PMO's voice to the justification process gains much favor in the project manager's eyes.

Basically the PMO, instead of acting like internal affairs needs to engage project managers, stakeholders, and project teams in a positive, collaborative manner that endears it to the organization and fosters success.

When to Formalize the PMO Function

Does every organization need a formal PMO? Of course not. Smaller organizations that only have a few projects in play can often manage the basket of projects informally without materially increasing risk. However, organizations sporting a poor record of delivering projects on time and on budget, no matter what their size are often well-served by a PMO function.

Typically organizations that have many (10 or more) simultaneous projects that are complex in nature and time sensitive need a PMO function to maximize the potential for success. The PMO becomes even more essential to success when the result of project failures impacts the organization's competitive position, community standing, profitability, or customer relationships.

If missing project delivery dates results in regulatory fines, law suits, or even enterprise financial disaster, a PMO is essential.

Finally, if the organization falls under Sarbanes-Oxley or other governance standards then a PMO might well be mandatory. What is important to remember is that the PMO is not a necessary evil but rather a means to increasing predictable project success.

PMO's Roles and Responsibilities

The last area to consider before exploring how to streamline the PMO is to review the PMO's roles and responsibilities. Understanding the roles and responsibilities of the PMO provides a framework for shaping the business processes that it deploys:

◆ Maintaining new project clearing house. PMOs serve as the clearing house for new project requests. In this role they must catalog the request, oversee the initial project justification process, oversee the approval process, and facilitate the proper prioritization of the project within the portfolio.

◆ Maintaining active project oversight. The majority of the PMO's time is spent providing oversight on active projects. Here they monitor project progress, prepare project and portfolio status reports for stakeholders, coordinate with project managers, and do whatever is appropriate to keep the project on track and on budget.

◆ Maintaining post implementation performance reviews. PMOs often drive the post implementation reviews on projects. They act as an independent source for evaluating if the project achieved its objectives in terms of outcomes achieved and procedures, tools, and protocols followed to achieve results. In this role the PMO conducts surveys, compiles statistics, and performs interviews to determine the overall performance of the project, the project manager, the team, and the stakeholders associated with the project. Often these reviews result in formal reports and scorecards.

◆ Providing leverage, mentoring, and coaching. PMOs often fail to provide the leverage, mentoring, and coaching project managers need to ensure sustainable success. World-class PMOs foster learning and growth by:
  ◇ Maintaining knowledge-based repositories consisting of all past projects (documentation, history, scorecards) so project managers can research quickly and learn from other project manager's experiences.
  ◇ Providing expert guidance for project managers, leveraging the project manager's ability to effectively lead.
  ◇ Maintaining estimating tools and standards allowing project managers to rapidly compile project estimates and work plans.

◆ Maintaining a talent registry so that project managers can find field teams comprised of the right people for the effort quickly.
◆ Facilitating improvements to project conduct and also the management processes.

Typical PMO Processes and Activities

Given the six major roles, it is reasonable to expect a PMO to have supporting processes that are well defined, procedurally efficient, and sound. Unfortunately many PMOs, while dictating standards by which projects are approved, conducted, and implemented are sorely lacking in their own internal maturity.

Most expect to have the PMOs processes and workflows well documented, policies well defined and procedures well specified. Ironically, for most PMOs it just isn't so. Instead, for far too many, the focus is on paperwork compliance supported by checklists.

Typically the PMO uses paperwork or the lack of it, to trigger actions. Often the operation is nothing more than a project updating and status reporting organization that runs on a weekly calendar (e.g. Thursday collect project updates from project managers, Friday post projects and prepare status and milestone reports, Monday distribute reports). The quality and insight is vacant from the process. It can be no wonder that so many PMOs are seen as merely a clearinghouse for processing project updates and producing portfolio status reports and alerts. A list of typical PMO processes and activities might include:

◆ New project request logging and tracking
◆ Project assessment logging
◆ Project charter inspection and compliance
◆ Project activation and prioritization logging
◆ Weekly project update processing
◆ Weekly project status reporting
◆ Monthly portfolio project reporting
◆ Stakeholder sign-off logging and form inspection
◆ PMO steering committee attendance and proceedings documentation
◆ Periodic project reviews and audits

The above activities are often supported by a vast array of forms of which the PMO inspects for quantitative completion and sometimes even for qualitative content (rare). These forms usually consist of:

◆ Project request
◆ Feasibility study
◆ Project charter

- Statement of work (scope document)
- Risk assessment and contingencies plan
- Time-phased staffing and resource requirements
- Work breakdown structure
- Work plan schedule and task assignments
- Communication plan
- Change requests
- Change impact analysis
- Status reports (project and portfolio)
- Budget and cash flow analysis
- Transition plan (from project into production)
- Post implementation review and assessment

The problem with so many forms (the majority of which contain endless amounts of redundant data) is that they become the focus of the PMOs existence; compliance to forms and procedures. Whether the project succeeds or fails, so long as the *i*'s are dotted and the *t*'s crossed all is good. No wonder so many PMOs are facing a constant state of resistance.

Streamlining the PMO for Value and Effectiveness

When streamlining the PMO it is important to understand that one size does not fit all. Even within a PMO there needs to be scalable processes that can be tailored to each project based on its complexity, size, and risk factors. It is also important to remember that there are two types of complexity; logistic and content. Logistic complexity is based on the overall breath of the project in terms of organizational impact. A project that requires enterprise wide involvement (e.g., an enterprise resource planning (ERP) system) is logistically complex, whereas a project that only impacts an individual (e.g., specialized reports) is not. Logistically complex projects need more structure and controls around them to ensure continuity and consistency.

Content complexity deals with the technical difficulty of the project. For example, a new algorithm might be intricate and difficult to conceptualize and program, yet the complexity from a project management point of view simple. The PMO's focus when scaling the process to the project complexity is more toward the process side not the content side of the scale. So when creating the processes that the PMO follows for vetting, overseeing, and supporting projects it is important that each project be identified in terms of its logistic complexity, which in turn indicates the level of discipline and formality the project needs to be governed by. In general, the higher the logistical complexity, number of tasks, number of stakeholders, and size of the project team, the more formal and structured the project process and oversight need to be.

For example, low-complexity projects that are under 100 hours might only require a project, request, statement-of-work, and work plan. The statement-of-work could provide a section for the project approval and acceptance and other authorizations.

In contrast a high complexity project might require vigorous vetting, approval by a C level executive, a multitude of milestones, comprehensive communication plans and more. Of course with complexity comes additional oversight and project management overhead; a form of insurance if you will.

To personalize this, consider home improvement projects. These could range from some minor maintenance, new landscaping, a new fence, a pool, or an extreme makeover. Certainly you wouldn't apply the same processes and procedures to all of them. It only makes sense to streamline the simple projects and to be more vigilant and careful on the more complex ones. Contracts, blueprints, permits, and inspections add to the complexity of a new pool or home addition and thus require more governance. The same holds true for IT projects.

Consider Figure 4.8 when assessing overall project complexity. Any given project likely contains a mixture of complexity components. The lower the overall project complexity profile the more simplified the oversight process. Conversely the higher the complexity profile the more formal and structured the process need be.

Given a framework for classifying projects as to their complexity we can now turn our attention to the angst-ridden area for most project managers and project teams when it comes to PMOs: the paperwork and perceived wasted effort associated with its upkeep. The impact of a single form can represent hours of

Project complexity

Influencing factors	Low	Medium	High
Cross-functional complexity	One person or department	One cross-functional business process (order processing)	Multiple cross-functional business processes (ERP, CRM)
# of stakeholders	One person or group	5 to 12 groups	Enterprise-wide
# of tasks	Under 30	31 to 500	Over 500
# of locations	1	2	More than 2
Project team size	Under 3	3 to 10	More than 10
Level of effort	Under 100 hours	101 to 300 hours	Over 300 hours
Political sensitivity	None	Low	Career threatening

Figure 4.8   Project complexity

effort. It has to be researched, filled out, and validated. A form that is deemed useless also creates negative tension and discontent among team members who are feeling the pressure of getting a project done on time and within budget. In addition people tend to be less diligent in completing forms if they do not appreciate their value. So streamlining the form set the PMO must administer and manage can shave at least a week of effort off of every project.

Instead of the traditional 15 forms found in most PMOs, a streamlined PMO only needs 7; less than half as listed in Figure 4.9.

Cutting the number of forms in half does more than just reduce documentation, it also eliminates hours and hours of labor that can be better utilized on project progressing tasks. This abbreviated forms set is far less imposing and daunting to project managers and stakeholders alike. Therefore compliance and buy-in to their use is enhanced and thus resistance reduced.

Getting Started on the PMO Project

Starting a PMO can seem monumental in scope for those who haven't done it before. To help you on your way it is beneficial to consider performing it in steps.

Develop an inventory of all known projects (in process, planned, and dreamed about). Having a comprehensive list of projects along with the stakeholders, including general scope and business justification is usually a great eye opener for management. Be sure to identify any interdependencies between projects.

Project complexity

Project document	Intended purpose of the project document
Project request	Contains the request that initiates the project process
Project proposal	Contains the project description, business case, feasibility and risk assessment, benefiting stakeholders, organizations involved, preliminary budget, resource requirements, rough work plan, and authorization to proceed
Project work plan	Contains milestones, activities, tasks, resource assignments, level of work, schedule of completion, capital outlays
Communication plan	Contains how the status of the project will be communicated to stakeholders, including sample reports, frequency, etc.
Project status reports	Contains the summary of the status of the project
Change requests and impact analysis	Contains the scope change information along with an impact analysis (costs, benefits, risks, etc.) and approval to proceed
Post implementation review and assessment	Contains a formal assessment of the projects overall conduct, team effectiveness, and outcomes achieved

Figure 4.9 Streamlined PMO forms

This helps in the prioritization process. Also identify the general talent and resource requirements (even if they are not available) so a resource GAP analysis can be performed later.

Develop an inventory of resources and talent that can be deployed on projects (IT, USER, Vendors.). This is critical when understanding the size of the project backlog and how it might be attacked.

Prepare a resource GAP analysis. This analysis provides insights as to how many projects could be conducted simultaneously and where the organization might need to engage outside support, which in turn effects the investment needed to achieve project objectives and thus the ROI.

Commission an IT project governance group and business process user groups (cross-functional). Critical to the success of the PMO is the establishment of an objective oversight committee that approves and prioritizes projects. Ideally this group's membership is comprised of stakeholders from various areas of the organization. In addition to this group, which meets monthly or quarterly, there needs to be a business process improvement user group. This group meets on a regular basis to review, identify, and explore process improvement opportunities that are frequently the source of new projects.

Formalize the PMO organization. Before convening the first group meetings, the PMO needs to be launched. Just like any other organization it needs a business plan, measurable objectives, performance metrics, compliance policies and procedures, an organization chart, and job descriptions. The first order of business with the newly formed groups is to review the PMO's business plan and communicate its purpose and objectives to everyone.

Develop project approval and prioritization methodology. In the absence of an objective way to establish project approval and priorities, urgency and politics usually win the day. It is therefore imperative that a mechanism be used. One approach is to score each project based on a set of consistent and weighted prioritization criteria. This involves creating a weighted average score for the project opportunity by establishing prioritization categories, criteria, scoring choices, and a weighted value, typically a percentage, for the category. Consider the following example of guidelines for categories, prioritization criteria, and scoring values:

- Urgency—when must this initiative be complete?
  - ◊ 10 pts = 3 months
  - ◊ 8 pts = 6 months
  - ◊ 6 pts = 9 months
  - ◊ 4 pts = 1 year or more
- Alignment—how well does this initiative align to organizational goals?
  - ◊ 10 pts = Directly supports
  - ◊ 5 pts = Moderately support
  - ◊ 1 pt = Does not support

- ◆ Productivity—how much does this initiative increase productivity?
  - ◇ 10 pts = 50% or more
  - ◇ 8 pts = 25%
  - ◇ 6 pts = 10%
  - ◇ 4 pts = 5%
- ◆ Costs savings—How much cost does this initiative save over the next 3 years?
  - ◇ 10 pts = 50% or more
  - ◇ 8 pts = 25%
  - ◇ 6 pts = 10%
  - ◇ 4 pts = 5%
- ◆ Income increases—how much does this initiative increase income?
  - ◇ 10 pts = 50% or more
  - ◇ 8 pts = 25%
  - ◇ 6 pts = 10%
  - ◇ 4 pts = 5%
- ◆ Morale—what is the morale improvement potential of this initiative?
  - ◇ 10 pts = Dramatically increases
  - ◇ 8 pts = General increases
  - ◇ 6 pts = Has no effect
  - ◇ 4 pts = Generally decreases
  - ◇ 2 pts = Dramatically decreases
- ◆ Time to completion—how long does it take to complete this initiative?
  - ◇ 10 pts = 3 months
  - ◇ 8 pts = 6 months
  - ◇ 6 pts = 9 months
  - ◇ 4 pts = 1 year or more
- ◆ Competitive position—how does this initiative improve competitive position?
  - ◇ 10 pts = Dramatically increases
  - ◇ 8 pts = General increases
  - ◇ 6 pts = Has no effect
  - ◇ 4 pts = Generally decreases
  - ◇ 2 pts = Dramatically decreases
- ◆ Customer service levels—how does this initiative improve customer service?
  - ◇ 10 pts = Dramatically increases
  - ◇ 8 pts = General increases
  - ◇ 6 pts = Has no effect
  - ◇ 4 pts = Generally decreases
  - ◇ 2 pts = Dramatically decreases

Based upon this common set of criteria and guidelines, the organization can evaluate and select the best fit projects of the mix of opportunities. Figure 4.10

Project selection scorecard

Category	Score	Weight	Weighted average
Urgency	10	5%	.5
Alignment	5	10%	.5
Productivity	6	10%	.6
Cost savings	10	15%	1.5
Income increases	10	15%	1.5
Morale	8	10%	.8
Time to complete	8	5%	.4
Competitive impact	6	15%	.9
Customer service	8	15%	1.2
Totals		**100%**	**7.9**

Figure 4.10   Project selection scorecard

shows one example of a project selection scorecard for the prioritization methodology.

Each member of the governance group scores each project. The scores are then consolidated and discussed, arriving at a group consensus score for each project. The projects are ranked by priority (highest score to lowest). This provides an objective and quantifiable means to establish a recommended sequence for pursuing projects. Each month newly approved projects are prioritized and added to the backlog. Projects that are in process are not re-prioritized but rather allowed to finish.

Develop standards. The PMO needs to be somewhat prescriptive in its deployment of compliance standards. That being said, it also needs to be flexible so as to allow some wiggle room for tailoring the standards to specific project situations. By creating a set of guidelines and support tools the PMO can provide quality levels of governance that is not prone to overkill or bureaucratic quagmires. Consider the creation of tools the project managers can draw from including:

- ◆ Standard templates and forms
- ◆ Checklists
- ◆ Pro-forma project plans
- ◆ Reporting
- ◆ Reusable project templates
- ◆ Application development

- Requirements discovery
- Requirements and design
- Construction
- Testing
- Training
- Deployment
- Evaluation
- Release management
- Application evaluation and selection
- Communication plans
- Risk assessment
- Infrastructure
- Business process improvement
- Project status reports

Launch the PMO. When launching the PMO it is important that the entire organization be educated as to its function and purpose. This can be accomplished in a variety of ways. Perhaps the best way is to conduct a series of orientation sessions for key staff and stakeholders. These can be coordinated through human resources as part of their training curriculum. In addition, as new project teams are formed they too can be given an orientation on the rules of engagement.

Conduct pilot projects using a streamlined PMO approach. Now that the PMO is launched some pilot projects can be pursued. In addition to getting the project completed on time and on budget these projects have one other goal—to exercise the PMO. During the pilot project period the PMO's processes can be tested and refined. The result is a more mature and efficient PMO that has been shaped to reflect *what works.*

Go to full PMO. Once the PMO has been fully exercised the entire portfolio of projects can fall under its domain. During the first year of operation it is prudent to conduct PMO effectiveness reviews, an operational audit of sorts. During these reviews, facts and perceptions of the PMO's value to the organization need to be considered. The review should be a 360 degree process and include stakeholders, management, project teams, and PMO staff.

Summary

There you have it—a practical, process improvement-driven guide for streamlining and launching a PMO that, by design, adds value, fosters buy-in, and promotes compliance. The next step is to get started. Good luck.

5

PMO Tools:
Establishing a PMO Architecture
vs
Implementing a Tool

Many organizations experience difficulties implementing the tools needed by the project management office (PMO). Figure 5.1 illustrates that there is never a shortage of vendors eager to sell their products. Nor is there a shortage of consultants anxious to provide implementation services or market analysts ready to provide their fee-based analysis and commentary. But at the end of the day, it is up to the PMO to select the tools that it needs. It is up to the PMO to rationalize how the various PMO tools all work together and to explain how they are to be used.

Naturally, prior to any discussion of tools, the organization must first determine that which is to be accomplished by the PMO. The goals and objectives to be achieved set the tone for the PMO strategy and shed light on requirements and needs. Different kinds of PMOs, in terms of their goals and objectives, no doubt have different kinds and levels of needs. Not just executive sponsorship, but true executive involvement and participation in establishing the PMO is tremendously important and has a direct correlation and impact on tools required. The PMO needs to provide the executives with the appropriate capabilities and required information so that they work together as a team as opposed to not participating or gaming the system to get the resources

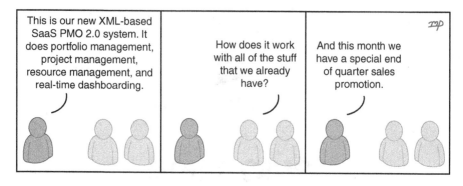

Figure 5.1   PMO comics—tools

they want or simply to get their projects through. The position of the PMO within the organization is also important. The location of the PMO is not only important to drive the strategy of the PMO, but it can also result in additional needs and requirements for collaboration and communication that need to be addressed.

Implementing a Tool Approach

Regrettably, for far too long, PMO enthusiasts and pundits have approached PMO tooling as merely a function of implementing a single project management tool or application. There are numerous problems with this approach and three quickly come to mind. First, this approach assumes that one tool can meet all of the needs of the PMO. Second, this approach assumes that the needs of the PMO are typically transactional in nature and can be addressed by the various features and functions of a single tool. Third, this approach tends to result in tool evaluation that oftentimes is oblivious to the wide variety of existing tools that the organization already has, knows, and uses.

One Tool Mindset

Can one tool meet all of the needs of the PMO? Of course not. A number of different tools are needed by the project managers to manage projects from the beginning to the end of the various project phases (see Figure 5.2).

In the initiating phase of the project, the project manager performs a number of activities that lead up to the creation of the project charter document. Project managers engage in brainstorming activities with clients and stakeholders to discover aspects of the conceived end product of the project using tools like MindMapper. The development of the business case, including feasibility

Project selection scorecard

	Initiate	Plan	Execute	Control	Close
Example activities	Brainstorming Feasibility analysis Business case Budget estimates Schedule estimates Scorecarding Collaboration Presentation	Requirements Scoping Scheduling Costing Quality planning Risk planning Collaboration Presentation	Kickoffs Assessments Contract reports Issues log Changes log Status reporting Collaboration Presentation	Performance Reports Budget update Scope update Risk register Approved changes Collaboration Presentation	Lessons learned Estimating updates Performance review Improvement plan Project archives Collaboration Presentation
Example tools	Word Excel Teamsites Document mgt PowerPoint Mindmapper	Word Excel Visio Project PPM Teamsites Document mgt PowerPoint Mindnapper	Word Excel Project PPM Teamsites Document mgt PowerPoint	Word Excel Project PPM Teamsites Document mgt PowerPoint	Word Excel Project PPM Teamsites Document mgt PowerPoint

Project manager tools

Figure 5.2 Project manager tools

analysis, budget and schedule high-level estimates, and project scorecarding are likely to be produced using standard project management templates and tools like Microsoft Word and Excel. To discuss work in progress with team members and to formally present findings to management, many project managers use presentation graphics tools like Microsoft SharePoint. To meet the collaboration needs of all those involved in the project effort, tools like Microsoft SharePoint that provide teamsites, document management, and communication and collaboration capabilities are used. Of course, email and all the features that the email system of the organization has is an indispensable tool used by the project manager and project team throughout the entire project.

As the project progresses from initiating to planning and through all the other phases of the project life cycle, additional tools are used by the project manager and project team. Special purpose tools like Microsoft Visio may be used to produce business and technical drawings helpful in the definition of requirements. Tools like Microsoft Project can be used to develop and manage a detailed project schedule as well as to control project work, schedule changes, finances, and resources. Some organizations may also have project portfolio management tools that extend upon the tool set of the PMO to provide additional project and resource management capabilities. More and more organizations are enjoying the benefits of platforms for collaboration like Microsoft SharePoint, IBM Lotus, and many others. No organization exists without an email systems. Collectively there are a number of tools, applications, and platforms used in the PMO and in the context of managing a project; the assumption that one tool can do it all or even should do it all is a bad one.

PMO Needs Are Not Transactional

The all-in-one approach assumes that the needs of the PMO are typically transactional in nature and can be addressed by features and functions. If that is the case, then perhaps one tool can do it all. But the PMO is not a transactional department. Operational work can lend itself to transactional applications, but project work is less transactional in nature and a great deal more collaborative.

Order entry is an example. The customer, in this case an external customer, wants a product. The product is readily available. The customer places an order from any one of many sellers of the product. The department of the seller that handles order entry receives the order. Using the order entry features of an accounting system, the user enters the order and prints invoices, credit notes, order confirmations, picking slips, and shipping labels. Any and all work required to satisfy the order is performed within the order entry features of the accounting system. Quickly and effectively, the order is processed and the product is delivered to the customer. That is transactional work and one tool can, and often does, do all the work.

Now take project management as an example. The customer, in this case an internal customer though it could be an external customer, wants to have a new capability. In particular the customer who is the head of sales wants to have better visibility into the status of sales opportunities, better management of the activities of the sales teams, and more accuracy in the forecasting of sales in terms of both timing and amount. The head of sales is no doubt aware of many vendor solutions, but does not have enough information and knowledge to purchase and implement a solution. There are many factors to consider such as the specific set of needs that the head of sales is seeking to meet, the needs of other organizations such as marketing and customer service, budget and time constraints, support requirements, and technology considerations, and alternatives for the solution. To successfully deliver the capabilities that the head of sales is seeking, a formal project is undertaken and a project manager is assigned to initiate the project.

To commence with the initiating of the project, the project manager meets with the head of sales to discuss the high-level requirements. Expecting to discuss a list of sales force automation needs, the project manager is surprised to hear about all of the frustrations and irritations. The head of sales is dissatisfied with the current system of spreadsheets, emails, and the Friday sales conference calls designed to find out if the forecasts are accurate and if they meet the sales quotas. The head of sales is in a hurried state and commits his marketing manager and one of his best regional sales managers to work with the project manager to further develop and define the business case for the project, key requirements, and the project charter for the effort.

In meeting with both the marketing manager and the regional sales manager, the project manager quickly discovers that there is not a great deal of common ground in terms of the needs of the sales department. The regional sales manager wants to keep things as simple as possible with minimal bureaucracy imposed on the sales teams, including following a rigid sales process, entering account, opportunity, and contact data, forecasting sales transactions, and preparing sales status reports. The marketing manager, on the other hand, wants the exact opposite; a sales force automation tool that provides both a disciplined approach for managing the sales process as well as a robust application for account, contact, and opportunity management, including all of the bells and whistles for management of the sales pipeline, forecasting, and reporting.

From the start of the project, the project manager is faced with a situation that is not straightforward and needs to be clarified. After documenting the various points of view of the requirements, the project manager reviews the input of the marketing manager and the regional sales manager with the head of sales. Shortly thereafter a working session is convened with all parties to discuss and vet out the core set of needs that the head of sales is seeking to fulfill. In this session the project manager makes use of a brainstorming tool called MindMapper to facilitate and add a bit of structure to the thoughts and ideas of the team. By the end of the working session with the head of sales, the marketing manager, and the regional sales manager, the project manager had guided the group to a consensus on key needs, requirements, and success factors. The results of this working session laid out a common vision of the needed solution; a vision that was more than the regional sales manager had in mind, not quite as much as the marketing manager had in mind, and exactly what the head of sales had in mind.

From that point the project manager went on to develop the project charter, which was reviewed and approved with management. The project manager next performed detailed planning utilizing numerous members of the sales and marketing department. The project plan, which was approved by management, was executed in a near flawless manner. The product of the project, in this case a new sales force automation application, was implemented and accepted and after a brief period of training and initial education, the new system was up and running and meeting the needs of the head of sales.

Over the course of the project the project manager used a collection of tools, including MindMapper to brainstorm effectively, Microsoft Word to document numerous aspects of the project, Microsoft Excel to perform financial modeling of costs and benefits, Microsoft PowerPoint to prepare summary presentations for management and the project team, Microsoft Project to manage and control the project work, Microsoft Project Server to communicate and collaborate with project team members and stakeholders, Microsoft SharePoint to manage the wide variety of project documents, and, of course, the many email and calendaring features of Microsoft Outlook. For those who advocate an all-in-one tool for project management, what kind of tool does all of that? There is none. The work to be done in a PMO environment requires many tools. Some of these tools are transactional to a degree, but most of the tools are collaborative and productivity tools. It is inconceivable to think that all of the work that a project manager must do can ever be performed through the use of one, and only one, tool.

Other Tools Exist

An all-in-one tool that provides all of the features and functions for everything that a project manager must do sounds nice in theory, but such a mindset tends to be oblivious to the wide variety of tools that every organization already has. Hence the opportunity at hand for the PMO is not that of simply implementing a tool or even a set of tools, but rather the establishment of a PMO architecture to deliver the capabilities and information required to perform all of the work at hand—both the management of projects and the management of the PMO.

Architecture Approach

With the exception of some in the vendor community who have a biased perspective toward their products and some in the community of pundits who simply have an outdated perspective, most contemporary information technology and PMO executives think in terms of architecture, not tools. Tools and applications are important, because they provide individuals and departments with rich feature sets and database-driven capabilities, but it is the architecture that provides integrated information management to the enterprise (see Figure 5.3).

What exactly is the PMO architecture and why is it important? PMO architecture is all about understanding the many different components that make up the PMO and how those components relate. The PMO in this context is not just the PMO but all those served by the PMO and linked by a common purpose. Components in this context are all of the tools, applications, platforms, technologies, processes, and organizational knowledge that reside within or is

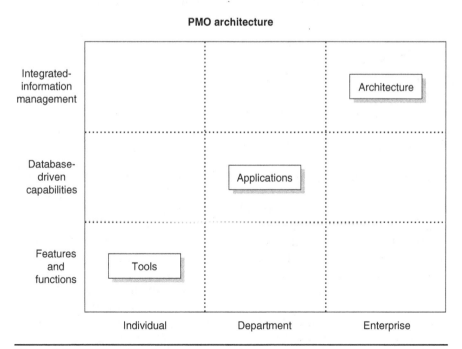

Figure 5.3 PMO architecture

available to the PMO. PMO architecture is important for a number of reasons, including but not limited to the reasons we discuss in the next section.

Keeping it Simple

PMO architecture like any architecture is a means of dealing with complexity. The complexity of the PMO takes many shapes and forms. Some of this complexity is related to the many different characteristics of the wide variety of projects that are found in nearly all PMOs. Project characteristics such as the degree to which the requirements of the project can be known, the amount of complex technology involved, the number of people resources required, the overall size of the project, expected duration, strategic importance, and competing demands all contribute to project complexity. As project management consultant and author Lew Ireland (2007) explains, "Projects have two primary areas for complexity—the technical aspects of the product with the degree of difficulty in building the product and the business scope (such as the schedule, cost, risk, communications)." Collectively, project complexity drives other areas of PMO complexity, such as tool and application, process and methodology, and communications and collaboration complexity. Therefore, PMO architecture is tremendously important and useful because it provides the means of breaking down these areas of complexities into usable and manageable components.

Enables Decision Making

PMO architecture provides a basis for decision making. According to IT and project management veteran Tom Mochal (2003), "At the most basic level, you can think of application architecture as an inventory and a process for managing and leveraging the inventory to make good business decisions." By defining the components of the PMO architecture, decisions can be made to select, implement, and use the best fit solutions and capabilities for these components. Additionally, the PMO architecture provides guidance in both addressing unmet areas of need as well as avoiding redundancies. Duplication of tool sets and redundancies of applications can exist for many reasons in an organization. For some organizations, mergers and acquisitions can result in multiple tools and approaches for managing projects and the PMO. For other organizations, such tool and application duplication can be the result of decentralized management decision making in which one functional department may use one set of tools and another department may use additional or different tools. Beyond project management offerings, many applications and tools such as email systems, collaboration platforms, sales force tools, customer relationship management (CRM) and enterprise resource planning (ERP) applications all provide overlapping and duplicate functionality as it relates to managing tasks and project work that nearly every employee in the organization has in one form or another. With so much from which to choose, it is not always obvious what tools are to be used for what work. The PMO architecture helps in the decision-making process and is important for the organization to effectively address unmet needs and to avoid making decisions that would result in tool redundancies and duplication of features and functions.

Process-Based Tool Usage

PMO architecture helps to define the properties and uses of the system components. As Cutter Consortium senior consultant Alexandre Rodrigues (2004) writes, "It is nowadays widely accepted that tools must be designed to fit the processes, and not the other way around." The PMO architecture provides the mechanism to instantiate components and tools relative to the processes for which they are used. Some of these components are function-driven, for example, how to develop and manage a project schedule. Other components are capability-driven such as how to communicate and collaborate with project team members. Other components are content-driven such as how to follow the project management process of the PMO. The PMO architecture is important and needed to provide the structure for the use of the components and tools as governed by the PMO processes and policies.

Longevity of Use

PMO architecture aids in establishing the long-term viability of the system. Tools and applications come and go, but the architecture is a lasting construct. It enables tools and applications to be implemented, used, and maintained. Over time, some tools are retired or replaced with others. The architecture allows the organization to improve its capabilities and tooling both in depth and breadth. For example, the PMO architecture might house sophisticated components for modeling and management of the projects of the formal portfolio while at the same time providing tools and streamlined best practices for the management of the line-of-business projects outside the formal project mix. Many PMOs need the ability to focus on the strategic needs of the organization while at the same time ensuring that broad areas of need are fulfilled. Complex functionality required to successfully manage the projects and resources associated with the formal project portfolio of the organization must be implemented and successfully used. At the same time, simpler and more cost-effective approaches must be effectively addressed and rolled out for the management of the ubiquitous informal project work throughout the organization. Without the PMO architecture, it is difficult to establish and maintain the long-term viability of the collection of applications, tools, and components.

Facilitates Continuous Improvement

PMO architecture provides the ability to implement continuous improvement. Continuous improvement in project management comes in many shapes and forms. It can be derived from formal initiatives such as the implementation of a program for organizational project management maturity as well as through ongoing management decisions and actions to address known problems and issues. Though day-to-day management decisions based upon such things as documented lessons learned and project team feedback are no doubt formal in nature, in the context of continuous improvement these continuous improvement opportunities are referred to as informal. But regardless of the formality or size of the potential improvement, there needs to be a way for the organization to incorporate and institutionalize the desired change. Nearly always, this requires modifying existing or implementing new processes and tools as well as effective communication of the changes. Without the PMO architecture to provide context and visibility into such things as processes and tools, it is extremely difficult to keep everyone on the same page once you get them there.

Examples of PMO Architecture

There are many examples of PMO architecture to consider in establishing the components of the PMO that are helpful for organizations. Most vendors and consultants who provide EPM products and services also provide representative architectures to help the PMO successfully implement, not just their offerings, but the other components needed to complete the PMO architecture as well.

PMO Architecture by BOT International

In 2002, one of the pioneer firms in PMO setup, BOT International, introduced and has continued to espouse an architecture approach to PMO setup. The PMO architecture approach, illustrated in Figure 5.4, advocated by BOT International consists of three layers of architecture; the user layer, the PMO layer, and the enterprise layer.

The user layer represents the components of the PC desktop such as the operating system, applications, and browser. The user layer is the gateway for the workplace professional to all of the tools and applications of the enterprise. Likewise the enterprise layer represents the information technology infrastructure and the vast number of applications of the organization. The

PMO architecture

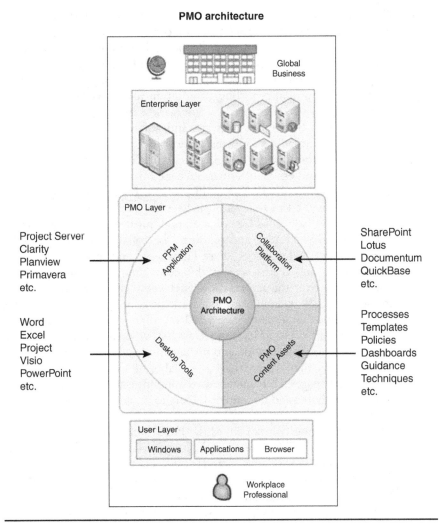

Figure 5.4   PMO architecture example

PMO layer, in essence, provides the PMO architecture for the organization and consists of four components; the project portfolio management (PPM) application component, the collaboration platform component, the desktop tools component, and the PMO content assets component.

   1. The project portfolio management component of the PMO architecture is represented by applications and solution offerings provided by project management vendors of all shapes and sizes. Popular offerings, such as CA Clarity, HP PPM Center, IBM RPM, Planview Enterprise,

Compuware Changepoint, Primavera Evolve, Dapiv PPM, and Serena Mariner represent the project portfolio management component of the PMO architecture. These application offerings provide capabilities and features for demand management, portfolio management, project management, resource management, financial management, methodology, workflow, and reporting. In addition to the well-known popular offerings typically covered by the market analysts, dozens of other vendors, both traditional software and software-as-a-service (SaaS) firms, provide solutions for project portfolio management.

2. The collaboration platform component of the PMO architecture is represented by vendor offerings such as Microsoft SharePoint, IBM Lotus, and many others. The ability to effectively communicate and collaborate is vital in today's businesses. As such, rather than having multiple point solutions for collaboration, most organizations have an enterprise-wide strategy and platform for collaboration that enables users to create workspaces, share knowledge and information across departments and teams, and at the same time maintain IT control and security over the information assets. Few organizations go about implementing a collaboration platform just for the PMO. For those organizations that already have a collaboration platform, the PMO no doubt makes full use of its features such as workspaces and document folders to share information and manage project documents. For those organizations that do not have a collaboration platform, the PMO and project teams likely collaborate using internal local area network (LAN) file shares and document folders to organize and manage project schedules, documents, and reports.

3. The desktop tools component of the PMO architecture is represented by the various PC tools and applications used by the PMO and the project teams. This includes standard PC desktop programs that most business professionals have such as those found in the Microsoft Office suites as well as project management scheduling tools like Microsoft Project and Niku Open Workbench and special purpose desktop tools like Visio and MindMapper. Collectively, the various PC tools used within the PMO and by those engaged in projects comprise the desktop tool component of the PMO architecture.

4. The PMO content assets component is represented by the various knowledge assets of the PMO consisting of, but not limited to, processes and templates, policies and procedures, executive dashboards, metrics, scorecards, tips and techniques, and guidance and training. Content assets exist throughout the PMO and project teams whether effectively organized and used as a managed PMO methodology and best practice framework or ineffectively left scattered about the organization. Establishing PMO content assets as a component of the

architecture is beneficial for a number of reasons. The content assets of a PMO are far more than just a methodology document and set of project management templates. Rather, it is a framework that is easy to access, use, and manage that provides such things as project management processes and templates (PMBOK®, SDLC, Agile), PMO processes (governance, portfolio management, continuous improvement), PMO policies (project type classification, team site and document management, roles and responsibilities), management dashboards, and training and skills improvement assets.

Nearly every PMO requires more than any one vendor product such as a PPM application can do. Organizations that simply implement a project management tool and expect to find all aspects of managing projects and managing the PMO to run smoothly are likely to be in for a surprise as some individuals seek out to effectively use supporting tools and collaboration platforms while others fail to do so. Likewise, organizations that develop lengthy methodology documents and expect them to meet the needs of all of the project teams might be in for a surprise as some individuals take the time and effort to understand and apply the methodology while many others do not.

The PMO architecture enables the required components to be placed, used in context, and continually refined and improved. It simplifies complexity and enables decision making. It brings a sense of order to an environment of people, processes, and tools that often has many different tendencies. The PMO architecture enables the PMO content assets component, a component that many organizations have difficulty addressing effectively, to be placed and effectively used as a key driver of the usage of the other PMO architecture components and a key enabler of the PMO strategy.

Enterprise Project Management Solution Architecture by Microsoft

Another example of architecture helpful to the PMO is the Enterprise Project Management (EPM) Solution Architecture provided by Microsoft (see Figure 5.5).

The Microsoft EPM offering is a complete, end-to-end, collaborative project and portfolio management solution. More than a single product, Microsoft EPM represents an architecture approach to meeting the tooling needs of the PMO. At a high level, the architecture provides an easy to understand view of how the various tools, applications, and enabling technologies work together.

The first layer of this simplified view of the Microsoft EPM architecture depicts the desktop tools and customer applications commonly used throughout the organization. For example, tools found in the various Microsoft Office suites such as Outlook, Word, Excel, and PowerPoint are indispensable to the

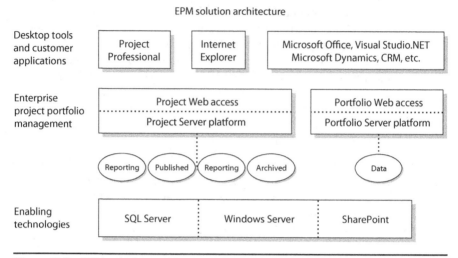

Figure 5.5   EPM solution architecture

---

work performed in the PMO. Additional Microsoft Office point tools like Visio for business and technical drawings and InfoPath for deploying forms and gathering information are helpful in the work efforts of the PMO. Microsoft Project is the de facto standard scheduling tool used by project managers all around the world.

The second layer of this view of the Microsoft EPM architecture represents the enterprise project portfolio management layer. Project Server provides such capabilities as resource management, scheduling, reporting, and collaboration capabilities and Portfolio Server provides the requisite features to enable organizations to best identify, select, manage, and deliver project portfolios that are aligned to the needs of the business. Collectively, Project Server and Portfolio Server enable the organization to manage all types of project work, enhance decision making through better insight and visibility to the project mix, effectively collaborate with all stakeholders and participants, and to establish a scalable platform for EPM.

The third layer of this view of the Microsoft EPM architecture depicts the enabling technologies such as SQL Server, Windows Server, and SharePoint. As these enabling technologies represent de facto standards that are commonly used, organizations are able to leverage skills they already have and to get more return on investment from their previous technology investments.

Many vendors and technology leaders like Microsoft realize that a decision to set up a PMO or a decision to implement EPM is more than simply a decision to implement a tool. Whether envisioned and planned upfront or accidentally arrived at after the fact, an architecture approach to the PMO provides organizations with the ability to leverage, use, and manage the various pieces of the puzzle. Microsoft's EPM solution architecture is one of many well-developed approaches.

Enterprise Performance Management Architecture by Planview

Another example of architecture helpful to the PMO is the Planview Enterprise Performance Management Framework (see Figure 5.6).

The Planview Enterprise Performance Management Framework presents an architecture that both recognizes the importance and leverages the existence of an organization's enterprise business applications, desktop tools, collaboration platforms, business intelligence and financials, and IT infrastructure. To develop such functions and capabilities with a project management application that are already inherent to an organization's existing tools, applications, and infrastructure results in the duplication of functionality and additional complexity.

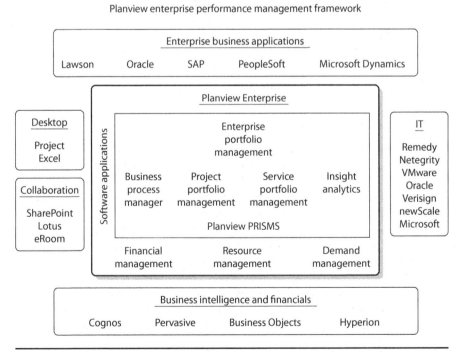

Figure 5.6 Planview enterprise performance management framework

The Planview Enterprise component of this architecture presents the applications and tools needed to effectively manage the project portfolio of the PMO. EPM enables the PMO to define and communicate organizational objectives and strategies, acquire a complete view of capacities and demand, and make optimal and transparent decisions to control costs, risks, and benefit delivery. PPM provides tactical execution of integrated work and workforce management, supporting workflows and daily reporting at the project level. Service Portfolio Management (SPM) enables the organization to catalog, quantify, and manage the resulting products and services. PRISMS enables the PMO to establish and integrate the supporting network of business processes, best practices, and supporting tools. Business Process Manager (BPM) automates these processes with a user-friendly interface that can track work as it traverses these processes as well as measure compliance using gates and supporting checklists. Insight Analytics enables the organization to monitor performance of all activities with meaningful drill-down metrics and graphics. Supporting functions help the organization to manage resources and money, collaboration capabilities, and data and request management.

The Planview Enterprise Performance Management Framework enables the PMO to establish an architecture approach grounded in the customer-centric reality of heterogeneous IT environments. This enables the integration of PPM with the other components of the overall architecture such as business service management, application life cycle management, productivity, and corporate resource planning and financial management. The Planview approach encompasses and simplifies complexity and it enables a wide range of decision making and selection of the best-of-breed alternatives represented in each of the components of the overall architecture.

It Takes an Architecture

These examples of PMO architecture serve to illustrate the point that no one tool does it all. For years, in numerous ways, market analysts have compared one vendor tool against another from the detailed features and functions of the product offering to the perceived ability to execute and the vision of the vendor. Regrettably, often missing from such analysis is any kind of assessment of the overall architecture in which the vendor product is a participant. One analyst may view that a particular offering is lacking in functionality, another analyst may appreciate the vendor's design strategy to integrate and interoperate with leading technology players rather than duplicate such functionality or compete with such vendors. This is not just an issue of complying with the customer's existing IT infrastructure; rather it is enabling the customer to invest in architecture and then leveraging that architecture to proactively meet the long-terms needs of their business units.

Summary

PMOs by nature are need-driven organizations. That is they are typically established not at the birth of a company but well after and usually as a result of organizational need or an impending crisis. By the time the PMO is established and the organization is seeking to address needs relative to the PMO and to PPM, the IT infrastructure, core applications, and collaboration platforms of the enterprise are usually already in place. To have a mindset that one tool can, or even should do it all is simply a theoretical mindset that is not possible or practical for most organizations.

While there is always a legitimate need to compare and contrast one vendor tool against another, for most PMOs such product comparisons are simply not that relevant. The combination of increasing application complexity and overlapping functional capabilities along with the fluid and changing roles of the PMO all but mandate that organizations approach the needs of the PMO from the perspective of establishing a PMO architecture as opposed to implementing a point tool. The benefits are numerous. For management and the leadership team, an architecture approach reduces complexity and enables decision making. For users an architecture approach rationalizes, explains, and makes available the various components that comprise the architecture, including enterprise applications, functional tools, and collaboration platforms and, let us not forget the important content assets of the PMO. Additionally the PMO architecture eases the burden of maintenance and support by standardizing components and leveraging technical skills associated with those components. By taking a holistic view, the PMO architecture is an enabler of continuous improvement and provides the means to institutionalize change whether in the form of new tooling or process improvement.

Questions

1. What are the problems of approaching PMO tooling as a function of implementing a single project management tool or application?
2. Why is it that one project management tool or application cannot meet the needs of the PMO?
3. In the initiating phase of a project, what kinds of activities are performed?
4. In the initiating phase of a project, what kinds of tools are used?
5. In the planning phase of a project, what activities are performed?
6. In the planning phase of a project, what kinds of tools are used?
7. In the executing phase of a project, what kinds of activities are performed?

8. In the executing phase of a project, what kinds of tools are used?
9. In the monitoring and controlling phase of a project, what kinds of activities are performed?
10. In the monitoring and controlling phase of a project, what kinds of tools are used?
11. In the closing phase of a project, what kinds of activities are performed?
12. In the closing phase of a project, what kinds of tools are used?
13. Why is the PMO architecture important?
14. How can the PMO architecture help address complexity?
15. How can the PMO architecture aid in management decision making?
16. How can PMO architecture help define the systems and the components?
17. How can the PMO architecture help address long-term viability of the system?
18. How can PMO architecture facilitate the implementation of continuous improvement?
19. What are the common components of PMO architecture?

References

Ireland, Lew. 2007. "Project Complexity: A Brief Exposure to Difficult Situations." http://www.asapm.org. (Accessed June 9, 2008)

Mochal, Tom. 2003. "Use Application Architecture to Reduce Redundancy." http://www.techrepublic.com. (Accessed June 9, 2008)

Rodrigues, Alexandre. 2004. "Developing Project Management Competency." http://www.pmo-consulting.pt. (Accessed June 9, 2008)

Executive Insights

Establishing a PMO Architecture

Rakan Saraiji

Vice President of Project Management,
SHUAA Capital, Dubai, UAE

Introduction

Great news, your organization has decided to establish a project management office (PMO), and since you are an experienced project manager, they decided to put you in charge of establishing it. Since everything to you is a project, you are thinking that the initiation phase of this project—to establish the PMO—is already done, and now you are in charge of completing the planning phase. One deliverable of this planning phase is the architecture of the PMO; this includes what resources are needed, the organization chart (org chart) for the PMO, and all the tools needed. How do you go about doing this?

This is the situation that I faced at SHUAA Capital and this case study gives you the steps that I followed with examples of the decisions and the outcome of these steps at my organization.

Study Your Current Organization

To establish the correct PMO architecture to benefit your organization, you need to first study your current organization. You should study the organization's structure, its business process, mission, and vision.

Organization Structure

You need to know the current structure of your organization. Is your organization project-based, function-based, or a matrix organization? The organization structure has an impact on how the PMO functions within the organization, which impacts how you architect the PMO.

SHUAA is a function-based organization. During project implement, the project team is in a matrix organization structure, which complicates the management of the projects. When thinking about the resources for my PMO, I had to keep in mind the need for excellent communication skills to enable them to communicate to resources at different levels and manage them in a matrix structure.

Organization Business Process

You need to know the current business process in your organization. How do projects gets started? Who approves their initiation and budget? How do they get prioritized? What is expected from the PMO in this area—will your PMO be part of the selection and prioritization process? Or, will the selected projects and their priority, in reference to other projects, be given to your PMO?

Currently at SHUAA, the PMO does not get involved in the selection and the prioritization of the projects; this is planned in the future once the PMO reaches a higher maturity level (see the discussion on PMO maturity levels later in this case study).

Organization Mission and Vision

To establish your PMO you have to have a PMO charter. The charter has the PMO mission and vision and these should be aligned with your organization's mission and vision. Therefore you should know and study these features of your firm.

Agree on the Project Management Office Charter

You need to finalize a charter for your PMO, which should be discussed and agreed upon by executive management. The main charter components that need executive management buy-in are the PMO mission, vision, goals, objectives, and reporting in the organization.

Decide on Mission, Vision, Goals, and Objectives

Your PMO is an integral part of the organization. The PMO affects the organizational efficiency and strategy, especially once the PMO reaches a high maturity level. Therefore it is prudent to be aligned with the company strategy from the start to get executive buy-in, which enables the growth and maturation of the PMO.

SHUAA is a leading financial service provider in the Gulf Cooperation Council and the Middle East and has been growing rapidly, but they wanted to keep their reputation of professionalism and best service. That is why SHUAA wanted to establish a PMO section; they will probably be the first local financial service firm to do so.

◆ Our PMO Mission is *"Establish standard project management discipline at SHUAA Capital throughout the organization."*

◆ Our PMO Vision (how to achieve our mission) is *"SHUAA Project Management will have standard project life cycle, collaterals, and management process. Projects will have standard reports and reporting mechanism in order for executive management to have a Dashboard view of all projects in the organization."*

◆ Our PMO Goals are *"1) Improve the delivery capability of project teams, 2) Improve project delivery, 3) Create real-time project status visibility to upper management, and 4) Analyze financial results of project returns (long-term goal)."*

◆ Our PMO Core Objectives are *"1) Establish project management standards, 2) Project quality control standards, and 3) Project reporting to management (Dashboard)."*

◆ Our PMO Supporting Objectives are *"1) Provide project management resources and technologies, 2) Audit and control on all projects, and 3) Conduct project management training and information sessions."*

Finalize PMO Place and Reporting in the Organization

You should finalize where the PMO fits in your organization. If the PMO is purely an IT PMO so that you are only concerned about IT projects, then you probably should be reporting directly to the Chief Information Officer (CIO) or Chief Technology Officer (CTO). If the PMO is involved in non-IT projects, then it should report to the executive responsible for the organization's operation, the Chief Operating Officer (COO) or equivalent.

Currently at SHUAA the PMO has been championed by the CIO and is being incubated within IT. Therefore, our PMO is reporting to the CIO. Once project management is recognized throughout the organization, the PMO is moved and we would report directly to the COO equivalent.

Assess Organization's Project Management Maturity Level

It's important to know where you are and where you are going if you want to know how to get there. The map that you use to do that for your PMO should be a project management maturity model. Just like the Software Engineering Institute's Capability Maturity Model Integration (CMMI) used for the software and system development projects and organizations, there are many maturity models out there for project management. Once you decide on a maturity model for your PMO, you determine the maturity level of your organization currently and to which level you want to achieve and when.

For the PMO at SHUAA, I used two project management maturity models: the first is Gartner's PPM Maturity Model, which has 6 levels 0 through 5 and the second is the PMO Maturity Model used in the Kendall and Rollins (2003) PPM book. In both cases SHUAA was essentially at the first level in both maturity models, which is appropriate for startup and/or growing companies.

Decide on Improvement Plan and Execution Strategy

Once you identified your current organization project management maturity level, your next step is to decide on an improvement plan base and what maturity level you want to get to in order to meet the PMO goals and objectives established in your charter.

Our goal for the PMO at SHUAA is to get to mid-level in both maturity modules mentioned previously. This is probably the most appropriate for our case based on the goals and objectives that we established. In addition, Gartner refers to Level 3, which is the fourth level of the six levels they have in their project management maturity models, as the *sweet spot* for most companies.

Establish the PMO Architecture

Now that you have finalized the PMO charter and agreed on the PMO strategy, you need to establish your PMO architecture. This architecture includes the type of PMO, what resources are needed, the PMO org chart, and all the tools needed.

PMO Type

What is the extent of your PMO involvement in the organization's projects? Will the PMO support, control, or manage these projects? This determines the PMO type for your organization. If all you need to do is to give other project managers in the organization the tools, templates, and general advice without any further involvement, then your PMO is the supportive PMO.

If in addition to support the PMO has the authority to enforce certain project management methodology, policies, procedures on the organization's projects that are not managed by the PMO, then your PMO is the controlling type; this is probably the most common type of PMO. If your PMO is managing all the projects within your organization, then your PMO is the directive type.

The directive type is not common and might only be possible to implement in small organizations.

We decided at SHUAA to initially have a hybrid PMO type—a combination of controlling and directive, but only on critical projects—with the aim of moving to controlling once project management is understood and the PMO is recognized throughout the organization.

Project Management Organization

Once you have decided on your PMO type, you need to decide on what resources staff the PMO and their org chart, in addition to what tools you need.

Resources Needed and Org Chart

You have to decide what skills you need in your PMO. Do you need only project managers? Or do you also need business analysts, quality control staff, and possibly other supporting staff like technical writers? In addition, what kind of experience does the staff have/need? Do they have to have prior experience in your organization's sector and hands-on experience in the kind of projects they review and/or manage? How many years of experience do they have to have? How will they be structured within the PMO—the PMO org chart?

All these questions have different answers for different organizations. The steps that we have taken so far, from establishing the goals and objectives to deciding on the PMO type, helps answer all these questions. For example, if your PMO is to be supportive only, then you need minimal staff, maybe only 1 to 3 for small- to medium-size organizations, prior experience in the organization sector is not essential, and you might need a technical writer if you are going to be creating templates and procedures. If your PMO is to be directive, then you probably need experienced project managers, who also have experience and knowledge of the organization's sector. You might also need a business analyst, who should have experience in the organization's sector, and a large staff if you have many projects.

At SHUAA, based on the goals and objectives listed before and since the PMO type is mainly controlling with some directive keeping in mind that we are starting under the CIO with the aim to move under the COO and control business projects, we decided on a staff of five in addition to the PMO Manager. Three of these staff members are project managers; two have prior experience in IT projects and one has prior experience in business projects within the financial sector. The other two staff members are business analysts, one with prior IT experience and one with prior financial sector experience.

All of these five staff members report to the PMO manager. If the company continues to grow and our PMO changes to controlling only, then we don't foresee adding any staff. But if the company continues to grow and the PMO continues to be controlling and directive to major or critical projects, then we will probably have to add more staff when needed.

Tools Needed

Finally, you need to decide on what project management tools you use within your organization and in your PMO. You might create your own project management templates or buy a tool that has all these templates. You will need a project management software/tool; this is the backbone to manage all the projects within your organization. You might also need a document management tool or a business analysis tool.

At SHUAA, we are using Microsoft® Project as our project management tool. We have the Enterprise version and also the served based product, Microsoft Project Server. We have integrated the Project Server with Microsoft® SharePoint and Outlook. Each new project created in Project Server has a SharePoint site to house all its documentation and is integrated to our active directory so that the project manager can assign the resources from the active directory and these tasks are listed as Outlook tasks on the resource Outlook interface; it makes it easier for the resource to update the status of their tasks straight from Outlook. We also have purchased a PMO content asset solution called Process On Demand (POD) with all its process documentation, guidance, and project management templates from BOT International. Finally, we purchased a business analysis tool, which helps us create use cases and test cases.

Summary

There is no magic formula on how to architect your PMO. It varies for different organizations, depending on the goals and objectives for the PMO and what PMO type fits best. I hope through this insight you have some general guidance and examples to best architect your PMO to be aligned with the organization's goals and objectives.

References

Fitzgerald, Donna. Barbara Gomolski, Lars Mieritz, and Matt Light. 2007. "Best Practices: Program and Portfolio Management Maturity Model," Gartner ID # G00149002, 13.

Kendall, Gerald, Steven Rollins. 2003. *Advanced Project Portfolio Management and the PMO: Multiplying ROI at Warp Speed*. Appendix A. Florida: J. Ross Publishing.

Method123. 2007. "Project Management Office—PMO." http://www.method123.com.

Pieces of the PMO Puzzle

Osama Bakir

CEO PMCT Quest, Oman

Introduction

Organizations always struggle with the concept of project managers having their own specialized office. In fact, one of our clients did not support the concept of separating—isolating—project managers from their functional departments, because the client believed that it is more beneficial and significant to keep appointed project managers within the functional department setup as well as to maintain the interaction between the project managers, technical subject matters, and decision makers.

While such thinking has certain aspects of acceptance, the functional organization has been in place since day one of the establishment of organizational theory. People tend to work better when they are assigned to a specific discipline or knowledge area. Moreover functional organization is the de facto standard approach for any new establishment and organizations do miss out on opportunities if they manage and work in this format.

However, life has changed. Organizations are beginning to think differently about ways to achieve better business results. IT is thinking differently about projects now due to rapid developments, new competitors in the same field, globalization and small-village tendency, high demands of clients, among other things. With the realization that the demands of projects are high, why not have a special discipline or knowledge similar to the finance department, procurement department, and human resources department in the organizational structure?

Hence, the word Project Management Department or Project Management Office has evolved. There is a need to have those who are doing project management and nothing other than project management tasks to work under one umbrella, under one department, headed by a manager for the PMO and chartered and committed to doing nothing except project management activities to fulfill the demands of the overall organization for change and improvement.

How to Approach the Idea of a PMO

In this context we began to have more clients who believed and trusted that under this setup they could do better. The focus of any organization is customer satisfaction and this needs to be driven by the ability to adapt to business change. Indeed many organizations are seeking to establish a new business

183

environment that is governed by projects and ultimately a strong need to manage these projects under a more focused concept of doing things *correctly* rather than just doing the *correct* things and, further, to be more efficient on overall project delivery. We have worked with clients who based their requirements, or intentions, on this overall idea; becoming more effective and efficient at the same time to deliver successfully in all projects dimensions—quality, time, and cost.

When a client first approached us to address their PMO needs, we were pleased to respond actively and thereafter arranged to be engaged in a timely manner. Clients have a great deal of confusion when it comes to the concept of their PMO. Some think of the PMO from the prospective of setup, structure, staffing, processes and procedures, authority, and policy as they do any other departmental office. Others believe it is a concept of getting together under one name. There are those who believe it is a virtual design, meaning we could have a PMO even though we don't work under one manager. Finally, there are those who look at the PMO as a collection of tools, applications, templates, forms, and processes without any real consideration for cultural change within the organization. Whatever form that the client envisions in a PMO, there is always a need to meet the client and to understand the client's point view as to what a PMO is and does.

The first thing that we do is to conduct a thorough project management assessment to address the existing status. Where are they now in terms of their current, as-is state. Then we work on the identification of the client's requirements to get them to the place that they want to be—the desired state. It is customary to face difficult challenges in this stage of engagement because the client is overwhelmed with the needs, the wants, and the wishes.

We always consider that the client is right. Our expertise and opinions are important, but it is the client who really matters. This strategy makes us spend more time, take nothing for granted, communicate effectively, and ensure that we arrive at the best answer directly from the client's needs and not our assumptions. The experience that we have gained from this approach has enabled us to become more practical in our questioning of needs in order to clarify the overall objectives from this entire exercise.

We spend a considerable amount of time working in this phase because it is crucial to ensuring that our resulting plans and efforts are on track. Our client sees this stage as a problem definition task and they tend to learn more on how to define their problems. They also tend to be more active and open to ideas and especially to getting everyone to become aware of the concept of the PMO. Quite often the client thinks about a small setup of their own PMO. To start with the idea in mind and to be as effective as an enterprise PMO is their wish.

Therefore, we look at refining and enhancing the client's points of view and clearly determine the borders between the three main PMO configurations:

1. Project level (project control)
2. Department level (project office)
3. Enterprise level (program office)

The stage of the analysis is important and valuable for the client, because we focus on the objectives of the business and what kind of PMO best serves those objectives rather than rushing in to deliver a recommendation, which might result in setting up a PMO that has no executive support or buy-in from the team.

Senior management support is important in this stage. We tend to work closely in getting them involved and we have found that senior managers provide support as long as there is a clear plan for a smooth transition. We rarely have clients who want to push a decision to have a PMO when there are those in the organization who might object or who might have concerns. There is nothing worse than someone steering the whole working environment, creating difficulties, and changing how team members must work without first having a good plan and strategy to add value and to keep things as simple and effective as possible.

Whenever organizations go about setting up a PMO without proper planning, strategy and participation of the necessary parties, the result is nearly always poor. Other departments, management, and staff view the PMO as an added burden. As soon as there are difficulties with the tools and processes, the users stop using them. Additionally people are quick to remember past experiences and failed attempts in which they ended up with overly detailed project management processes; volumes of paper nicely prepared and saved in the system without being utilized even 20 percent of the time. The signs of a PMO that is failing or soon will be in trouble are:

1. Lengthy processes that are theoretical and too detailed
2. Complex applications that require special expertise to apply and adhere to
3. Overstaffing of specialty functions in the PMO with backgrounds in planning, quality, risk, and documentation before first getting the core project management and business analysis team in place and working on projects
4. Management and the board in the company not knowing what projects to do, when the projects can start and finish, and how the projects progress

We valued such experiences from our clients and recognize the problems to overcome and pitfalls to avoid.

Project Management Office Implementation

The PMO implementation business is not all about documents, processes, and systems; we emphasize that it is about culture change. PMO implementation is an approach of giving the project management processes or the organization more attention than what they used to get. Therefore we believe it is important to consider all surrounding resistances and to try to address their concerns in ways that are more productive. Some of the concerns that we hear from our clients are:

◆ Do we need this change? What is the importance of doing this?
◆ Does this affect our current practice?
◆ How complex is the change?
◆ What is the impact on our job position, job role, and what is the impact in terms of simplicity vs complexity?
◆ How much effort is required to implement this new change?
◆ Does this jeopardize my job? Is there any threat of losing my job?
◆ We have more important things to do. Why can't we do our projects the old way?

Concerns and questions such as these are always in the minds of those involved with a new PMO. It is more about the principle of change than it is about the PMO. We recognize that as a key requirement to what an organization needs to address and a key focus of our efforts when helping our clients with their PMOs.

When dealing with this culture change, we tend to work closely with end-user staff and not just the management decision makers. We seek to involve and get the strong buy-in from those staff since they are the ones who make this change work under the approval of their management. We spend as much time as is needed with those who are the most resistant to change or who have had the worst of prior bad experiences. We find that once they learn the key concepts of the PMO and learn a few of the basic elements of project management such as scope planning, enhanced schedule development, cost budgeting, quality, and risk management, they are quick to recognize the value. What may have seemed to be extra work at the time, in fact, saved much more work later in the project.

By this phase of the new PMO effort, we work with all of the members of the PMO, project team members, the management team, and all of those who are part of the change. It is important at this stage to establish a common positive view of the PMO and of the objectives that we are all working to achieve. This enables the staff to contribute more effectively, sharing their opinions and perspectives on how to make improvements, and, of course, becoming part of setting up the PMO.

Rather than present our project management and PMO services and skills to our clients, we find brainstorming sessions to be an effective technique to gather key customer requirements for success and options for meeting needs. We find it interesting to realize that our client's needs are more or less answered by our offerings. Clients need solutions that work for them and not against them. They need such things as:

◆ A clear and concise methodology for how to manage a project. This has to be customized toward their specific industry and modular enough to be used when managing small, medium, and large projects.
◆ A useful and usable set of standard templates and forms to easily understand how to use the methodology and effectively apply it to any level of project needs.
◆ A robust tool that provides seamless user access, collaboration, and flexibility to be used by all the team members, anytime, and anywhere.
◆ A governance framework that provides all types of organizational policies, authorities, and guidelines to all members with the organization.

These needs are:

1. A proven structure of project management processes and procedures for managing projects, not a collection of processes and procedures that are not applicable to your business-related industry.
2. A way to communicate easily and a tool that enables sharing, collaborating, and communicating that is available to all involved in the project, anytime and anywhere, as per the set of authority levels.
3. A project management application that allows project planning, scheduling, resource optimization, cost budgeting, prioritization, and the best utilization of overall project resources.

Clients find such a summary helpful and, accordingly, are eager to have us help them set up their PMO. Toward that goal, we first develop a clear plan to get the overall business solution formulated and executed in a stage-by-stage format. We like to divide the overall project plan for the setup of a new PMO into five stages, each with its own final objectives:

◆ Stage 1: Exploration and organization culture smoothing stage
◆ Stage 2: Planning and solution design stage
◆ Stage 3: Implementing and delivering the key elements of the PMO
◆ Stage 4: Finalizing the PMO setup, testing, verifying, and rolling out
◆ Stage 5: Post implementation review

Stage 1—Exploration and Organization Culture Smoothing Stage

In the first stage we work diligently to determine all related parties and meet with them individually and in group brainstorming sessions to develop ideas and approaches toward culture change. Additionally, we discuss all details needed for the deployment of the new project management methodologies (PMM). We define the structure of the team as well as individuals required and resources needed to establish a centralized PMO at this level. A starting point is often to have a center of excellence, which is tailored to the needs for establishing a centralized resource of project management specialists.

Stage 2—Planning and Solution Design Stage

At this stage we formulate a workable plan that addresses the scope of work and required tasks to be completed for all related areas, including physical location, human resources, processes and procedures, systems and tools, and training required as well as defining the guidelines and policies to govern the overall work. These efforts and tasks are performed in a coordinated effort with the entire team and reviewed by management to establish an accurate baseline for the PMO setup that includes costs, time frames, and possible issues, for example, risks and dependencies.

Stage 3—Implementing and Delivering the Key Elements of the PMO

The plan is implemented at this stage. Knowing that budget is always tight and time is always constrained, we focus on delivering as quickly as possible the most important components of the plan as well as the components of the plan that deliver value. These supercede the work on less important components and those that do not deliver as much value. We ensure the key members of the team get the training they require. We plan for all members of the PMO to come on board as early as possible by providing them with required tools and training. At this stage it is important to meet the needs of the executive management team, which is often at a higher level than the PMO staff and other mid-management.

Stage 4—Finalizing the PMO Setup, Testing, Verification, and Rollout

Finalization of the overall PMO setup is completed at this stage. We work on concluding the remaining elements of the implementation, final testing, verification, review, validation, completion of training, documentation, and final acceptance of and satisfaction with the PMO.

All of the PMO setup work that has been planned is completed, reviewed, and approved. The planned staffing is put in place and roles, job descriptions, and other organizational matters are completed. The project management system is deployed. This includes all PPM elements such as project prioritization, project selection, policy development, project planning, project scheduling, status reporting, and the use and updating of the project management information system (PMIS). The final delivery of the PMO is secured and smoothly transitioned so that every member in the office is aware of his/her roles and responsibilities, including project management, planning and scheduling, cost control, document control, quality control, risk monitoring and control, and overall project communications.

Stage 5—Post Implementation Review

Once the PMO has been put in place and the organization deployed, there is an essential need to review all of the deliverables and assess all of the results after the deployment is completed. At the third and sixth month mark, we conduct an after-project implementation review exercise. The tools used for this stage are measurement tools needed to measure the status before and after implementation. We use a questionnaire to gather data in a format that facilitates analysis. The data gathered is compared to measure how well the PMO has performed as compared to both the plan for the PMO and the performance level of the organization prior to the set up of the PMO.

Summary

We quickly learned that our clients are extremely concerned when they go through the process of PMO implementation. They expect things to change for the better when compared to what they are used to doing, and they are overwhelmed as to what the impact of the PMO is to the organization. Despite the promise of the PMO, deep down many clients are concerned that the way projects are managed will not noticeably or quickly improve because it is difficult for organizations to adapt to change.

PMO implementation and the improvement of project management is not an easy task. It involves a great deal of *perceived* uncertainty and a *real* fear of major changes is always the norm. To accomplish this mission in an effective way from day one, it is essential to obtain senior management's continuous support as well as the involvement of all parties related to the PMO. Setting up a new PMO is like putting together a puzzle. There can be a lot to do; there is never just one piece to the puzzle. However, the overall effort and change to the organization can go smoothly and be accepted easily as long as all parties are involved and engaged in the process and active during the implementation activities.

6

Executive Reporting:
Keep It Simple

For many organizations and not just the project management offices (PMOs), the cartoon in Figure 6.1 portrays a situation that many recognize. In today's busy organizations, management and the leadership team need to be kept informed in order to provide the executive oversight for which they are responsible as well as to step in and exercise their decision-making authorities as appropriate for the project portfolio at hand. Yet, far too often, executive reporting does not meet this need. In some cases the reports provided to executives, though well-intended, are simply too detailed and provide too much inaccurate information and not enough accurate information. In other cases executive reporting is overly graphic to the point of being flashy and more focused on looking like the dashboard of an F-16 fighter jet than on providing the summary and control information needed by the executive and the leadership team.

Case Study

Consider the dilemma faced by Harold, the new PMO manager for a regional health care provider. In response to the executive reporting needs expressed by management and the leadership team, Harold embarked on an effort to establish an executive report that would summarize the status of the projects of the PMO. Prior to Harold's arrival at the company, Harold's predecessor had implemented an enterprise project management (EPM) application which was used extensively by the PMO and the members of the project teams. The project mix of the PMO consisted of 100 projects of which 15 were large, major projects in the eyes of the executive and leadership team and the remaining

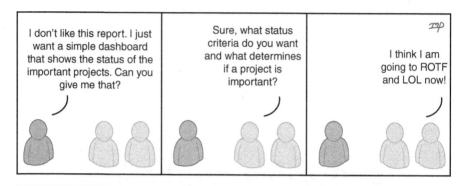

Figure 6.1   PMO comics—the dashboard

85 projects were small, minor projects typically completed with little difficulty within three to four months.

While the EPM application provided capabilities for project and resource management and some degree of custom reporting, it did not provide the kind of high-level, executive reporting that management and the leadership team wanted. For example the EPM application was quite complicated, especially in the eyes of casual users not familiar with the system. Some of the executives with access to the EPM system found that it did not provide them with the summary information that they were seeking; others complained that the system was complicated and that it was easy to get lost in the various areas of the tool. Furthermore, as the EPM application was licensed on a per user basis, not all of the executive and leadership team were licensed to access and use the system as a matter of cost, expected usage, and degree of need.

Harold's predecessor did provide management and the leadership team with a monthly executive summary report but they did not like it. The report was an extract from the EPM application in the form of a PDF document that provided, in essence, a complete list of all of the active projects of the PMO— all 100 of them. The report was tabular, providing a number of columns of information for each project, including the sponsoring department, project number, name, description, manager, budget and its status, project schedule and its status, project issues, and the overall project status.

The report provided ample data, but it did not provide the meaningful executive summary information that the executive and leadership team wanted. Harold met with all of the members of the executive and leadership team to find out what they wanted in the way of executive reporting. Rather than meet with them collectively, Harold thought it was more beneficial and more efficient to meet with them individually to discover what the collective preferences for the executive reporting were.

Over the course of the week Harold met with all 22 members of the executive and leadership team. The feedback Harold received could be placed in three areas of thought. In the first group the executives wanted to see a report that simply showed the major projects. These major projects totaled 15 out of the PMO project mix of 100 projects. In addition to only wanting to see this subset of important, larger projects, this group of executives did not want to see all of the project administration information (project name, number, and the project sponsor) because this information was not needed in the executive summary report. For each of the top 15 projects they merely needed a few project status indicators, including the statuses of the budget, schedule, risk, and the overall status. For this group the simpler the executive summary report the better.

In the second group Harold received similar feedback. This group did not like the current executive summary report. It included all of the projects, which the group didn't like. Additionally, they didn't like the information that was provided because it didn't provide enough of a management context in the form of an assessment of the health of the projects. The data provided didn't portray an intuitive picture or understanding of the projects' progress and if any management attention or intervention was required.

There was no call to action so, in effect, the executive report did not provide any real value. This group was similar to the first in that it only wanted to see the status of the top 15 projects; however, it was different from the first in that it wanted the executive summary report to provide a PMO manager call out, or flag, indicating whether or not a project needed the attention of the executive and leadership team. To this group, such a capability would make the executive summary report a useful and actionable information tool.

The third group was the most sophisticated. They agreed with the first two groups regarding the report extracted from the EPM system. They only wanted to see the top 15 projects. They didn't want to see or need to see the project administration information. They thought that it only cluttered up the summary report. They wanted to see a streamlined, graphical dashboard that contained both selected information from the EPM system and PMO manager assessment information that would be qualitative in nature and that would provide further context to the system data as well as a call to action if required.

Additionally, this group insisted that the executive summary report be limited to just one page and that for further information on a particular project, they should refer to the project status report. It was expected that the status report would provide more detail on such things as open project issues, project manager plans to address those issues, and management action that was needed along with the other status report informational items. The team also suggested that rather than sending the monthly executive summary report in PDF format and via email that the PMO manager should post the report on the PMO portal where the executive could find it along with other information as desired.

With all of this collective input Harold produced a summary of findings and recommendations and emailed the team for their feedback and confirmation that he had a grasp of what the team wanted from the PMO. Harold listed the as-is state of the executive summary report along with the desired state of the report in accordance with the feedback that he was given (see Figure 6.2).

Over the course of the day Harold received email replies from all of the members of the executive and leadership team thanking him for his time and attention into the matter and expressing interest and enthusiasm in seeing the new executive summary reports. With little effort Harold met all of the requirements provided by the executive and leadership team for their executive summary report. He posted the summary report on the PMO portal along with links to the project status reports. Additionally, Harold created a few custom reports within the EPM application and provided descriptions for those reports along with hyperlinks so that those with access to the EPM application could easily access useful information without having to navigate through the complexities and nuances of the system.

Common Executive Summary Report Mistakes

There are many mistakes that PMOs make when producing and providing executive summary reports. Consider the follow:

1. **Executive reporting is not status reporting**. The executive summary report is not a project status report. Some executives like to see a summary report, keeping each project to a one-line description with

PMO executive summary report
"Feedback from leadership team"

As-is state	Desired state
1. Report timeframe—monthly	1. Report timeframe—monthly
2. Length of report—more than one page	2. Length of report—one page
3. Distributed via email	3. Posted on PMO portal
4. Too many projects listed	4. Top fifteen projects listed
5. Too much project administrative detail	5. No project administrative detail
6. Not enough context to project status	6. Context top project status added
7. No PMO manager assessment	7. PMO manager assessment provided
8. No call to action	8. Call to action provided
9. No link to additional project details	9. Link to project status report provided

Figure 6.2   PMO executive summary report

various status traffic light-style indicators—green for good, amber for caution, and red for trouble. If the executives want more information, they can follow up with the PMO manager or the project manager directly. Other executives like to see a full status report for each project, which provides project performance information as well as other project details. Many PMOs struggle with producing an all encompassing executive summary report that seeks to meet both needs. For most organizations it is a mistake to interchangeably use the terms executive summary report and project status report or to try to make them one overall report. The executive summary report and project status report are two distinct reports that meet very different needs.

The executive summary report needs to be intuitive, simple, and concise. It should not provide detailed data. In fact, only a small amount of the executive summary report should be project data. The major focus of the executive summary report should be providing contextual information, management assessment of the data, and a clear flag, or call to attention, and the action taken. Project details can be found in the EPM application and in the project status reports. The need of the executive status report is not to simply abstract that data, but rather to provide meaning to it.

2. **Project management reporting is not operational reporting.** Project management reporting is not the same thing as operational reporting. Oftentimes PMOs are established within the information technology (IT) department and managed by people with operational, not project management, backgrounds. The reporting of project work at the executive level is different than the reporting of operational work.

Operational reporting is typically time sensitive in terms of the frequency of the reporting. The reporting of operational work, such as a help desk, might provide executive summary information for hundreds, even thousands, of incidents, for example, help desk calls summarized by trouble tickets received, resolved, and still open and by various timeframes or by various degrees of severity. Operational reports are generated by the help desk or IT service management software, often daily, and there is little need to assess or place a context on the data.

The executive summary reporting of the projects of the PMO, on the other hand, is not nearly as time sensitive in terms of report frequency. Few executives would want daily or even weekly summary reports for the top projects of the PMO because the project timeframes are longer. The top projects of the PMO, such as an IT PMO, can easily have project durations of six months to a year, or even longer. As such, daily reporting is of no value to the executive team.

3. **Executive status reporting is not real-time reporting.** In the zeal to throw technology at every problem, many PMOs make the mistake of thinking that executive reporting should be done in real time. In *The Complete Project Management Office Handbook,* Gerald Hill (2008, p. 144) writes, "The executive dashboard can be viewed as a condensed and graphical representation of the project status report in real-time." There are several flaws with this thinking.

   First, project status reports are not maintained and updated in real-time; hence neither is the information in the executive summary report or dashboard. Certainly it can be accessed from a real-time online network or collaboration platform, but the data is not real-time data.

   Second, for dashboarding or executive summary report data that is coming from an EPM application, it is important to note that an EPM application is not a transactional application like an order entry. An EPM application does not run on auto pilot. Project work might be progressing, but until the project manager enters or updates the data in the EPM application there is no current news for management in the system.

   In most PMOs project managers do not sit at their desks in front of their PCs all day. Many PMOs consider it a resounding success if the project managers and team members enter their data and complete their project status reports on a weekly basis. Any executive summary report or dashboard abstracted from the EPM application might be accessed via a real-time online mechanism, but the data contained in such reports and dashboards is simply not real-time data.

   Third, executive summary reporting and dashboarding is all about providing information not just in a condensed form, but in a form that provides a context for the data, an assessment of what the data means, and a call to attention or action as desired per the reporting or dashboarding policy. Suggesting that an executive summary report or dashboard is a real-time online condensed version of the project status report sounds good in theory but makes little sense in the practical reality that most PMOs face.

4. **Executives don't want daily summary reports.** In most organizations executives want to see report period data, usually monthly, rather than daily or weekly summary reports. The reasons for this are simple.

   When it comes to the top projects of the PMO, which are typically larger and longer-term projects, the interval of time between reporting periods needs to be sufficient to allow for a meaningful comparison of project work performed from one period to the next. Perhaps for some organizations this interval of time is daily, but for most organizations it is monthly and possibly even quarterly for large PMOs with longer-term projects.

Without an appropriate interval of time and comparison of work to plan, it is difficult for executives to get any value or make decisions. Executives meeting on one day to review and discuss the top projects of the PMO would be wary that whatever information they are reviewing is subject to change the very next day. Typically executives want to align the frequency of executive summary reporting with the frequency in which the executive team meets. If the executives and leadership team meet monthly to review the top projects of the organization, then their summary report should be prepared monthly.

5. **Executives want substance, not form.** Don't place form over substance when creating executive summary reports. Executives appreciate technology when it is applied in a meaningful way to solve a problem or to improve a process or to facilitate decision making. But executives rarely prefer form over substance. Oftentimes it is easy to get caught up on the latest gadget or technique to the point of spending more time learning how to play with gadgets than managing the business.

For the top projects of the PMO, executive dashboards can be effective and of value if implemented correctly, but they can also be time consuming and of little value if done incorrectly. The first point of focus should be on the substance of the report or dashboard and meeting the needs of the executives who are reviewing the summary information. The novelty of creating an executive summary report that looks like the dashboard of an automobile or some other creative graphical construction soon wears off if the summary information is not intuitive, correct, easily accessed, and pleasing to view.

6. **Executives want information, not complex data.** Don't forget to keep it simple. Many executive summary reports for the top projects of the PMO start off simple, but over time become more and more complex. Executives are keen to see information in different ways, therefore, rather than having two, three, or even four executive summary reports with different levels of information, there can be a tendency to morph what was once an intuitive straightforward executive summary report into a complex amalgamation of text, shapes, and figures.

It is best to continually confirm with the executive and leadership team the level of detail that they want to see in their reports. If the increase in complexity and level of details are driven by their needs and the requests of the executives, then there are few if any problems. If, on the other hand, the executive summary report becomes increasingly detailed and less intuitive just because someone in the PMO thinks it is a good idea to populate the executive summary report with as much detail as possible, for example a detailed earned value management (EVM) project performance analysis, then the executives might or might not appreciate or benefit from such changes. For most PMOs it is better to keep the executive summary report simple and intuitive and to provide, if necessary, additional summary reports or drill downs for further information and detailed analysis.

Simple Executive Summary Reporting

PMOs can provide simple, intuitive summary reports to the executive and leadership team in a number of ways. For many PMOs the idea behind executive summary reporting of the top projects is to both provide an easy to understand synopsis that periodically portrays the status of the top projects as well as to provide a front door to further information and details that can be accessed as needed.

Organizations that have complex applications for project portfolio management (PPM) and organizations that do not have such tooling can benefit from executive summary reporting of the top projects of the PMO. For organizations with an enterprise PPM application, executive summary reporting can provide the high-level top projects status information that the executive and leadership team want to see. It can also provide a summarized context and PMO assessment that might not be readily apparent from the data, reports, and lists of the enterprise PPM application. Executive summary reporting can also alleviate the need for casual users to have to login and chance navigating around a complex PPM application to find the information they are seeking.

Organizations that do not have an enterprise PPM application are also well served by the top projects executive summary reporting of the PMO. Without an enterprise PPM application, the PMO can deliver tremendous value by providing the executive and leadership team a common view and status of the top projects of the organization. Ideally every PMO should have the tools that they need to manage the project mix. But no two organizations are alike nor do they have the same needs relative to project management tools. While larger PMOs might use their PPM application as the bedrock of the PMO and the centralized depot for all projects, smaller PMOs might not have the need, ability, or resources to approach tooling for the PMO in the same way. In environments in which the PMO does not have the luxury of a PPM application, effective executive summary reporting of the top projects is essential because it can often be the only reporting and review mechanism that is available at a summary level.

Irrespective of the level of PPM tooling that different organizations have, more and more PMOs are addressing executive summary reporting as part of their overall PMO architecture strategy. As discussed in Chapter 5, whether deliberately designed or arrived at by accident, PMOs typically have three key components that collectively make up the PMO architecture:

1. The tools for project management
2. The platforms for collaboration
3. The content assets of the PMO

Project management and collaboration tools might be Microsoft Project Server and Microsoft SharePoint or any of the other various leading and quality solutions. The content assets of the PMO are all of those non-application things such as project management methodologies, project management templates, software development approaches, tips and techniques, training and learning materials, policies and procedures, and executive scorecards, dashboards, and summary reports.

For many organizations the content assets of the PMO are well-organized and rendered via an internal framework of some kind such as an intranet site within the organization (see Figure 6.3). Executive summary reporting of the top projects of the PMO is typically provided as part of the PMO content asset framework. Here the executive and leadership team can find and view periodic executive summary reports, in this case monthly, which provide an easy to understand assessment of the status of the top projects via text, data, graphical icons, and bar charts.

As an example, the executive dashboard-summary status view shown in Figure 6.3 provides a tabular graphic that lists the project name and the name of the project manager. The status reports column provides graphical indicators that show whether or not the project manager has updated the project status report. For many organizations it is far more effective to simply highlight the timeliness of the status report rather than to chase down project managers to ask them to turn their report in on time. The summary status view also provides the traditional project management traffic light—red, amber, and green—status indicators along with the appropriate graphical enhancements such as smiley faces for trouble, caution, and good enabling colorblind users to understand the dashboard, which happens to be a requirement of Section 508 of the US Rehabilitation Act of 1973. These indicators are used to show the overall project status as well as the schedule, cost, and risk statuses.

In addition to the executive summary reporting provided within the PMO content asset framework, other project details can be accessed through the organization's PPM tool via URL hyperlinks to Microsoft Project Server. Further, project document information, including detailed status reports and project plan documents, can be accessed for the organization's collaboration platform via URL hyperlinks to Microsoft SharePoint. Whether Microsoft Project Server or another tool for PPM (e.g., Planview, CA/Clarity, HP PPM, Primavera) is utilized or whether Microsoft SharePoint or another tool for collaboration

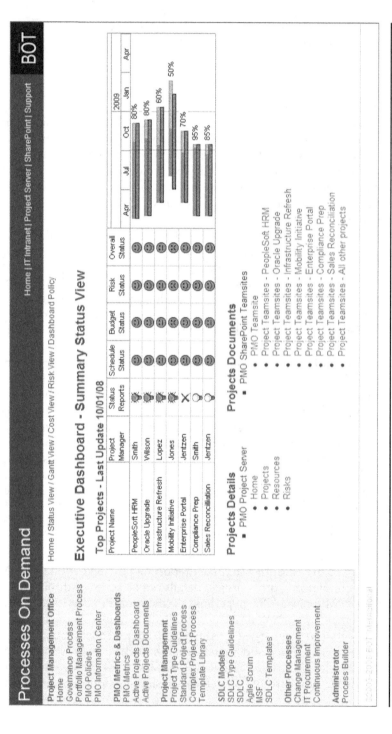

Figure 6.3   PMO executive dashboard—summary view

(e.g., IBM Lotus, Documentum eRoom) is utilized, the user is able to seamlessly navigate to and from the components of the PMO architecture—project management tooling, the collaboration platform, and the PMO content assets. Additional executive summary reporting is provided to show more intuitive and useful executive summary level information (see Figure 6.4).

The Gantt view executive summary report provides the traditional project management schedule view of the top projects. Further summary information, including project duration, start, and finish are provided along with the planned schedule, percent complete, and project baseline provided in bar chart form.

The cost view executive summary report provides the traditional project management cost view of the top projects (see Figure 6.5). Summary information, including the plan, actual, and estimate at completion (EAC), is provided along with the planned schedule, percent complete, and project baseline. The risk view executive summary report (see Figure 6.6) provides the traditional project management risk/return view of the top projects.

The four quadrants of the risk/return analysis are Blockbuster, High-wire Act, Cash Cow, and Least Attractive. The Blockbuster quadrant represents projects that provide a high return and incur a low amount of risk. The High-wire Act quadrant represents projects that provide a high return and incur a high amount of risk. The Cash Cow quadrant represents projects that provide a low return and incur a low amount of risk. The Least Attractive quadrant represents projects that provide a low return and incur a high amount of risk. The projects are listed and ordered numerically and plotted in the appropriate area of the risk/return quadrants. The size of the circular plot of the project is relative to the alignment of the project to the strategic business objectives of the organization.

With Microsoft Internet Explorer 7.0 and Microsoft Office 2007, many organizations and PMOs are enjoying the enhanced RSS support and ease of use. One of the many areas of fit for internal RSS feeds is in support of routine, periodic information distribution. In addition to providing simple executive summary reporting within the PMO content asset framework, many PMOs can now take service and support to the next level by providing PMO RSS feeds that enable the executive and leadership team to subscribe to the PMO dashboards and summary reports. This enables the executive and leadership team to immediately receive the PMO updates and reports from either, or both, the browser (see Figure 6.7) or their email inbox.

Most knowledgeable workers open their browsers daily, therefore, PMO RSS feeds help to ensure the timely distribution and benefit of executive summary reporting. In addition to accessing RSS feeds from a browser, Microsoft Office 2007 now provides a mail folder for RSS feeds that acts just like the inbox mail folder. RSS feeds are listed and managed in the same way that incoming mail is handled (see Figure 6.8). New RSS feed items are highlighted

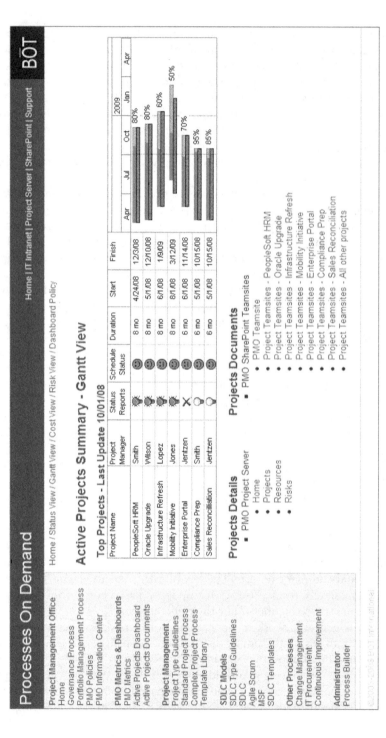

Figure 6.4   PMO executive dashboard—Gantt view

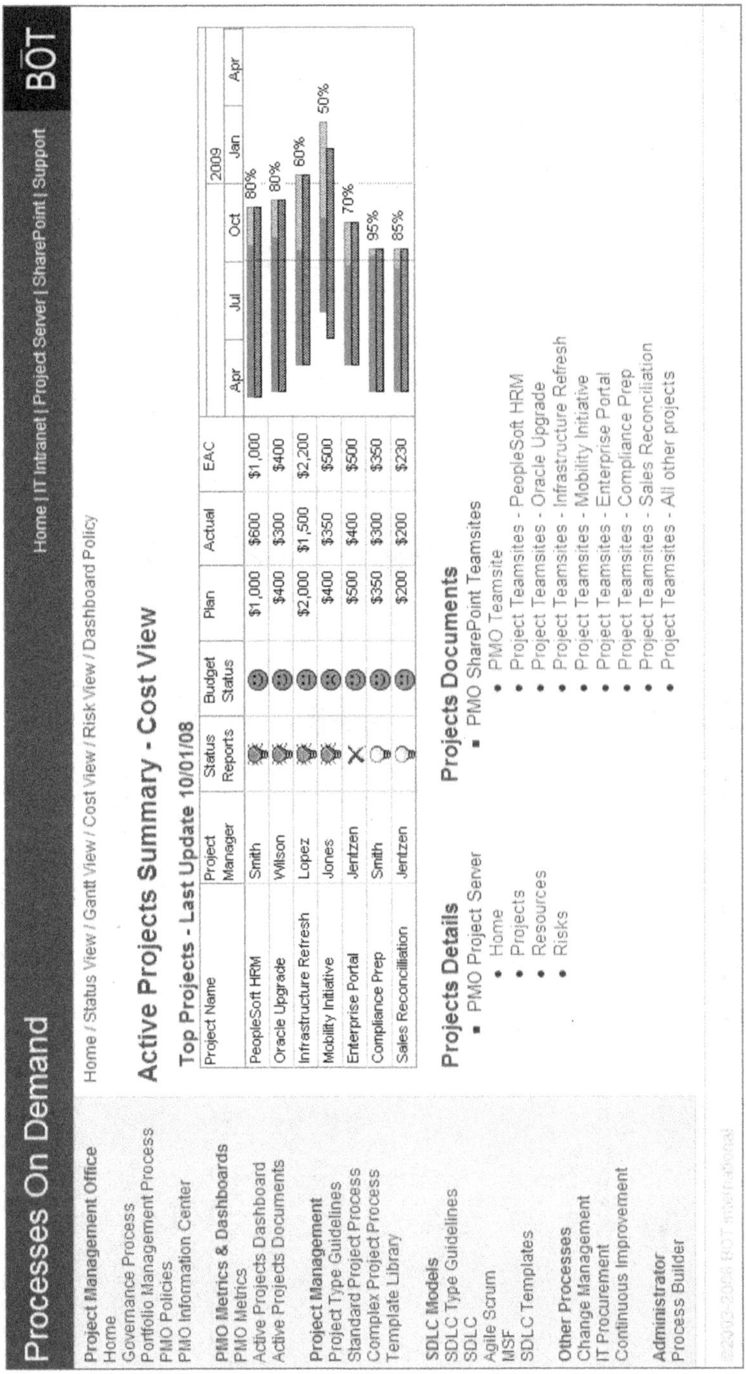

Figure 6.5 PMO executive dashboard—cost view

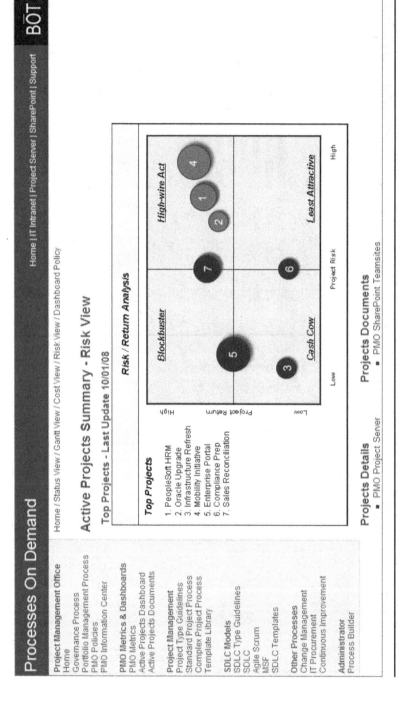

Figure 6.6 PMO executive dashboard—risk view

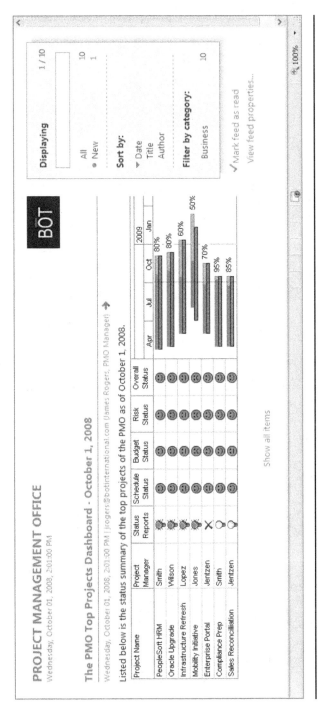

Figure 6.7   PMO executive dashboard RSS feed—E 7.0

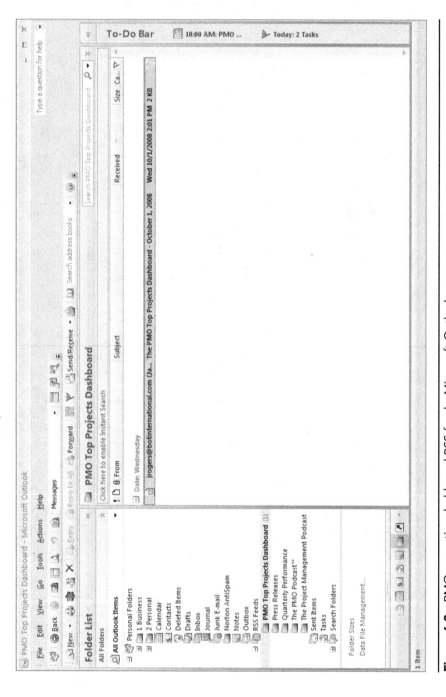

Figure 6.8 PMO executive dashboard RSS feed—Microsoft Outlook

and can be opened, read, and saved just like email. RSS feeds are an ideal mechanism to distribute executive summary reports directly to the mail client of the user (see Figure 6.9).

When opened, the RSS feed item, in this case the current PMO executive summary report for the month, renders both the graphical summary information to the executive and leadership team as well as provides a *view article* link. When clicked it takes the user to the dashboarding and executive summary report of the PMO content asset framework. Hence, the PMO RSS feed expands on the PMO executive summary reporting that is completed periodically and provides the best possible customer service to the executive and leadership team in the form of timeliness, convenience, and ease.

In addition to PMO executive summary reports, PMO RSS feeds can be useful in communicating and distributing many kinds of information, including training schedules, announcements and events, project management tips of the week, and other information useful to those served by the PMO.

As Oliver Young (2007) of Forrester writes, "Information workers today are drowning in content-email newsletters, releases, and spam—and the problem is getting worse. To deal with this tsunami, workers are turning to RSS (Really Simple Syndication)." While RSS does not replace email within the PMO, it offers two key areas of benefit. Rather than requiring the users to come to the PMO to find updates and reports, the PMO immediately brings this information to the user. Unlike a PMO email distribution list that requires periodic maintenance to add or delete users or to update user information, there is no distribution list to be maintained. Users simply subscribe to the PMO RSS feed.

Sophisticated Executive Summary Reporting

In addition to the executive summary reporting that is periodically performed by the PMO, most of the leading PPM offerings provide functionality for dashboarding and executive summary reporting. While keeping up with all of the various providers of PPM offerings can be a daunting task for nearly all PMOs, research firms such as Gartner and Forrester provide insight into the drivers of the market, the needs faced by today's businesses, and an assessment of the leading firms and products.

For example, Gartner provides research and analysis in PPM and they are renowned for the annual Magic Quadrant reports that position qualifying vendors, per Gartner's inclusion criteria, according to their ability to execute and their completeness of vision. Those with a high degree of ability to execute and a high degree of completeness of vision earn a place in the coveted leaders' quadrant.

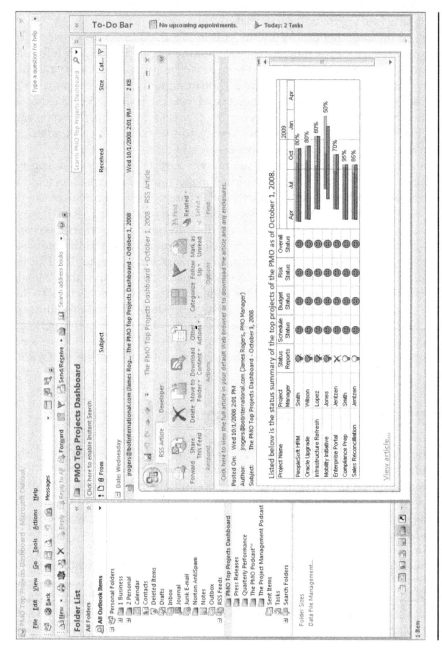

Figure 6.9 PMO executive dashboard RSS feed item—Microsoft Outlook

According to Matt Light and Daniel Stang (2008), the PPM vendors who qualify as leaders are:

◆ CA Clarity (formerly Niku)
◆ HP PPM (formerly Mercury)
◆ Planview Enterprise
◆ Compuware Changepoint PPM
◆ Primavera Systems
◆ Microsoft EPM
◆ Daptiv (formerly eProject)

Each of these market leaders represent best-in-class products found in PMOs around the world. These products have sophisticated capabilities and features enabling PMOs to manage projects and portfolios, achieve high degrees of alignment to business strategy, prioritize and optimize resources, and provide integrated views of the statuses of portfolios, projects, resources, and service levels. Additionally, they all provide a high degree of dashboarding and executive summary reporting inherent to the application.

Figure 6.10 is a screenshot of the Planview Enterprise provided by Planview. The executive and leadership team can access and view dashboards that provide high-level views of trends occurring within a portfolio. In this view all of the projects within the portfolio are automatically assessed based upon real-time system data. Graphical icons and status meters provide an intuitive understanding of the health and trend of the portfolio components. Radial picks on the dashboard enable the user to toggle back and forth between viewing information in the form of showing data and showing buttons. More detailed information can be found for each portfolio component simply by clicking on its name.

Figure 6.11 offers another screenshot of Planview Enterprise. In this view the executive and leadership team can access and view dashboards that provide high-level views enabling users to plan, manage, and track projects. These executive dashboard examples are just two of many within the Planview Enterprise application that enable the executive and leadership team to access the information they need.

Much like Planview, most providers of PPM, and all of the leading providers, have capabilities and features that enable the PMO to provide the reporting required to meet the needs of the executive and leadership team. For users with authorization and login rights to the PPM application, they can directly access these executive dashboards and summary reports in real-time.

For others, such as casual users, who have a business need to view project and portfolio executive summary reports but do not require or want a login to the PPM system, the PMO can make use of the PMO content asset framework to provide this information on a periodic, time-stamped basis such as weekly, monthly, or quarterly. This can ensure information flow from the

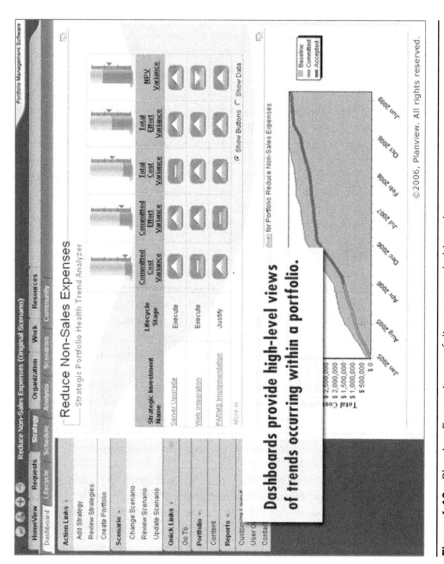

Figure 6.10 Planview Enterprise portfolio strategy dashboard

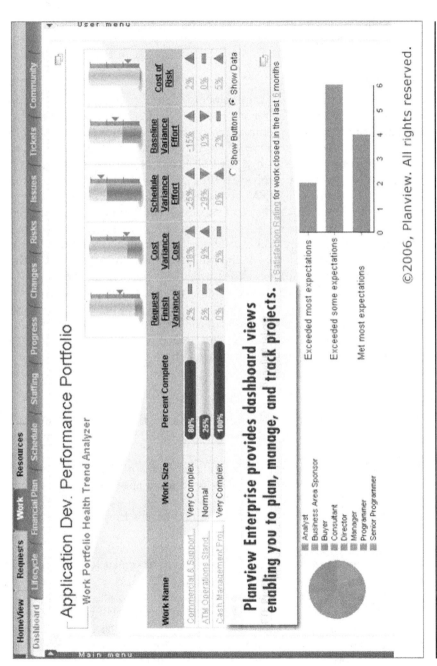

Figure 6.11 Planview Enterprise portfolio work dashboard

PMO to those served by the PMO and at the same time effectively manage the use, complexity, and per-user licensing expenses associated with the PPM application of the PMO.

Summary

The executive summary report requirements of the executive and leadership team are always the same. The reports need to be timely, accurate, and easy to understand. Simple, intuitive summary reports to the executive and leadership team can be provided in a number of ways from emails with attachments to more structured approaches such as the PMO content asset framework.

For many PMOs a major epiphany is the realization that, in addition to the tools of the PMO, including PPM applications and collaboration platforms, a collection of content in the form of processes and templates, policies and guidance, tips and techniques, dashboards, and reports exists. Organizing this content into a PMO content asset framework can be beneficial to the PMO for many reasons and at many levels. At the executive level, one key benefit of the PMO content asset framework is that it provides a mechanism for the PMO to deliver executive dashboards and summary reports that provide context, assessment, and an intuitive understanding of the status of the most important projects of the organization. The efforts of the PMO to provide a comprehensive and useful PMO framework for execution and review and, in doing so, to keep things simple is also appreciated by executives.

Questions

1. What are some of the common problems that executives and the leadership team can have with PMO monthly executive summary reports?
2. What executive summary reporting problems might be encountered when the summary report is produced as an abstract or export from the EPM system?
3. How is an executive summary report different from a project status report?
4. How is project reporting different from operational reporting?
5. How is real-time online reporting different or similar to the executive summary reporting of the projects of the PMO?
6. What information components typically make up an executive summary report of the overall status of the top projects of the PMO?
7. What information components typically make up an executive summary report of the schedule status of the top projects of the PMO?
8. What information components typically make up an executive summary report of the cost status of the top projects of the PMO?

9. What information components typically make up an executive summary report of the risk status of the top projects of the PMO?
10. How can RSS feeds be used to support the executive summary reporting of the PMO?
11. In what ways can a user access a PMO RSS feed?
12. What kinds of information can be displayed in an RSS feed item?
13. In addition to executive summary reporting, what other uses of RSS within the PMO are beneficial to users?
14. In what ways can organizations with PPM applications that provide real-time dashboards and reports benefit from providing periodic, time-stamped executive summary reports?
15. In what ways can periodic, time-stamped executive summary reporting complement the PPM application and enable decision making for organizations that have PPM applications?
16. In what ways can periodic, time-stamped executive summary reports reduce per-user costs for large organizations with many formal and casual users of the PPM application as well as users without access to the PPM application?

References

Hill, Gerard. 2008. *The Complete Project Management Office Handbook.* Florida: Auerbach Publications.
Light, Matt, and Daniel Stang. 2008. "Magic Quadrant for IT Project and Portfolio Management." Connecticut: Gartner. (Accessed June 9, 2008)
Young, G. Oliver. 2007. "Enterprise RSS Tackles Information Worker Overload." http://www.forrester.com. (Accessed June 9, 2008)

Executive Insights

The Value of Proper Stakeholder Management

Brian Rabon

PMO Director, XSP, and President of Braintrust Software, LLC

All too often projects live and die on communications and, unfortunately, sometimes project management offices (PMO) do as well. This is a strong statement, but it highlights the point that communications are vital to ensuring project management success. Like it or not, we all need to realize that executive support is one of the keys to a successful project. Therefore all project managers should make properly managing communications with all key executive stakeholders one of our primary responsibilities.

Properly managing communications means taking the time to identify stakeholders, gather their requirements, and manage them throughout the life cycle of the project. In addition, you must find the most effective means of simple, precise, and high-bandwidth communication available. By ensuring that you have well-informed and engaged stakeholders, you are providing yourself with a supportive group of individuals who help the project along in critical times of need.

Understanding Stakeholder Management

Before we get into the heart of executive stakeholder management, let's take a minute to look at the definition of a stakeholder. According to the Project Management Institute (PMI) (2004, p. 24), a stakeholder is a "Person or organization (e.g., customer, sponsor, performing organization, or the public) that is actively involved in the project or whose interests may be positively or negatively affected by execution or completion of the project. A stakeholder may also exert influence over the project and its deliverables." The key phrases here are *positively or negatively affected* and *exert influence*, and both of them apply directly to executive stakeholders.

Executives within the enterprise are going to care about the outcome of the project, because odds are it impacts their organization. The affected executives are going to want to understand the extent of the impact in order to ascertain

214

what the return on investment is for them. Depending on their understanding of the two previously mentioned points, they will choose either to support or fight the project. Either way it is essential that project managers carefully manage communications with their executive stakeholders if they want their projects to be successful. Effective executive stakeholder management begins with analyzing who the impacted stakeholders are, determining their communication requirements, and then carefully managing them throughout the life cycle of the project.

Many project managers falsely believe that only the executive sponsoring the project should be considered a stakeholder. While these individuals might be their most important stakeholders, certainly they are not the only ones. During the initiating phase of the project it is essential that every project manager uncover all of the executive stakeholders. This can be accomplished easily by first asking the project sponsor what areas of the business the project impacts.

For every identified functional area it is important to interview the executive head of that group. Ask each executive interviewed the same question and soon all of the stakeholders are identified. By taking the time to interview executive stakeholders face-to-face, you are on the right path to successfully discovering all of the project stakeholders.

Once all of the executive stakeholders have been identified, turn your attention to gathering their communication requirements. This activity typically takes place during the planning phase of the project. Take the time to sit down with each stakeholder and find out what information they want specifically, how they want it formatted, and how often they want to receive it. It is a best practice to document this information as part of the stakeholder analysis section of the communications plan (see Figure 6.12).

By investing the time to gather communications requirements from the executive stakeholders, you are demonstrating your commitment to keep them informed as to the status of the project based on their specific needs. In 9 out of 10 cases this practice ensures that your stakeholders' communications needs are fully met. When properly managed, the executive project stakeholders are your best allies throughout the life of the project. A well-managed stakeholder is one who is informed and up-to-date on the project status. In addition a stakeholder who is engaged and actively participating in the project helps to

Stakeholder analysis template

Stakeholder name	Stakeholder department	Report type	Report format	Report frequency

Figure 6.12 Sample stakeholder analysis template

clear roadblocks when they appear. In contrast a poorly managed stakeholder is one who is akin to a vulture, circling the project from afar, waiting patiently to swoop down and take a bite out of you or the dying project. Don't allow disgruntled stakeholders to stew; be proactive in your communications and follow up frequently to determine their level of satisfaction. By carefully managing your communications with executive stakeholders you are assured that you have their full support of the project and that there aren't any landmines lying in wait for you.

In summary, don't overlook the value of properly opening the lines of communication with the executive stakeholders. Spend time during the initiation of the project to uncover each and every stakeholder. Meet one-on-one and get to know them and understand their specific needs regarding communications. Finally, take the necessary time to carefully manage the executive stakeholders throughout the life of the project. Remember that a well-managed stakeholder is a happy stakeholder, and these individuals are your greatest allies.

Effective Communication with Stakeholders

Now that you understand proper stakeholder management it is time to examine the *how-to* of communicating effectively with the stakeholders during and beyond the execution phase of the project. Remember these key points: keep communications simple and straightforward, shield executives from complexity, and avoid unnecessary duplication of effort. These points are accomplished by taking advantage of the resources at your disposal.

Some of you probably have access to an on-line Wiki or project web site; if not, use less high-tech means—whiteboards or flipcharts—for communicating status. Another best practice is that of creating an executive summary or one-page status report. Finally, take full advantage of the project resources' time by carefully managing in-person meetings. By utilizing the appropriate tool for the job, you are assured that the message is effectively communicated and that the stakeholders are well-informed.

A best practice concept from the Agile Project Management camp is that of utilizing an information radiator. Coined by Alistair Cockburn, an information radiator is a *publicly posted display that shows people walking by what is going on* (Alistair Cockburn, 2008). Cockburn recommends building information radiators that are "big, very easy to see, and change often enough to be worth revisiting." More often than not, information radiators are low-tech devices that might include blackboards, flipcharts, or even sticky notes. In practice, however, on-line project web sites or Wiki's work just as well, if not better, in most situations.

The trick is to keep the information radiator current and filled with useful project information. Documenting project status, milestones, and key performance indicators are all essential best practices. By providing a one-stop shop for gaining in-depth project status, you are empowering the executive stakeholders to check-in on the projects as often as they deem necessary.

One of the most effective means of communicating project status today is that of the executive summary or one-pager. While the concept of a one-page status is easy to grasp, distilling large amounts of data down to a few bullet points can prove difficult. By keeping the following points in mind, you greatly simplify the task at hand.

◆ Include only the projects that are strategic in nature. To determine which projects are truly strategic, it is important to sit down with the executive team and prioritize the entire project portfolio.

◆ Only report on the key performance indicators that matter the most to the enterprise. There are a multitude of measurements of project performance, but again, take the time to ask the executive team how they measure success and what kind of indicators bring value to them.

◆ Use an indicator such as traffic light coding—red, amber, green status to indicate change (Wikipedia, 2008). Highlighting critical areas in red calls attention to danger signs and gives the executive team an opportunity to step in and assist. When properly written a one-page status is an excellent tool for communicating the overall health of the project portfolio to your company's executive team.

Many project managers utilize project meetings as the only means of communicating project status. These drawn-out meetings typically drag on for hours as members of the project team drone on and on about their progress to date. It is little wonder that executive stakeholders avoid these meetings like the plague.

Project managers can collect status from team members at any time; when the executive team is in the room is neither the proper time nor place. Make sure that the project meetings are focused and have a set agenda. Cover only the topics of interest to the stakeholders; high-level status, major roadblocks, and risks. Give the executives time to ask questions and make suggestions; this gives them a sense of ownership and participation in the project. By limiting the amount of low-level details covered in the status meetings, you begin speaking the language of the executives and encouraging them to attend. Additionally, they become more engaged in the project and supportive of your efforts.

By utilizing the appropriate communications tool for the right setting, you maximize your ability to keep executive stakeholders informed. Information radiators provide an easy method for executives to gain an in-depth understanding of project status whereas one-page executive summaries provide them with a complete view of portfolio status at a glance. Blend in project meetings that cover high-level details and risks and you have a winning combination of communication techniques that meet the needs of a broad audience.

Don't be afraid to experiment with new tools and techniques, including RSS feeds, micro-blogging, and project dashboards, which all have value. The trick is finding the appropriate tools, which keep the executive team informed and in touch with the project's progress. Before concluding let's look at an example that highlights some of the key points in this section.

Case Study

Robert is an experienced project manager with a mid-sized industrial manufacturing company. Robert reports directly to the company's PMO headed by Andy the vice president of the department. First thing Monday morning Robert is summoned into Andy's office and told that the company wants to implement a new enterprise resource planning (ERP) system and that he is just the guy to accomplish it.

Robert instantly realizes the magnitude of the project and is a little hesitant, but quickly decides that he is up to the task. Andy pledges his support and the full support of the PMO for the project, but cautions Robert of some challenges that he might face soon. As it turns out the CEO of the company, Lisa, selected the project herself and is looking forward to a quick and seamless implementation. In addition, Fran, in the accounting department, is vehemently opposed to the project. Further complicating matters, Fran is old-fashioned and tied to paper-based systems and she doesn't like the idea of introducing a new technology into her department. Robert thanks Andy for the insider information and assures him that he will do everything in his power to make the project a success.

After spending the rest of Monday researching ERP systems on the web, Robert decides to set up meetings with Lisa and Fran separately. Lisa is ecstatic to see Robert as he enters her office the next morning. During the first few minutes of their conversation Robert quickly realizes that Lisa has a false expectation for how fast and easily an ERP system can be implemented.

Right off the bat, Robert tries to reset Lisa's expectations in regard to the complexity of the project. In addition he asks her who else in the enterprise is affected by the project. Robert discovers that the project touches on many more areas of the company, including sales, customer service, inventory control, and, most importantly, manufacturing. Robert thanks Lisa and reluctantly treads into Fran's office.

After learning the purpose of Robert's visit a deep scowl surfaces on Fran's face. Realizing that he has just stepped into hostile territory, Robert quickly sets out to sell Fran on the benefits of implementing the new ERP system. Even though Robert doesn't seem to persuade Fran to support the project, he has managed to find another stakeholder, the procurement department. For the remainder of the week Robert schedules and interviews the executive heads of each identified department. Finally he is confident that all of the stakeholders are identified and that he can proceed with the planning portion of his project.

Now that planning is underway, Robert has more time to sit down with each executive stakeholder and complete a full stakeholder analysis, the results of which are given in Figure 6.13.

Because of the sensitivity with Fran and her opposition to the project, Robert decides to meet with her more frequently to keep a close eye on her mood. In addition Robert has discovered that the project would have the greatest impact on the manufacturing department's daily operations so he sets up more frequent meetings with James the departmental VP as well.

Once the project planning is complete and the execution phase begins, Robert is proactive with his status reporting. He sets up the project on the company's PMO Wiki and lists all of the key project information. He updates the project Wiki every Friday, including important milestones and key performance indicators. Every couple of weeks, Robert compiles his Wiki updates into a detailed status report and sends it out to Timothy, Casey, Michelle, and Patricia. Once a month Robert compiles a one-page executive summary for Lisa; in fact, she liked the format so much she insisted that it be reprinted in the company newsletter. Finally, Robert arranges a monthly company-wide

ERP project—stakeholder analysis

Stakeholder name	Stakeholder department	Report type	Report format	Report frequency
Lisa	CEO	Executive summary	Written	Monthly
Fran	Accounting	Status report	In-person	Bi-weekly
Timothy	Customer service	Status report	Email	Bi-monthly
Casey	Inventory control	Status report	Email	Bi-monthly
James	Manufacturing	Status report	In-person	Bi-weekly
Michelle	Procurement	Status report	Email	Bi-monthly
Andy	PMO	Status report	In-person	Weekly
Patricia	Sales	Key milestones	Wiki	Bi-monthly

Figure 6.13 ERP project—stakeholder analysis

meeting at which he is able to communicate the successes of his project to the enterprise and answer any outstanding questions.

After about a month of meeting bi-weekly with Fran, Robert finally had a breakthrough. Fran began to open up to the idea of utilizing technology and realized how substantial the benefits to her and the accounting department would be. She discovered that a significant percentage of her staff's day would be freed to work on more important matters. With the additional time she could finally implement a key strategic program that had been on the back burner for years.

The greatest shock of the project came in month three when Fran came to Roberts's aid. As it turns out there was a software/hardware incompatibility with some manufacturing equipment that had been missed during the requirements phase of the project. James, head of manufacturing, was furious and ready to shut down the project. Fran came to the rescue and devised a plan to lease new manufacturing equipment that was compatible with the software and actually saved the company thousands of dollars a year. Fran's quick thinking and win-win strategy truly spared the project from failure in Robert's eyes.

The remainder of the project wasn't without incident, but Robert managed to complete everything on-time and on-budget. During the gathering of lessons learned, at project closeout, all the executives really honed in on how effective project communications had been. They all felt like they were well-informed and a contributing member of the project team.

At Robert's next performance review Andy praised him on how effectively he had managed executive stakeholder communications during the implementation of the ERP system. Robert told Andy that he had learned long ago that the secret to a successful project was to communicate early and to communicate often.

Summary

Fundamental to the successful practice of project management is the importance of properly managing stakeholder communication. By actively taking part in identifying, gathering requirements, and managing the communications needs of the stakeholders, you are one step closer to completing the project. In addition, providing clear and concise communications through information radiators, one-page executive summaries, and productive project status meetings ensures that key information about the project is always at the fingertips of the executive team. Failure to communicate with key executive stakeholders can lead them to work against you, and that in turn can lead to failed projects and even failed PMOs. However, engaged stakeholders clear roadblocks and work hand-in-hand with the project team turning them into your greatest asset. By making executive stakeholder communications the number one priority, you ensure that you are setting the project up for success from the start. The value of stakeholder management is substantial; when done poorly it can place the project in immediate jeopardy, when done well it can contribute significantly to the success of the project. The latter is much preferred.

References

Cockburn, Alistair. 2008. "Information Radiator." http://www.alistair.cockburn.us/Information+radiator.

Project Management Institute. 2004. *A Guide to the Project Management Body of Knowledge Third Edition (PMBOK® Guide)*, Project Management Institute.

Wikipedia. 2008. "As a rating mechanism." http://www.en.wikipedia.org/wiki/Traffic_lights#As_a_rating_mechanism, 2008

7

Project Management Office Leadership:
MBWA 2.0

As the cartoon in Figure 7.1 satirically illustrates, even the best of leadership techniques can go awry when applied ineffectively. Management, by its very nature, lends itself to meetings, many of them. For many organizations, meetings are the way in which information is formally communicated and shared. They are necessary. But while meetings serve a purpose and are beneficial, too many meetings can be time consuming and overly taxing to an organization. Good managers seek to hold meetings to a minimum and one way to do that is to employ management techniques that enable management to continually get the information they need and to stay on top of the workplace without calling a meeting every other day just to stay informed.

Management by Walking Around

One such technique that has passed the test of time is *management by walking around* (MBWA). Some people say managing instead of management and other people say wandering instead of walking, but the idea is the same and it has been around for a long time. Though MBWA was a common management technique employed by the executives of leading companies such as Hewlett-Packard, IBM, General Electric, and many others, it was made popular by Thomas Peters during the 1980s because of his book, *In Search of Excellence*.

What is MBWA exactly? Chances are, if you are a manager and are over fifty years of age, you know what MBWA is. Back in the days when companies had business departments or divisions all in the same office building and

Figure 7.1   PMO comics—acknowledgment

executives managed face to face, MBWA was the recommended leadership technique. But in today's business environment with all of its organizational constructs such as satellite offices, remote offices, virtual offices, home offices, corporate *hoteling*—desk and phone on demand offices, if you are a new manager or just a young guy or gal, you might not have ever heard this term.

Case Study

I formally learned about MBWA in new manager training years ago, though I experienced it firsthand before that in 1983. I was an account manager in Dallas. I was having lunch with my customer, a value-added reseller of ours and point of contact for our relationship. We were at their company cafeteria and, for no particular reason, a well-dressed gentleman sat down and joined us for lunch.

After taking his seat the gentleman proceeded to ask us our names. *He* needed no introduction. He went on to ask us about our areas of responsibilities and our measurements as well as how business was going. By *how business was going,* he didn't mean good or bad. He asked for details, including year-to-date percent of plan, forecast for the year, and the top three opportunities for the month. Throughout the conversation he offered ideas and suggestions. As our lunch chat came to an end he gave me his business card and offered his help if I ever needed it or had a problem working with the company and to give him a call. He also asked for my business card and told me how important my efforts and support were to the company. He then told the two of us to give him a call as soon as we achieved our reseller objective for the year so he could congratulate us. He added, the sooner the call, the better. We learned quite a bit from this man's suggestions and ideas.

We were also quite inspired to achieve our goals, and we continued with our working session with renewed vigor and resolve. That is the end result that effective MBWA has on others. Who was that executive who sat down at our table and joined us for lunch? It was Ross Perot, the founder and chief executive officer (CEO) of EDS.

Not Just for Executives

MBWA is noticeable and memorable when it is performed by high-ranking executives such as a CEO or division head, but it is a mistake to limit its use and practicality to just the high-ranking members of the executive team. MBWA is especially well suited to working environments with high degrees of collaborative activities and there is no better example of such an environment than project management.

MBWA for Project Managers

As Gary Heerkens (2002) writes in his book *Project Management*, "Management By Walking Around (MBWA) might seem cliché, but for effective project leadership it's absolutely vital. Maintaining control is often more than just recording information. It's assessing the motivational level of your team members, evaluating or confirming the accuracy or validity of the information you receive, and uncovering problems or issues that might not surface in a team meeting."

Heerkens, like many seasoned project managers, understands that the information that is communicated and shared in a formal meeting such as a project status meeting or project management office (PMO) staff meeting might not be provide the same insight and context that can be obtained via informal walking around, asking good questions, listening to the answers, and observing the workplace. Additionally, in some organizations management expects to see nothing but good (green) status indicators in the project status reports. A status report with caution (amber) or trouble (red) indicators is deemed to be a reflection of poor project management. In such environments the project manager is motivated to report favorably at all costs and to handle project issues offline and out of the view of management, rather than to report the project status accurately.

Not surprisingly it is common that in many organizations there is a marked difference between how management views how work is accomplished and how employees actually go about accomplishing their work. Whereas management always uses reports and metrics to manage their departments, there is no substitute for getting out of the office and seeing firsthand how the cow eats the cabbage. In commenting about the value of employees, William Piker

(2008) writes, "Enjoy getting out from behind the desk, or the top floor and practice 'MWBA', that is management by walking around . . . You may actually be amazed at how different it all is compared to what is presented to head office."

MBWA Japanese Style—Genchi Genbutsu

MBWA is not just a U.S.-based management technique and it is certainly not a fad du jour. The concept of MBWA is closely aligned to the Japanese attitude of Genchi Genbutsu, meaning go and see for yourself. In Joaquim Menezes (2008) interview with Hao Tien, the chief information officer (CIO) of Toyota Canada, Tien acknowledges that the attitude of Genchi Genbutsu is a key part of the management philosophy that's behind the success of Toyota. At Toyota managers are encouraged to go out into the field and witness firsthand the needs and problems of their employees, customers, and business partners. The idea is that rather than hear about a problem or issue raised in a meeting or conference call or email, management should go to the source and see the problem or situation firsthand. Being in the workplace and observing the activity and work output provides a context that far too often is missing from the status meetings of the management team.

Experts Advocating MBWA

MBWA in all of its many forms not only complements formal meetings and reports, but it helps to ensure effective communication and control of the project effort, including, not just the schedule and budget status of the project, but the management of problems, issues, and risks as well. According to Donna Fitzgerald (2002), "One of the best ways to collect status is by walking around." This doesn't have to be invasive and there can be rules set for flagging when a developer is in the zone and shouldn't be interrupted.

The key to good MBWA is observing, asking, and listening. Tim Landgrave (2001) writes, "While it's impossible for a CIO to be effective if he or she questions every decision made by a manager or project leader, it's also impossible to be successful if he or she accepts every report without the proper level of inspection." Landgrave advocates inspecting what you expect and he performs his inspections by MBWA and spot demonstration. In addition to visiting with team members to discuss their progress and issues, Landgrave asks his development team to be prepared at all times to give spot demos. While some might argue that it is unfair to ask developers to be prepared to give a spot demo at the drop of a hat, Landgrave advises that spot demos result in the entire team continually thinking about the project as a whole rather than made up of their individual sub-parts. As any team member might be called upon to give a spot demonstration, there is a high degree of teamwork and communication regarding the project's progress as a whole. Landgrave writes, "In fact, in my organization, there's a direct correlation between the success of the project and the amount of MBWA that's been applied during the life of the project."

The value of MBWA goes in both directions. Not only do managers benefit from using the technique and staying more informed on the progress of the project and needs of the project team, but the project participants benefit as well. When managers make it a point to be aware of what's working and what's not, they are in a much better position to correctly understand the needs of the project and to help solve project problems. As Jon Emmons (2006) writes in speaking of MBWA, "As a natural byproduct of this technique a trust relationship builds up between employees and manager. The employees feel like their manager knows what they're doing and the manager has a better rapport to address issues, both good and bad, with their employees."

While MBWA can be an effective technique and be of value to all involved, it can also be applied ineffectively. Ian Buchanan (2008) writes, ". . . some managers walk around for effect and simply to be seen. Their attitude is to keep employees on their toes, and to sniff out deficiencies of any kind that can keep the employees on the defensive. This type of MBWA is completely destructive to the original concept . . ."

And John Reiling (2008) offers, "Many of us have experienced ineffective managers at one point in our careers. Typically one of the distinguishing factors of a poor manager is that they do not ask good questions and they have little to offer in the way of help, support, or suggestions."

MBWA 2.0

To be effective and to meet the business and technical challenges of today's PMOs, the traditional approach to MBWA needs an upgrade. In keeping with popular nomenclature, let's call it MBWA 2.0. As shown in Figure 7.2, MBWA 2.0 needs to provide not only the time-tested management technique of managing by walking around but also needs to address the opportunity for situational leadership and the opportunity to take advantage of current Web 2.0 technologies.

As Tom O'Dea, information technology (IT) veteran advises when a project is in real trouble, "There are (at least) four areas where you have the opportunity to demonstrate situational leadership and good (or bad) judgment. In each of these areas, you are going to be making choices as to how to behave, whether you make them consciously or unconsciously."

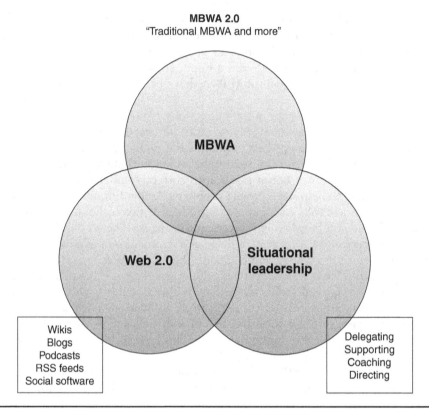

Figure 7.2   MBWA 2.0

O'Dea summarizes those areas as follows:

◆ Urgency vs panic. If nothing has a sense of urgency then you can expect project delays and slippages. If everything is a top priority then nothing is really the top priority. The leadership behavior you demonstrate affects everyone. Acting in accordance with the situation is more effective than losing your composure.

◆ Accountability vs blame. Rather than placing the blame you must be accountable and hold others accountable. Project sponsors want to see you take ownership and responsibility when project problems develop. It is essential for all involved in the project that you correctly assess the cause of the problem and the appropriate approach to mitigate the problem. Avoid public criticism even when seemingly justified because it quickly takes on the appearance and characteristics of the *blame game*. Offer individual coaching and counseling to project team members in private.

◆ Increased involvement vs taking over. When the project encounters difficulties, increase your involvement and your visibility. If necessary hold status meetings and report the status of the project to management more frequently. Avoid taking over tasks or reassignment of project resources unless there is simply no other viable alternative.

◆ What actions to take. When a project is in trouble you must take action rather than allow the project to fall further behind. A useful axiom to remember is that if you find yourself in a hole, stop digging. If a project problem can be resolved quickly without pausing the project, then do so. But if the project problems are severe and the appropriate action is to formally pause project work and reassess the project, then as project manager don't be hesitant to recommend this course of action to management.

Project managers and PMO managers have unlimited opportunities to display situational leadership, though few have had any kind of formal training or exposure to situational leadership strategies and techniques. Many project managers have natural soft skills and the judgment required to always act appropriately for the situation. Others have difficulty and find themselves wishing, after the fact, that they had taken a different approach or used a different tone in the heat of a project conflict.

Situational Leadership

For PMO managers and project managers seeking to improve their leadership skills, there is perhaps no better model than the Hersey and Blanchard Situational Leadership Model. Their model involves analyzing the needs of the situation at hand and then adopting the most appropriate leadership style. Proven effective for many years in work environments of all kinds, the Hersey and Blanchard Situation Leadership Model is a popular executive development program staple that is increasingly finding its way down to first line management and functional specialist training as well.

Blanchard (2001) characterizes four leadership styles—S1 to S4—that emerge out of combinations of supportive and directive behavior; directing, coaching, supporting, and delegating (see Figure 7.3). They are:

◆ S1: In the directing style the situational leader closely controls and monitors the worker and the end results achieved by the worker. The leader defines the role of the follower and explains the tasks that the follower is to perform. The leader supervises the follower, makes the decisions, and their communication is largely one-way.

◆ S2: In the coaching style the situational leader explains what the job entails and discusses ideas and suggestions while still staying in control of the worker and how the work is performed. Like directing leaders, coaching leaders define roles and tasks, but they also entertain ideas and suggestions from the follower. Decisions are still made by the leader, but their communication is much more a two-way communication.

◆   S3: In the supporting style the situational leader fosters a team approach emphasizing support of the follower rather than close control. As much of the day-to-day decision making as possible, regarding work and tasks is left to the follower. The leader seeks to facilitate and take part in decisions, but overall control of the work effort and tasks is in the hands of the follower.

◆   S4: In the delegating style the situational leader empowers the follower and turns over responsibility to complete assigned work and tasks to the follower. The leader is still involved in major decisions, but overall control of the work effort and tasks resides with the follower. Communication is open and two-way and the follower decides when and how the leader is to be involved.

Of these four leadership styles, no one style is considered the best or optimal style for leaders to possess and exhibit. Rather, effective leaders need to be able to apply the leadership style that is most appropriate for the situation. As most leaders have a natural style that is one of these four, it is important to recognize that intrinsic style and not let it overshadow the effective use of

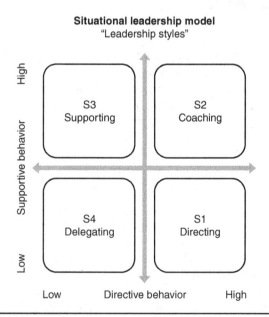

Situational leadership model
"Leadership styles"

	S3 Supporting	S2 Coaching
	S4 Delegating	S1 Directing

High / Low — Supportive behavior

Low — Directive behavior — High

Figure 7.3   Situational leadership model

the other styles. Some leaders are control-oriented, want to make all decisions, and find it difficult to empower workers and delegate tasks. Other leaders enjoy managing competent and enthusiastic workers and struggle when asked to closely monitor and control performers who require explanation of tasks and regular follow up.

Hersey and Blanchard also suggest that the optimal leadership style depends solely upon the development level of the follower as determined by the follower competence and commitment. Using the traditional matrix analysis, they categorize four levels of development of the follower—D1 to D4:

♦ D1: Low competence, high commitment. Followers lack skills but are eager and willing to learn, to take direction, and to produce results.

♦ D2: Some competence, low commitment. Followers have some skills but are unwilling or cannot perform the work without assistance.

♦ D3: High competence, variable commitment. Followers are skilled but might lack the confidence or motivation to perform the work independently without leader involvement.

♦ D4: High competence, high commitment. Followers are skilled, often more so than the leader, and motivated to perform all tasks independently without leader involvement.

Naturally, the development level of the follower is situational to the task at hand. A competent and committed worker can drop from D4 to D1 when placed in a new situation and faced with tasks that require skills they don't possess. In such an event it is critical that the leader recognize the development level and exhibit the appropriate leadership style.

As the Situational Leadership Model has evolved over time to be more applicable to the workplace, the concept of the development level of the follower has expanded to address the follower performance level and to include indicators of follower behavior for each level of follower readiness. Again, using the traditional matrix analysis, four follower readiness levels—R1 to R4—are provided:

♦ R1: Unwilling and unable. The follower is unwilling and unable to complete assigned tasks.

♦ R2: Willing but unable. The follower is willing to perform assigned tasks but does not possess the required skills.

♦ R3: Unwilling but able. The follower has the ability to perform assigned tasks but is unwilling.

♦ R4: Willing and able. The follower is willing and able to perform all assigned tasks.

The style of the leader—S1 to S4—should correspond to the readiness level of the follower. Important to note, it is the leader who must always be cognizant of the situation and adapt, not the follower.

One of the reasons that situational leadership is such a critical skill for PMO managers and project managers is that even though they are nearly always willing and able (R4) performers, the members of the project teams and all those involved in the projects of the PMO span all levels of follower readiness.

Case Study

A new project manager joins the PMO. The new project manager has exceptional skills in project management, but has no previous experience in the use of the PMO's project portfolio management (PPM) application. Even though the project manager needs little direction in how to manage projects, the project manager does require a bit of initial direction and explanation in the use of the PMO's PPM application and any related policies surrounding use, frequency of project data updates, and reporting. The leader, the PMO manager, needs to identify the project manager's readiness level and exhibit the appropriate leadership style. As the project manager might be willing but not yet able to use the PPM application of the PMO, the PMO manager needs to exhibit a coaching leadership style.

In another example a project manager is managing a difficult order-to-cash (OTC) project with a number of shared resources that are assigned to the project. One of the shared resources, a highly skilled developer, is supporting another project that he views as more important and higher in priority. Though this developer and his manager have committed to the OTC project tasks, the developer is well behind in his assigned tasks for the project. How should the project manager react? What kind of project leadership style should the project manager exhibit? Clearly the developer has the ability to do the assigned tasks so there is no need to direct or coach the developer. But in this particular case the developer is uncommitted and unwilling to complete the tasks on time. As leader the project manager needs to recognize this readiness level (R3) and to exhibit the appropriate, supportive leadership style to achieve commitment by the developer to complete his assigned tasks as already outlined and agreed to.

For many organizations setting up a PMO for the first time or introducing project management as a discipline within the organization for the first time, the leadership team might be faced with a number of followers who do not have the needed project management ability. Of these followers some might appreciate the value of project management and be eager and enthusiastic to acquire new abilities; yet others might view project management differently and be reluctant to develop new skills or to follow a structured approach. As a result the leader needs to recognize the follower readiness and be prepared to exhibit coaching and even directing leadership styles.

Extending the Effectiveness of MBWA

Situational leadership is a key component of MBWA 2.0. It complements the normal use of MBWA and provides a key skill that the leader can effectively use. By its very nature, MBWA fosters follower to leader communication and an open and penalty-free dialog. In many instances, MBWA creates and reinforces a high level of teamwork, morale, and recognition for the end results achieved in the workplace. But MBWA also serves to identify areas that are not going well and to pinpoint, in the eyes of the follower, what's wrong and what should be done about it. The effective leader needs to be able to understand what the follower is communicating.

The perspective of the follower is framed within their readiness level. An able and willing follower likely will have a different perspective than an unable and unwilling follower. Both perspectives are valid and need to be taken into consideration and it is up to the leader to immediately and effectively interact with the follower. Issues that need management attention should get it. But non-issues or areas that simply cannot be addressed at present by management should be met head on and not allowed to affect workplace morale. For example, consider an organization that is implementing a PPM system for the first time and there are execution difficulties on account of new and additional work that is required of the project team members in the use of the tool. In their MBWA the leader has to both take heed of the useful feedback and constructive criticisms of the team and at the same time help to ease the natural frustration that might exist and to dissuade if not eradicate workplace mischief and ill-intended commentary.

Situational leadership is a valued skill that can be applied and effectively used in organizations of all shapes and sizes. Project management and the PMO are all about situations; they're called projects. By default, the PMO manager and the project managers are all leaders. In today's project management environment, MBWA and situational leadership go hand-in-hand and can help the PMO more effectively manage projects and resources.

Web 2.0

In addition to traditional MBWA and situational leadership, the concept of Web 2.0 is a key component of the new MBWA 2.0 model. Adding the number 2.0 to the end of something usually indicates a new way of thinking. In the context of the PMO, Web 2.0 means incorporating new capabilities and taking advantage of the new behaviors that today's knowledge workers are all too eager to engage in. Web 2.0 is not a product; rather it is the idea of using such things as blogs, wikis, social software, podcasts, and really simple syndication (RSS) feeds to improve the effectiveness of the PMO and its ability to achieve its goals and objectives.

Commenting on Web 2.0 Kumar Sarma (2008) writes, "Web 2.0 is all about democracy and participation; it provides the project manager with an opportunity to introduce some changes in the way the whole team communicates and shares information." Likewise, PMO 2.0 is viewed as a continually evolving, adapting, and improving tool set. In this context PMO 2.0 tools are simply Web 2.0 tools applied and used by project organizations and project managers.

In With the New

Much like email and voicemail initially were, not all new-age tools are immediately understood, appreciated, and welcomed. In the early days of email, many workplace professionals felt overwhelmed by the volume of email they received and the time it took to respond to it all. Enthusiasts and early adopters of technology embraced email while others were less convinced of its merits. Voicemail was even worse. Many workplace professionals refused to use voicemail and were frustrated with the early voicemail systems that often required them to get their voicemail messages from separate, standalone communications hardware kiosks peppered about the workplace. The tools of Web 2.0 are no different. Innovators, enthusiasts, and early adopters are already using Web 2.0 tools in the PMO in a number of ways.

Blogs

Tim Duckett (2005) states that, "Blogs aren't just for marketing—there are many areas of the business where they can help improve information flow, reduce clutter, and avoid the dreaded 'but I didn't know about that' situation." Duckett outlines ten ways that blogs can be used for managing projects; four of which are:

◆ Keeping project team members updated. Today's project teams are made up of individuals who are geographically dispersed. Some teams might exist all in one location, but many project teams are spread out over multiple departments, divisions, and even time zones. Private project team blogs enable project team members to communicate with one another, keep abreast of progress and issues, and develop enhanced working relationships.

◆ Communicating with project stakeholders. Blogs can be used to keep project stakeholders informed of the status of the project. Blogs can be used to post key weekly, daily, or even hourly accomplishments. Stakeholders can peruse blog webfeed summaries and quickly discern if they need to immediately respond or simply be advised.

◆ Maintaining project logs. Anyone involved in the project should be able to raise issues, communicate risks, and question what is needed to meet requirements as well as if the requirements are complete, technically possible, or still relevant. For project organizations without a PPM system or collaboration platform, email is typically used to manage project logs. While email is great for quick communication, it has its limits when it comes to team collaboration and information exchange. Project blogs offer an alternative to email in which anyone can view and post to a project log. Discussion threads can facilitate resolution and provide an audit trail.

◆ Replacing paper. Project management is inherently paper intensive. Detailed project management methodologies (PMM), systems development life cycles (SDLC), and even Agile approaches to project management all have one thing in common; documents. Project blogs do not replace all project documents, but they can replace the need for many kinds of project documents such as project status reports, project logs, and performance summaries.

In addition to internal use within the PMO and by the project teams, project blogs can also be an effective tool for use in projects in which a large number of project participants might be external to the organization such as customers, vendors, consultants, and contractors. The project blog might be the best fit or only tool that is available and appropriate for project team communication and collaboration.

Wikis

Duckett (2005) also comments on ways to use wikis, another 2.0 tool, for project management. What is a wiki? Wiki (from the Hawaiian word meaning quickly) is a collaborative website or set of web pages that allows the user to add, remove, or edit the content. Wikis can be used in project management in a number of ways including:

◆ Maintaining documents. For project organizations without a collaboration platform such as SharePoint or Lotus, wikis can be an effective alternative to storing project documents on network file shares. Wikis have built-in version control and change tracking, so it is easy to see what changes have been made and who made them. For project documents that are created collaboratively or that change often, including the product of the project training plan materials, testing scripts, and application screenshots, wikis can be used to provide a central source of the document, including team member changes.

◆ Planning meeting agendas. Planning meeting agendas for the project team are typically the responsibility of the project manager. On large projects, however, project team members frequently need to share information that the project manager might not have considered or allowed time for on the agenda. Using a wiki page to plan the agenda allows anyone who needs to add and agenda item to do so, along with supporting notes and information. Once the agenda is set, the project manager can lock it and issue the agenda to all those invited by simply forwarding the link.

◆ Taking minutes in real-time. For many project teams the minutes of a project meeting, if taken, don't always capture the topics discussed and key points made. Documenting decisions and actions are critical, but it takes time to type minutes up and once they have been emailed there is no assurance that all project team members take the time to read them. As with much of the daily email traffic, the item might be summarily deleted or filed and forgotten. Wikis can be used to capture meeting minutes while the meeting is still in progress. As each agenda item is discussed, decisions and actions can be documented on the agenda wiki page. Additionally, information not discussed or available at the time can be added, so that project team members can update the agenda wiki page in the context of the meeting and discussion.

◆ Developing and giving presentations. Preparing team presentations can be extremely difficult, especially as the participants involved increase in size. Whereas tools like PowerPoint are great for preparing presentations, when multiple authors are involved and creating content simultaneously there can mishaps. Wikis can be used to brainstorm presentation outlines, add slides, and edit topics. You can export pages in a format that can be imported into PowerPoint or you can run the wiki presentation from a browser.

Perhaps not every project team needs a wiki nor wants to use wikis. However, for those project teams that need a way to communicate and collaborate and that do not have access to enterprise collaboration platforms, wikis can be a high-value and low-cost approach, which any project team can effectively use.

Social Software

Like blogs and wikis, social software tools belong in the PMO 2.0 arsenal. Twitter and Yammer are two good examples of extremely simple social software that serves a useful, niche purpose. With Twitter the central question is "What are you doing?" and with Yammer it is "What are you working on?"

Why do users need this when email and instant messaging can do this and more? For many organizations email is no longer used as an active response communications tool. More and more workplace professionals make use of email in a near batch-mode manner reminiscent of the punchcard days of the past. In the morning emails are sent out. Over the course of the day emails are collected and reside in the inbox awaiting further action. Some emails, if urgent, are read and responded to; others are left for the end of the day at which time they are perused and handled as needed. Hence, tools like Twitter and Yammer appeal to those users who want to engage in active response communications.

For many project teams, communication is the key to project success. In fact, project communications is so vital to the success of the project that it is one of the nine project management knowledge areas that make up the Project Management Institute's Project Management Body of Knowledge (PMBOK®). In some project environments, there is a need for the project manager and project team members to actively communicate frequently. Phone calls can be overly disruptive and emails can be too passive, therefore social software tools like Twitter and Yammer can keep the project team lines of communication continuously open and actively responsive.

Social Networks

Another example of social software in a PMO and project management context is Gantthead. Gantthead provides an enormous professional oasis of project management information, resources, and collaborative features (see Figure 7.4).

What is Gantthead exactly? Gantthead is a community for IT project managers with over 500,000 members worldwide. It provides informational resources in many forms:

- ◆ Departments headed by subject matter experts
- ◆ Processes for nearly every known approach to managing a project
- ◆ Downloads of project management templates and example documents
- ◆ Tools and training resources that are categorized and searchable
- ◆ White papers and articles along with reader ratings, reviews, and comments
- ◆ Discussions groups and blogs
- ◆ Social features such as professional profiles, networking, and interest groups

Like any online social community, Gantthead enables its members to draw upon a vast population of like-minded professionals. If a PMO manager or project manager is searching for information, looking for new ideas, or wanting

Figure 7.4 Social software

feedback on their own idea, online social communities like Gantthead can be a tremendous resource.

Podcasting

Another 2.0 tool for the PMO arsenal is podcasting. Project management podcasts are already commonplace. Popular podcasts such as The Project Management Podcast, The PMO Podcast, Controlling Chaos, PM411, and many others offer listeners hundreds of podcast episodes featuring tips and techniques, interviews with subject matter experts, and topical information of interest to the project management community. Such podcast resources provide today's knowledge workers the ability to make full use of their handheld devices and free time. Whether driving to work, commuting on the train or bus, jogging, or doing lawn work, podcasts provide an opportunity for ongoing learning in an incredibly convenient and flexible way. As an example, The PM Prepcast is a podcast consisting of over eighty episodes that provides the topics and information that project managers need to learn in order to take and pass the PMI Project Management Professional (PMP®) exam.

PMOs and project teams can benefit not only from listening to the wide variety of project management-related podcasts that are already available, but by using podcasting themselves. Podcasts can be used internally in a number of creative ways. The project manager can interview the sponsor to provide a summary of the project and its benefits to the organization so that project team members and others can hear first hand from the sponsor what the project is all about. The PMO manager can make use of podcasting on a periodical basis—weekly or monthly—to highlight the progress of the PMO and the status of the top projects of the PMO. While at a project management conference or training session, the PMO manager or project manager can conduct an informal interview with a subject matter expert or a colleague so that all those not attending can benefit from the PMO's investment to send an attendee to the event.

Podcasting is neither complicated nor expensive. Anyone with a laptop and microphone can create a podcast and for a small amount of money, sound quality can be improved with a quality microphone and a mixer/preamp. Free software, including Audacity and GarageBand enables the podcaster to easily edit the sound file and even add additional tracks for such things as introductions, closings, and transitional and background music. As re-takes are easy to edit, neither the podcaster nor guest have to extensively prepare or seek to be perfect in their dialogue and commentary.

RSS Feeds

One more 2.0 tool for the PMO arsenal is RSS feeds. RSS feeds have been around for a long time. An RSS feed is a document that includes full or summarized text along with metadata such as publishing dates and authorship. RSS feeds enable the publisher to quickly and automatically release content and the user to subscribe to the content. Many project management professionals are already familiar with RSS feeds and syndicated content having subscribed to news, sports, and entertainment.

With today's technology and enhanced support for RSS such as Microsoft Office 2007 and Internet Explorer 7.0, it is much easier for users to subscribe to and manage their RSS feeds. With Microsoft Office 2007, for example, RSS feeds can be subscribed to directly from Outlook and new feed items appear in the Outlook RSS Feed folder much like new mail appears in the Inbox folder.

A natural fit for RSS feeds within the PMO is in the area of dashboarding the status of the top projects. Busy executives don't have enough time to do all of the work that they would like to do or to make themselves available to all those in the organization who want and need their time. They certainly don't have time to login and navigate around complex PPM systems just to get a quick update. Most executives appreciate any tool or technique that adds value and will save them some time. A PMO RSS feed for executive dashboarding provides busy executives with the key top projects summary information that they require (see Figure 7.5).

After subscribing to the PMO RSS Feed, executives receive new updated dashboards in their Microsoft Outlook RSS Folder. When the feed is updated, the RSS folder and new item are displayed in bold font type just as the Inbox folder and new email items are. The PMO dashboards are immediately rendered to the executive subscribers keeping them informed and abreast of project progress. Additionally, the PMO summary dashboards serve to pique the curiosity of the executives who, when interested, might take the time to login and visit the PMO's PPM system for further information and details.

Using Web 2.0 Tools

Web 2.0 tools for the PMO are a concept more than a reality. Certainly the tools (blogs, wikis, social software, podcasts, RSS feeds) are real, but it is up to the PMO to put them to use in a sensible way or to just make them available and allow the users to use them. Web 2.0 is about providing a social element to the organization in which all of those involved can generate and distribute content, often with the express desire and consent for sharing and re-use. Web 2.0 is a philosophy, not a policy, and it suggests that all those involved in the organization are best served by mutually maximizing the collective intelligence

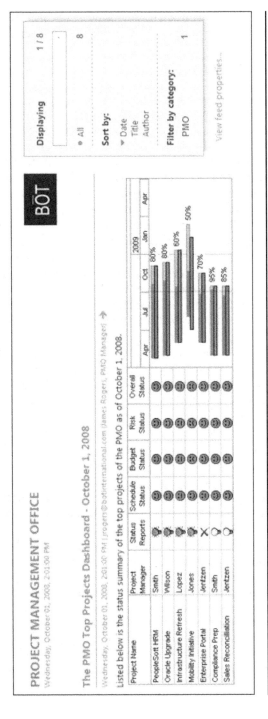

Figure 7.5   PMO dashboarding—RSS feed

of the team rather than allowing such intelligence to be privately hoarded and secretly kept, whether intentionally or by accident and oversight.

Summary

Today's PMOs are all about leadership. PMO managers are leaders, project managers are leaders, and in many cases project team members are also leaders. But exhibiting leadership is far more than the ability to schedule a meeting and actually have people attend it. For many, leadership in a PMO is a skill that doesn't come easily. In many companies, leadership training is viewed as being mainly for executives or management. Until employees reach a certain level in the management hierarchy, they might not receive or qualify for the organization's leadership development and training programs. Besides, many of the tried and true leadership techniques have aged over time and are no longer as applicable and useful as they once were.

Enter MBWA. The Japanese call it Genchi Genbutsu. There is no better way to find out how things are going in the workplace than to go out and see for yourself. In yesterday's world if there was a problem in the customer support organization, management would walk down to the department and have a look. Today that customer support team might be in India, Ireland, Israel, or the Philippines. Hence, there is a continual need to adapt the tried and true leadership techniques so that they can be of use and practical value to today's organizations. As a concept MBWA 2.0 is a natural extension to the original MBWA. By adding situational leadership and Web 2.0 tools and techniques, MBWA 2.0 provides today's PMO leaders (PMO managers, project managers, and team members) a leadership framework to enhance communication and collaboration and to more effectively manage the projects of the PMO.

Questions

1. At what level in an organization can MBWA be undertaken?
2. What behavioral characteristics are important to demonstrate when using the MBWA technique?
3. When applied effectively, what are the benefits of MBWA?
4. When applied ineffectively, what are the problems that MBWA can potentially cause?
5. In what ways can project status information collected from MBWA compare and contrast to project information provided in project status reports?
6. In Japanese business, in what ways does the attitude of Genchi Genbutsu compare to MBWA?
7. What is the purpose of the Situational Leadership Model?

8. What are the four leadership styles of the Situational Leadership Model?
9. What are the four follower development levels of the Situational Leadership Model?
10. What are the four follower readiness levels of the Situational Leadership Model?
11. If a follower is unable and unwilling to perform an assigned task, what readiness level does the follower have and what leadership style should the leader exhibit?
12. If a follower is unable to perform an assigned task but is willing to do so, what readiness level does the follower have and what leadership style should the leader exhibit?
13. If a follower is able to perform an assigned task but is unwilling to do so, what readiness level does the follower have and what leadership style should the leader exhibit?
14. If a follower is able and willing to perform an assigned task, what readiness level does the follower have and what leadership style should the leader exhibit?
15. How does the concept of PMO 2.0 compare and contrast to the concept of Web 2.0?
16. Describe three ways in which project teams can benefit from the use of blogs?
17. What advantages can blogs potentially have over email for project team members?
18. Describe three ways in which project teams can benefit by the use of wikis?
19. How can social software be used in a PMO?
20. In what ways can an online community for project managers be of value to PMO managers and project managers?
21. What kinds of podcasts are available to PMOs and project managers?
22. What are the business use cases and potential benefits of podcasting within the PMO?
23. What are RSS feeds?
24. How can a user subscribe to RSS feeds?
25. What potential uses of internal RSS feeds can be of benefit to the PMO?

References

Blanchard, Ken. 2001. "The Color Model, A Situational Approach to Managing People." Blanchard Training and Development. Escondido, California.
Buchanan, Ian. 2008. "Defining Management by Walking Around (MBWA)." http://www.helium.com. (Accessed June 11, 2008)

Duckett, Tim. 2005. "10 Ways to Use Blogs for Managing Projects." http://www .adoptioncurve.net. (Accessed June 11, 2008)

Duckett, Tim. 2005. "Four Ways to Use Wikis for Project Management." http:// www.adoptioncurve.net. (Accessed June 11, 2008)

Emmons, Jon. 2006. "Management By Walking Around." http://www .lifeaftercoffee.com. (Accessed June 11, 2008)

Fitzgerald, Donna. 2002. "Adopt Nimble Status Reporting for Your Shop." http://www.buiderau.com. (Accessed June 11, 2008)

Heerkens, Gary. 2002. *Project Management.* McGraw-Hill. http://www .briefcasebooks.com. (Accessed June 11, 2008)

Landgrave, Tim. 2001. "When Good Software Projects Go Bad: Three Telltale Signs." http://www.articles.techrepublic.com. (Accessed June 11, 2008)

Menezes, Joaquim. 2008. "What's Driving Toyota Canada's Success—CIO Reveals All." http://www.itbusiness.ca. (Accessed June 11, 2008)

O'Dea, Tom. 2008. "Leadership Tips—When a Project is in Trouble." http:// www.articlesbase.com. (Accessed June 11, 2008)

Piker, William. 2008. "MBWA—Management by Walking Around." http://www .articlestars.com. (Accessed June 11, 2008)

Reiling, John. 2008. "MBWA: Managing by Walking Around (What It Is and What It Is Not). http://www.pmcrunch.com. (Accessed June 11, 2008)

Sarma, Kumar. 2008. "How Can the Project Manager Seize the Web 2.0 Movement to be a PM 2.0." PM World Today. http://www.pmworldtoday .net. (Accessed June 11, 2008)

Executive Insights

PMO Leadership: An Unusual PMO Assignment

John Chrystal

President, Intrepid Diverse Services

Introduction

In the fall of 1997, an IBM Global Services Europe, Middle-East, Africa (EMEA) general manager asked me to go to Paris to discuss a new assignment. This began the most unusual PMO leadership role in my IT career. The role was to set up a Pan-EMEA PMO to identify, define, mitigate, and remove Y2K-related systems failure and the associated litigation risk in IBM EMEA's Professional Services Portfolio. To be clear, I was to have absolutely no responsibility for selling Y2K compliant services to clients in the field, nor was this role a customer facing one. Rather, my challenge was to create and lead a PMO team to scrub a $15 billion professional services portfolio, to remove Y2K-failure and litigation risk, and to provide cross-functional leadership to the *in-country* management and project executive ranks within IBM Global Services EMEA.

Assignment Environment

Risk Management

In the fall of 1997, IBM Global Services EMEA had established solid transactional risk management practices and every bid was scrubbed for technology and commercial risk by an independent risk management team before bid submission to the client. However, there had been little focus on Y2K compliance and there were no Pan-EMEA *Portfolio* risk management tools available to me as I took this role. Additionally, a prior attempt to conduct the exercise I was about to undertake had failed badly.

Media and Legal Attention

By this date the Y2K issue set was receiving significant media coverage with some of our more pessimistic journalists predicting a *Silicone Winter*, including the shut down of all vital safety and health services, utilities, and food supplies.

In the United States, IBM's CEO had just appointed a new chief legal officer (CLO) who had extensive prior experience in the tobacco industry. In this prior role he had witnessed the success of *pattern litigation*, resulting in increasing plaintiff wins in cancer-related litigation against the tobacco industry and was strongly focused on preventing pattern litigation success against IBM on the Y2K issue set.

Portfolio Structure

The portfolio structure mainly consisted of multi-year systems integration projects and multi-year outsourcing contracts. At that time IBM was using phrases such as five by five and ten by ten for its outsourcing contracts, indicating the contract duration in years and the revenue yield per year in millions of dollars. However, EMEA's portfolio differed from the U.S. portfolio to such an extent that the first time I presented it to corporate management in the States, I was reprimanded for presenting inaccurate staff work. While the United States had a significant number of high-value managed operations contracts, EMEA was skewed to a much larger volume of medium and small value outsourcing and systems integration contracts in its portfolio. At the time I assumed this role, IBM Global Services EMEA held 427 significant managed operations contracts and 16,610 significant systems integration contracts, with the majority of these having a total contract value of less than one million dollars. I believe this initial effort to define EMEA's detailed contract portfolio footprint, and its marked difference from its U.S. counterpart, provided some good early insights for the follow up work and was a valuable first contribution in its own right to the IBM Executive Team.

IBM Culture

Traditionally, IBM executive management time had been heavily skewed toward new business, rather than improving the ongoing integrity of the existing portfolio of business. I tried to change that during the pre-millennium era. Figure 7.6 is the slide that I presented to IBM executive management, indicating the traditional balance of executive focus and time and what would happen post millennium if this refocusing was not accomplished.

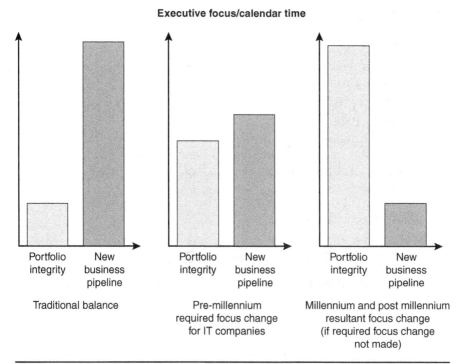

Executive focus/calendar time

Figure 7.6   Culture change

As a leadership challenge I tried to change the culture, priorities, and mindset of the executive team during the pre-millennium era in order to obtain focus on portfolio integrity; a significant challenge well outside IBM's normal management culture and prioritization schema. Had I simply requested more time, involvement, and support, I would likely have received little attention from the executive team. But by presenting the real scenario that failure to focus on Y2K compliance in the late nineties could all but halt their ability to focus on new business in the 21st century, we gained the full attention and support of the executive team.

Approach

Given all these environmental factors, and the pressing millennium deadline itself, I decided to set up a highly structured, somewhat rigid management system for running the PMO. This approach was not universally welcomed across EMEA, but it got the job done on time without Y2K-related litigation during my tenure in the role.

PMO Mission Execution

PMO Mission Statement

The PMO mission statement that I agreed to with EMEA headquarters (HQ) management was:

- Establish IBM's Y2K liability exposure within EMEA's professional services portfolio
- Establish action plans to prevent or minimize these exposures
- Direct and control the execution of these plans at a high level
- Provide all required support to field, line, and staff organizations to ensure success
- Strive at all times to avoid Y2K-related tarnishing of the IBM Global Services brand image

Recruiting and Organizing the PMO Team

Project Management Office Organizational Overview

Clearly the scrubbing of thousands of professional services contracts across EMEA, in the sort of detail required to guarantee Y2K compliance, was not going to be a single person staff job. After some initial set up and approval cycles, we had in excess of 80 fulltime individuals assigned to this role across EMEA. Most of this headcount was in the EMEA regions and countries, with a slimly staffed PMO in EMEA HQ.

This diversion of highly skilled talent away from winning new business or performing existing business was not universally popular. Country general managers did not receive any relief on headcount or revenue objectives as we mounted this exercise. Additionally, IBM was experimenting with some new job titles in EMEA at that time; my title became *Primus*, which roughly meant *first among equals*. Even though this was at least a Stage 4 PMO as defined by Gerard "Gerry" Hill (2003, p. 102) somewhat famous "PMO Competency Continuum," the IBM nomenclature at the time was Readiness Office.

I reported to the French Professional Services Director for EMEA, a man I respected highly and who supported me and the organization (see Figure 7.7). The first two levels of the organization indicated by solid lines represent EMEA HQ Readiness Office staff and the third level indicated by dotted lines represents EMEA Regional and Country Readiness Support Staff. Although exactly half of the EMEA HQ Readiness Staff were devoted to regional and country support issues, in the stressful third quarter of 1997 with many of my regional and country colleagues racing to make their year-end performance targets, many of them viewed this as a *fatty* organization; but knowing the size of the playing field by this time, I did not. The EMEA director of professional services became my reporting executive and my executive sponsor for this effort, but I implemented a slightly different reporting structure in the EMEA regions and countries whose teams took functional guidance from me but reported in-region/country.

Readiness Office (PMO) Structure

Each regional process and policy manager had his/her own multidisciplined team:

◆ Commercial and business leadership team comprised of:
  ◇ Finance representative
  ◇ Industry sector focal point
  ◇ Field communications and service letters representative
  ◇ Legal representative
  ◇ Contracts management representative
◆ Technical and professional services leadership team comprised of:
  ◇ Y2K subject matter expert
  ◇ Systems integration expert
  ◇ Managed operations expert
  ◇ Network services expert
  ◇ Product support services expert
  ◇ Application development expert
  ◇ Business partner liaison representative

The Commercial and Business Leadership Team and the Technical and Professional Services Leadership Team are shown in Figure 7.8. Within each such regional team, each representative managed, drove, and leveraged its respective community in the execution of the Y2K Readiness Office Mission and established buy in from and interfaced to their respective regional leaders. Additionally, each regional process and policy manager had access to, and executive sponsorship from, his regional Global Services general manager to ensure the correct level of management focus on this compliance exercise.

Whereas all regional team members were recruited with considerable care, special focus was placed on recruiting the Industry Sector Focal Point (ISFP) in each regional team. Key recruitment criteria for these team members included proven global services experience in at least two industry sectors and some experience in life preserving/life sustaining/safety domains, an important factor as we discover later in this chapter.

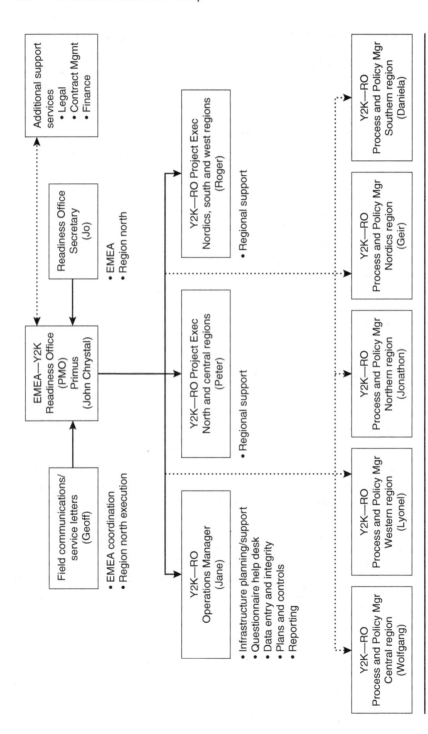

Figure 7.7 IBM EMEA organization

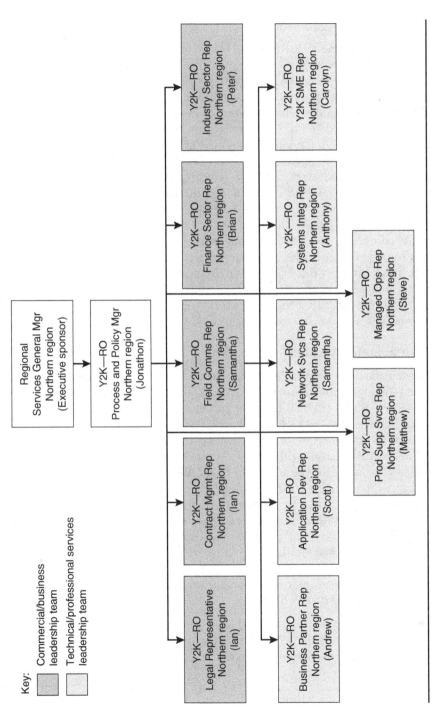

Figure 7.8 Regional headquarters organization

Country Level Organization

Whereas most of the Y2K Readiness Office (PMO) support infrastructure resided at the EMEA HQ level, the key Y2K audit and assurance work was to be completed at ground level by IBM project executives engaged with implementing specific contracted projects within their individual country and industry sector organizations. For these reasons, the regional ISFP had an organization that reported to him from within the country. At the time of this exercise IBM EMEA Region North consisted of four countries; the United Kingdom, Ireland, The Netherlands, and South Africa. Using EMEA Region North again for the example, the in-country organization was reporting to the regional ISFP (see Figure 7.9). Across the entire organizational hierarchy, we implemented an alert/response communications and governance system, which is described later in this chapter.

This completes the organizational and leadership model that we put in place for this exercise. The reader has probably concluded by now that the really heavy lifting in this exercise was delegated to and completed by the in-country industry and project executives who had the role of inspecting every single contract for Y2K compliance; fully supported by the EMEA HQ and Regional Y2K PMO teams, where necessary.

Prioritizing the Workload of the PMO

With thousands of contracts to scrub across EMEA, it was obvious that we needed some prioritization schema in order to attack this work. The first point to note here is that the Y2K issue set presented an *asymmetrical* threat to IBM Global Services. We could diligently scrub and remove risk from ninety-nine contracts out of every hundred and still have the hundredth fail dramatically for Y2K-related reasons with severe impact to a client's mission-critical services and the associated tarnishing of IBM Global Services brand image.

Since September 11, 2001, the world in general, and counter-terrorism organizations in particular, have come to understand asymmetrical threat axis in some detail; the Readiness Office just stumbled into it a little early in the fall of 1997, deciding that a sampling approach was non viable and that every contract had to be inspected.

With this first decision, made we examined a number of approaches to prioritizing the workload and decided on a triage approach similar to that used in medical emergencies. Ours became:

◆ Life critical and safety-related contracts first
◆ Other mission critical-related contracts second
◆ Client convenience-related contracts third

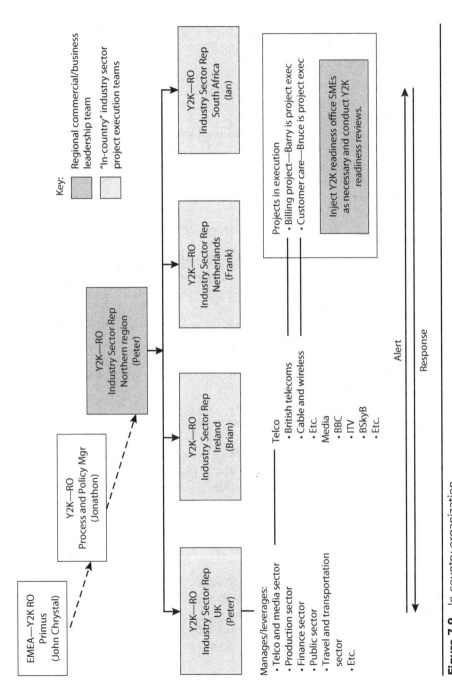

Figure 7.9 In-country organization

The reader will notice the absence of *total contract value* in this schema. It was a secondary prioritization parameter within the classifications defined. In October 1997, I presented the following life critical and safety definitions and structures to EMEA HQ management.

Life Critical

- ◆ Life threatening
  - ◇ Military-related contracts and platforms (planes, ships, tanks, missile systems)
  - ◇ Civilian transportation-related contracts and systems (planes, ships, trains, automobiles)
- ◆ Life preserving
  - ◇ Directly
    - Police, fire station, ambulatory support, and Coast Guard air sea rescue infrastructures
    - Traffic system infrastructures (traffic lights, air flight control systems, port authority control systems)
    - Hospital, operating theatre, and dental surgery support infrastructures
    - Pharmaceutical and prescription drug infrastructures (date/time stamping issues)
  - ◇ Indirectly
    - Utilities, including electricity, gas, oil, coal, and telephone infrastructures
    - Food chain infrastructures
    - Sewage disposal infrastructures
- ◆ General safety
  - ◇ Manufacturing and process shop floor safety infrastructures
  - ◇ Building management infrastructures
    - Heating and air conditioning
    - Elevator control
    - Fire control and sprinkler
    - Emergency exit infrastructures
    - Site security systems (to avoid a Y2K-related window of opportunity for criminals!)

This early work was refined somewhat because the European Union and U.K. House of Commons Y2K-related *white papers* were published some time after we had finished this classification schema. In general, it held up rather well throughout the exercise. Some of us, myself included, received the highest security clearance of our careers in order to inspect the status of military-related contracts.

PMO Plan of Record

With the organizational model and contract prioritization model in place and agreed by EMEA Management, it was time to put the project plan in place; and at a high level the Readiness Office Plan became:

◆ Phase 0: Infrastructure set up (9/97 to 11/97)
◆ Phase I: Account awareness/contract assessment (12/97 to 1/98)
◆ Phase II: Process and position test IBM position with clients (2/98 to 4/98)
◆ Phase III: Engage client for accountability and closure (5/98 to 6/98)
◆ Phase IV: Integrate Y2K plans and return to business as usual (7/98 to 8/98)

A high-level PERT Network Plan, for Phase 0 and most of Phase I, is illustrated in Figure 7.10.

Integrated into this Plan of Record was a program-customized "Alert/Response" process (see Figure 7.11).

There are many things that I could say about this process, but let me just hit the high spots here:

◆ I did not engineer this process myself; it was engineered by executives on IBM's corporate staff.
◆ It was an extremely solid, robust attempt to implement a single IBM global approach to Y2K compliance, from the corporate staff down to the account level, in a manner that treated each client in the same equitable and fair manner.
◆ I had the responsibility for implementing this approach on a Pan EMEA basis, which was certainly quite challenging enough for me at the time.
◆ I spent a lot of effort with my team at the time focusing in on Pan EMEA consistency, position scenarios, project executive *scripts* and *dress rehearsals* for client engagement.
◆ While the alert/response process originated as a key part of the high-level plan, it was quickly adopted for many other issues; for example:
  ◇ Alert: IBM's CLO wants an IBM legal position letter sent out to every professional services account
  ◇ Response: Confirmation counts that every professional services account has received such a letter
  ◇ Alert: A business partner application solution is known to fail on 9/9/99
  ◇ Response: All IBM professional service accounts integrating such an application in an IBM engagement informed, with confirmation that client has been properly briefed

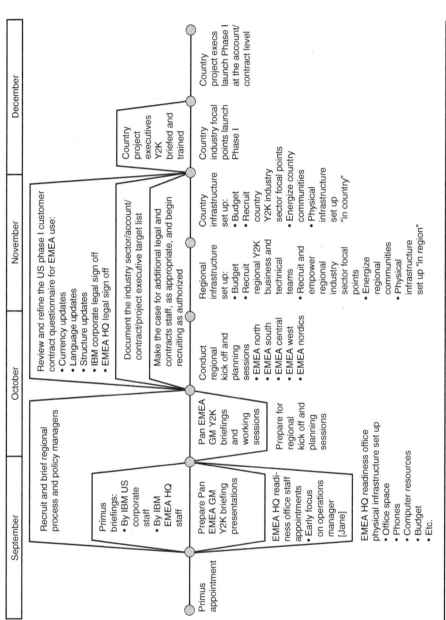

Figure 7.10   EMEA Y2K readiness PERT network plan

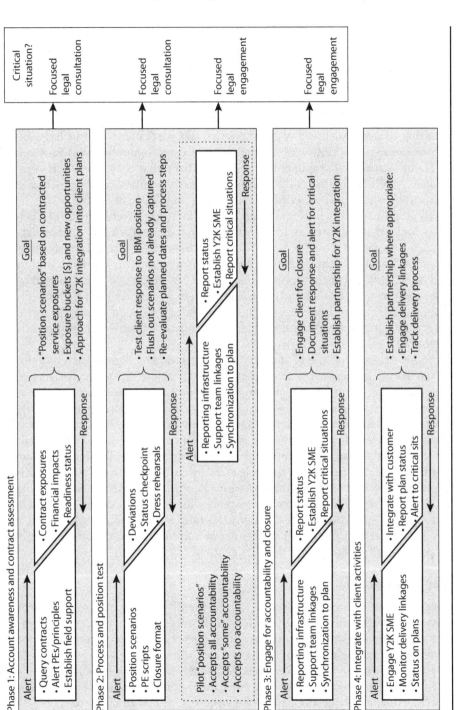

Figure 7.11   The alert/response system

◆ I have continued to use this approach in any major global or theatre role I have had since this assignment, and perhaps most notably during a later assignment as infrastructure and operation executive for IBM's direct sale channel (ibm.com).

Event Horizon Analysis

In trying to put myself in my client's shoes, and particularly for our large enterprise and selected international account clients with hundreds to thousands of IT infrastructure components, I quickly realized that they faced Y2K compliance prioritization issues of their own obviously wanting to bring increased focus to life- and business-critical IT Infrastructures early, as we did.

To help our clients in this domain, we worked extensively with IBM Divisions and Business Partners to try to identify the precise *event horizon* date when a component would either fail, or begin to produce seriously misleading, possibly dangerous output. Many of these organizations worked hard with us and our clients on precise event horizon dates, but predictably some organizations did not want to undertake this analysis. They wanted to sell their clients the new Y2K compliant versions of their products as soon as possible with no real guidance on when the older, non-compliant versions of their products might fail.

While I always felt the IT industry could have done a slightly better job for its clients in this respect, many clients themselves left Y2K engagement and internal PMO set up far too late for effective project management disciplines to be used with right to left scheduling in evidence in many, many such accounts. The associated miseries of a *forced march* plan that such an approach entails were clearly visible. Whereas many accounts felt they could circumvent such problems by a rapid implementation of an ISV Application Solution, (with SAP and Oracle among the leaders fostering and capitalizing on this approach), even here the absence of early client project planning and analysis produced miserable results in some instances. In one such account, the Oracle Enterprise Applications Y2K solution direction was implemented in such a forced manner that it left its key client communities still complaining bitterly more than half a decade into the 21st century.

Contract Data Gathering

Given a failed historical project to address the EMEA Y2K risk management domain, and with time a factor, we decided to implement a single, comprehensive questionnaire structure with one such questionnaire to be completed for each contract in the portfolio.

Furthermore, the EMEA Readiness Office edited all such questionnaire input for some reasonable level of accuracy and completeness of key answers, and for evidence of questionnaire review and signature/sign off by the contract project executive, the appropriate services contracting specialist/executive and the regional services executive. Questionnaire submissions that did not meet these criteria were returned to the EMEA regions for rework, and while the word quickly got out that we were not going to accept poorly completed questionnaires, it created some rumblings of discontent along the lines that I was running the program/project office too tightly. However, at this stage, I still had my original French contact executive in Paris who supported such discipline, and we continued in this manner despite some grousing!

The form factor of this book does not permit us to publish the entire questionnaire here, but in summary it was comprised of these sections:

- Customer definition data
- General contract data
- Managed operations specific contract and delivery data
- Systems integration specific contract and delivery data
- Contract summary data
- Legal supplement

Included in this was a six part, nine-page comprehensive questionnaire accompanied by a governance philosophy that I was advocating at the time—complete it once, complete it correctly with zero defects and no rework. An overview of this data capture process is shown in Figure 7.12.

While the EMEA country teams had responsibility for the integrity and completeness of the contract data at the transactional level in the field and undoubtedly kept shadow databases of their contract data submissions at their own individual geographic levels, the EMEA Y2K Readiness Office was given the responsibility, as a matter of executive mandate, for the accuracy and completeness of the contract data at the Pan-EMEA portfolio level. Hence, the PMO process and discipline for capturing this data in a thorough manner were justified at the time. In the contract summary section of the questionnaire we not only captured Y2K contract risk assessment, but we also captured the contract commercial risk assessment and technical risk assessment, disciplined contract assessments that were already in place, and transactional-level visability in EMEA but not tracked or visible on a Pan EMEA portfolio basis.

Contract Y2K Risk Classification

The PMO established five Y2K-related contract risk classifications, in escalating order of severity, as follows:

- Type one—green status
  - ◊ Client accepts all Y2K responsibility
  - ◊ Client needs no IBM services
  - ◊ Client relationship not impacted by Y2K compliance issue set

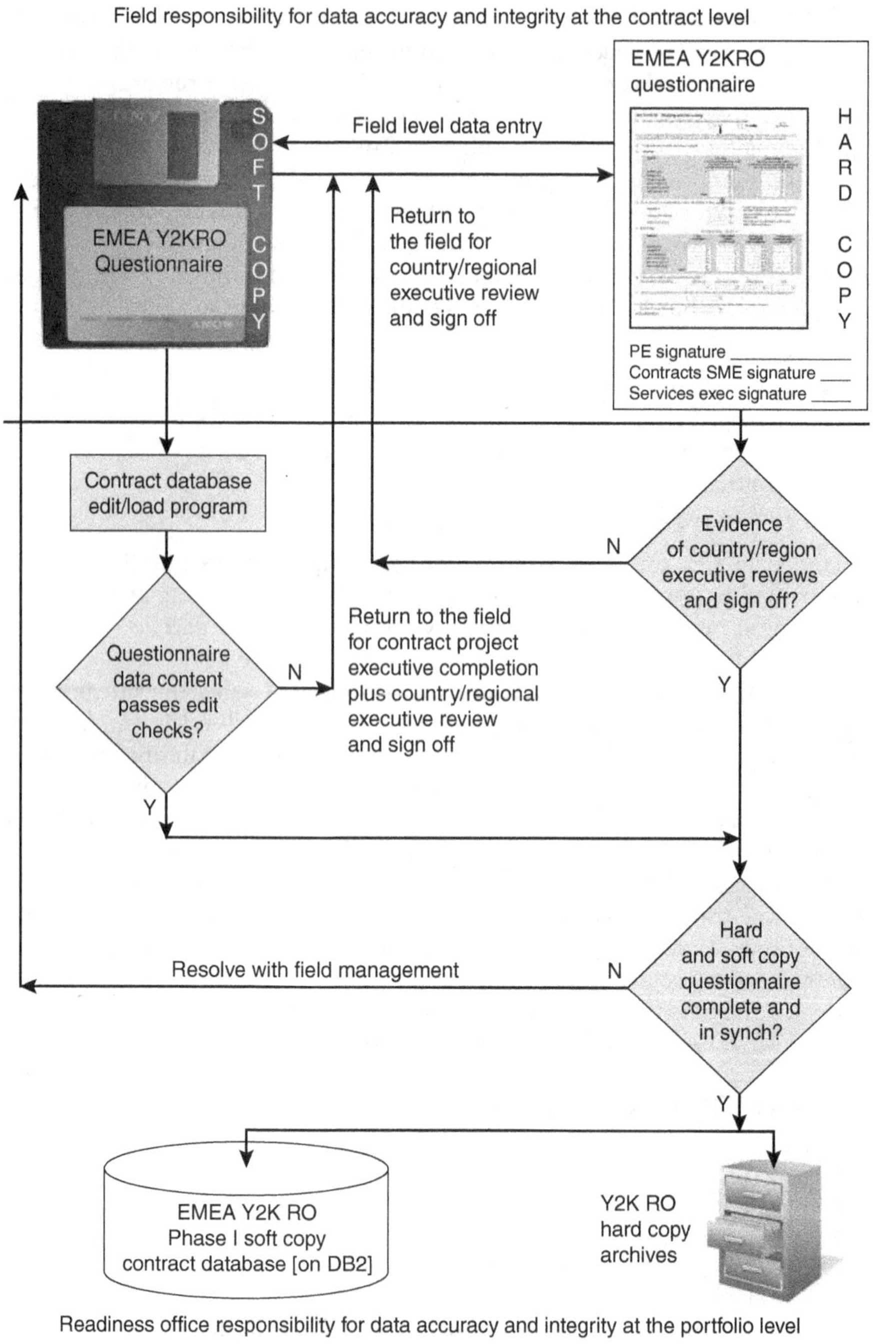

Figure 7.12 Contract data capture process

♦ Type two—green status
◊ Client accepts all Y2K responsibility
  • Might need some IBM services
◊ Client relationship unlikely to be impacted by Y2K compliance issues
♦ Type three—amber status
◊ Client accepts most Y2K responsibility
  • Might need some IBM services
  • Successful negotiation probable
◊ Client relationship unlikely to be impacted by Y2K compliance issues
♦ Type four—amber status
◊ Client accepts some Y2K responsibility
  • Might need some IBM services
◊ Some litigation risk
◊ Successful negotiation probable
◊ Client relationship might become *tense* through the Y2K compliance negotiation period
♦ Type five—red status
◊ Client accepts no Y2K responsibility
  • Expects IBM to fix all the Y2K issues at IBM expense
◊ High probability of litigation

Risk Classification Check and Balance

Since the contract Y2K risk classification accuracy and level was going to be the key parameter on which ongoing, senior, highly paid IBM Global Services resources were to be deployed, we developed a computerized assessment tool to check and balance the first pass risk classification that came in on the questionnaires. In essence this check and balance was structured as shown in Figure 7.13.

In this manner, questionnaires/contracts that attracted a loading figure of 13 or more came up for a formal check and balance review to ensure Y2K risk assessment level accuracy and completeness. From memory only, this turned out to be around 15 percent of the total contract database, with a smaller number actually having their Y2K risk assessment level changed during this exercise. The EMEA Y2K Readiness Office appointed a red team and a blue team to conduct these reviews and update the Phase 1 questionnaire/contract database. A summary of the process used is shown in Figure 7.14.

Even though the Readiness Office (PMO) teams conducted these check and balance reviews, they were done in full cooperation and participation with

Computerized assessment tool

Questionnaire field	Data entered	Risk loading	Reason
Client Y2K status snapshot	None Aware only Assessed	5 3 1	Indication of the degree of attention being given to the Y2K issue set by the client and IBM
Existing client relationship	Fragile	7	Risk due to fragile client relationship
Clean management clause	Yes	4	Indicative of specific IBM obligation
Master contract reviewed	No	5	Possible "in country" lack of attention to the Y2K review process
Contract component inventory Y2K compliance checked	All "no"	5	No granular component analysis/assessment of contract Y2K readiness
Contract pricing methodology	Fixed Other Mixed	SI 5, MO 3 SI 5, MO 3 SI 3, MO 1	Differential between systems integration (SI) and managed operations (MO) contracts in this category
Existing contract risk assessment Commercial risk Technology risk	Each high Each blank	2 1	Anticipated that high risk contracts should have this reflected in a higher classification, no assessments may be indicative of a potential risk
Triage category	Life critical	3	Add emphasis to life critical contract situations

Figure 7.13 Computerized assessment tool

the in-country project executive/contract engagement team, the in-region contracts SME, and the in-region services general manager; all of whom were required to sign off on a revised hard copy questionnaire submission as part of this process.

Reporting

We studiously avoided the *garbage in* syndrome, and by the time we had finished, we had scrubbed the contract data submissions data well beyond my earlier hopes. So as this data was now stored on a relational database, accurate reporting to EMEA HQ and IBM corporate management became simple. Some of the key reports we generated were obvious in nature:

◆ Y2K-related contract risk by risk classification and geography (EMEA total, region, and country)
◆ Y2K-related risk by risk classification and industry sector (production sector, finance sector, public sector)

But some reports that we generated were far less obvious:

◆ Contract commercial risk to Y2K risk correlation
◆ Contract technology risk to Y2K risk correlation
◆ Contract *client satisfaction* to Y2K risk correlation

Client Y2K Contract Negotiations, Execution and Closure

For this phase we executed along similar lines of the alert/response management system (see Figure 7.11). Y2K-related Type One, Two, and Three contracts were generally negotiated to closure quite quickly and in good faith by both parties with few hiccups and only a handful of exceptions. Although we certainly had some tense moments during the negotiation of the Type Four and Five contracts, ably assisted by IBM legal counsels where appropriate, I am pleased to say we had no litigation during my tenure in the Primus Role, which was not universally the case across IBM or the larger IT industry.

Change Of Guard

In late fall of 1998, or thereabouts, my French contact executive, (and comrade in arms) in Paris decided to retire, and he was replaced by an American executive on international assignment. As is often the case in large international companies, he brought a new culture and perspective to the role and advised me fairly early during his tenure that he wanted to reduce the headcount and management system disciplines and controls associated with the Y2K Readiness Office because we now seemed to have most of the risk under control.

For my part, I had now been on international assignment myself almost continuously since 1991, first in Tokyo, then in Singapore, and now in London.

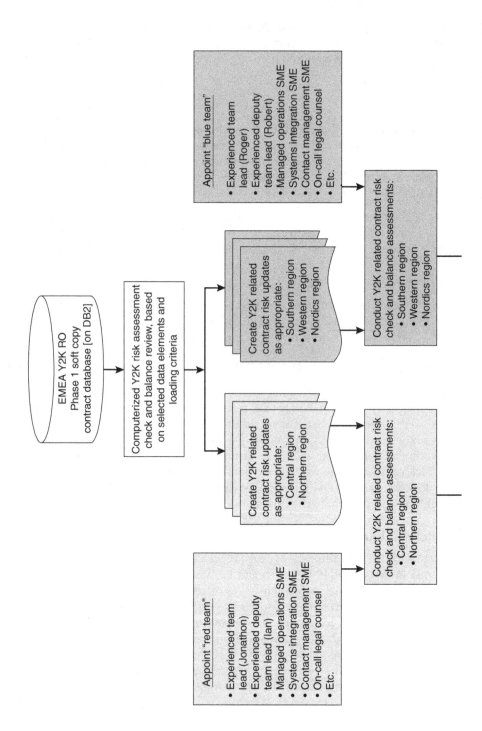

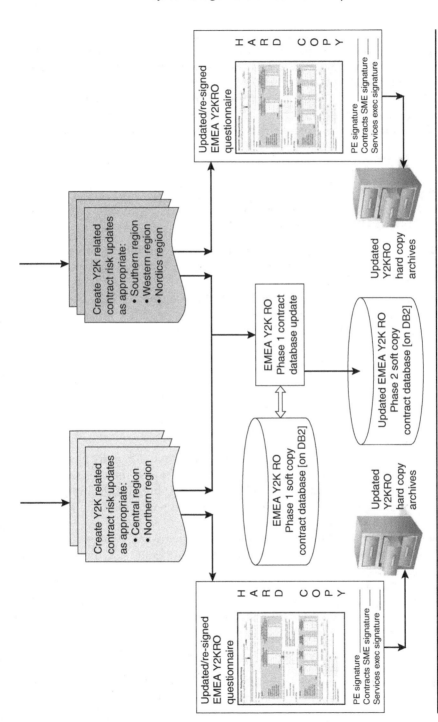

Figure 7.14 Risk classification check and balance process

Perhaps it was time to think about returning to Connecticut to give my young sons the opportunity to put down roots and enjoy more lengthy friendships and schooling environments in the land of their birth. (And since I was the only international assignee in the Readiness Office, I was also the most expensive headcount it supported.) So I stepped down from this role in late fall of 1998, handing it over to my operations manager who had been with me on the program from day one when I shared her office for the first few days until an office of my own was found.

Summary

There are many things I could say about this hugely interesting assignment, but I will touch only on the highlights:

- First and foremost, this was a *business* Program Office effort that just happened to be operated inside an IT company; it was not a traditional IT Program Office effort.
- Our world is changing quickly, and the concept of business Program Office initiatives is no longer as radical as in earlier years! Now I am consulting to a business Program Office in the health insurance sector. The program director reports to the senior vice president of sales who reports to the division president; there is no IT executive anywhere in her reporting line.
- Even for conventional IT projects, it's probably worth a healthy debate on where the Program Office resides; within IT reporting up to the CIO or within the user of record function reporting up to the executive sponsor.
- For one shining moment in 1998 (perhaps two), I had my finger on the pulse of one of the largest IT contract portfolios then on the planet! We understood not just the Y2K-related risk, but also the more general commercial risk and technology risk in the portfolio at the geography and industry sector levels among others.
- Some of the techniques and frameworks that we developed for this exercise were also used by the EMEA Euro Readiness Office. I had the pleasure of kicking off the first piece of work on Euro readiness before I left London at the end of 1998.
- I have occasionally reflected on whether I ran the program in a too disciplined fashion and if I could have managed the risk adequately with fewer resources. My own answers to these questions vary a tad, depending upon the nature of a current consulting engagement or world events going on around me.
- Now I live in lower Fairfield County in the United States, a stone's throw from Wall Street. I do wonder if some of the disciplines described

in this chapter would port well into the finance industry in general, and the subprime market place more specifically.

◆ Had I stayed in Europe it would never have been my intention to maintain the Y2K Readiness Office at the resourcing levels described in this chapter. In my view these resources were initially necessary to set up the program, to recover from at least one abortive attempt at this exercise by a predecessor, to manage the key data collection and data scrubbing at the individual contract level, and to meet the dependencies of a deadline I could not move, specifically our entry into the 21st century.

◆ Before leaving Europe, and on a couple of later occasions, I did recommend that a much smaller team in each IBM theatre HQ organization, (EMEA, Americas, Asia Pacific) leverage the Y2K work as the basis for ongoing contract database maintenance and post-millennium *business as usual* portfolio risk management.

◆ I lost touch with such thoughts and disciplines as I reentered IBM United States after nearly a decade abroad in a number of global expatriate assignments, being initially assigned on return to IBM's Corporate Technical Committee on Pervasive Computing.

◆ In late 1999, I was appointed the IBM Global Services E-Finance Practice Leader for the Americas.

◆ By spring of 2000 it was clear to me that the millennium event was over. In general IT industry executives around the world were refocusing aggressively on new business development with portfolio risk management integrity becoming a second priority.

◆ In my own small world, I started to manage an Americas E-Finance services contract portfolio of around $75 million with no IBM Americas portfolio risk management tool sets at my disposal, and only my Y2K Readiness Office experience and some rudimentary Excel Spreadsheet skills to guide me. It was managed almost exclusively on a business growth and practice utilization measurement system, which further reinforced my belief that we had all returned to a business as usual paradigm.

Conclusions

The Y2K phenomenon clearly forced a portfolio risk management focus on practically every IT company on the planet. But the intriguing question remains "How many of these companies leveraged the infrastructures they set up to be Y2K compliant for ongoing portfolio risk management and integrity management in the post-millennium era?"

References

Hill, Gerard. 2008. *The Complete Project Management Office Handbook*, Florida: Auerbach Publications.
Most of the data for this chapter comes directly from my personal archives. I am indebted to several members of the British Arms Forces, then as now, on the military view of asymmetric threat axis. I believe industry in general, and chief security officers specifically, have much to learn from this community.

8

Project Management Leadership:
Servant-Leader
vs
Subject Matter Expert

As the cartoon shown in Figure 8.1 suggests, it is actually quite important for leaders to know what they are talking about and to lead in the right direction. But what makes a good leader? As long as there have been groups of people, there have been leaders. Whether borne out of necessity or appointed, leaders occupy a position of authority. But do leaders have to be experts? Do leaders have to make strategic decisions? Do leaders have to micromanage followers? Do leaders have to brandish their power?

Conventional leadership has taught us that the answer to all of those questions is yes. To a considerable extent, our natural concept of leadership is really about heroic leadership such as the Viking warrior slaying the beast or the cowboy prevailing over the outlaws or the come-from-behind quarterback who pulls victory from the jaws of defeat in the last two minutes of the football game.

Fortunately, there are many more forms of leadership other than the conventional, heroic style of leadership and many argue they are more effective. In speaking of quiet leadership Joseph Badaracco (2002, p. 1) writes, "The most effective leaders are rarely public heroes. These men and women aren't high-profile champions of causes, and don't want to be. They don't spearhead

Figure 8.1   PMO comics—project planning

ethical crusades. They move patiently, carefully, and incrementally. They do what is right—for their organization, for the people around them and for themselves—inconspicuously and without casualties."

And in highlighting what's wrong with conventional leadership, Mitch McCrimmon (2006) takes it a step further and writes, "[Traditional] Leadership theory is out of step with today's knowledge driven world where power has shifted from the top down force of personality and the quest for dominance to the power of innovation and widely dispersed knowledge."

So in the context of today's project management leadership, what style of leadership is likely to be most effective? There are many leadership types for PMO managers and project managers to choose from, including:

♦ Autocratic leader. This style of leadership gives total power and authority to the leader to make decisions. This style is appropriate for work environments in which followers need continual instruction and close supervision to perform their tasks.

♦ Bureaucratic leader. This style of leadership is structured and follows policies and procedures. Ensuring adherence to process and organizational structure takes precedence over exploring new ways to solve a problem. Levels of authority are in place and formal escalation is required to obtain approvals.

♦ Charismatic leader. This style of leadership invigorates followers. Oftentimes, followers place their allegiance with the charismatic leader over their allegiance to the company or division. If the charismatic leader is deeply committed to the organization, for example the founder of a company, then the energy and inspiration passed on to followers can lead to long-term success. If the charismatic leader fails or leaves the company, however, it can take a long time for followers to regain their confidence and some might even follow their charismatic leader and leave the company.

◆ Democratic leader. This style of leadership openly involves the followers in the decision-making process. However, the leader maintains the final decision-making authority. When used effectively, a democratic leadership style is respected by followers and viewed to be a leadership strength, not a show of weakness or indecisiveness.

◆ Laissez-faire leader. This style of leadership allows the followers to make their own decisions. The leader is still responsible for the end results achieved. Laissez-faire leadership means delegation, but not abdication. The leader sets objectives and priorities and delegates work to capable followers.

◆ People-oriented leader. This style of leadership involves supporting, training, and developing their followers. A focus is placed on achieving a high degree of job satisfaction by the follower.

◆ Task-oriented leader. This style of leadership focuses on the work to be performed and the immediate set of tasks at hand. As completion of work takes precedence over follower considerations, the task-oriented leader needs to be careful to not alienate their followers.

◆ Servant-leader. This style of leadership seeks to achieve objectives by providing followers with what they need to be productive and happy. The servant-leader is a facilitator in reaching the goal rather than a commanding and directing voice that shouts out orders. This style of leadership seeks to achieve a high degree of follower participation, enthusiasm, and commitment to performing the work tasks.

Of the many leadership types for project management professionals (PMPs) to choose from, perhaps the most effective and best choice for today's PMOs is the servant-leader style.

What is Servant-Leadership?

Servant-leadership as a concept has been with us for thousands of years. Around the time of 600 B.C., the Chinese sage Lao Tzu wrote a treatise on servant-leadership called *The Tao Te Ching*. In this work, Lao advised that great leaders do not think about themselves, but attend to the development of others. In 375 B.C. the advisor from ancient India, Chanakya Arthashastra, suggested that leaders shall consider as good, not what pleases them, but what pleases their subjects. Nearly 2,000 years ago, Jesus said that the greatest among you shall be your servant (Matthew 23:11). The philosophy espoused by these and many other early, historic figures recognized the paradox of true leadership. Even though it is the leader who is placed forefront and at the center of attention often in heroic proportion, it is putting the follower first and serving that follower who makes the leader a great and effective leader.

The modern concept of servant-leadership was coined in 1970 by Robert Greenleaf who published, "The Servant as a Leader." Servant-leadership at its roots is a practical and philosophical approach to leadership in which the leader first chooses to serve. For most servant-leaders, the desire to serve others is a natural desire; for others it can be a learned and beneficial behavior. The servant-leader has an innate desire to make a difference and to do so in a way that helps others achieve success and the fullest of their potential as opposed to a desire that is inwardly focused and for their own gain.

Some contend that the characteristics of servant-leadership cannot be taught and unless a person has a natural calling to serve, servant-leadership is not a realistic or compatible leadership style for them to exhibit. Others disagree with that premise altogether. Information technology (IT) veteran, Benjamin Lichtenwalner (2008), suggests that servant-leadership can be developed and he advises, "If organizations seek long-term results, sustainable growth and leaders who are out to benefit the organization, not themselves, they need to identify and promote servant leaders."

Examples of Servant-Leadership

Examples of Servant-leadership are not hard to find. In Spears and Lawrence's (2001, p. 126) book, *Focus On Leadership*, Nancy Larner Ruschman cites three organizations in *Fortune* magazine's yearly ranking of the "100 Best Companies to Work for in America" that are renowned to be servant-led organizations: Southwest Airlines, TDIndustries, and Synovus Financial Corporation.

At Southwest Airlines, Herb Kelleher, founder and CEO, advocated and practiced servant-leadership. Kelleher did not want blind obedience, rather he sought out people who wanted to work toward a worthy objective and displayed initiative to achieve their objectives. Kelleher believed that the best leader is the best server and that if you are a servant, then by definition you are not controlling.

At TDIndustries, Jack Lowe, the chief executive officer (CEO), advocated servant-leadership and described it as the kind of trustworthiness that requires character and competence and can only flourish with leadership that trusts, supports, and encourages. At Synovus Financial Corporation, James Blanchard, CEO, fostered a servant-leadership culture that placed special emphasis on balancing work with the rest of life. Blanchard, an outspoken advocate of servant-leadership, believes that every person who labors has great worth and deserves to be treated so.

Other executives who have achieved phenomenal success and have credited servant-leadership include Howard Behar, CEO of Starbucks, and James Autry, CEO of Meredith Corporation. At Starbucks, Howard Behar, known simply as

HB, spread the gospel of servant-leadership throughout Starbucks worldwide. He popularized the now famous and often quoted line; "Starbucks is not in the coffee business serving people. Starbucks is in the people business serving coffee." In writing about servant-leadership and Howard Behar's legacy, John Moore (2005) writes, "For those not in the know, Servant Leadership eschews the classical definition of a leader being a stand-alone hero. Instead, Servant Leadership asks leaders to focus on creating a shared vision for all employees, fostering a spirit of interdependence, and managing with respect, honesty, and empathy."

At Meredith Corporation and in his book, *The Servant Leader*, James Autry stressed "service to others" as the most efficient and effective way to lead. Autry places a high level of importance on the degree to which colleagues, under his tenure, have grown professionally. A key focal point of success is on successfully developing a talented, enthusiastic, and engaged community of followers who in turn have the ability to periodically assume leadership roles.

Describing James Autry's servant-leadership, Max Douglas (2003) writes, "As James Autry suggests refer to your employees as participants. This means organizational and professional goals are co-determined with employees and adequate resources are provided to help them achieve their objectives. Servant-leaders must coach employees to stretch their abilities without allowing them to overextend themselves. The goal is to set employees up for success, not failure."

Servant-Leadership in Project Management

Unquestionably, there are untold examples of CEOs from leading companies who have had considerable success and credit much of that success to servant-leadership. But can a project manager really be a servant-leader? According to Barbara White (2004), the answer is yes. In her reflective critique, White writes, "Using servant leadership skills creates synergy on projects. It allows each of us to use our special gifts to get the most positive outcomes. Teams work better than one individual. A project manager needs to be less in control and more a team member exhibiting servant-leadership for the best positive outcomes."

Project managers seeking to apply the principles of servant-leadership in their projects still experience project difficulties and need to rely on sound project management best practices. The need to properly initiate, plan, execute, monitor and control, and close the project is not lessened. Servant-leadership in project management works because at its core it seeks to ensure that the members of the project team have what they need to be successful. Ensuring that each member of the project team has what they need to be successful cannot guarantee the success of the project, however, team members not having what they need might compromise the project from the start.

Also attesting to the value of servant-leadership in project management is Brian Rabon (2008) who recommends practicing servant-leadership as one of five secrets to successfully implementing Agile Project Management. Many project managers struggle with the concept and principles of Agile Project Management. Rabon suggests that it is important to realize that Agile Project Management is all about the team, not the project manager.

Rather than command and control tactics, dictating what the project team should be doing, and regularly checking the status of project tasks, a different mindset and approach is required. The Agile project manager seeks to lead and develop the team into self-directed participants. Continual focus is placed and effort is expended by the project manager to remove roadblocks that stand in the way of the team such as lack of needed resources or changing management priorities. It takes great skill to lead and develop a group of individuals and turn them into a cohesive team and it is well worth it.

Characteristics of Project Management Servant-Leadership

In 1992, Larry Spears surveyed the servant-leadership writings of Robert Greenleaf and identified the ten most frequently mentioned characteristics. In his servant-leadership Research Roundtable article, Spears (2005) discusses these characteristics:

1. Listening: Leaders are known for communication and decision-making skills. These skills need to be reinforced by listening intently to others and being receptive to what others say and do not say.
2. Empathy: Leaders empathize with their followers. This empathy must be sincere and far reaching. People need to be accepted, recognized, and valued for their special and unique gifts. Workers must be accepted not rejected, even when refusing to accept the behavior, performance, or results achieved of the worker.
3. Healing: Learning to heal one's self and others is one of the great strengths of servant-leadership. It is natural for humans to become hurt. Overcoming hurt is a powerful force for transformation and integration.
4. Awareness: All leaders need to have good awareness skills. Awareness is the key to understanding issues involving ethics and values and in solving problems. Awareness is not gentle solace; rather it is a disturbance and an awakener. Those who truly seek awareness and the truth of a situation are not looking for serenity.

5. Persuasion: Leaders have authority and can use it. Servant-leaders rely upon persuasion, not positional authority, in making decisions within the organization.
6. Conceptualization: To conceptualize, leaders must think outside the box and beyond the day-to-day constraints of the organization. Many of today's leaders are focused on short-term operational goals. Servant-leadership requires leaders to have the ability to take a broader view, at times, to see the full range of possibilities.
7. Foresight: Closely related to conceptualization, servant-leaders have the ability to foresee the likely outcome of a situation. Foresight enables the servant-leader to understand the lessons learned from the past, the realities of the present, and the likely outcome of a decision for the future.
8. Stewardship: Servant-leaders have stewardship and hold in trust their institutions and their people. Servant-leaders recognize stewardship and are committed to serving the needs of others.
9. Commitment to the growth of people: Leaders recognize that people are the greatest asset of an organization. Servant-leadership involves a commitment to the growth and satisfaction of workers and acknowledges that people have an intrinsic value beyond the measurable end results they achieve as workers. In practice, this can include formal employee development planning as well as informal mentoring and professional development.
10. Building community: Leaders recognize that a sense of community and belonging is important to workers. It is impossible for workers to be committed to their workplace environment and jobs without it. Servant-leaders recognize that much has been lost in terms of community and belonging. The servant-leader seeks to build community and show the way among those in the workplace.

Each of these characteristics can be applied to project management. Over the last decade working with PMOs and project managers as well as overseeing the projects of our firm, the project management community has seen firsthand project management servant-leadership in action and many have come to believe in the value that servant-leadership has to offer to today's PMOs and project managers. Consider the following project manager scenarios each demonstrating one of the ten characteristics of servant-leadership:

Project Manager Listening

Dave is a hard-working project manager who goes beyond the call of duty without reservation. His project management and technical skills are superb. However, of all of Dave's skills it is his listening skills that are his greatest asset. One day Dave and a team member, who was responsible for a major component of the project, had a meeting with the customer to discuss the project status and open issues. Dave's team member took the lead in the discussion of how his component of the project was going. Quickly thereafter, the customer and Dave's team member began to argue about how that part of the project was going, project issues that had been encountered and not yet resolved, and previous agreements on how to get that particular component of the project back on track. Both the customer and Dave's team member were becoming increasingly agitated to the point of jeopardizing the relationship.

Dave listened intently to both sides of the discussion and quickly realized that neither party was hearing and understanding what the other had to say. So Dave interrupted the discussion and asked his team member if he could clarify what the customer was saying. Dave repeated his team member's words to the customer and asked the customer if that was what he meant. The customer responded that that wasn't what he was saying and meant at all. Dave asked his team member to clarify again what he thought the customer was saying. The second was still not correct. Finally, on the fourth try, Dave's team member clarified what the customer was saying and meant. Dave repeated his team member's words to the customer and the customer nodded in agreement.

Not stopping there, Dave asked the customer to clarify what his project team member had been trying to say. Dave repeated the customer's clarification to the project team member and the project team member shook his head indicating that the customer had it wrong. A few tries later the customer had clarified accurately the position of Dave's project team member. Realizing that they had each completely misunderstood the other, the customer and Dave's project team member began to laugh and then they continued with their meeting and productively and successfully addressed all of the open project issues.

On the way back to the office after the meeting, Dave mentored his project team member emphasizing the importance of good, effective and personable communications. Dave stressed the importance of truly paying attention to what is said and using the technique of replication to ensure that all parties have a clear and common understanding. Dave's motto was that a problem clearly understood and communicated effectively is already half solved.

Project Manager Empathy

Tom is one of those senior project managers who have seen it all. A veteran in IT and highly skilled project management practitioner, Tom uses his years of experience to keep a balanced perspective on the priorities and pressures of an intense workplace and to keep calm under pressure. Tom is with a major telecommunications company that has outsourced all of its support center and much of its IT department. Tom is managing a development project with the firm's outsourcing partner and at the end of the project Tom, and most of his internal staff, will be let go.

Though the company has announced the reductions in staff that are coming, they have not finalized their decisions regarding which of the employees will be let go and which of them will be asked to stay. As one expects in such an environment, the morale of Tom's internal team, like the company at large, is poor. Rather than ignore the increasingly poor morale of the internal team, Tom called a meeting of the internal project team. There was no agenda in the meeting request; just Tom's request for all of the project team to attend a thirty-minute meeting.

Tom didn't know exactly what the outcome of the meeting would be, but he knew exactly what he was going to say. Tom shared with the team that they all had a life outside of work and that their life, their families, and the pursuit of their dreams were far more important than any one job or any one company. Tom empathized with each of the project team members, which came easy for Tom since he was in the same situation as they were. Although Tom was not their functional manager and it was not his job to manage their morale, as a leader Tom could not escape his calling to best serve his team.

To the project team, Tom's meeting and words were like medicine to an ailing patient. They all felt miserable about the current work situation and the prospect of losing their jobs in a down economy. As professionals they all wanted to perform their duties and maintain a positive attitude, but it was difficult to put aside the reality that the waters ahead would likely be turbulent. Tom couldn't change the situation or make the problem go away, but he did offer two important things. He offered sincere empathy to the team that was truly appreciated. He also gave the team an opportunity to share that empathy and to keep a balanced perspective on their lives.

Tom didn't ask the team to put aside their feelings in order to perform their duties on the project. In fact, Tom didn't even talk about the project. However, as a result of Tom's empathy and leadership, the morale of the project team vastly improved. The care that Tom showed his team spilled over to each of the team members and they in turn supported each other, emotionally, as they continued work on the project and faced all but certain termination from the company.

Project Manager Healing

Susan was a professional recruited by a university to head their new PMO. Prior to her arrival, one of the senior project managers was named acting PMO manager and asked to get things started. He achieved quite a bit. The strategy of the PMO was put in place and reviewed with management. A project portfolio management (PPM) system, Microsoft Project Server, was implemented and the project managers were trained to use it. The project management methodology (PMM) framework was updated and made available for use within the IT department. Although the acting PMO manager did a fine job of setting up the components of the PMO, he did not have experience or a background in strategic planning or working with the executive team and they wanted to hire a PMO manager with experience and a proven track record in these areas.

Upon Susan's arrival, it did not take long for her to recognize that the senior project manager who had been named acting PMO manager felt passed over. It was obvious to all that he was a little dejected and it could be seen in his attitude and comments. He had done a good job in getting things started and would have liked the opportunity to be the PMO manager. The senior project manager was a valued employee and contributor and the management team all believed that he had long-term potential. Although the management team made it clear that his role as acting PMO manager was only temporary and that a PMO manager would be hired from outside the organization, the senior project manager had hoped that if he did a good job as acting PMO manager then maybe the management team would offer him the job. Alas, it was not to be, and the senior project manager now reported to the new PMO manager.

Rather than ignoring the obvious pain the senior project manager had, Susan called a lunch meeting with him. She took him to a nice restaurant, not a quick in and out place. Susan made it clear that she was picking up the tab as it was she who had called the meeting and wanting to talk over a few things. She also set the agenda and said that before discussing the matter on her mind she wanted to first enjoy the opportunity to get to know each other a little better while having a nice meal.

After they had both finished their meal, she order coffees for each of them and then began to discuss the situation at hand. Susan expressed empathy and concern and made it clear that she understood that the senior project manager couldn't help but be a bit disappointed in not being named the PMO manager. After all he had performed as acting PMO manager for nearly six months. It would be unnatural not to feel hurt. Susan's words and attention were comforting to the senior project manager. By the end of their meeting, he had felt much better about the situation and rather than feeling rejected and dejected, he felt that he could learn from his new boss as she had been a PMO manager with two other organizations and had experiences and knowledge that he didn't.

Susan could have chosen to take no action and wait for the senior project manager to come around, but she didn't. She recognized that the senior project manager was hurting and needed healing. Rather than leaving the senior project manager alone to his own devices to get through it, Susan chose instead to act and to be a healer. Her actions were effective in both helping to heal the wounded senior project manager as well as to help him see the positive side of the situation.

Project Manager Awareness

Steve was a seasoned project manager who was asked to take over a failing project. The project lacked definition. The project charter document provided few details other than the fact that the sponsor of the project wanted to implement a particular vendor software package. The project team members each had their project work packages to develop and test and progress seemed to be taking place at the unit level, but the project was not coming together as a whole.

There was no clear view of the project completing on time or within the prescribed budget. The greatest challenge was that the sponsor had not clearly specified the key requirements and needs to be addressed by the system and the sponsor was not involved nearly enough in the development of the product of the project. No amount of iterations and walk-throughs with the sponsor was enough to arrive at an acceptable solution without more definition and direction from the sponsor.

Steve could have continued on with one development iteration after another, but instead he chose to disturb the project by calling for an immediate review and update of the requirements with the sponsor. He felt that there wasn't enough awareness by all involved in the project of the project goals. He also felt that there was not sufficient project definition to enable the team to even arrive at a real completion for the project.

Steve's project team and the sponsor initially complained and suggested that Steve simply didn't appreciate their *agile* approach to the project. But, Steve knew better. His sense of awareness and effort to reveal the disturbing truth of the project, rather than turning a blind eye to the lack of definition, was the key factor in rescuing the project.

Project Manager Persuasion

Chuck was the most senior and experienced project manager in the IT department. Though he had little formal authority, he had a great deal of informal authority and influence with everyone in the organization, including management, co-workers, and project team members. Chuck's greatest strength was his people skills and in particular his ability to persuade others to commit to a course of action when they really didn't want to.

Not too long ago, Chuck managed a software development project. One of Chuck's project team members was a new developer to the organization. The new developer was highly skilled and previously worked at a software development company that was always on the leading edge in terms of adopting the latest in trends and approaches for software development. Though the developer was tremendously talented, we continually lamented that the PPM of the organization was out of touch with current best practices for software development.

Recognizing that the ongoing negative commentary by the developer served no useful purpose and might even compromise the morale of the project team, Chuck persuaded the developer to refrain from his negative commentary. But more importantly, Chuck persuaded the developer to start a dialog and exchange of ideas about leading approaches for software development within the IT department. Chuck suggested that the monthly IT department lunch and learn meetings were an ideal venue to share ideas and promote change in a positive, forward going way, as opposed to the continual kibitzing at meetings that the developer had been doing. Chuck also planted the seed with the developer, both praising his skills and motivating him to seriously apply his knowledge and demonstrate his value to the organization.

Within a few months of sharing ideas and information in a more productive manner, the head of IT and the applications manager asked this new developer to assist them in modernizing their approach to software development and systems implementation. Although Chuck had no formal authority over the developer, it was his servant-leadership persuasion skills that, in effect, brought about the change in the behavior of the developer needed for not just Chuck's project, but the company as well.

Project Manager Conceptualization

Julie was a project manager at a growing software company. She was asked to manage the project to implement the company's first customer relationship management (CRM) system. Everyone knew what CRM was and most of the management team and sales and marketing staff had some kind of previous experience in the use of a CRM system.

There were several business needs that led to the decision to implement a CRM system spanning marketing, sales, services, and support. From the start, Julie's greatest problem was the fact that there was no common view of what the CRM system should do. Also adding to the problem was the resistance of the management team to take the time needed to discuss and determine the core requirements of the system. Everyone was busy and presumed that they were all in agreement. In actuality there was little discussion and agreement to anything. The head of sales wanted better reporting and managing of the sales pipeline and quarterly revenue forecasts. The marketing manager who reported to the head of sales wanted a system that provided marketing automation features in support of their lead generation programs and investments. The head of professional services wanted the system to provide billable services reporting and resource management capabilities. The manager of customer support, who reported to the head of services, wanted the system to provide features for customer support and, in particular, customer self service.

Julie recognized the situation as being ever so similar to the classic story about the blind men and the elephant. As the story goes, each of the blind men approached the elephant from different points of reference and, hence, all of the blind men were quite wrong in their perception of what was before them. And so it was with Julie's management team. They all were in agreement to implement a CRM system, but none of them had a clear idea of what the CRM system, as a whole, needed to do.

After meeting individually with each of the four key members of the management team and discussing their perspectives and requirements, Julie put together the conceptualization for the CRM system and called a working meeting to review and finalize it with the management team. Although Julie didn't get the entire picture totally right, her approach enabled the management team to participate, contribute, and reach agreement on the key requirements for the system.

Project Manager Foresight

Robert was a project manager with years of experience managing projects in Japan. He spoke Japanese fluently and worked for a Boston-based software firm that provided billing and customer care solutions to high-end telecommunications firms. Robert was happy to learn that the Asia Pacific sales team had made a major sale in Japan and he would be the project manager for the implementation of the firm's product.

A typical implementation of the firm's product required six months onsite and involved six project team participants; the project manager, one business analyst, and four developers. When Robert found out the members of his project team, he immediately became concerned. One of the project team members, a developer who he had worked with in the past, was not a good road warrior and Robert had concerns that the developer would not survive working on a complex project in a foreign country.

Robert took his concerns to management and suggested that a different developer be assigned to the project. Rather than being irritated by Robert's concerns, management took them seriously and decided to have Robert and the VP of the Asia Pacific organization have a pre-project, orientation discussion with the developer. The developer was quick to admit that she didn't really want to be on the project team because of the travel and excessive time away from home that was required.

Management was able to make the appropriate adjustments both to get a developer who was a better fit for the Japan implementation project and to reassign Robert's developer to a project that required far less travel and time away from home. Robert's foresight prevented the all too likely scenario that midway through the project the developer would become increasingly unhappy compromising the project and the customer relationship.

Project Manager Stewardship

Michelle was a project manager responsible for a software development project. The project wasn't overly complex and the project team was made up of talented individuals. However, the project was running behind schedule and management decided that to make the schedule commitment promised to the customer by the sales team that the developers would have to work Saturdays for the last four weeks of the project. None of the developers complained because they were accustomed to working nights and weekends from time to time. It was not unusual, just a bit inconvenient.

As project manager, Michelle didn't have any work that really required her to come in on Saturdays. It was the developers who had all of the "real work" to do. Nonetheless, Michelle came in each Saturday. She brought in two boxes of Krispie Kreme donuts for the team, which didn't last long and ordered pizzas for lunch, which was also much appreciated. But far more important than feeding the team, Michelle was able to handle a number of small problems that the team faced while working Saturdays.

On one Saturday the air conditioner was not working. It had been turned off automatically by the facilities management system. Though notified to keep the air conditioner running, the facilities personnel did not make the necessary arrangements and the team started work quite uncomfortably and it was getting worse. Michelle made calls and was able to track down a facilities person who could come into the office and activate the air conditioner. On another Saturday the vending machine was sold out of cold drinks. Michelle went home and came back with an iced-down cooler full of sodas, sports drinks, and water.

Michelle's service to the team not only helped with their morale and immediate needs, but the time she spent resolving the various small problems that the team faced each Saturday was time that would have otherwise been spent by one of the developers. Her presence and efforts ensured that the developers could best use their time on those Saturdays doing their development and remaining focused on the project tasks at hand, nothing else.

Project Manager Commitment to the Growth of People

Eldon was a senior program manager with years of experience. Over the course of his career he had technical positions as well as positions in management. One of Eldon's project managers was having a difficult time.

One day Eldon overheard his project manager, whose cubicle was not far away, having a heated discussion over the phone with one of the project team members. Eldon calmly walked over to his project manager's cubicle and took a nearby seat listening to the conversation. The project manager changed his tone, but was still clearly agitated. After the call was over Eldon asked the project manager to calm down, explain the problem to him, and tell him why he allowed himself to lose his composure. The project manager, though highly skilled technically, admittedly had an anger management problem and sometimes it got out of control.

No one had ever thought to confront the project manager about his behavior. It was simply tolerated by others; some even made fun of it. Even though it didn't significantly impact anyone else's attitude or work yet, it did impact the attitude and work of the project manager. Eldon took the time to discuss the anger management problem with the project manager and encouraged him to overcome it. Rather than lecture him on the inappropriateness and lack of professionalism that losing one's temper can have in the workplace, Eldon viewed the heated phone discussion that he witnessed as an opportunity for growth and improvement.

Project Manager Community Building

Linda was an experienced project manager in the PMO of a large, successful company that had thousands of employees all over the world. Over the years Linda had the opportunity to work with other project managers in all of the company's theaters of operation; North America, Europe, Asia Pacific, and Latin America. She enjoyed travelling and learning about other cultures, but mostly she developed a deep appreciation for the tremendous skills and talents of all the people she had an opportunity to work with and get to know.

Linda took it upon herself to start a project management community of practice (PMCOP) within the company. She developed her vision and business case and took it to management. Her objective was to harness and grow the collective talent of all of the project managers of the company. Management loved the idea and Linda was surprised at how eager they were to help her. As it turns out, for years the management team had been discussing ways to share information more effectively and take advantage of the many subject matter experts they had throughout the company.

The PMCOP soon became a reality and the benefit to the participants and to the organization was tremendous. Participants shared best practice tips and techniques, lessons learned feedback and reviews, risk management strategies related to the company's known and likely risk events, how-to guides for using the company's suite of project management tools, and a wide variety of training and professional development resources. The community was supported by management, but it was led by the collective participants.

Linda's sense of community building quickly caught on fire, continued to evolve, and grew to proportions far greater than her original vision. Had Linda not taken the initiative to follow through on her ideas and convictions, this special community would not exist.

Summary

What is the best leadership model for project managers to exhibit? As always the answer is, it depends. There are many models to choose from and each has its special and unique qualities. But of all of these models, perhaps the model most conducive to project manager leadership is the servant-leadership model.

In many ways project managers are servant-leaders. Project managers do not exercise positional authority and power; rather they listen, think, and persuade others to a call of action. What servant-leader enthusiasts call foresight, project managers call risk mitigation. What servant-leader enthusiasts call building community, project managers call community of practice. The similarities go on and on.

Conventional leadership teaches us that it is all about the hero. The hero has special abilities that no one else has. The hero always saves the day no matter what obstacles must be cleared and no matter what perils must be faced. But, heroes as a business strategy do not scale well. As organizations mature, they quickly come to realize that hero worship is a tell-tale sign of a process defect.

An alternative to the conventional thinking of hero-based leadership is the servant-leadership model. It has been around for centuries and has passed the test of time. Critics might scoff at servant-leadership and complain that it is soft and takes too much time. But at the heart of the matter, servant-leadership is all about collaborative skills, trust, listening, and ethical behavior. It is hard to argue that a project team is poorly served by a project manager exhibiting these traits.

Questions

1. What are the characteristics of an autocratic leader?
2. What are the characteristics of a bureaucratic leader?
3. What are the characteristics of a charismatic leader?
4. What are the characteristics of a democratic leader?
5. What are the characteristics of a laissez-faire leader?
6. What are the characteristics of a people-oriented leader?
7. What are the characteristics of a task-oriented leader?
8. What are the characteristics of a servant-oriented leader?
9. In what ways do the teachings of early historic figures such as Lao Tzu, Chanakya Arthashastra, and Jesus praise servant-leadership?

10. What three companies are listed in the *Fortune* magazine's "The 100 Best Companies to Work for in America" list and are recognized for their servant-leadership?
11. What are the ten characteristics of servant-leadership?
12. What examples illustrate the applicability of servant-leadership to project management?

References

Badaracco, Joseph. 2002. *Leading Quietly*. Massachusetts: Harvard Business School Press.

Douglas, Max. 2003. "Servant-leadership: An Emerging Supervisory Model." http://www.allbusiness.com. (Accessed June 12, 2008)

Lichtenwalner, Benjamin. 2008. "Servant-Leadership." http://www.lichtenwalner.blogspot.com. (Accessed June 12, 2008)

McCrimmon, Mitch. 2006. "What's Wrong with Leadership Theory," http://www.leadersdirect.com. (Accessed June 12, 2008)

Moore, John. 2005. "The HB Way." http://www.brandautopsy.typepad.com. (Accessed June 12, 2008)

Rabon, Brian. 2008. "The Top Five Secrets to Successfully Implementing Agile Project Management," http://www.braintrustsoftware.com, (Accessed June 12, 2008)

Spears, Larry. 2005. "The Understanding and Practice of Servant-Leadership" http://www.regent.edu. (Accessed June 12, 2008)

Spears, Larry, and Michelle Lawrence. 2001. *Focus on Leadership*, New Jersey: John Wiley and Sons.

White, Barbara. 2004. "Can A Project Manager be a Servant Leader? A Reflective Critique." http://www.maxwideman.com. (Accessed June 12, 2008)

Executive Insights

Situational Project Management Leadership

Jennifer Arndt

PMO Manager, American Chemical Society

In the complex world of project management we are confronted by many challenges: navigating business demands, financial pressures, and personality conflicts are all part of the job. Things change moment by moment, and nothing ever works out quite the way you planned it. In IT we've seen the rise of Rapid Application Development (RAD), Extreme Programming (XP), and Agile software development as we struggle to respond to the (seemingly) capricious whims of our all-important customers.

In addition to applying Project Change Control and Communications Management, PMOs have begun to incorporate and borrow from an increasing array of complimentary disciplines and methodologies like Knowledge Management (KM), Business Process Management (BPM), and Information Technology Infrastructure Library (ITIL), all in a desperate attempt to keep key projects from spinning further and further out of control. And in the end, when the project has been declared complete, we're often left wondering whether we really accomplished the goals we all agreed to in the beginning or if it was sheer exhaustion that drove our decision to close the effort.

According to Gartner (2007), it doesn't look like the situation will improve any time soon. Their 2007 annual report on IT indicates that, "ad hoc requests will be the norm, not the exception. Decisions cannot wait for formal governance cycles ... The flexibility required to enable enterprises to exploit all these capabilities cannot be delivered by traditional PPM practices." In this atmosphere, leading from the front isn't enough—you're likely to turn around and find that your team has wandered off in some unforeseen direction while you struggle to catch up. It's become absolutely critical to develop the skills required to allow you to lead from the heart of your team.

Over the years of managing people, projects, and programs, I've developed a few leadership rules that I live by. I'd like to share these with you in the hope that my lessons learned help you to make a positive impact on your organization as a leader in project management.

Don't Reinvent the Wheel

The profession of project management (Coppens, 2008) is at least as old as the pyramids. While we all know people who do it, managing people or projects by the seat of your pants is rarely a pleasant experience—either for project managers or for the teams they are trying to lead. The good news is that there are lots of great ways (many of them low-cost or free) to get educated on the issues that your PMO is facing today. The even better news is that sharing what you learn quickly makes you an invaluable resource to your organization. Here are a few of my favorite ways to keep up on project/program/portfolio management knowledge:

1. Network. There are few problems that haven't already been analyzed and solved by your colleagues, and most of them don't mind sharing their stories of defeat and success on the way to a solution. One of the first places to make contacts is within your own organization. Look for the people who have been there for a while and who have successfully navigated the corporate culture. Even if they don't know much about project management in practice, they are a fantastic sounding board as you consider which tools and techniques to deploy in your environment. There are any number of ways to meet skilled PMPs in your community and around the world. A few of my favorites include:
    ◊ Attend local Project Management Institute (PMI) chapter meetings. Volunteer to speak on your favorite topic or help with a PMI headquarters initiative. That earns you introductions to some interesting and knowledgeable folks.
    ◊ Attend project management-oriented conferences (PMI, Gartner, PMO Summit) and lectures.
    ◊ Participate in Webinars offered by vendors.
    ◊ Join project management groups on networking sites, for example, LinkedIn.
2. Get credentialed. I have heard many arguments against obtaining project management credentials. In particular, I've heard many say that it's just a measure of whether you can pass a test, and not of whether you are a good project manager. This might be true, but it also indicates that you have taken the time to read and absorb standard definitions for project management terms and practices and can speak the project management language with your colleagues around the world. Perhaps most importantly, earning your credential shows that you are willing to make a commitment to your profession.
3. Build a library of resources. A great way to be known as an expert is to have a variety of resources at your fingertips. Relevant books are an obvious choice, but it's also helpful to have a subscription to Gantthead.

com, ProjectConnections.com or another site that offers articles, advice, and valuable templates. You might also want to hang onto those catalogs from Learning Tree, ESI and the like; the next time someone stops by your office asking if you know of a class in Microsoft Project, you'll be able to quickly point them in the right direction. You can also ask the project managers in your organization to contribute to an online library of resources, with links to helpful articles and templates for successful deliverables used at your organization.

4. **Participate in training.** While traditional classes are helpful and can generate new ideas, I personally find that, at more advanced levels, conferences and Webinars are most likely to cover the latest trends and usually leave me eager to get back to work and try out some of those new ideas. Another great way to catch up on training is to download podcasts. PMI's Information Systems Specific Interest Group offers a number of video podcasts that are not only informative, but can also apply to maintaining your project management credentials.

One of my best educational experiences happened organically at work. In 2001 there were several of us who wanted to attain our PMP credential. After several months of hallway conversations we decided to prepare together, and agreed to meet for brown-bag lunches every two weeks. Each person in the group volunteered to lead a session covering a chapter of the Project Management Body of Knowledge (PMBOK). Everyone read the section before the discussion, and the leader prepared a high-level walk-through of the material along with providing supplemental material for additional background.

I happened to be the first graduate of this study group, and obtained my PMP certification just a few minutes before one of my colleagues. Eventually every person in the group obtained their certification as the rest of us encouraged and celebrated each success. While providing each of us with a strong foundation in a common PMM, this shared experience has also led to a more productive workplace.

Get Out of the Ivory Tower

After mentioning some ways that you can gain expertise and improve your project management knowledge, I would be remiss if I didn't throw in a word of caution: It's easy to get so caught up in theory that we in the PMO can forget what it's like for the project team down on the ground. It's easy to get intrigued by the many ideas and theories, while forgetting that methodologies must be carefully tailored to each unique work environment. Here are some suggestions to help ensure that you don't become one of *those people* full of enthusiasm and ideas, but without a strong understanding of the real world consequences:

1. Mentor. Look for opportunities to help that aspiring project manager to learn the ropes and gain confidence and success. This doesn't just mean meeting for coffee every few weeks; if your mentee is willing, find ways to work shoulder to shoulder with them. Providing valuable, constructive, and sensitive feedback on documents and performance not only helps others learn, but gives you the opportunity to find out first-hand what's happening elsewhere. Best of all your helpfulness and eagerness to teach enhances your reputation as a leader in project management.
2. Manage a project. There are many roles in the modern PMO, not all of which involve managing projects. If you find yourself in one of these positions, it can't hurt to find opportunities to flex your project management muscle now and then to ensure that you don't get rusty. These don't need to be work projects—in fact, volunteering to manage a project for your local community, or applying your skills to a minor home improvement project, can be great learning opportunities. The point is to practice what you preach to help cement and perfect all of the knowledge that you've gained.
3. Collaborate. Partnering with others to address real world needs is a wonderful way to stretch your knowledge and skills while showcasing your ability to lead—often beyond your responsibilities in the PMO. Working with your colleagues to improve your organization not only helps bring you out of the realm of theory, but can also provide you with the opportunity to showcase your leadership potential beyond project management.

Looking back on my career, my most interesting and challenging projects were those that solved complicated, immediate needs—and required me to go well beyond my expertise in project, program, and portfolio management to ensure success. For example, several years ago I was asked to manage an enterprise architecture planning (EAP) effort for our organization. For various reasons I also ended up filling the role of enterprise business analyst on the project. While the work was difficult and required many hours of effort, I learned a great deal about the way our core business functioned. Because I was responsible for modeling these business processes, I left my safe haven in IT and spent days just talking to the people who make our organization run every day.

In addition to my work with our business partners, I spent many hours working shoulder to shoulder with a knowledgeable consultant, and our architecture team. In those days we had vigorous debates about the role of portfolio management in relation to EAP (the architects felt that the portfolio management function should be subsumed by EAP—I begged to differ). Now several years after our initial effort was completed, I find that I continually draw on the contacts I made during the EAP project, and I count the members of the

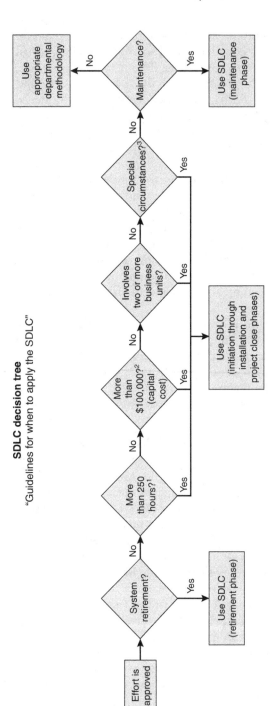

NOTES:

1. Includes all work hours, from staff or consultants, required to complete the effort.

2. Efforts meeting the hour, capital cost, and business unit visibility criteria should follow the methodology for SDLC phases from the "define project" step of the initial phase through the installation and project close phase. This applies to all efforts, including those categorized as enhancements and maintenance.

3. If a unique situation applies to the project, then the SDLC may be used to manage the associated risks. Examples of these exceptions may include the implementation of a new system or technology, a change that affects financial systems or an effort that has visibility at the executive or board level.

IMPORTANT: This document should be viewed as a set of guidelines for the thresholds at which the SDLC will apply to projects. The final decision regarding the appropriate application of the SDLC remains the responsibility of each individual technology owner.

Figure 8.2 SDLC decision tree

architecture team as some of my closest friends and allies at work. Stepping out of my role as PMO manager and jumping into a completely new way of working broadened my knowledge of the organization I work for, and gave me insight into a completely different discipline—lessons that continue to shape and inform my current work.

Don't Be Afraid to Break the Rules—for the Right Reasons

In project management we learn numerous rules: always have a signed charter document, create a work breakdown structure, and keep your communications plan up to date. The list goes on . . . These recommendations are made for good reasons and in many cases following a PMM by the letter results in success.

On the other hand, we've all experienced situations in which the rules just don't apply. A small effort is decreed a project, but requires such minimal effort that writing and getting signed approvals for the charter and work breakdown structure would take longer and involve more risk than implementing the change. The project is internal to your department and only a few people already working on the effort are affected, so a communications plan seems like overkill.

As someone responsible for leading project managers, it is critical that you be prepared to make decisions about when the rules must be followed, and when they should be bent or broken. Ideally these decisions should be documented so that, eventually, you can create policies and guidance that reflect the needs and culture of your organization.

For example my organization rolled out a Software Development Life Cycle (SDLC) methodology several years ago as shown in Figure 8.2. As we learned more about how project managers were (and weren't) using our SDLC, we developed guidelines to help staff determine when they should use it.

Summary

While there are many tools at the disposal of a project manager, true leadership is knowing when to use the hammer for the nail and the thumb for the tack. When neither works, it's time to get creative and find an innovative combination of tools to achieve results.

Being seen as a leader in project management requires much more than knowledge of the profession, or even a strong track record of managing projects. Leadership also requires you to champion project management as a legitimate solution to the specific challenges faced by your organization. You don't need to have all of the answers, but you do need to know how to look for them, and then tailor them to your environment. Most of all, you should be willing to freely share what you know, and be enthusiastic about working with others to find the best solution for your unique situation.

References

Coppens, Philip. 2008. "The Great Pyramid: A Course in Project Management." http://www.philipcoppens.

McGee, Ken, Christopher Ambrose, et al. 2007. "The 2007 Gartner Scenario: An Annual Report on the Current State and Future Directions of the IT Industry." Gartner Research G00149904 (September 15).

How to Get What You Want

Michelle LaBrosse

Founder and CEO, Cheetah Learning

There's a Joe Jackson song with a great line: "You can't get what you want 'til you know what you want." That line is not only applicable to many aspects of life, it's applicable if you're starting or rejuvenating a PMO.

Set Expectations

If it's control and accountability that you're looking for, a PMO is a great place to start, but you can't stop there. Don't make the mistake of putting a placard on a door and waiting for the benefits to magically build up and boost your bottom line. Instead, define your goals from the start; set expectations, manage those expectations, keep your team motivated, and make sure you're streamlined for virtual team management. Let's start with your goals.

Define Your Goals

What are your organization's goals and how is the PMO supporting those goals? Do you want a PMO that is enterprise wide or does it make more sense for you to start your PMO as a boutique inside the organization and then expand the size as you get more successes under your belt?

Decide What Type of PMO You Want to Establish

There are two basic models: a consultancy hub that provides project managers in business units with training, guidance, and best practices; and a best practices center with project managers on staff who are loaned out to business units to work on projects. Build a good team with solid leadership and clear ownership. Don't employ people with down-time to lead the PMO. Choose strong leaders who have a direct line to you.

Track the PMO's Success and Share the Results

Don't treat the PMO as a top-secret international space mission. Share the mission and its successes, failures and benefits with the entire organization. Be open and inclusive and have a communication strategy for sharing information regularly. Using baseline controls, decide what you want to track and set expectations for what you want to benchmark against. *Hint*: track things that senior management cares about. If you don't know what they care about, download the latest annual report or go back and read what the CEO is saying to clients, investors, or other stakeholders. If you're in a smaller more agile organization, make friends with someone in corporate communications or human resources and make sure that you are aligned with the hot issues du jour. Be relentless in your pursuit of performance. Results come from diligence and dogged determination. Support your PMO with clear commitment and support from the senior most levels of your organization. This support generally comes when you are working on issues that they care about. I can't stress enough that you have to make sure that your PMO is working on initiatives that matter to the organization. When can you see the bottom-line impact? Once you have a baseline to measure against, you can see results in less than three years. You'll save money by empowering better resource management, reducing project failures, and prioritizing and supporting those projects that offer the greatest payback.

Make It Actionable not Administrative

Avoid the pitfall of making the PMO a purely administrative office. Instead make it the center of change, a catalyst for improvement across your organization with tangible and realistic strategic goals. When you're pitching the PMO, don't present it as the fix-all to organizational woes. Instead give management a clear idea of what a PMO can do.

Seven Things a PMO Can Do

1. Improve PPM: Develop the capability to select the right mix of projects to most effectively and efficiently meet strategic objectives.
2. Provide project support: Build a conduit for project management guidance to project managers in business units.
3. Create project management process/methodology: Develop and implement a consistent and standardized process.
4. Conduct training: Build training programs and develop a staff of program managers who can manage multiple projects across the enterprise.
5. Establish a home base for project managers: Create a centralized office from which project managers are a cohesive team that works across an enterprise.
6. Become internal consultants and mentors: Advise employees about best practices.
7. Assess project management software tools: Select and maintain project management tools that are useful for the capabilities of the staff.

Manage Expectations

You can boost organizational efficiency, cut costs, and improve on project delivery, but even more important is the path to get there. The PMO provides discipline that is often lacking in organizations. It helps you to deliver strategic projects with more consistency and efficiency. But you need to let management know that it won't happen overnight. Once you have a baseline that you are measuring against, you can show improvements; but at the beginning you are building the foundation so you have good data and information that is meaningful to measure against.

Standardization and Sarbanes-Oxley

PMOs can provide the structure needed to both standardize project management practices and improve PPM. A PMO can help your organization determine methodologies for repeatable processes. The Sarbanes-Oxley Act has been a huge driver for the development of PMOs in the United States. The Act requires companies to disclose investments that might affect a company's operating performance. Many large projects fall under that definition. With or without Sarbanes-Oxley, PMOs give a company a central brain for project management and provide companies with a systemic way to keep a closer watch on project expenses and progress.

Focus on Culture

Many PMOs fail when they are not set up to work in a company's culture. If you look at other important strategic initiatives in your company that were successes, you'll generally find that they worked because they flowed within your business culture. Make sure your PMO does the same. Don't isolate it as some solo test project. Make it part of the organization's very fabric.

Time Matters

According to a survey by *CIO* and the PMI, there is a strong link between the length of time a PMO has been operating and project success rates. The longer a PMO has been operational, the better its results. In this survey, 37 percent of those companies who had a PMO for less than one year reported increased success rates; those with a PMO operating for more than four years reported a 65 percent success rate increase.

Keep Your Team Motivated

In my career I've found that getting what I want nearly always involves getting other people behind me and excited in what I'm doing. Don't think of team building as one of the rare activities that you do at an off-site retreat. Instead, incorporate inspiring your team into your daily activities. Here are my top tips for keeping my teams infused with energy.

Be Enthusiastic about Each Person's Contributions

Remember how good it felt when a teacher recognized your contribution? You glowed all day and nearly flew home. It costs nothing to tell people how they're doing. Recognizing what they're doing well, and also giving ideas on how they can work even better, goes a long way.

Wear Your Blue Hat and Leave the Black Hat at Home

You might have played the game where you wear different hats to assume different roles. The black hat starts with the negatives and tells you everything that's going wrong. This is the person who can kill idea generation in any meeting. When you're inspiring a team wear the blue hat and encourage others to do the same. Creative meetings and events rarely happen because someone followed the same formula. See the possibility and opportunity in every challenge. Begin with what is working and then build on it.

Focus on the Strengths of Each Person

One of the greatest myths in business is to focus on weaknesses instead of building strengths. It's a backward way to approach problem solving—like fitting the proverbial square peg into the round hole. It's faster and more effective to focus on the strengths of your team members and develop them. Not only will you see results faster, you'll also have a happier team because people are doing what they're good at and contributing at their highest level.

Clear Hurdles Like a Super Hero

How do you get your team to feel like rock stars? Think like Superman and clear any hurdles that are in their way. When you remove obstacles, you show your team that you've got their back.

Get the Slackers Off the Team

Nothing brings down a team like slackers. When people aren't pulling their weight, it lowers the standards of everyone and makes it seem like quality doesn't matter. When you remove people who aren't performing, it improves morale because it shows your team that you're serious about the best results. Roll up your sleeves. When you work with the team in the areas where you can contribute, you send a strong message because you are showing that you are part of the team with your actions.

Acknowledge People's Contributions Every Week

Many managers make the mistake of recognizing people once a year. Recognition isn't a holiday. It should be a regular part of your team dynamic. Take the time every week to tell people how they've contributed to the team. This is even more important when you're under a crucial deadline or working on the most important meeting of the year.

Be the Model of Accountability

If you're telling people to be accountable while not meeting your own deadlines, it doesn't take too long for the eyes to roll. Keep your team inspired by keeping your commitments to them and meeting every milestone. Show and communicate your progress. Don't make the mistake of doing project updates only at milestones. Communicate the progress of the project every week to make sure you're on track.

Create a Safe Environment

If people laugh and talk freely, you have a safe environment. If everyone shuts up as soon as you walk into a room or jump on the conference call, you need to change the dynamic. Focus on being open to new ideas, to listening more than you talk, and letting your team take the credit when credit is due.

Get Streamlined for Virtual Team Management

When we think of successful management today of any project or initiative, often the old rules don't apply. Nowhere is this more evident than when we think about the impact of virtual teams on project success. Getting what you want today is about knowing how to manage projects and people when everyone isn't in the same place. Even if your PMO is in one central location, chances are that the departments you're working with and your team might be in several locations. So it's important to build some virtual management best practices into your roadmap for success.

Manage Results, Not Activity

In the physical office environment, busy work often gets mistaken for real work. In the virtual environment, when you can't see what people are doing, the key is to manage results. Monitor and measure the results and be clear about the goals.

Schedule Regular Communication

It's important that there is a regular time for reporting both progress and potential pitfalls to the team. This keeps people on track and gives every one the discipline of a team check-in. It's ideal if there is a standing time every week or every month—depending on your project milestones. Remember to build in time for feedback, coaching and support. Create communication that saves time. Have you created an email culture that wastes time with endless *daisy-chain* conversations that take several hours to read? Does your team spend hours trying to solve an issue with an email conversation that could have been solved with a thirty-minute conference call? Email is a critical tool in our work environments, therefore it's important to create a new culture of effectiveness around it. Have people learn to write meaningful subject lines that communicate what the email is about. Also, make sure they lead with what is important and who needs to take action on what. Many deadlines can be missed when the action is buried in paragraph 12.

Create Standards that Build a Cohesive Culture

What are your standards of quality? How do you define excellence? What does your brand mean to each employee? Making sure everyone knows the answers to those three questions is even more important when people are scattered geographically. Virtually, you need to create cohesion with excellence and a sense of pride in what your company stands for.

Rules of Responsiveness

When people are working remotely, it's important that you define what the rules of responsiveness are for your culture. How quickly are people expected to return an email, an Instant Message or a phone call? What is your protocol when people are out of the office or on vacation? If you're in a customer service environment, it's important to have clear expectations regarding how to respond to all customer inquiries.

Use Collaborative Tools like the Wiki

Working virtually is *not* about platitudes. It is about systems, creating the systems that enable people to do their work from anywhere and everywhere. There has to be a strong commitment to giving people the tools they need to help run the business and serve the customers. If they have to go somewhere to answer the phone to serve the customers, they cannot work virtually.

The Wiki is a central hub for our work in which we coordinate our projects and processes. We started this for the marketing group to reduce the email and to better capture the various marketing initiatives and decisions. Within one week it was adopted by all the people in the company: IT projects, facilities to coordinate facility work, accounting to coordinate budgeting with the different parts of the business, and course development to keep track of course upgrades. It has increased our productivity and also created a central memory for all of our work.

Pay Attention to Cultural Cues and Time Zones

When you're working on a global team, you need to be sensitive to the time zones that you're working in. For example, which time zone are the deadlines relevant in? Are you scheduling calls at a time that works best for all time zones? Also, remember that cross-cultural communication becomes even more of an issue in email. Pay attention to how your colleagues communicate in email. How formal is it? How are they addressing each other? Don't automatically assume an informal tone until you have gained the trust and respect of your team.

Create an Attitude of Gratitude

Reward people when they do well. Especially when people are working virtually, they need to know when they've made a difference. We created a program called *The Attitude of Gratitude* in which people have 2000 points every month to distribute to their coworkers to thank them for whatever they did during the month. The top three people with the most points at the end of the month win. First place is something worth $500, second place is worth $300, and third place is worth $200. It's a company-wide employee recognition program that everyone participates in and it creates both buzz and community.

Summary (No Shoving Necessary)

So, getting what you want is not about shoving your way to the front of the line. When you define your goals from the start, know what to except, manage expectations, keep your team motivated, and make sure you're streamlined for virtual team management, there is nothing you want that you can't get! Go for it!

Servant-Leadership for the IT Project Manager

Benjamin Lichtenwalner

Senior Manager, Whirlpool

IT project managers are on the front lines of organizational leadership. These individuals are exposed to some of the most cross-functional personnel and therefore possess some of the greatest opportunities to practice and embed the company's leadership style and beliefs. Countless IT projects necessitate the involvement of individuals across the organization. From back-office subject matter experts to front-office implementation personnel and of course, the many technical experts necessary for development, most IT initiatives touch many departments.

While the board, CEO, and other executive leaders should set the tone and culture for the company, the PMO and project managers are in position to deliver the most effective leadership for the organization on a daily basis. As a result, the leadership style that the PMO and individual project managers practice is critical. Conventional wisdom suggests the domineering, fear-inducing, hero-worship style of manager would prevail and get the greatest results, but focusing on this ego-fueled style of leadership is damaging in the long run.

We've all seen it—the project managers who are out for themselves first, the company, customer, employees, and all other stakeholders are secondary to their personal success. These individuals seek fame and fortune through short-term wins that often cost the organization by diminishing the opportunities for sustainable success. These are the managers who don't understand that their employment is not an opportunity for them to promote themselves over their peers, but a responsibility to drive sustainable benefits for the organization. It is a responsibility to ensure the greatest return on the investment the organization placed in them, their team, and the assets they control.

In contrast, the narcissistic project manager sees each new project as another opportunity to promote themselves—to show how they get it done, not how they lead others to greater success and sustainable results. We intuitively know there is a better way. That better way is called servant-leadership as depicted in Figure 8.3.

What Is Servant-Leadership?

When it comes to leadership, there are many named styles, variations within those styles and countless evangelists and critics of each. I have been fortunate

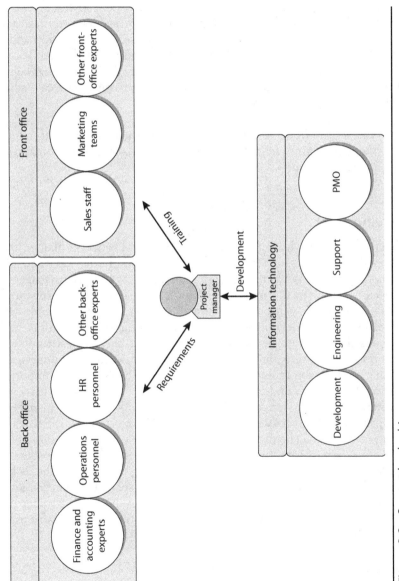

Figure 8.3 Servant-leadership

enough to work under many different leaders. In fact, I have worked with organizations that actively promoted servant-leadership, some who expressed indifference and even some who intentionally resisted servant-leadership. From these experiences I found the servant-leaders delivered the greatest benefits for all stakeholders, while still generating optimal long-term, sustainable growth. As a result I researched the concept of servant-leadership and found it to be ideal for all forms of leaders. However, I also found limited knowledge of servant-leadership in most industries, especially IT. Below I highlight some of the core attributes of servant-leadership in an attempt to reveal its benefits, particularly for today's IT project managers.

> *The servant-leader is servant first. It begins with the natural feeling that one wants to serve, to serve first. Then conscious choice brings one to aspire to lead.*
> —Robert K. Greenleaf (2002)

Serving First

Robert Greenleaf who coined the term "Servant-Leader" explained that the servant-leader wants to serve first and then finds leadership their optimal method of service. When the primary motivation for a project manager is their own career growth, the main aspiration is not placed on the organization's sustainable growth, but on the actions that most quickly promote that individual's success. Unfortunately these actions often directly conflict with the methods that generate sustainable results. In fact, the shortest route to near-term project success is through overworking staff, stretching budgets, and extending assets beyond their intended capacities. This is why it is important for the PMO to identify and promote individuals who seek to serve first.

There is nothing wrong with the career-minded project manager. Certainly few people are successful professionally who care little about what they achieve personally. The problem rests with individuals who do not understand they are a part of something larger than themselves. When the sole or even primary motivation is selfish gain, they are taking their eye off the ball that is the corporation's sustainable success. The proper servant-leader therefore can, and should still, pursue career growth. However, the servant-leader pursues their career aspirations as secondary to serving others—their staff, customers, organization, and stakeholders.

Stewardship

The Merriam-Webster (2008) dictionary defines stewardship as "the conducting, supervising, or managing of something; especially: the careful and responsible management of something entrusted to one's care." Servant-leaders understand their role as a steward of the company's resources. Servant-leaders, for example, are more likely to say *our team* rather than *my team* and *the budget* rather than *my budget*. Stewards recognize that resources are not given to them, but temporarily placed in their care with the expectation of strong returns. The best leaders therefore understand it is up to them to leverage those resources for optimal performance for the organization, not for their career. As stewards, servant-leaders do not possess anything the organization provides, but accept responsibility for the return of investment (ROI) of those resources.

Humility

It is difficult to find publications referencing servant-leaders because of the inherent humility these individuals possess. By nature, those who want to serve first are unlikely to seek public attention for their accomplishments. In fact the servant-leader often defers credit for accomplishments to their team, while accepting responsibilities for the team's failures. As a result these humble individuals rarely grace the covers of *Business Week*, *CIO* magazine, or other trade publications. There are exceptions though, for example, outstanding servant-leaders like Herb Kelleher, founder and former chairman and CEO of Southwest Airlines, who still receives press coverage for Southwest's success. Still, the vast majority of servant-leaders understand the success is not about them, but about their organizations, their staff, customers and other stakeholders who they serve. The result is humility that contradicts the over-the-top, self-promotion so dominant in more narcissistic managers.

Sustainability

Quick wins at the cost of future success is not an option for the servant-leader. Instead, in their role as servant first, good leaders understand that any solution that is not sustainable is not acceptable. Successful project managers realize their track record does not end when they move on, but instead, just begins to play. The successor who was developed and ideally chosen by the servant-leader is the final determinant in the predecessor's success. Leaders who insist team members find their own replacement before accepting promotions have the right idea. In contrast, managers interested in self-promotion often hop around, stretch the resources to the furthest extent, and leave a shell of an organization behind.

    Obviously deriving quick results is great and even necessary. Working hard and expecting your team to do the same is important. Pushing for results, stretching the project team for development, and driving unnecessary costs out of the system are all expectations of good project managers—especially in turnaround scenarios. The difference is that servant-leaders draw the line when cuts become too deep, excessive hours drag on too long or engineering cuts result in abysmal quality. The servant-leader does not achieve immediate success at the cost of sustainable solutions.

Continuous Development

All too often leaders who achieve a certain level of success feel they have *made it* and cease to focus on developing their skills. Assumptions are often made that because they have *been there, done that* for positions beneath them on the traditional organization chart, they know all they need to know to lead. In contrast, servant-leaders understand that we never stop developing our abilities and they recognize the importance of continuing to develop leadership skills. In fact, most good leaders do not consider themselves deserving of the description servant-leader. Instead, most of these individuals consider themselves students of servant-leadership, striving to develop the skills, but recognizing that becoming a full-fledged servant-leader in all one does is a nearly impossible achievement. As a result, most servant-leaders are life-long learners, excellent at proactive listening and never afraid to say, "I did not know that".

Servant-Leadership for Project Managers

So why should project managers care about servant-leadership? After all the very nature of a project is that it is not continuous—shouldn't we be focused on delivering the success of the project only? Of course not. Whether a contracted project manager or a regular employee, the company has invested in you to deliver the best results for the organization. You are expected to deliver a solid ROI from the project. That does not simply mean meeting the business objectives defined in your project charter. This does not mean just making sure the system works efficiently when delivered. And this certainly does not mean that the results delivered the day you close the project are the final determinant of the project's success. Instead, the PMO should define the project's success based upon the complete ROI.

The complete ROI for a project as depicted in Figure 8.4 looks far beyond the cost savings, efficiency improvements, or other direct benefits of the project deliverables. The servant-leader project manager recognizes that equally important are factors such as employee morale, staff development, sustainability of the solution and net impact to all stakeholders. If you have a reasonably defined scope, budget and time line, any project manager can deliver results when they care little for the complete ROI. If the PMO sets a tone that only the immediate results are important, then the solutions will not be sustainable. Employee burnout results in higher turnover and lower knowledge retention. Limited employee development stunts organizational growth and innovation. Maintenance costs bring the credibility of the team and solution into question,

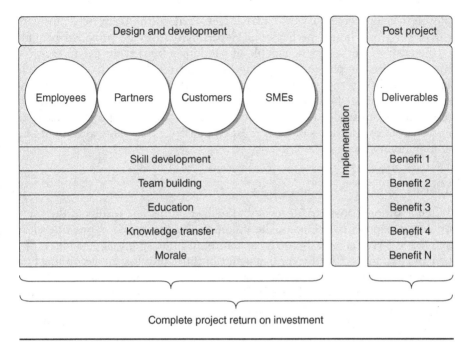

Figure 8.4 Complete project ROI for servant-leaders

resulting in lower acceptance levels and potential system replacements. Last but not least, a single-focus on the predefined users or customers might result in costs to other stakeholders who net out limited benefits or even an overall cost to the organization.

Turnaround Projects and Times of Crisis

The best project managers are often tasked with the immediate turnaround of failing projects. If you're reading this, it's clear your dedication to the field has probably placed you in at least one such environment. In these cases, the argument has been made that an emphasis on servant-leadership is not possible as the narrow focus on immediate results is necessary at the expense of factors such as complete ROI. While I agree these situations necessitate somewhat of a tunnel vision, it should not come at the cost of servant-leadership opportunities. The difference is in the messaging and the follow through.

When a crisis occurs in an organization, the servant-leader in everyone—from the CEO to the line worker—requires that we all focus on the near-term results that return the organization to sustainability. And so yes, perhaps employee development must take a back seat. Perhaps the team needs to work excessively long hours, perhaps one department must be provided benefits at the cost of another more capable of handling a burden for the foreseeable future. Maybe the project's complete ROI must result in an overall negative for the viability of the greater organization. This is not an unheard of circumstance. What must be clear though, is the overall emphasis on and commitment to servant-leadership. More than ever, servant-leader project managers in turnarounds and times of crisis must emphasize clear vision, alignment and accountability.

Vision

When additional costs are necessary to deliver immediate results at the trade off of other potential benefits, the vision on the greater good must be clear and precise. We can all espouse great communication spin that generalizes the benefits of a project to the company. But in times of crisis the vision must be precise. If the company is failing financially and the project delivers cost savings, the team must be told exactly the planned savings. Show how their time and commitment to the project nets the result that could save, or at least contribute to saving, the company. Translate those results into potential employee jobs that could be saved and then balance that with the costs to the team. As a servant-leader project manager it is up to you to ensure the project team clearly sees the benefits gained for the costs to those on the project.

Alignment

If your team is required to drive hard for results with a more narrow focus on the less-than-complete ROI, you need to ensure the greater organization is aligned with your charge. While the project team is heads down in their work, the last thing they need to worry about is whether or not an external contributor understands the importance of their work and therefore meets their deliverable timelines. If your boss charges you with getting the project done at potentially greater costs, you must respond appropriately. Ensure that your boss is doing everything in his power to provide you with all the necessary resources. If this crisis project has resulted in negative perception of project team members, it is your responsibility that they receive the credit due when they rally behind the effort to a successful implementation.

Accountability

Accountability now has a negative connotation, but in fact, the objective of accountability is a positive result. When a project fails, the servant-leader does not go on a witch hunt. However, they do ensure the same mistakes are not made again. If a failing project results in a negative impact to the team, the servant-leader project manager must be accountable for ensuring the same mistake does not resurface.

This goes beyond the standard postmortem analysis. Accountability for troubled projects and costs to employee morale or development means a follow through on any missed commitments during that project. Did the project team work excessively long hours for extended durations? Then it's time for a little rest and relaxation. Did staff members miss scheduled training events? Then it is time to reschedule the training that was missed and ensure their attendance. Did somebody go above and beyond the requirements of their role? Then it is time to recognize and reward them as well as ensure their performance review captures the contribution. Too often accountability results in documenting where a project went wrong and misses the accountability and follow through to staff. The servant-leader designed PMO ensures the process captures the sacrifices made and repays those sacrifices as needed.

Does a turnaround project or organizational crisis mean sacrifices are necessary from staff for a return to viability and sustainability? Of course. Does that mean it is an excuse to ignore the principles of servant-leadership? Of course not. In the end most projects face bumps in the road that must be resolved through additional sacrifices by servant-leaders at all levels. The occasional extra hours and the periodic over-extensions in different areas are all part of the responsibilities of servant-leaders, at all levels of the organization. Every time someone is required to put in a little overtime or miss a happy hour with co-workers is not an excuse for a bonus check or huge proclamation of success.

These are all realities of today's business environments. But when the hours are excessive for too long or large sacrifices are made as a result of a crisis or failing project, the servant-leader project manager must ensure the vision, alignment, and accountability are in place for the staff and resources entrusted to them.

Summary

I laugh a bit to myself when I hear someone suggest that servant-leadership is soft management or too weak for today's tougher business climates. It is clear to me that these individuals do not fully understand the concept. After all, when you consider the challenges in balancing the paradoxes of servant-leadership, it is by far the most challenging leadership style. The servant-leader must care about the team deeply, but must discipline them quickly and clearly when necessary. The servant-leader must be humble while effectively influencing leaders across the organization. The project manager who is focused on servant-leadership must still deliver rapid results but never at the cost of long-term benefits.

Balancing these issues effectively while remaining focused on the long-term sustainability and benefits of the organization is anything but soft or weak. In

Figure 8.5   Servant-leaders wanted; no wimps allowed.

fact those critics who do understand servant-leadership argue that it is too idealistic or impossible to achieve in today's work environments. It might surprise others that I agree.

I agree in the sense that becoming a perfect servant-leader is as impossible as becoming a perfect leader, period. We are, after all, human. We do make mistakes. Nobody reading this will become a perfect servant-leader. Is this a hard pill to swallow? Perhaps it is, but only if you aren't able to recognize your own shortcomings and therefore lack humility. This, by the way, means you are not a perfect servant-leader. But that does not excuse us from striving for the idealistic leadership character that servant-leadership represents. In the same manner that your best programmer, CEO, mailroom clerk, or leader of the free world still makes mistakes, so too do we as servant-leader project managers. Where you can set yourself apart from others, though, is by avoiding the mistakes of toxic leaders and by striving for the better way. How you ask? You do this by striving to be a servant-leader in your role as a project manager and by setting the example for other project managers in your organization to follow. There are many other authors, teachers, and practitioners of servant-leadership in the world, thankfully. Many of whom explain the concept and challenge you to succeed in a different manner than I have here. To that end I am glad this book includes a reference to the importance of servant-leadership for today's project managers. If this is your first introduction to the concept, welcome to the club. I now challenge you to further develop the greatest project management attribute of all by honing your skills of service to your team, organization, and greater community through servant-leadership (see Figure 8.5)

References

Greenleaf, Robert. 2002. *Servant Leadership: A Journey into the Nature of Legitimate Power & Greatness*. New York: Paulist Press.

Merriam-Webster Online Dictionary. http://www.merriam-webster.com/dictionary/stewardship. (Accessed 2008)

9

Creating High-
Performance Teams

For many organizations, not just project management offices (PMOs), the cartoon in Figure 9.1 strikes a familiar chord. Sometimes the actions of management, though well intended, can simply dampen the spirits and challenge the attitude of even the most committed and capable of high-performing employees. Aside from seeking to avoid the obvious miscues, how should management go about creating and maintaining high-performance teams and an environment that is conducive to high performers? But first, to answer the question there needs to be a clear understanding of what a high-performance team is and the value to an organization that such a team is capable of producing.

A Common Challenge to Creating
High Performance

Not long ago, creating a high-performance PMO team was a challenge faced by Alberto, a first time PMO manager. Alberto wanted to build a best in class PMO and high-performing team of project managers. He had inherited a newly formed PMO that was struggling in a number of areas, namely people, process, and tools. The PMO team members represented a mix of good technical talent and experiences, but none of them had any kind of formal project management training. There were few processes to speak of for both doing the right projects and doing projects right. Other than desktop tools, there were no systems in place for project and resource management and no platforms in place for collaboration and document management.

Figure 9.1   PMO comics—managing performance and morale

Alberto wanted to do a gap analysis to assess the true current state of the PMO and to determine what improvements in capabilities needed to be addressed to get the PMO off the ground and performing at a higher level. Management, however, did not want to take any more time and effort to conduct studies and present findings as they had gone down this path three times in the last five years with consultants and on their own. They wanted action; mainly, they wanted Alberto to implement a project portfolio management (PPM) system for the organization and the sooner the better. Additionally, prior to any discussion about forming a steering committee and putting in place processes for project selection and governance of the PMO, which they already had with consultants on previous occasions, they wanted to first see the PPM system in action.

Against his better judgment, Alberto implemented one of the leading PPM systems that management had looked upon with favor. With the support of the vendor, the installation of the system and training of the team went quite smoothly. Project managers were using the tool effectively, in terms of features and functions, but there was quite a large inconsistency in the degree to which the project managers followed any kind of methodology for managing their projects. Some project schedules were overly simplified and incomplete. Other project schedules were overly detailed with no discernable structure to the tasks. Beyond a basic project charter, project schedule, and project status report, few if any of the project managers had a project plan or any of the supporting project plan components such as a document of requirements, a scope plan, a risk management plan, a plan for quality, a communications management plan, work packages and a work package list, and other useful checklists.

By the end of the first year, which passed by all too quickly, Alberto was extremely frustrated. He had not built his best in class PMO and his PMO team was not performing at a level that could be described as high. The PPM system, however, was implemented and there was a lot of data in it, but the integrity of the project data was highly suspect. Without the project management training that the team needed and the organizational project management processes that the PMO needed, the overall results achieved in the management of projects was no better than it actually was in the days when the organization did not even have a PMO nor a PPM system. Despite a year's worth of hard work and best intentions, not to mention expenditures, the high-performance team and best in class PMO that Alberto wanted to make a reality did not come to fruition.

Recognizing High-Performance Teams

So what are high-performance teams and how do you create and maintain them? High-performance teams are groups of skilled people who are committed to a common goal, performance measurements, and an approach for which they hold themselves mutually accountable. With this definition, it is easy to see why Alberto failed in his efforts to build a high-performance team. He did not provide his team with the skills, goals, measurements, and approach to performing the work that they needed to far exceed, not to mention barely meet, expectations. Additionally, high-performance teams are created by being genuinely interested in helping each team member excel, not just implementing management edicts without adequate planning and preparation. In Alberto's case, the rush to prematurely implement the PPM system demonstrated more interest in pacifying the ill-placed wishes of management than in ensuring the PMO team had what they needed to be successful project managers. It was far easier for Alberto to kowtow to management and avoid a sensible management discussion than it was for him to place the needs of his direct reports, first and foremost, at the center of attention.

When a high-performance team is working well together, they can achieve results that are only limited by imagination. High-performance teams are a tremendous asset to the organization and they are not limited to only those large multi-national firms with a large number of employees and tremendous budget for employee development. Commenting to the importance of high-performance teams to organizations of all sizes is Chris Musselwhite (2007), the founder and CEO of Discovery Learning, "An important leadership competency for any size organization, the ability to build and lead high-performing teams is especially critical in small-to-midsize businesses." Musselwhite offers the following three characteristics of highly effective teams: effective teams understand the big picture, effective teams have common goals, and effective teams work together as a unit.

In high-performance and effective teams, each member of the team thoroughly understands the goals and outcomes to be achieved by the team. They have a full and complete vision of that which is to be achieved and a context for what represents adequate achievement, better-than-expected achievement, and extraordinary achievement. High-performance teams do not seek to *gold plate* their work; that is, performing additional scope beyond that which has been agreed to by the project sponsor. But they do seek to exhibit excellence in their work, the results of which are extraordinary. For example, successfully planning for and mitigating risks to keep the project on time and on budget can be an example of very tangible project work that when performed well can pay a big dividend and when omitted or not performed well can jeopardize the potential success of the project. Likewise, taking the time and effort to understand project procedures and communications can be the difference between a project team that performs well and a project team that encounters endless execution difficulties. Understanding the big picture inherently leads to an understanding of the context of project team roles and responsibilities.

High-performance teams have common goals. These common goals are clear and concise and provide measurable objectives such as how much and by when. High-performance teams make use of their objectives. They are not simply viewed as an end point; rather they are used to gauge progress, make improvements, and of course achieve the final objective. High-performance teams understand that team goals take precedence over individual goals. A developer might produce great functionality in a system, but if the requirements are wrong the stakeholder of the project will not be satisfied. Likewise, a business analyst might provide a detailed analysis of functional requirements, but if the developer doesn't understand the business use case models presented by the business analyst the project could very well be at risk from the start. High-performance teams work together toward a common goal, not just completion of their assigned tasks.

Additionally, high-performance teams communicate and collaborate well. They have a heightened sense of awareness about the project and the progress of the project that is being made by each team member. High-performance teams seek to understand and alleviate risks and constraints. Team effectiveness is enhanced through cooperation and assistance to one another. When execution difficulties are encountered, high-performance teams seek to fix the problem and then the process, but never look to blame.

Creating High-Performance Teams

So how do you create high-performance teams? Far too often for many organizations there is a belief that all that is required to create and maintain high-performance teams is to hire the best of the best and pay them well. There is nothing wrong with hiring the best possible people and paying them competitively, however, more is required to bring a team together and have it perform at a consistently high level. There are a number of management strat-

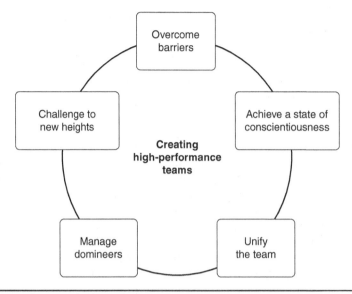

Figure 9.2 Creating high-performance teams

egies for building high-performance teams that organizations of all sizes have used successfully. At the core of nearly all of these strategies are five key steps that transform just about any group of individuals into a high-performance team (see Figure 9.2).

Overcome Barriers

The first step of the process involves overcoming barriers to effective teaming. As Lauren Keller Johnson (2005), renowned business writer for Harvard Business School Publishing, explains, "It's not easy, pulling a group of diverse individuals together to work as a team. Barriers abound, in the form of fierce territoriality, incentive systems that reward individual rather than collective achievement, and mistrust spawned by an acquisition, merger, or major internal restructuring." Some barriers can be truly difficult to overcome, but many barriers can be reduced in size or knocked down altogether. One critical success factor in dealing with barriers is information sharing among the team. High-performance teams do not work in a vacuum. They inherently need to know the context of both the project and the work environment. In order for skilled individual contributors to blindly give their commitment and loyalty to the team and the work effort at hand, they need to first be given all of the *truth cards*. Once they have processed and internalized the pertinent facts to the satisfaction of their real and perceived need to know, then these high-value individual contributors can set aside their concerns and become allegiant to the cause and to the team.

Sometimes sharing information can be difficult. Some information is not going to be pleasant no matter how it is given, but that doesn't mean that it is not the right thing to do. Richard was a PMO manager at a telecommunications company with eighteen direct reports. The company was outsourcing its information technology (IT) department and an announcement had already been released to the employees. Richard's PMO would be completely eliminated and the transition plan called for 14 of the 18 members to be given a separation package at the end of the quarter. Richard and the remaining four members of his team would stay on for another three months to transition the work and train the new team, the staff of the outsourcing vendor. After that they would be given a separation package. Though this news and the details were not pleasant to give or receive, sharing information did enable the team to perform their expected and needed duties as well as plan for their departure in the best possible, most productive manner.

Sharing information, however, doesn't mean that you disclose company secrets or highly confidential and sensitive information. Paul, a professional services PMO manager for a private company, found this out the hard way. During the height of the dotcom era, a rumor was spreading within the company that it was in discussions with a much larger firm to be acquired by that firm. All of the employees had stock options and IPOs, mergers, and acquisitions were occurring throughout the industry, therefore, it was hard to keep secrets a secret.

One day in a state of excitement, Paul's manager, the VP of sales and marketing for the firm, let it slip that the rumors were true and the company was in serious talks with two firms, each of whom wanted to acquire it. Paul then told just one person on his team, a trusted senior project manager and by the end of the day the entire PMO team knew. Day after day went by with more hall talk and office gossip about the status of the acquisition rather than the real work of the company.

At the next PMO staff meeting, one of junior project managers asked Paul for an update on the acquisition talks. Rather than squelch the discussion, Paul took it upon himself to share with the team whatever information that he had. After a few weeks of PMO meetings and updates, one of Paul's project managers confronted the CEO of the firm who was also the founder and majority shareholder and demanded that the he wrap the deal up quickly before the window of opportunity closed.

Naturally the CEO was extremely unhappy about the leaked information and traced it back to Paul and the head of sales and marketing. In the end the acquisition did not go through largely because the CEO felt the price offered for the firm was not commiserate with its value. Nonetheless, many of the employees of the firm, including most of Paul's project managers, were disappointed and felt resentment toward the CEO and management for not reaching a deal. Paul's sharing of information, though it seemed like a good idea to him at the time, resulted in countless hours of productivity being squandered away with more of the same to come. Rather than overcoming a barrier, it simply raised it.

In additional to sharing information there are other tactics that can be used to overcome barriers. Barriers can exist on account of lack of processes, tools, and training. For those not familiar with how organizations mature their capabilities, processes can be viewed as bureaucracy and a barrier to creativity and innovation. If such processes are a barrier, they need to be improved. If the mindset of the performer is simply one that is a low level of maturity, then that mindset needs to be refreshed. Similarly, not having the right tools and needed training can result in a significant barrier that makes it difficult for the team to achieve a high level of performance. For many organizations seeking to create high-performance teams, there are no better tactics for overcoming barriers than to equip the team with streamlined and effective processes, useful and usable tools, and training and learning resources.

Achieve a State of Conscientiousness

Step two of the process requires achieving a team state of conscientiousness. Though it might seem inconsequential and unnecessary, the high-performance team actually needs to know that it is a high-performance team and not just a collection of skilled individuals. This is their state of conscientiousness. Leadership guru Kevin Eikenberry (1997) presents seven key attributes that describes teams that are highly productive and successful and suggests that a discussion of these attributes with the team enlightens them and moves them to higher levels of performance. This enlightenment and inner challenge to perform at the highest of levels is the esprit décor of team conscientiousness. The seven attributes Eikenberry identifies that serve to define team state of conscientiousness are:

1. Commitment. To be committed, individual contributors must see themselves, not just being a part of the team, but belonging to the team. Nearly always they report to a manager who is not on the team and who does not belong to a functional department. However, for the duration of the project, their allegiance to the team needs to trump their loyalty to their functional department.

2. Trust. Trust is given. Team members must give their faith to each other to work as a team, to support each other, to complete their assigned work, and to behave in a professional manner. Trust is reinforced through actions such as completing assigned tasks and providing early notice of issues and execution difficulties.

3. Purpose. A strong purpose is required to create a team state of conscientiousness. If the purpose is not understood or of no importance, the team does not come together. Teams that understand how they fit in the organization, know their roles and what is expected of them, and see how their efforts make a difference have a sense of purpose and state of mind.

4. Communication. Effective communications are required for the team to establish and maintain its state of conscientiousness. Good communications facilitate constructive dialog and teamwork. Poor communications almost always makes a problem bigger than it is and harder to solve than it should be. Effective communications requires continual humanization. Emails to distribution lists and use of collaboration platforms and tools can always be effectively employed, but they need to be reinforced with direct, face-to-face dialogue.

5. Involvement. To maintain the team state of conscientiousness, everyone has to be involved. Though some work is clearly more important than other work, everyone on the team has a role to play and work to produce. Despite differences in skills, knowledge, and experiences, the involvement and contributions of all team members are honored and respected.

6. Process orientation. Process orientation enables the collection of individuals to come together and perform as a single team. Members of high-performing teams are typically highly skilled individuals who are accustomed to process-oriented thinking and often have additional insights to offer to streamline and improve processes. An occasional process deviation is warranted, but too little adherence to the process might well be a sign that the team could be performing at a higher, more consistent level.

7. Continuous improvement. High-performance teams understand the value of continuous improvement. First time errors and execution difficulties are acceptable, but repeat errors and difficulties are not. If the team allows repeat errors to occur and does not take advantage of improvement opportunities, it soon loses it state of conscientiousness. Conversely, the more that team focuses on improvement and reduction of errors, the more heightened its state of conscientiousness becomes.

Whether discussing these seven attributes, a subset of these attributes or even identifying additional attributes to discuss with the team, bringing out the factors that are required for the collection of individuals to come together as a high-performance team is a critical step to take. It sets a teaming expectation beyond the accomplishment of individual tasks and it fosters a state of conscientiousness that can be seen and felt and that produces results.

Unify the Team

In the third step of the process, the team is unified. There has been much written about approaches to unify teams and the discussion is, of course, not limited to just project management teams. Regrettably, far too often, the discussion of how to unite teams goes far beyond practical tips and techniques and into a world of theoretical dimensions and proportions with untold workshops, classes, and situational exercises that can be applied. Not long ago I was asked to audit a team unification workshop. Over the course of three days the participants, who were members of large companies sent out to receive leadership training, listened to a few lectures and mostly engaged in one after another team unification exercise such as building bridges with popsicle sticks and paperclips, building towers with index cards and scotch tape, and designing an egg package with foam, Saran Wrap, and paper to save an egg from breaking when dropped. Over the course of working together in these team unifying activities, a number of lessons were learned and everyone had an enjoyable time. However, at five grand a pop most companies, and certainly PMOs, cannot afford to invest the time and money that it takes to send the managers and team leaders to these venues. At the end of the day it is the practical learning points of the class, not the games, which need to be brought back and put to use.

For many PMOs, a spot on excellent approach for unifying teams that is easy to grasp and implement is offered by Lonnie Pacelli (2005), internationally recognized author and President of Leading on the Edge™ International. In his article "Five Simple Strategies for Unifying Your Project Teams," Pacelli highlights reasons why project teams don't gel and offers a five-step approach to unify them:

1. Establish clearly defined roles that make sense for the project team. Use whatever standard the organization has to configure the team, but don't hesitate to add to that standard if additional roles are needed as well as to eliminate non-performing roles or roles that simply don't make sense for the project. It is not uncommon that projects, especially larger ones, encounter execution difficulties and in some cases out right fail. Statistics of project performance by such organizations as the Standish Group show time after time that project management is a discipline that has room for improvement. Even with the best of people, processes, and tools, anything and everything can, and often does, go wrong. With less, the odds are highly against the project completing on time, on budget, and within the agreed to level of quality. Hence, it is terribly important to recognize the natural tendency of those on teams to spend more time and effort on fixing the blame, rather than the problem.

2. Foster loyalty. Pacelli advises that a penalty free and confidential environment must be established so that the team can debate ideas and solutions openly and passionately without unfair fighting, personal attacks, and finger pointing. A good rule to observe that has a catchy undertone is 'What happens in the project team meeting, stays in the project team meeting.' There is no faster way to jeopardize a unified team than to have its members engage in gossiping and to be bad mouthing each other to outsiders.

3. Establish the team's rallying cry. Just a few words such as *Where's the beef*, or *Just do it*, or *One for all, all for one*, can go a long way to unify the team around a common purpose. If a team needs to be conscious about the need to quickly get a workable product out as opposed to engaging in the gold plating of the features of the system, a rallying cry and mantra of *that's good enough* can help keep the team on point. If on the other hand the team needs to be challenged to innovate and separate the product of the project from that of the product capabilities of the competition, a rallying cry of *dare to be different* might serve the team well.

4. Hold them accountable. High-performance teams are typically comprised of overachievers, however, the team and each of its members individually need to be held accountable for not just showing up and working hard, but for delivery. Team members must not only deliver their assigned components, but they must also have an understanding of what all the members of the team are doing. Project team members are like pieces of a puzzle. Rarely do they work in a vacuum without the need to interact and exchange issues and ideas. One approach that might alleviate a difficulty for one project component might negatively impact another. For example, a decision to improve on the user help of a product being developed might result in a reduction in the amount of training documentation required as part of the project effort. While the team member responsible for delivering the training documentation component might be in favor of this, the team member responsible for developing the user help might not be as favorable to the idea. Hence, the project team needs to realize that it is not only accountable to the project manager, but also accountable to each other.

5. Recognize them. Unifying project teams and keeping them unified requires finding ways to frequently recognize the team. Project victories come in many shapes and forms and you don't have to wait until the end of the project to celebrate success. In fact, long, complex projects are arduous and they take quite a bit of effort to drive through their completion. Project teams, even high-performance teams, can get discouraged from time to time. Celebrating project milestones along the way can help the team keep in perspective all that they have achieved

and enable the team to remain committed and enthusiastic finishing that last, long mile of the project. A good practice for recognition that many PMO managers advocate is to publicly recognize team results but to privately recognize individual heroism. This can be wise for two reasons. First, sometimes individual recognition, especially for heroism, can be a sensitive issue to other members of the team that might have performed brilliantly all along the way thus making their contribution seem less heroic. Rather than being a positive event, the individual recognition only serves to demoralize the team. Second, individual recognition can often be viewed, whether accurately or not, as hero worship. For many organizations, hero worship is a tell-tale sign of a process defect. Rather than fix the process, the organization encounters the same problem over and over often rewarding work around efforts rather than ensuring that such difficulties do not continue to be experienced. Naturally, if individual recognition among the project team is warranted it should be given. Also, if it is appropriate for the recognition to be public, that is perfectly fine too.

Manage Domineers

In step four of the process for building a high-performance team, high performers who are domineering are identified and properly managed. In many organizations, highly successful and results-oriented contributors can exhibit strong Type A personalities and can become difficult to work with. Though the concept of Type A and Type B personalities emerged in the 1950s as a personality theory useful in determining risk factors for coronary heart disease, the term was quickly adopted in the business community and to this day is used to describe worker personality types. The Type A worker is impatient, highly competitive, aggressive, and incapable of relaxation. The Type B worker, in contrast, is laid back, relaxed, and easy going. Needless to say the aggressive and sometimes egotistical behavior of some Type A employees can be over the top and impact even the best of teams in a negative way.

Commenting on managing high-performance nightmares, Marcus Miller (2007) advises, ". . . there's a price to pay if overachievers aren't properly managed. It's important to recognize when a drive to succeed creates destructive behaviors, and to intervene with a solution to grow corporate performance for the long term." Though most people think of domineering high performers in a role of sales management in which results are to be achieved at any and all costs, such performers exist in all areas of the organization, including the PMO.

Domineering performers are not always a problem. In fact, in many cases they can drive their component of the project through helping other team members with their components at the same time. However, sometimes domineering performers can have a negative impact on the project team in two ways. First, they are reluctant to consider that the project might be in trouble and require changes to the project baseline. Rather than proposing needed changes, they are inclined to continue to push ahead harder and faster in the hope of achieving their objectives and the objectives of the project team. Sometimes this is simply not possible. Second, the excessive drive and aggressive relations with others can quickly sour the project team. Though generally well-intended, overly eager Type A personalities tend to rush through things. They always have the time to do it over or to work late to meet an unreasonable schedule, but they seldom have the time to patiently plan the work in the first place. Domineering performers on a high-performance team need to be managed. Left to their tendencies and predilections, more times than not domineering performers find a way to make both significant contributions in some areas of the project and in other areas alienate and irritate the members of the project team. It is usually best to manage domineering performers in the quiet sanctity of one's office as opposed to on the spot in the heat of an altercation. Members of the team take notice of management action and it is typically not necessary to make more of an incident than it actually is. They see and appreciate your attention to the matter as well as any improvement in the behavior of the domineering team member.

Challenge to New Heights

In the fifth and last step of the high-performance team building process, high performers are challenged to reach new heights and rewarded for the results. The key is to challenge project team members to new levels of performance that are achieved both individually and as a team. Whereas many organizations like to think they are committed to improvement, it is not all that uncommon to find in organizations of all sizes and types that a high degree of resistance to change exists and can be as hard to break through as a brick wall.

Approaches that aid in challenging high-performance teams to reach new heights are to foster a mindset that is always open to, and awake for, embracing change and turning conflict into motivation. What motivates people to be open to change and to view problems as opportunities? For most individual contributors, including project team members, it is a combination of three things: a positive attitude, a sense of recognition both internally and by others, and money.

For most people a positive mental attitude simply does not pop in mind by itself. How we choose to feel is a decision that each of us makes every day. Some people view the glass as half empty and others as half full. But attitude problems really manifest themselves when people view a half full glass as nearly empty. There are obviously physical aspects to maintaining a positive attitude such as regular exercise, eating healthy, getting the rest you need, and giving yourself enough time to work through the day's activities and tasks at a civilized pace. But there are also common obstacles that all but ensure the demise of positive thinking. Exaggerating problems, ignoring the positive aspects of a situation, and taking things too personally make it almost impossible to maintain a positive attitude. In setting the high-performance team up for success, it is important to ensure a positive attitude by the team and all of its members. Nothing propels a positive attitude more than success. An inability to produce a successful outcome is a failure only if the team and organization are not able to learn from the experience and, therefore, to do considerably better the next time.

As a leader of a high-performance team, it is essential to recognize good performance. High performers especially do not like being taken for granted; often all they want is that their efforts do not go unnoticed and unappreciated. To recognize good performance, you have to see it and preferably see it first-hand. You must not only take time to recognize what your team is doing well, but you must provide timely and accurate feedback that is sincere. It is of little value if the feedback is inaccurate and late and even worse if the feedback is insincere. These things can greatly demoralize and irritate high-performing teams and high-performing individuals. Give out compliments whenever they have been deserved. When you have challenged the team to higher levels of performance and you observe them working exceptionally well together and meeting the challenge, a simple *great job, keep up the great work* goes far in keeping the momentum strong and morale high.

When you have challenged the team to higher levels of performance, to be open to change, and to turn conflict into resolution and problems into solutions, remember to show them the money. The individuals who make up high-performance teams need to have incentive compensation. There is nothing worse than paying an employee a fixed salary with no ability to be rewarded for their contributions to the team and to the organization. Management teams that are serious about continuous improvement and challenging performers to new levels are eager to tie-in some form of direct compensation. As project managers are expected to deliver projects on time and on budget, many PMO managers view that as the core expectation of the job and sufficiently addressed by one's salary and appraisal. Rather than incentivize expected performance, a pool of incentive compensation is established for the team that is potentially available based upon the contributions of the team and individual team members to the development and implementation of continuous improvement suggestions. There is no shortage of opportunities to improve on the capabilities of the organization especially when problems are truly viewed as opportunities in waiting.

Approaches for such compensation can be based upon a fixed, budgeted amount that is established annually or even more exciting are approaches that pay the team or individual a percent of the assessed and expected benefits to be realized for the improvement suggestion. Some organizations choose to leave the incentive opportunity uncapped; others might establish a ceiling that represents the highest level of payment. High-performance teams enjoy a challenge. When that challenge is backed up by real money, it is taken more seriously.

Summary

Creating high-performance teams is more of an art than a science. While there are a vast number of opinions and points of view for what works best and prescribed roadmaps for how to create and maintain high-performance teams, no two groups of individuals come together as a high-performance team in exactly the same way. For companies that have a track record of not being able to get the most out of their teams and numerous institutional obstacles to teaming, it might be worth the time and expense to attend team building workshops offered by reputable firms with experience and a successful track record in helping organizations build teams and develop teaming and leadership skills.

In the context of the PMO in which teams typically work well together as a matter of formal training in project management and the almost inherent nature of project managers and project team members, elevating the game to higher levels of team performance need not be an elusive goal. Practical steps to create high-performance teams that are relatively easy for any PMO to take include removing obstacles that stand in the way of the team, achieving a team state of conscientiousness, unifying the team, managing domineering personalities, challenging the team to higher levels of performance, and rewarding them for their achievements.

Building high-performance teams makes for good business and most organizations are quick to acknowledge that any investment made in building high-performance teams is quickly returned as measured by better end results achieved. The optimistic team views the glass half full and the pessimistic team views the glass half empty, but it is the high-performance team that tops up the glass and gives it to the customer.

Questions

1. What are three characteristics of high-performance teams?
2. Why is it important for high-performance teams to see the big picture?

3. Why is it important for high-performance teams to have common goals?
4. Why is it important for high-performance teams to work well together?
5. What five steps transform groups of individual contributors into high-performance teams?
6. What kinds of barriers can prevent teams for performing effectively?
7. In what ways can information sharing help to overcome barriers that teams face?
8. In what ways can information be detrimental to the team?
9. To what degree can processes, tools, and training facilitate the removal of barriers that teams face?
10. From a high-performance perspective, what is the difference between exceeding expectations and "gold plating" one's work?
11. What is a high-performance team state of conscientiousness?
12. What are the attributes of the high-performance team's state of conscientiousness?
13. Why is it important to unify the high-performance team?
14. What five steps facilitate unification of the high-performance team?
15. In what ways can Type A domineering performers both serve the team as well as exhibit destructive behaviors?
16. In what ways should domineering performers be managed?
17. What techniques can be used to challenged teams and individuals to higher levels of performance?
18. In what ways can incentive compensation lead to higher levels of performance and organizational improvement?

References

Eikenberry, Kevin. 1997. "7 Key Dimensions of High Performance Teams." http://www.ezinearticles.com. (Accessed June 12, 2008)

Johnson, Lauren. 2005. "Overcoming Barriers That Destroy Teams." Harvard Management Update, vol. 10, no. 9. (Accessed June 12, 2008)

Miller, Marcus. "Managing the High-Performance Nightmare: High-Performing Managers Can Torpedo Team Performance . . ." http://www.allbusiness.com. (Accessed June 12, 2008)

Pacelli, Lonnie. 2005. "Five Simple Strategies for Unifying Your Project Teams." http://www.asme.org. (Accessed June 12, 2008)

Musselwhite, Chris. 2007. "Building and Leading High Performance Teams" http://www.inc.com. (Accessed June 12, 2008)

Executive Insights

Project Management and Successful Teams

Tom Boyce

Program Manager, Nuclear Regulatory Agency

Introduction

I recently assisted my youngest daughter during a high school activity that is part of the school's homecoming celebration. Each of the classes is provided a theme in which to design and decorate one of the hallways around the school. This year's theme was *Let Us Entertain You*, and my daughter's sophomore class decided to decorate their hall as if it was a monopoly board game with some expansion of that idea.

The parents are only allowed to be involved in limited supporting roles. The students must design, identify materials, and produce all art work and structure. In other words, the parents provide food and materials and get out of the way. The students are extremely limited in the amount of time available to them—they start at 10 am on a Saturday morning and must have the hall completely done by 7 pm that night; completely transforming a 100-foot hallway. It is clear that there are some budding project managers among her classmates. Even more encouraging is that they naturally adopted one of the key approaches to successful project management.

The students who did the planning also completely delegated various construction elements to other students so the Free Parking, Boardwalk, GO and other board pieces were handed off for painting and construction to teams of two or three students each. These students clearly delegated responsibility for delivering to others. They also knew that given the time constraints they could not possibly oversee individual activities to the extent they liked, therefore they needed to trust each team to deliver on time. Their roles were to coordinate, not execute each phase. The teams working on the individual pieces for the hallway knew that by 7 pm that evening they had to be finished and lined up in the order their parts were to be placed in the hallway—meaning they also understood their responsibility and knew that delivering late or incompletely was simply not an option. Over the next few pages I explore how what these students seemed to intuitively understand applies to formal project management practices.

Project Management Leadership and Team Success

So what does my example have to do with formal project management and engaging a PMO in executing projects? In my example there wasn't anyone trained in project management practices to designate as the master project manager. Most PMOs I have been involved with seem to assume that having the PMO accountable for the delivery of all facets of the project is the natural way to run projects.

Leading from the PMO with an overarching project manager who is going to be held accountable for all facets of a project is, in my view, the opposite of good project management. Typically the project manager is skilled in the project management discipline, but unlikely to be an expert in the subject area of the project. I have established PMOs in some of the organizations I have worked in and I needed to convince the PMO director that they were not instantly in charge of all projects.

This is not because team members do not know what is needed or how to deliver. Your staff is typically quite skilled and knows what they need from other parts of the organization in terms of project support. Depending on one person, the individual from the PMO, to manage every aspect of delivery from all the various groups on a complex project is expecting too much of the project manager.

The project manager might be an expert in project management practices and earned value management, but it is highly unlikely that they are an expert in software development or all facets of building construction. The PMO might argue that they are responsible for ultimate delivery on time and on budget and therefore must be fully in charge of all aspects of the project. However, this is not acknowledging that clear accountability and definition of team member's roles and responsibilities is one of the key success factors to executing and delivering a project's goals. After all, it is the team members that you must depend on to deliver those board game pieces on time and designed correctly. Correspondingly, the project manager and the PMO must vest responsibility with the teams across your projects for success to be a reasonable option.

Cause and Effect

So if the PMO are experts in project management practices, and we have application developers and other team members who know their jobs, why do so many projects fail to meet budget or on-time delivery promises?

In some cases it appears that the PMO and its processes support these mistakes. Project status meetings are held in which team members expect to gripe about other teams not delivering on time. They look to the PMO's project manager to track who is behind and flag potential problems in the schedule. Status meetings discuss how others might crash the schedule or use slack somewhere in the schedule to allow the other teams to meet the next milestone.

It has to be clear to the teams and team members who are responsible for those milestones. The teams must be empowered to raise risks and trust that other teams deliver as expected. Not only must everyone's roles and responsibilities be clearly defined, but these roles and responsibilities must be known across the project.

This approach needs to come from the beginning and be designed in. Usually by the time the PMO realizes there is a problem, it is too late to do anything to correct it besides adjust the schedule, which is what disciplined project management practices are trying to avoid.

In the Beginning

One of my basic assumptions is that if the team has any control, it is over the scope of the project. Teams typically do not have budgetary control and usually have little input into setting the project due date. Starting with a clear project success definition provides the foundation for team control over the project scope. It often falls to the project team to succeed or fail with little or insufficient sponsorship and involvement of project stakeholders. Defining success and getting at least initial written approval of the goals of the project by the stakeholders is the first step in this success.

Simply defining the project goals in terms of scope, significance, and time is critical to identifying the staff and skill sets needed. Knowing what success looks like to the project sponsor helps the project team member's focus on a successful outcome. It is assumed that all of this is documented in some form of a project charter, and this charter identifies not only the business objective, it provides a high-level description of the project objectives and initial milestones and deliverables. It is not often that you have a Monopoly board to replicate with the design clearly laid out well in advance.

The project charter is the basis for delegating the responsibilities to the individual teams, and if used correctly, should help the team members control scope and change throughout the project. The next step is to make sure the teams know what is expected.

Clear Roles and Responsibilities

With the project charter identifying the skills needed, you can identify teams and individuals for your project. You also need to develop a project-oriented organization chart. I caution against linking this to any thoughts of existing organizational hierarchy or reporting structures. This document should be all about the project. Regardless of whether the teams are co-located physically or geographically dispersed, the idea behind this chart is to make it clear to everyone on a team what they are responsible for, and what the other teams are responsible for.

This chart can identify key responsibilities for each team member as it relates to the project milestones. The goal is to not have some fuzzy definitions like software development team, but rather concrete deliverables that support the project's success. There should be zero ambiguity about what the teams, and to the extent possible, the team members are responsible for; not only to each other, but to the overall project. This chart should be formally documented, published, distributed, and posted. This is a hugely important step in shared accountability. The message is clear that the project or program leadership knows who and what it takes to succeed.

Enabling Success

So if the project charter clearly defines what is needed, and the teams understand their roles, the project is off to a good start. The PMO can help track project status, assist with scheduling, and provide feedback to everyone as to how things are proceeding. Is this alone enough?

You must demonstrate to the project members that they have input and control over the project throughout. They need to understand that it is the team's responsibility to hold each other and the project sponsor to the original scope. If an important part of the project, interim deliverable, or key component was initially overlooked, it must be understood that any changes impact either the schedule or cost. Having a defined and accepted change management process should partially address this need. Part of the early acceptance of the project charter should be the acknowledgment that any later changes have to be signed off on by the project sponsor and accepted by the team.

While scope control is an obvious tenet of project management concepts, you must also provide the team with some way to raise concerns when the change management approach is either ignored or not accepted by the sponsor or others. The best means for this is to establish a simple but formal risk management approach in every aspect of the project.

I have found that risk management tends to be the most underutilized, yet most powerful tool available to allow everyone a voice in identifying potential problems. Used correctly, team members at any level can establish a risk, which must be addressed. It must be clear that there is no intent to *shoot the messenger*, but rather that formal risk identification is expected and encouraged. Every process, document template, work package, and nearly every meeting should have someone asking the question, 'what have we overlooked, what could go wrong?'

It should be expected that the team regularly reports on risks, and combines the risk reports with regular feedback on project progress. Risk management taken together with change control is crucial to the team in managing the project to a successful outcome.

Communication and Leadership

You have delegated responsibilities to the teams and made it understood they should let you know if you are not abiding by the original agreement. The program, project, or organization leadership needs to be open to input from the team members and demonstrate that they are truly supportive. This goes beyond recognizing that risks and problems occur. Management must listen and provide feedback throughout the life of the project (Ladika 2008, pp. 71–73).

Management must be open to discussing any issue or concern, even if it does not directly relate to project outcomes. On almost any team there seems to be the one or two dominant personalities who tend to overshadow other voices around the table. These other voices need to be heard—and it up to the leadership to make sure that happens.

Project Control

The PMO plays a major role in coordination, tracking, and monitoring project status. The teams must be enabled to have direct control over their pieces of the project. What the team wants and needs is some way to raise concerns that are heard across the project, and know that they can count on other teams for delivering on time and on budget.

The PMO can enable this transparency across the project and, as mentioned, organizational leadership must listen and act effectively. If the project leadership demonstrates through their actions that they are there to assist the teams in getting the right resources and addressing concerns, the teams knows that they truly have a voice in controlling project outcomes.

Team Staffing

I was tempted to move this discussion up behind project definition and establishing the project charter, which is where it naturally fits in the project planning process. Given the complex nature of organizations, the varying maturity and structure of project management offices, project sizes, and project types, there are no set answers to team staffing. In the best of all worlds, a program or project manager is able to hand pick the best people for the tasks at hand, be given 100 percent authority for all necessary resources, and have a project backer who is engaged on a daily basis.

You seldom get to pick the perfect team. This ideal concept of project management seldom occurs. The students involved in the hall decoration project were the ones who happened to show up that day. They represented a random 10 percent of the total class population.

In your work place you probably have more control than this. However, given the nature of projects and the order that tasks need to be performed, you might well need to restructure teams or bring in specialists with specific business knowledge at certain points. The approaches to empowering the teams through clearly defined roles and using change and risk management should be applicable to whatever team staffing approach is needed by your organization. If your teams know you are listening, they should not hesitate to point out when they need your help.

Conclusion

Put the project first! Despite the many books and articles on project management office styles, project matrices, project management tools, and high-performance teams, it is all about completing the project successfully. For the students, the hall judging competition occurred at the end of the day, ready or not. They had to put aside some normal teenage personality issues and focus on completing the project. Defining the project and project success through a clearly defined business objective is step one.

Establish project leadership from those who know what needs to be done. The PMO plays a large role in project success, but true subject matter experts need to be in control of the project. Project management practices are necessary for success, but not sufficient to guarantee success.

Use the project charter to establish what skills are needed and clearly outline the roles and responsibilities of the team members. The project charter identifies, at a high level, the key milestones and deliverables for the project. It should also be clear to each team member what their role is and how they help achieve the goal.

Publish and make widely known not only a synopsis of the project goals but a team organization diagram. Establish an expectation of shared accountability early—make it widely known what is expected of the teams and to the extent possible, what is expected of the individual team members. This is even more important in today's world of geographically dispersed teams (Bourgault 2008).

If nothing else you have to give the team the responsibility and authority to control what they can control. This does not mean the project will not change, or that the project sponsor does not get to add features after the project starts, but it does mean that this cannot happen without gaining input and feedback from the project teams. Without being given this control; the project simply becomes another job to do.

Listen, communicate, and act. Let the teams know they can come to you or the organizational leadership with problems. Use the risk management reports to know what needs to be dealt with, and act. Listening effectively is not all about problems; let the project teams know that they can come to you with a variety of issues and that you want to hear their views.

Understand that staffing the team can be more art than science. Regardless of the structure the Project Management Institute has provided us in terms of formal project management practices, it is all about the people. If you are given the chance to pick your team among the best people your organization has to offer, congratulations!

Otherwise you need to be flexible in your approach to team staffing; there is no one answer on any given project or usually throughout the project life cycle. If you are listening and paying attention, you know when a change needs to be made. Finally, recognize their achievement and celebrate your successes!

References

Bourgault, Maro, Nathalie Drouin, and Émilie Hamel. 2008. "Decision Making within Distributed Project Teams: An Exploration of Formalization and Autonomy as Determinants of Success." *Project Management Journal*, vol. 39. S97–S110.

Ladika, Susan. 2008. "Positive Response." *PM Network* vol. 22, no. 9.

Better Processes Mean Better Performance

Steve Romero

IT Governance Evangelist, CA

Improving the performance of personnel is a constant goal for organizations in every industry today. Companies make significant investment in countless approaches and programs designed to increase the performance of their people. Most of these approaches are focused on affecting human behavior and the capability of individuals, including leadership development, management skills, shared values, business acumen, core competency knowledge, and technical proficiency. Companies seldom pursue process improvement and process management as a means to make their people perform better.

Process improvement efforts are almost always associated with increasing business efficiency or reducing cost. Process management is generally viewed as an operational discipline rather than a means to get people to perform better. In fact, processes are usually viewed negatively and thought of as inhibitors of individual and team performance. Mention the word process and you are likely to hear:

- ◆ Processes are bureaucratic!
- ◆ Processes slow me down!
- ◆ Processes take too long!
- ◆ Processes are too complex!
- ◆ Processes are difficult to understand!

Processes in and of themselves are not inherently bad, but we hear these statements over and over again. In fact, they are true . . .

- ◆ when it is a poorly designed process;
- ◆ when the process is inadequately implemented; and
- ◆ when the process is not properly managed.

Some companies even go so far as to say, "We don't really have processes." Let's dispel this myth. All enterprises, companies, and organizations have processes. They might not be apparent because the processes are unknown, unnamed, and therefore unrecognized. They are ad hoc, informal, and inconsistent. They might not be formal processes, but they are still there.

For companies that do recognize they have processes they frequently find them to be fragmented, haphazard, disjointed, and disconnected. They are incoherent, complex, and chaotic. They lack continuity, coordination, and integration. They are likely neither managed nor measured.

It is the lack of good process management discipline that makes processes bad. In addition to the primary goal of increasing customer satisfaction, well-managed processes make work possible and practical. In fact, improving the performance of people is what I personally consider to be the number one benefit of processes and good process management. Good process empowers workers and enables them to succeed . . .

- ◆ when the process is defined and well designed;
- ◆ when the process is established by thoughtful, thorough implementation; and
- ◆ when the process is properly supported, managed, and governed.

I have found that few organizations realize how processes improve the performance of their people. In fact, organizations are more concerned with how to force the processes on their workers. "How do I get people to follow the process?" I hear that question again and again. It is actually a kinder, gentler version of the question I am frequently asked (with a more menacing tone), "How do I *force* people to follow the process?" Or, "How do I get the *authority* to force people to follow the process?" Many people believe processes require an iron fist.

The words force and process should never be used together. Force never succeeds when it comes to process compliance. Please note I used the word compliance as opposed to enforcement. Even the word compliance is problematic. Consider the formal definition:

Com-pli-ance, n. 1. the act of conforming, acquiescing, or yielding. 2. a tendency to yield readily to others, esp. in a weak and subservient way. 3. conformity; accordance. 4. cooperation or obedience.

I am comfortable with only one word in this definition—cooperation. That is the human behavior I am seeking if I want my process to be successful. I want people to willingly participate in the process, as opposed to conforming, acquiescing, or yielding. I want people to embrace the process because the process makes them perform more effectively.

I wince when I hear the question of how to force people to follow a process and I always answer the question the same way—with a story. In this story I am the director of the PMO and the process owner of all project management processes. One day a furious project manager approaches me and says, "This process is terrible!" It is natural to assume that this negative statement causes me to have a negative reaction. You might think I would react defensively to this indictment on my process. Not at all.

My first response upon hearing this angry statement is to wonder to myself, 'What is wrong with my process design?' I then review the design and find it to be reasoned, rational, thoughtful, creative, meticulous, and valid. The process is completely aligned with the customer and it is delivering the appropriate value. It is devoid of nonvalue-added tasks that result in waste and it is a great example of a best practice. So the process design is not the problem.

My next thought is, 'What did I do wrong when I implemented the design?' I review my implementation project deliverables and find I appropriately documented procedures, established tools and templates, implemented support systems, provided and validated thorough communication to all stakeholders, and successfully delivered training to process team members. So it wasn't the implementation.

My next thought is, 'What is wrong with my management of the process?' I take a look and determine I am doing a good job of monitoring customer requirements, best practices, and process performance. My metrics and measures are sound. However, I may not have been responding to process issues and problems as quickly and forcefully as I should have been to ensure success. Therefore, my management of the process life cycle could be improved.

So, it is not a process design problem or flawed implementation, but rather some mismanagement. After taking a hard look at the process, it was not a problem with the complaining project manager. Yet, this three-tiered thought progression is the exact opposite of most responses to somebody upset about a process. In just about every case when somebody complains about the process the first reaction is that something is wrong with the person who is griping and we need to figure out how to force them to follow the process. I contend that in nearly every one of these cases the problem is not with the person, but with the process. It is due to either the design, the implementation, or the management of the process. It is rarely because there is something wrong with the person.

I have yet to see force work when it comes to process compliance, or how it is otherwise mistakenly referred to, process enforcement. The iron fist approach nearly always fails eventually. People find a way to avoid something they don't want to do or undermine something in which they don't believe.

How do you get people to follow the process? By showing what is in it for them—*employee empowerment*. I have mixed feelings about using that term because I have found it to be overused and misunderstood. I have seen plenty of companies that say they empower employees but I have seen few that do what is necessary to actually empower them. Consider the following critical dimensions of employee empowerment:

- Defining and designing work that is possible and practical
- Providing employees with the knowledge, skills, and competencies required to do the work
- Assigning accountability and giving employees the authority to make decisions to successfully complete the work

Processes and good process management provide all three of these dimensions. A well-designed, properly implemented, expertly managed process is enabling, liberating, and empowering for the people participating in the process. Processes and good process management improve performance by:

◆ Focusing the work on customers, products, and services
◆ Providing workers the knowledge and perspective to make their own decisions, which reduces or eliminates nonvalue-added work i.e., checking, supervising, and controlling
◆ Reducing disputes because everyone is aligned around a common goal
◆ Increasing efficiency by reducing overhead, errors, and cycle time
◆ Making work repeatable and predictable, which enables greater flexibility and performance improvement

The primary goal of any process is to produce a product or deliver a service that delights a customer. This requires everyone working on the process to have an acute understanding of the outcome of the process (product or service) and an appreciation of the customer it serves.

A good process design defines and describes the activities and tasks needed to get the work done in the most efficient and effective manner. An adequately implemented process provides the mechanisms (systems, tools, templates) and the knowledge and understanding (through appropriate and thorough communication and training) required to complete the activities and tasks. The process provides customers the ability to initiate the work. The process makes team members accountable for completing defined activities and tasks and provides workers with the authority to make decisions to ensure customer and enterprise needs are met.

Processes promote collaboration and team behavior. The process provides an end-to-end view of all of the work required to succeed. This understanding and appreciation aligns everyone on the process team around a common goal instead of on individuals preoccupied with isolated tasks. This helps to foster an appreciation for how each team member contributes to that common goal, which enables and encourages team members to assist one another. Processes discourage finger-pointing and advance problem-solving because everyone associated with the process functions as a team.

The process provides the metrics and measures necessary to determine if targets are met. Process management provides the mechanisms to continuously improve team performance and increase customer satisfaction. Processes provide stability and predictability to everyday work and reduce the frustration and anxiety of constant firefighting. This stability also enables agility in the face of change because precise adjustments can be made in a systematic way with measureable results. People willingly follow a good process because:

◆ They understand how it benefits the customer
◆ They understand how it benefits the enterprise
◆ They understand how it benefits members of their team

- They understand that the process makes the work possible and practical
- They understand that process improves their performance
- They understand what it is in it for them

I must admit that not everyone is ready to join process teams. Employees have worked in environments where they were not required or even allowed to make decisions for a long time. Their work was not defined by process and initiated by customers. They were told what to do by their managers and when to do it. This function-centric model is very different from a process-centric model. A process team member needs to think and make decisions to succeed. To do this effectively, they must:

- Execute select process activities per the design but think process
- Act with understanding of the customer, business, and process
- Be a self-directed member of a process team that shares a common purpose and works toward a common goal with the context and empowerment to make decisions
- Appropriately takes initiative to meet customer needs
- Perform work, solves problems, owns results
- Contribute to continuous process improvement

Organizations need to be aware of the transformation that must take place to move people from a function-centric to a process-centric model. This is a major change in culture for most enterprises and the people in them. Essential elements to establishing and institutionalizing processes are:

- Foster and build enterprise expertise and capability in process design, process implementation, and process life cycle management
- Foster and build enterprise expertise and capability in organizational change management because establishing and managing processes is a transformation effort intended to affect human behavior
- Involve as many people as practical—in every phase and aspect of process management—and listen to them
- Communicate, communicate, and communicate! And when you think you're done communicating, communicate some more

It seems like a relatively simple formula for success, but it is incredibly difficult. It requires courage, diligence, and patience because it is a major transformation and the path to success is uncertain and unpredictable. It requires fortitude, perseverance, and stamina because there are missteps and mistakes. It requires process management knowledge, skill, and competency, which few companies have.

Summary

The benefits of good process have been studied and well documented by renowned industry leaders such as Michael Hammer, Geary Rummler with Alan Brache, and Jack Welch of General Electric. Companies have seen significant performance improvements through Six Sigma and LEAN process frameworks. There is a mountain of evidence and numerous examples of the power and promise of good process. But what excites me the most is what good process means to people—to the workers in an enterprise. Processes bring meaning to all work, no matter how small the task. People are no longer vague cogs in the machine. They are critical members of a process team. They are the ones with the accountability and authority to delight the customer. They know they are essential to the success of the enterprise. They matter and they know they matter. Place them in this situation and just watch how they perform.

10

Establishing a PMO:
A Practical Roadmap

Organizations have struggled with establishing their project management office (PMO). Though every project management consultant and vendor has a roadmap on hand for how to go about setting up a PMO, for most organizations many of these roadmaps lead to costly expenditures and time-consuming management and consultant activities that could have been avoided, or better utilized, at a different time in the birthing and maturity of the PMO. And in some cases the directions of the PMO setup journey as prescribed by some of these project management vendors and consultants seem to be in the incorrect order as if someone clicked on the reverse route button (see Figure 10.1).

Case Study

Consider the following real-life scenario. Let's introduce George, the chief information officer (CIO) of a fairly large firm. George decided that it was time to establish a PMO within his information technology (IT) department. As the firm had an ongoing relationship with a Big 5 consulting firm, George and the leadership team brought in the consulting firm to provide a recommendation and expert opinion for how to best go about setting up the PMO. George's company enjoyed a healthy and growing industry and with their strong financial performance, budget for the PMO was available and expenses were not an issue, at least not initially.

Figure 10.1   PMO comics—PMO setup

Gap Analysis

The first order of business was to engage the Big 5 consulting firm. George had hoped to get a roadmap from them for quickly getting the PMO up and going and he had hoped to get it sooner rather than later. The initial scope of work that the consulting firm took on was to perform an assessment of the as-is state. This involved taking an inventory of tools, processes, and skills as well as performing interviews with members of the leadership team, both within and outside of IT, to arrive at a prioritized list of needs for the PMO. This effort alone took six weeks and cost over fifty thousand dollars.

Presentation of Findings

Next the consultant findings and recommendations were presented. The assessment findings came as no surprise to George and the management team. In essence they just paid the consultant to tell them what they already knew. The main and immediate recommendations of the consultant dealt with organization, tools, and training.

Organization, Tools, and Training

Shortly thereafter, George and the leadership team re-organized the IT department, established the PMO, and named the PMO manager and the initial team of project managers and staff that made up the PMO.

After organizational decisions were made, the PMO manager was given the task to implement a project portfolio management (PPM) system. The prevailing thinking was that without a PPM system the organization could not select the appropriate projects to manage, manage those projects correctly, or utilize the shared resource pool of technical professionals effectively. Through no particular fault of any one person, the effort to implement the PPM tool took over a year. Furthermore the collective project management capabilities of the team did not improve with the new tools; rather they got worse because of tool limitations and usage issues. Additionally, all those involved, the project managers, the project team members, and the stakeholders were becoming increasingly frustrated as project work was becoming more and more bureaucratic without any noticeable or appreciable gains.

Following the PPM tool implementation was a series of project management training classes. Designated project managers in the PMO were streamed for project management certification training. Other members of the team and project participants, including management, were streamed for training in project management fundamentals. The project management training initiative phase of the PMO plan took almost one full year. By the end of this period a few of the project managers in the PMO had become certified project management professionals (PMPs). Though there was appreciation by all involved that the training in project management provided by the project management training firm was professionally conducted, the overall sentiment was that the project management performance of the team post training was no different than the project management performance of the team prior to the training. There was also considerable frustration and disappointment that, though the project management instructor was entertaining and made the classes enjoyable, the fact of the matter was much of the project management training in the classroom simply could not be effectively applied to the workplace and everyone knew it.

Aftermath

What followed was the logical conclusion that despite reorganizing the IT department and forming a PMO, despite implementing a PPM tool, and despite delivering a curriculum of project management training, processes really do matter. Though the organization had a legacy systems development life cycle (SDLC) model that was the approved and formal approach for managing projects, it was in fact out-of-date and did not serve any of the project types of the project mix of the PMO particularly well. Over the next three months George worked with the PMO manager and two of the senior project managers to truly put in place the much needed processes and knowledge assets for project management. They also put together the requisite policies for governance, tool usage, and management of the PMO. By the time George and his PMO team were done with this process effort, they had also intuitively and iteratively arrived at a short list of well-defined PMO goals as well as metrics for measuring the performance of the PMO. This also led to a common and shared vision throughout the organization for the PMO, something that had been lacking since its inception, and an understandable and agreed to value proposition for the PMO as a key enabling, perform, and support organization.

George's subjective assessment and conclusions were twofold; first, the perceived value of the PMO only started to resonate with the leadership team once processes and metrics were put in place; and second, the investment made in time and money of the various PMO setup phases were disproportionate to this perceived value (see Figure 10.2).

It was then that George had an epiphany. Everything that he had done in the last two and a half years to get the PMO established, staffed, and operating had been done in the incorrect order. If George could do it all over again, he would have gone about establishing the PMO in the reverse order of what actually had been done.

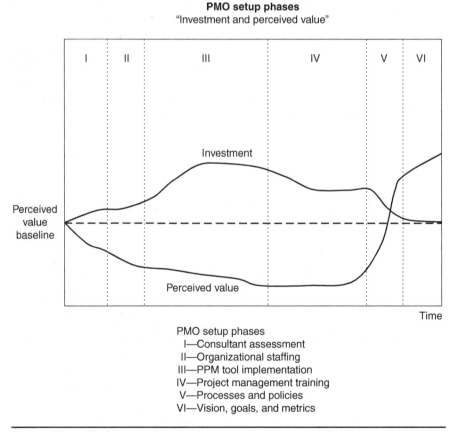

PMO setup phases
"Investment and perceived value"

PMO setup phases
I—Consultant assessment
II—Organizational staffing
III—PPM tool implementation
IV—Project management training
V—Processes and policies
VI—Vision, goals, and metrics

Figure 10.2 PMO setup phases—investment and perceived value

In hindsight, the initial study, assessment, and recommendation by the Big 5 consulting firm was not money well spent. The lengthy and expensive implementation of the PPM tool was not only problematic because it did not have effective processes in place first, but the PPM tool selected might well have been the inappropriate tool for the company. By the time that was discovered, it was too late to change that decision. The organizational structure and staffing decisions that were made early on without enough accompanying structure, in terms of processes and policies to ensure a smooth and effective PMO operation, resulted in too much disruption, confusion, and execution difficulties. The investment in project management training could have been much better spent had some, if not most, of the training been based upon specific needs and problem areas as opposed to a curriculum mostly designed to meet the certification needs of project managers per the Project Management Body of Knowledge (PMBOK®) framework of the Project Management Institute (PMI).

Until the processes and policies of the PMO were established, debated, vetted, communicated, and strictly adhered to, the operations of the PMO did not start to run smoothly and effectively. Additionally, the time and attention given to the vision, goals, and objectives of the PMO proved to be far more than a trivial exercise or organizational lip service, rather it became a solid foundation and guiding set of boundaries for what was to be in, or outside of, the purview and scope of the PMO.

A Practical Roadmap

Vision

A practical roadmap for establishing a PMO starts with visioning (see Figure 10.3). Few would argue that an organization needs a vision. But for many people, vision is unnecessarily either an abstract construct or it is an endeavor that is believed to be limited to the top executives of a company. Nothing could be further from the truth. Every business unit, from a one-person virtual business unit to a fully staffed organization needs and can benefit from having a vision, including the PMO. Consider the following:

◆ The business unit is responsible for producing new capabilities and breakthrough results for the organization
◆ The business unit is responsible for turning around specific areas of poor performance
◆ The business unit is responsible for prioritizing a limited amount of investment dollars and organizational resources
◆ The business unit is responsible for developing short- and long-term goals in key performance areas

- ◆ The business unit is responsible for institutionalizing new processes, tools, collaboration, and behaviors
- ◆ The business unit is responsible for providing cross-functional support and skills improvement
- ◆ The business unit is responsible for eliminating duplication of effort, repeat mistakes, and misallocation of resources

If any one of these statements is true, an organization is well-served by having a vision and strategic plan. Though most business units of an organization, such as a PMO, need a vision and strategic plan, few actually have them and, in some cases, some organizations *think* they have them, but in fact they don't.

There are a number of barriers that prevent PMOs from establishing a clear vision. In many cases, awareness of the value of vision is a key issue. Is it enough for the PMO to deal with the projects and issues it faces on a day by day basis? Probably not. The absence of a vision and plan nearly always causes organizations to become reactive and remain in a continuous firefighting mode of operation, rather than proactively meeting the needs of customers and stakeholders. The symptoms of lack of awareness of an organization's vision can take many shapes. Organizations with too many initiatives, such as

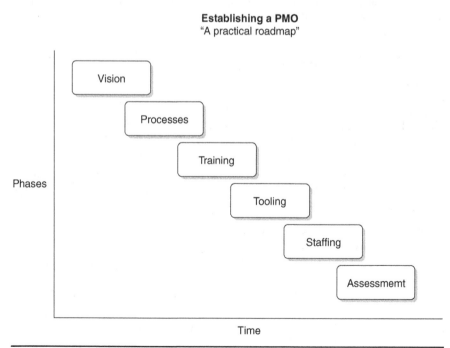

Figure 10.3 Establishing a PMO—a practical roadmap

PMOs with too many projects, are in a constant state of activity, but much of the activity does not produce successful results. Another symptom of the lack of awareness of the vision and strategic plan shows itself when it comes time to prioritize projects and allocate budget and resources because it is not possible to accurately discern how much money to give, whom to give it to, and how to identify the top, most critical projects to the organization.

Desire can also be a real and pressing barrier to clarifying a vision for the PMO. In many cases there can be a lack of desire to take the time needed to create the vision and strategic plan for the PMO. Sometimes this is because of previous experiences and attempts to create an organization vision that in the end proved to be an unproductive exercise. Most business executives and organizational managers and leaders have more than a few good stories to tell about lengthy offsite meetings and heated discussions all intended to produce a single vision statement. However, more often, the lack of desire to do this work comes from the lack of training and first hand experience in how effective vision and plans can be in energizing and driving an organization.

Perhaps the most significant barrier to the PMO in establishing its vision and plan is the amount of know-how that is required. How do you go about creating a vision for the PMO? Who needs to be involved? How do you go about it? How do you recognize a strong vision and plan from a weak one? How do you gain executive support and sponsorship? How do you communicate and engage with other groups to achieve organizational buy-in for what you are doing? Gaining this know-how is critical for creating and sustaining the vision and plan of the PMO.

One approach to use in considering the basic elements for a vision and plan is shown in Figure 10.4. Far more important than attempting to establish a PMO aligned to a prescribed theoretical model is the determination of the elements that make up the raison d'être of the PMO. Few if any vision statements include the desire to be a project management control tower, a fighter squadron, a weather station, or even a strategic PMO. As the PMO evolves from birthing to various stages of growth and maturity and takes on additional areas of scope within the enterprise, the vision of the PMO evolves along with it. Most importantly, it is not the goals and objectives of the PMO that determines how advanced or mature or valuable the PMO is, rather it is the metrics and demonstrated measure of attainment that is the best indicator of how successful the PMO is and of how much value to the organization it has delivered. Hence, it is critical and imperative for the PMO to first clearly establish its vision, goals and objectives before any other decisions and activities.

Processes

Processes do matter. Effective and usable processes are nearly always the most significant indicator of an effective PMO. Yet time after time organizations

Vision and planning checklist

Check each box (yes or no)	Our vision includes	Alignment to customer needs and business strategy	Executive sponsorship and support	Organizational buy-in and adherence
A clear statement of who we are				
Clear goals to be pursued				
Measurable objectives to be acheived				
A defined process model				
Technology architecture and tools				
An optimized work environment				
Metrics to measure organizational progress				

Figure 10.4   Vision and planning checklist

have difficulty even talking about PMO processes much less defining and adhering to them. Three common pitfalls can be summarized as follows: assuming that processes exist when in fact they don't; implementing tools prior to establishing processes; and confusing processes with methodology.

Why wouldn't a PMO take the time to first establish its processes and best practices? One reason often cited is the belief that many PMOs, maybe most, are simply not created with the idea in mind to spend much time on process documentation but rather to solve a pressing business problem. For example, noted PMO expert Mark Mullaly (2008) writes, "For most organizations, the establishment of a PMO has emerged out of crisis." Many attribute the period of time leading to Y2K as the definitive acceptance of PMOs within the IT department. Virtually every large firm implemented one or multiple IT PMOs or program offices for Y2K readiness. The task at hand was not to define PMO processes and best practices, at least not initially. Rather, it was to assemble a team of non-existent experts to quickly develop a plan to understand and mitigate the risks and to perform the application upgrades and maintenance work required to ensure that corporate systems and applications would run in a new date-field world.

The decision to establish PMOs can be also driven by the business necessity of implementing complex applications with a higher degree of success as measured by cost and schedule overruns. It is becoming increasingly common to see PMOs established and solely dedicated to the implementation and ongoing development and support of such applications as Enterprise Resource Planning (ERP), Customer Relationship Management (CRM), and Business Intelligence (BI). Companies like Chicago-based Wrigley's are known within the SAP community for their exemplary operational excellence running the entire firm on a single SAP image. Driving the implementation, management, and use of SAP is the Wrigley SAP PMO. In addition to SAP, PMOs are being strategically used to successfully implement other high-value enterprise applications and platforms including Siebel, Oracle, Lotus, Hyperion, and Business Objects. Sometimes these PMOs are established and intended to operate for a fixed period of time, but often they become a permanent fixture of the organization because of the value they deliver.

For many large worldwide companies, minimizing the duplication of projects and more effective utilizing, as well as reducing technical support resources has led to the creation of PMOs. For such global corporations, it is not uncommon to find multiple versions of the same project underway with little to no cross organization management or sharing of information. Such projects can range from the periodical upgrades of the desktop operating system and applications to the wide variety of infrastructure projects and everything in between. While enterprise PMOs are often thought of as advanced PMOs that are engaged in a high level of portfolio management and alignment of the project mix to the strategic priorities of the company, the reality is that for most enterprise PMOs the first order of business is to conduct a thorough project inventory and to put in place the management mechanisms to consolidate and better manage duplicate projects and resources. This effort alone can take an enterprise PMO two to three years to accomplish.

For these PMOs that are created out of an existing or impending crisis, it is understandable that attention to process detail might take a back seat to the pent up and pressing business priorities and project workload awaiting the new PMO. It is not that these organizations don't value processes rather that they often assume that whatever approaches to project management and processes that are already on hand such as the Systems Development Life Cycle (SDLC) or the Solutions Delivery Model (SDM) would be sufficient for the needs of their PMO. In effect, they fall into the common pitfall of taking for granted that effective and usable processes exist when in fact they do not.

The urgency to implement tools is another leading pitfall that can interfere with or minimize the attention given to processes. In some cases, there is a tendency to rush through the much needed process and policy work of the PMO to focus on the implementation of a project management system or portfolio management application. In other cases, there is a tendency to intentionally put off this work until later under the belief that it is easier to address PMO processes and policies once all of the tools are in place. Both of these tendencies contribute to a snow-ball effect in which more and more problems and execution difficulties are encountered and collectively enlarge the impact to the organization until such time as the PMO addresses its processes and policies. Surprisingly the rush to implement tools before processes is typically not vendor-driven. In fact, some of the project management vendors are the strongest proponents and advocates of process. Leading PPM software companies provide comprehensive process frameworks as a core part of their offerings. Noted PMO guru Terry Doerscher of Planview often makes the important distinction between an approach framework that describe processes in a general manner and a functional framework that goes several steps further and serves as an integration platform to graphically depict process interdependencies and provide step by step contextual guidance and tool integration. Doerscher (2008) writes, "I don't care whose process framework you use; the important thing is that you HAVE one."

Implementing tools before processes can be problematic for several reasons. It can be timely, costly, and exhaustive to roll out a project management application without first having a clear view of the business use case. What business problems are we seeking to solve? What modules and features enable us to address specific areas of need? How and when do the various users within the organization use the application? What tool usage behaviors need to be learned or changed? What decisions does the application enable us to make and when do we make them? All of these questions must be answered and the degree to which an organization answers them is typically represented by the presence or absence of processes. Whether accidental, ad hoc, or found within the playbook of a process framework, processes exist inherently.

Another problem that often occurs when implementing tools before processes is the after-the-fact, and regrettable, conclusion that the project management tool selected was not the appropriate tool for the PMO. Take the case of Tom, a PMO manager in a mid-sized IT department. As a Microsoft-centric shop, Tom and the team were quick to implement Microsoft Project Server for their new PMO. The company already used Microsoft SharePoint quite extensively, so the decision to implement Microsoft's enterprise project management tool seemed to be a natural one. Six months into the implementation Tom and the team realized that despite their best efforts the project management application wasn't meeting their needs, and that it was primarily a process problem not a tool issue.

After spending the time needed to establish an effective process framework for the PMO, it became clear to Tom and the team that their business needs could have been better met by a simpler, lower cost, Software-as-a-Service (SaaS) solution. Fortunately for Tom they were able to change course. Oftentimes, once a tool decision has been made, it can be difficult if not impossible to switch to another, better-fit tool. That a tool switch can be done technically is of no great debate, rather it is organizational tolerance, or intolerance, for management decision-making mishaps that more times than not leads to sticking with a bad tool decision.

Confusing Methodology with Process

Perhaps the most challenging pitfall in establishing processes that PMOs face is the confusing of process with methodology. As described in Chapter 3, although some people use the terms process and methodology interchangeably, there is in fact, a significant difference. For example in the context of a PMO, a methodology such as a project management methodology (PMM) is typically limited to the description of the approach that is to be taken. Noted project manager guru and PMI Fellow Max Wideman (2006) defines a PMM as the set of guidelines and principles that are applied to a type of project. Methodologies usually exist in a document format. Many organizations, typically large companies, have a methodology document in Microsoft Word or Adobe PDF format that, when printed, exceeds several hundred pages.

Such methodology documents give the appearance of good project management, but in reality lengthy methodology documents have many limitations. Often they are out of date and even more often they are simply not read by those in the organization for whom they are intended. But the greatest limitation of all to the PMO is that methodology documents only provide descriptions of the *what to do* of the work to be performed and even that is limited to just the project effort.

Methodologies do not provide the much needed organizational context for how the *what to do* of the work to be performed actually gets done. What management policies need to be adhered to in order to start the work effort? How do the project review mechanisms actually work? For each work step, what outputs are mandatory and what outputs are optional? For each functional task of the project including communication and collaboration, what tools, platforms, and applications are available and/or required to be used? Where multiple tools and platforms exist, what is the prescribed guidance or policy for tool usage? What interdependencies, relative to the projects of the PMO, exist within the organization and how are they managed? A PMM document does not answer these questions. Hence, it is inherently of limited practical value.

Processes as a Functional Framework for Doing the Work

Project management processes, on the other hand, do answer all of these questions and provide a functional framework to the organization for doing the work, for exhibiting the appropriate techniques relative to the project type characteristics and needs, and for using the appropriate tools, applications, and enterprise infrastructure of the company. Where a PMM tends to be rarely read static documents that are seldom updated and almost always offline to the project effort, project management processes are typically found in the form of intranet-based project management process frameworks that are frequently accessed, continually updated, and used as a driving part of the project effort.

As noted project management expert George Pitagorsky (2004) writes, "It is widely accepted that when a process is described in common terms, and is repeatable and managed, performance quality is higher and more consistent." Simply put, project management processes drive higher levels of performance whereas a PMM, at best, potentially provides a theoretical common approach and common language for project management.

It is well worth the time and effort for PMOs to avoid these traditional pitfalls related to establishing effective and usable processes. Three good rules of thumb are: don't assume processes exist, don't implement tools prior to processes, and don't confuse process with methodology. Failure to address processes prior to tool implementation leads to execution difficulties and increased time, cost, and organizational frustration. Sooner or later the leadership team has an epiphany; they need to urgently establish a process framework and they wished they had done it earlier. The importance of processes to a PMO can't be overlooked or taken for granted. Borrowing from the punch line of the famous A-1 Steak Sauce commercial, "Yeah. It's that important."

Training

There is no better training strategy for the PMO than to take full advantage of both the outside training opportunities, including those provided by registered education providers in project management and the internal use and leverage of the project management process functional framework. There are those who would also advocate the establishment of a community of practice, but the community of practice should not be a replacement or substitute for the functional process framework, rather custodians and ombudsmen of it.

For many PMOs, taking advantage of outside training is a worthwhile endeavor. Most project management training classes provided by reputable firms provide excellent content and knowledgeable instructors. However, there are hidden costs to project management training; especially fee-based training provided by registered education providers, training vendors, and third party consultants that need to be taken into consideration. There are hidden costs to all fee-based training in the form of applicability of the agenda and ability to retain and project management is no exception.

For example, project managers attend training for a number of days, study and learn a great number of new topics, capabilities, and areas of knowledge. Some might even apply for and take testing to achieve a professional credential. But after the class ends and after the professional credential has been attained, the initial enthusiasm from attending and participating in the class quickly wanes as the project management practitioner returns to the office and quickly realizes that it is not possible to effectively apply the material learned in the classroom in the workplace.

Soon the inability to apply that which was learned in the classroom becomes an inability to retain. Adding to this hidden cost of training is the fact that oftentimes in project management classroom settings the agenda of the training class is filled with many topics that might not be immediately applicable to one's job or one's company. Tom, a project manager who recently attended a three-day project management class states, "In my last class, many of the topics were stretched out to fill the agenda. The three day class could have been easily held over just one day. Little of what was covered will have any real impact at our company."

The hidden cost of project management training can be seen by a high-level assessment of the degree to which such training is paid for and realized (see Figure 10.5). For example, if 100 percent of the training is paid for, but only 70 percent is realized, then the amount of the hidden cost is 30 percent. In determining the overall effectiveness of the training investment, a number of factors are useful to consider. Three key factors are the applicability of the training to the job, the applicability of the training to the workplace, and the ability to retain the training.

It is not uncommon for many PMO managers to lament the fact that the hidden cost of project management training can be as high as 75 percent of the actual cost. For example, such would be the case if only half of the training agenda was truly applicable and of that applicable amount only half of that could be, in fact, realized and retained. Of course this is a subjective measure

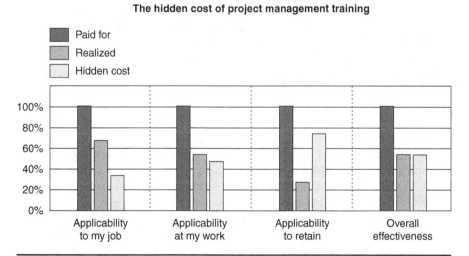

Figure 10.5 Hidden cost of workplace training

and, once training is paid for, that money is gone. But think about it. If you send 20 project managers to a three-day class at a cost of $3000 per project manager and, in your best judgment, you assess that only 75 percent of the class is applicable and of that applicable amount only one third of it is truly realizable and retainable, then 50 percent of what you have paid for has no value. Of the $60,000 spent, $30,000 was wasted.

As a more practical and cost effective means of project management training, many PMOs are using their project management process functional framework for training purposes. This makes all too much sense. The project management process functional framework is in effect both the always-on real-time playbook for the PMO that guides execution as well as the de facto PMO knowledge framework that provides practical training and continually improves via process owner stewardship.

Assume the PMO determines that improvement is needed in project risk management, for example. Rather than send the entire team of project managers to a risk management class and potentially incur the hidden cost of training related to applicability and retention, send just the process owner responsible for the project management process framework risk processes.

In some cases this might be the PMO manager. In other cases it might be a senior project manager or delegate of the PMO manager. In either case only this individual, as process owner, attends the fee-based class. The process owner has the prescribed duty to determine how best to tailor and apply the risk management training back into the project management process *functional* framework for the PMO. If needed, in-house training by the process owner can be scheduled and provided for the team. Otherwise the appropriate PMO communication can take place informing all involved that the designated project risk management areas of process framework has been updated and is available for both functional guidance and on-the-job training use.

Fee-based project management training and the project management process functional framework of the PMO naturally complement each other. There are those who advocate that all fee-based training should be attended with the added intention of incorporating it into the working fabric of the PMO, the project management process functional framework, to ensure that as much of the training investment as possible is realized and retained.

Communities of practice, in terms of an informal network of professionals within the company, can also play a key role in both project management training and in promoting the project management process functional framework of the PMO. Few, if any, companies have ever been harmed by a community of practice and in many cases, those in the community can play a key role in and be a critical asset to help management get things right.

Once again the degree to which an organization has a project management process functional framework will greatly determine whether or not the community of practice can institutionalize knowledge and thought leadership throughout the organization or if it will simply become an irrelevant monthly social gathering with limited or no real value to the organization.

Tools

Tools and applications for project management and the PMO come in many different shapes and sizes. Anyone researching the web for information on project management tools or PPM applications no doubt finds a potpourri of solutions. But unlike the mixture of dried, naturally fragrant plant material which produces a desirable gentle scent of nature, the project management mix of solutions produces a far less desirable, if not understandable, concoction.

Terms such as enterprise project management (EPM) and project portfolio management (PPM) have overlapping and duplication of meaning to the point that most people use them interchangeably. Adding to the confusion are such terms as IT governance, knowledge process outsourcing (KPO), business process outsourcing (BPO), and many more that resonate well at conferences and seminars but that don't fit the everyday vernacular of the PMO organization and leadership team of most companies. In effect these tools, applications, and solutions are all about aligning people, resources, and projects to the business goals of the company. It is crucially important that the tools phase of a PMO's practical roadmap for setup follow the vision, process, and training phases as each of these predecessor phases provide tremendously viable insight in the form of actionable needs and critical success factors.

Based upon the business needs and critical success factors determined in the previous PMO setup phases, the PMO can start the process of tool evaluation and selection. But before evaluating and examining any of the potential best fit tools for the PMO, it is helpful for the PMO and leadership team to first discuss how all of the pieces of the PMO puzzle fit or *should* fit. This is the PMO architecture introduced in Chapter 5 and shown in Figure 10.6.

There are a number of reasons why it is important for the PMO management and leadership team to understand and fit these PMO architecture puzzle pieces. It is important to understand what work is performed, or should be performed, with which tool and the degree to which the various tools interface. The key point is that one tool does not do it all for the PMO.

In addition to how the puzzle pieces of the PMO architecture fit, it is also important to understand and optimize the investment that is required to provide users with easy access to the tools. Which tools are desktop tools? Which tools are server-based tools? Which tools are accessed via subscription? Which tools require per-user licensing? Which tools require site licensing? Which tools require term or usage commitments? Which tools provide unlimited usage within the enterprise? Which tools have limitations or protections on vendor-copyrighted content? From a pure financial perspective,

The PMO architecture
"Fitting the pieces of the PMO puzzle"

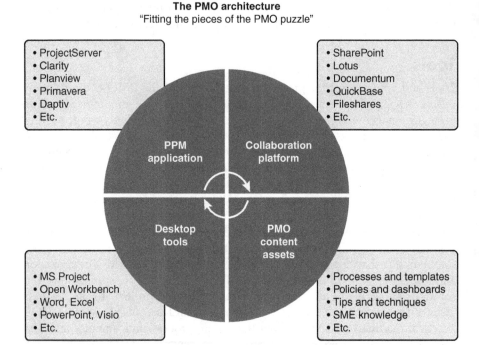

- ProjectServer
- Clarity
- Planview
- Primavera
- Daptiv
- Etc.

- SharePoint
- Lotus
- Documentum
- QuickBase
- Fileshares
- Etc.

PPM
application

Collaboration
platform

Desktop
tools

PMO
content
assets

- MS Project
- Open Workbench
- Word, Excel
- PowerPoint, Visio
- Etc.

- Processes and templates
- Policies and dashboards
- Tips and techniques
- SME knowledge
- Etc.

No one tool does it all . . .

Figure 10.6 PMO architecture

few organizations can provide all users with access to all tools. Another consideration is the fact that some users are regular users of the various tools and other users are occasional users of the tools.

For example an organization might well have a PPM tool that is used by a defined set of users, including the IT executive team, the PMO, the project managers within the PMO, and the project team members of the shared resource pool and functional units. In additional to the application functions of the tool, there are likely to be reporting features and dashboarding capabilities. To meet the periodic status and update needs to the many occasional users, two approaches can be taken.

One approach provides the occasional users with full license access to the application in which they can view reports and access dashboards at any time. The advantage of this approach is that the occasional users get access, at any time, to the reports and dashboards that they would like to view. The disadvantages of this approach are not only cost, but added complexity. While the per-user licensing fees that would be incurred because of providing occasional users access to the tool can be significant, many times the added complexity to the informal user who requires management in the form of training and support is more problematic.

The second approach provides an alternative to the cost and complexity associated with the first approach. In the second approach the occasional users are not provided direct login access to the tool. Rather, the reports and dashboards that the users want to see periodically are rendered to the user in the form of time-stamped export files such as PDF reports and graphical dashboards.

For PMOs that have an intranet-based project management process functional framework, such reports and dashboards are placed there by the PMO team where they can be easily found by the occasional users. The benefit of this approach, in additional to avoiding per-user license fees for occasional users, is that the occasional users can easily access the reports and dashboards that they want without having to learn the intricacies of a new and complex tool.

Additionally, the PMO is better able to control and ensure an accurate understanding of the report and dashboard information that it periodically prepares. Otherwise, occasional users not aware of how and when project teams enter and update the tool data, might find that the reports and dashboards that they are viewing have differing levels of updated project schedule and status data from day-to-day and throughout the week. The disadvantage of this approach is of course the fact that the occasional user is not being provided direct access to the tool, which might or might not be a bad thing. As always there is no one approach that is categorically correct all the time. A good rule of thumb is to keep tool usage as simple as possible for all those involved.

One last practical consideration for tools is the relationship between tools of the PMO and the processes and policies of the PMO. While more and more tools, especially PPM tools, are being provided by vendors along with some kind of methodology or project life cycle to be followed, a question that must be answered, 'is methodology part of the tool or is the tool part of the methodology?' Many people have different opinions and answers to this question.

For example, as noted project management expert George Pitagorsky (2004) writes, "The organization needs tools to deliver the methodology to people at the desktop, when they need guidelines, templates, examples, and the other methodology components. Methodology tools must be fully integrated into the PM tool set." In theory this sounds fine, but in practical application it is the other way around. That is, you don't want to integrate your methodology into your PM tool set, rather you want to integrate your PM tool set into your methodology and the reasons are many.

First, if you integrate your methodology into your PM tool set, you limit the access and adherence to the methodology to just those that have the PM tool. For example, let's say that you have integrated your methodology into your new SaaS PPM tool. How do people who do not have per-user licensing or subscription to the tool access the methodology? Is it assumed that everyone in the organization has a per-user license to access the tool? Is it assumed that only those in the organization who have access to the PM tool need to access, or can benefit from accessing, the methodology. For most organizations and PMOs, this is not a viable option.

Second, if the tool is replaced, you have lost your methodology until such time as you can integrate it into the new tool.

Third, if you have multiple tools for differing divisions or geographical business units, you need to integrate the methodology into each of these tools and maintain it.

Fourth, for most PMOs there are process steps, activities, and tasks that need to be performed both before and after the point at which the PM tool set comes into play. For example a PMO might be using a project and resource management system like Project Server. While Project Server is the functional tool of the PMO, not all work relative to the project management process of the PMO is necessarily performed within the functionality of Project Server. Is the work omitted, compromising the project management process? Is the work, not performed within the tool, included in the embedded methodology of the tool, confusing users?

And lastly, integrating the methodology into the tool has a tendency to promote an incorrect and backward way of thinking about processes and tools in general. A far more practical approach is to integrate the tools into the methodology. In this approach, the methodology of course is the project management process functional framework and the tools are any and all of the tools that can or should be used over the course of following the processes of the PMO. By integrating tools into the process steps of the PMO's project management process functional framework instead of the other way around, user's are provided with clear and concise guidance that explains not only the what is to be done of the process but that also describes and provides access to the specific tools that are available to be used in adhering to the process.

Implementing tools for the PMO is no different than implementing tools for any other part of the organization. Three helpful rules of thumb to remember are: (1) the vision, process, and training phases of establishing a PMO should precede the implementation of tools; (2) establish a clear view and understanding of the PMO architecture; (3) integrate your tools into your processes and not the other way around.

Staffing

Many PMOs have struggled out of the gate because of making ill-advised and untimely organizational decisions. Like our CIO friend George did as described in the beginning of this chapter, the PMO organizational model that is adopted is more aligned to theoretically approaches instead of aligned to concrete goals, objectives, and needs of the business and, quite often, the PMO organization is established much too early in the PMO setup process.

Let's take the organizational model issues first. According to Levatec (2006, p. 6), "One of the first important considerations that must be addressed by any organization considering the implementation of a PMO is the basic structural model that will be used within the organization." Those who advocate this approach are quick to then offer a few structural models to choose from. At one end of the continuum you have the functional organization and at the other end you have the projectized organization (see Figure 10.7).

The functional organization has projects, but the scope of these projects is managed by staff within each functional department. In the projectized organization, project team members are often collocated and most of the performance resources of the organization are involved in the project work. Of course in today's businesses most organizations are neither totally functional nor totally projectized. Matrix organizations are often presented as an attempt to explain this and are shown as a blend of the characteristics of both functional and projectized organizations (see Figure 10.8).

But the fact of the matter is that in most of today's businesses you do find all of these matrix organizational structures and characteristics present to one degree or another. As organizations embrace project management as a core competence and strategic skill set, they find not just one, but many PMOs beginning to appear throughout the lines of business, divisions, departments, and functional business units.

What can start out as a single PMO, typically started in the IT department, can quickly evolve to multiple PMOs from not only a strategic PMO at the uppermost executive level but to a wide variety of other PMOs throughout the organization, each providing significant value to the organization (see Figure 10.9).

Why are PMOs popping up like hedgehogs in so many areas of today's businesses? As certified PMP Tim Jaques (2001) writes, "With so many companies adopting the project-based approach to completing work, it is no wonder that the concept of the project management office, or PMO, is gaining popularity." This popularity is driven by the business value that PMOs of all shapes and sizes deliver and it is not absolutely limited organizationally to just those in the IT department or in the strategic project office.

PMO guru Gerard Hill (2008, p. 209) wisely advises, "The PMO should conduct initial planning to establish its own structure, and then ongoing planning to expand its structure and reach to the desired level of organizational alignment." Hence, too much focus and obsession on aligning the PMO to the various theoretical models is misplaced and of little value. It is far better to focus, not on theoretical PMO organizational models, but rather on practical business goals and the delivery of value.

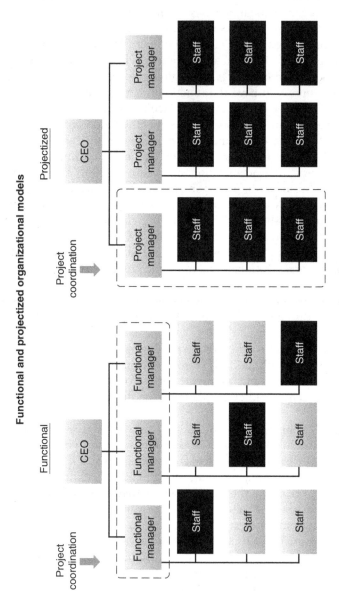

Figure 10.7   Functional and projectized organization models

Matrix organization models

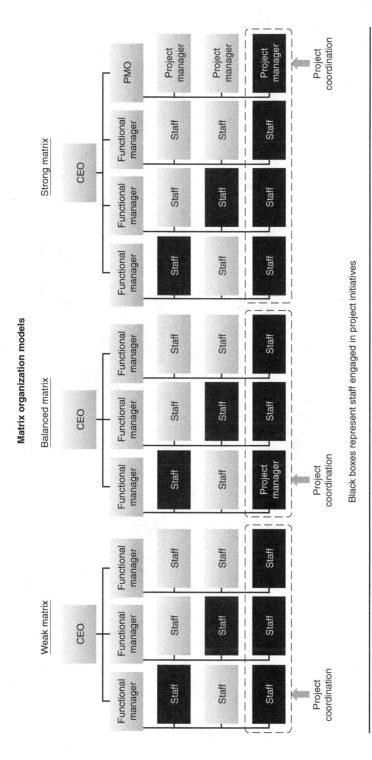

Figure 10.8 Matrix organization models

Black boxes represent staff engaged in project initiatives

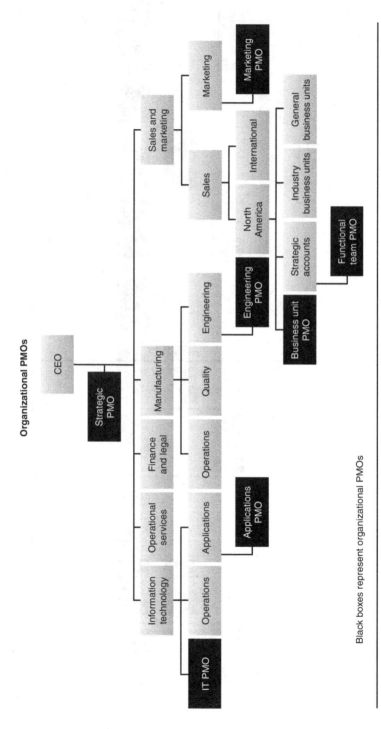

Black boxes represent organizational PMOs

Figure 10.9   Organizational PMOs

Coupled with too much attention on the PMO organizational model is the rush to establish the PMO organization. This can lead to organizational structure and staffing mistakes as well as the missed opportunity to best phase in the PMO organization and staff as PMO setup activities are completed. Unlike our friend George, the CIO, who rushed into creating his PMO organization, a far better approach is to gradually create and staff the office of the PMO as specific PMO setup objectives are accomplished and phases are completed.

For example, naming a PMO manager and then immediately announcing the organizational structure of the PMO, open positions, and plans to engage in reorganization and resource realignment distracts the management and staff from their day-to-day duties. This can lead quickly to organizational politics and people mischief as staff inquires about, if not competes for, open positions. Even among professionals feelings can be hurt and relationships can be jeopardized as is always the case when management is evaluating and selecting people for positions.

Even more problematic than the politics of it all is the fact that for most PMOs there is a significant amount of work that could, and should, be done prior to staffing. The initial work of developing, reviewing, and committing to the vision, goals, and objectives of the PMO is often best accomplished as a collaborative effort between the new PMO manager, their immediate manager, and the participating executives and leadership team. Though this work should be carried out before any decisions on PMO organizational models and levels of staffing are made and executed, this is not often the case. Additionally, the requisite PMO process and policy work is another effort that can be completed prior to organizational decisions and staffing changes and in some cases it might influence and drive staffing. Likewise most organizations can benefit greatly by addressing the training and tooling plans and strategies, prior to staffing the PMO. Collectively, these important PMO setup and readiness activities can take quite a bit of time and dedication of purpose to get right.

Figures 10.10 through 10.14 illustrate that the organizational approach best suited for most new PMOs is a phased staffing approach. To get started quickly and effectively, the PMO manager should first be named. After the PMO manager has developed, reviewed, and obtained commitment to the PMO plan by the leadership team, then attention should be placed on establishing the processes and policies of the PMO. At this point the PMO manager might bring on board an individual, such as a PMO administrative assistant or project manager, to assist with this work. After approval of the PMO processes and policies, the small PMO team can turn their attention to development of the PMO plan for training and tools. Depending upon the size and complexity of the business organization for which the PMO exists to serve and the goals that the PMO is seeking to achieve, it can easily take from several weeks to several months to truly get through this step. At this point in establishing a PMO, the

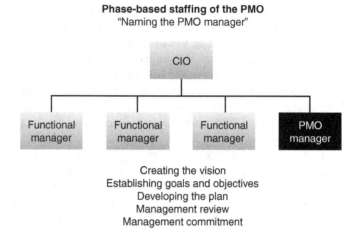

Figure 10.10   Naming the PMO manager

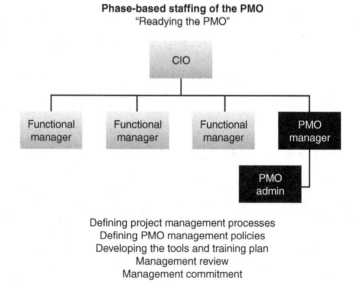

Figure 10.11   Readying the PMO

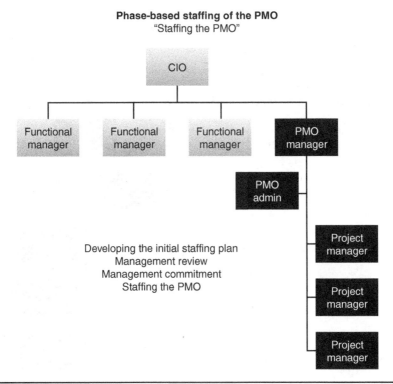

Phase-based staffing of the PMO
"Staffing the PMO"

Figure 10.12   Staffing the PMO

organizational structure of the PMO is ready to be announced, including additional staffing of the PMO if necessary.

There are those who claim that if a new PMO does not show results within six months then it is doomed to failure. While this is a good rule of thumb, it is often misapplied as activity can be confused with results. Consider the following observation, "We trained very hard, but it seemed that every time we were beginning to form into teams we would be reorganized. I was to learn later in life that we tried to meet any new situation by reorganizing, and a wonderful method it was for creating the illusion of progress while producing confusion, inefficiency and demoralization." One might think that this quote was the sage advice and wisdom of a leading management consultant, but no, it was penned in 50 AD by Titus Petronius, a Roman writer in the Age of Nero. Though rushing to staff a PMO and to implement a PPM system might look like progress, if these things are done prematurely the consequences are always disastrous as measured in wasted time, additional costs and rework, and organizational frustration.

Phase-based staffing of the PMO
"Expanding the PMO"

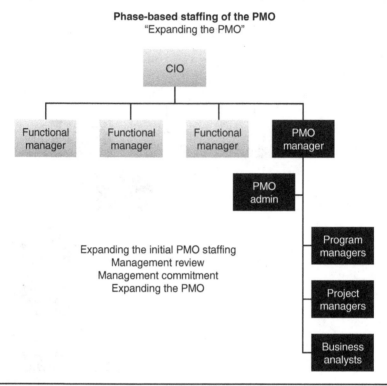

Figure 10.13   Expanding the PMO

One of the biggest misconceptions of establishing a PMO, and it relates to staffing, is the idea that the PMO should be, or needs to be, sold to management. There are those in the project management community who advocate a PMO start-up roadmap that begins with a gap analysis to assess project management needs followed by an explanation of how the PMO meets the assessed project management needs, which in turn is input into a business case to be used to sell the PMO concept to management. At best this is just bad advice. In many cases it quickly leads to backward thinking or a *the answer is* mentality in which the answer is known in advance and all efforts are focused on justifying it to others. The goal of the PMO is neither to meet project management needs nor to establish an additional organizational entity within the company. These things are no doubt by-products of a successful PMO. But the goal of the PMO is to best deliver value to the organization for which the PMO exists to serve. Kendall and Rollins (2003, p. 285) speak at length about

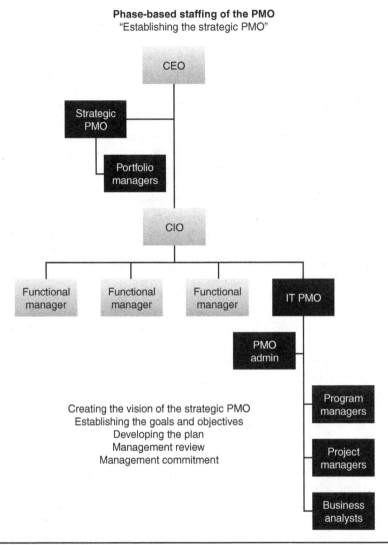

Figure 10.14   Establishing the strategic PMO

this and even propose a Deliver Value Now PMO Model that takes PMO value delivery to the next level for a strategic PMO. Whether the correct approach for an organization is to staff a PMO of whatever type and style or to not staff a PMO, this should be an unbiased decision based on objective analysis and facts, not spin and salesmanship.

Assessment

Whether one is shooting a gun or establishing a PMO, it is always good to have a ready-aim-fire mindset. However, many organizations fall into the common pitfall of performing far too much analysis at the wrong time and not enough analysis at the right time. Once again, let's take the case of our good friend, CIO George. The first order of business that George undertook was to engage with the firm's Big 5 project management consultant to perform a gap analysis and assessment of findings. Though George and the management team had a clear idea in mind of what they needed to do to get from their as-is state to their desired state, no one objected to bringing in an outside expert to help.

The consultant proceeded to conduct a gap analysis according to their prescribed gap analysis methodology. Key members of the management team, project managers, and project team members were interviewed over a three week period and within six calendar weeks the gap analysis had been complete and the assessment of findings had been delivered. The assessment summarized the perceived maturity of the organization by various knowledge areas of the PMBOK® (see Figure 10.15).

So after six weeks and fifty thousand dollars, George and his management team were entreated to a presentation of findings that revealed to them nothing that they did not already know with the possible exception of the revelation of a numeric score indicating their level of assessed project management maturity. Of course the consultant presented the details of his interviews and analysis as well as his recommendation for additional consulting services that his organization could provide to help George and the team to get on with setting up their new PMO.

This is the problem with performing detailed assessments at the wrong time. When it comes to establishing a new PMO, detailed gap analyses and maturity assessments might sound like a good idea in theory, but the universal reality is that for PMOs, much like with living organisms, maturity comes only after birthing, not before it. George came to the conclusion that the detailed gap analysis and assessment was of minimal value so early in the life cycle of the PMO and that the potential value, obvious to all, of the consultant engagement would have been far greater if it had been performed after the initial PMO setup steps had been completed. Could George have done a better job of limiting the scope of the gap analysis and assessment to just those essential areas to be considered in establishing a new PMO? Could the consultant have done a better job in quickly arriving at an actionable roadmap for setting up the PMO? Absolutely, but this rarely happens.

In the case of our friend George, the CIO, he had squandered fifty thousand dollars and six weeks of calendar time. For some organizations, perhaps not George's, this would be a tremendously poor outcome. The overly detailed assessment that was conducted prior to any of the other PMO setup activities

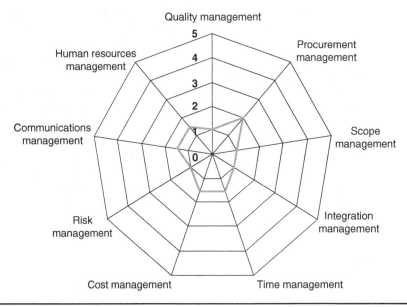

Figure 10.15 Assessment summary by knowledge area

provided little to no value. However, important to note, after the initial PMO setup activities, including goal setting, definition of processes and policies, carrying out a basic level of training and tooling, and establishing the initial PMO organizational structure, a detailed gap analysis and maturity assessment would be of much greater value and practical use and this would not have been a poor outcome. It is not that analytical information isn't nice for management to know or have on hand, rather that the timing of when to perform the analysis is nearly always more important than the analysis itself.

Summary

Many PMOs have struggled with getting off the ground. While there is no shortage of PMO setup roadmaps to follow, oftentimes these roadmaps are aligned to and arrive at predetermined PMO organizational models or they assess and provide a generic path of maturity. While well intended, for the new PMO such roadmaps and paths to maturity can quickly become expensive exercises as measured not just in cost, but in loss of time and organizational enthusiasm for the tasks and journey ahead.

Business speed is important and it is true that the early bird gets the worm. But it is also true that it is the second mouse that gets the cheese. For many organizations, rushing to implement tools prior to establishing purpose and processes are nearly always met with execution difficulties. In some cases, organizations might come to find out that they implemented the inappropriate tool or that the tools that they already had were all that was really required. Likewise, rushing to make organization changes can give the appearance of progress, but if carried out at the wrong time and in the incorrect manner, such organizational changes might well result in confusion and inefficiencies at best and chaos and organizational mischief at worst.

To avoid these calamities, a practical roadmap for establishing a PMO must be followed. In the case of setting up a PMO, the practical roadmap that has proven successful time after time consists of vision, processes, training, tools, organization, and assessment. As with any roadmap, there is ample opportunity to change lanes and vary speeds, but it is rather important to stay on the road.

Questions

1. What are some of the leading factors that contribute to the establishment of a PMO?
2. In terms of a practical roadmap for establishing a PMO, what are the phases and order of phases that a PMO should seek to follow?
3. List three characteristics faced by business units that drive the need and value for a clear vision and strategic plan?
4. What are the basic elements of a strategic plan?
5. List and describe the three barriers that often prevent a PMO from establishing a clear vision?
6. What period of time is attributed to be the definitive acceptance within IT departments of the PMO?
7. List and describe three business necessities that drive the business need and management decisions to establish a PMO?
8. Why do many organizations have an urgency to implement tools rather than the patience to first develop processes?
9. What are the differences between a project management process *approach* framework and a project management process *functional* framework?
10. Why is implementing project management tools before project management processes problematic for most PMOs?

11. What are the differences between a PMM and a project management process?
12. In establishing project management processes for the PMO, what are three good rules of thumb to follow?
13. What three factors results in the hidden costs of fee-based project management training?
14. If 75 percent of a project management training class is applicable to a PMO and one third of that applicable amount can be realized and retained, what is the hidden cost amount of this project management training to the PMO?
15. How can the project management process functional framework of the PMO be used to provide practical project management training?
16. What essential requirement is needed to ensure that a project management community of practice within an organization can provide lasting value?
17. What are the components of the PMO architecture?
18. What two approaches can the PMO take in making periodic report and dashboarding data available to occasional users?
19. Why is it important for the PMO to integrate its tools into its methodology and not the other way around?
20. What are the differences between and characteristics of functional and projectized organizations?
21. What are the differences between and characteristics of weak, balanced, and strong matrix organizations?
22. What is PMO setup phase-based staffing?
23. What are the pros and cons of have a "selling" the concept of a PMO mindset?

References

Doerscher, Terry. 2008. "Do You Have a Process Framework?" http://www.planview.com/pmo. (Accessed June 16, 2008)

Hill, Gerard. 2008. *The Complete Project Management Office Handbook.* Florida: Auerbach Publications.

Jaques, Tim. 2001. "Imaginary Obstacles: Getting Over PMO Myths." http://www.gantthead.com/articles. (Accessed June 16, 2008)

Kendall, Gerald I., and Steven C. Rollins. 2003. *Advanced Project Portfolio Management and the PMO.* Florida: J. Ross Publishing.

Levatec, Craig. 2006. *The Program Management Office.* Florida: J. Ross Publishing.

Mullaly, Mark. 2008. "The Multiplicity of PMOs." http://www.ganthead.com/ articles. (Accessed June 16, 2008)

Pitagorsky, George. 2004. "The Business Value of Embracing a Unified Project Management Methodology." International Institute for Learning. (Accessed June 16, 2008)

Wideman, Max. 2006. "Project Management Methodologies." http://www .maxwideman.com/issacons. (Accessed June 16, 2008)

Executive Insights

A Practical Approach to the PMO

Jimmy Char

CEO, Skills Group, Bulgaria

Last summer I participated in an international seminar in which lots of interesting presentations and discussions were held. I participated in most of them trying to learn as much as possible from these experts. The last day I was in a presentation concerning the PMO establishment in the organization and I was told by a PMO guru that the new era and all his findings show that the PMO is a temporary endeavor and no matter what its role, value and position in the organization, it must start delivering within the first six months and must dissolve itself after two years within the organization!

Like others in this seminar I had already started to establish a PMO with one of my clients and our plan was to establish the PMO, implement its deliverables, train the project managers, and complete its maturity cycle within the first five years!

I might agree with the first half of the PMO guru's message but I definitely do not agree with the last half of it. The guru finished his presentation and, after several minutes of silence, asked for questions. While I was lost in my thinking, I wanted to manifest my thoughts and ideas, but I did not know where to start. I had hundreds of reasons not to accept what I had heard, but at the moment of truth I could not find many except this and I asked the guru, 'But what do you do with continuous process improvement and the next maturity levels to reach?' and the guru said with a nice smile that told me how stupid I·was to ask, 'Well . . . just forget them.'

Maybe I was naive to believe everything that I had learned and experienced, or maybe I was too naive to listen to what the guru said. How can we establish a PMO, develop the business operation methodologies, document the corporate and/or operational governance and all related processes, procedures and guidelines, train the project managers and the project management teams, and implement the deliverables organization wide and assure their compliance and continuous improvement to achieve the required maturity level in just two years and just disappear?

Besides the comfortable hotel, nice city, sunny days, long happy nights, the beach and the golden sand memories, I went back home with disappointment

371

and painful demotivation. As a matter of fact, I go beyond the definition that the guru offered about temporary endeavor and insist, from experience, that the establishment of a PMO is a series of short (couple of months) and long (couple of years) projects interrelated and split by production periods where outputs of one project become the inputs of others and thus group in a clear program definition.

After twenty-five years working in an international organization as project manager, program director, systems integration manager and then general manager of one subsidiary where I tried earnestly, and without success, to find the right expert to develop the PMO, I left with a clear vision and mission in mind; to establish a consulting firm that helps struggling companies efficiently organize themselves and effectively run their projects through the foundation of a serious, adequate, and added-value PMO units.

The Story

Let me share one of my experiences, hoping that it more effectively explains how things, I believe, must happen. Over ten years ago I had the chance to work with a partner, an IT solution provider in Europe (let us call it hereafter the PARTNER) and we both had the time to know each other fairly well and to identify the strengths and weaknesses of each. I was, at that moment, the project director for a relatively large and complex project that had spanned over two years.

Several years passed in which I got involved in many other projects in Europe that ended with me and some good friends knowledgeable in this field establishing our own consulting firm focused on establishing governance and processes in challenged organizations. I was called by an old friend working for the PARTNER to help in setting-up a centralized PMO coping with the complexity and challenges of the projects the PARTNER was running. While discussing the problems, I understood that a year ago this PARTNER tried to launch its PMO using internal resources and failed. The PARTNER recognized that it would be necessary to bring in an external subject matter expert to launch and develop the PMO functions based on the required objectives and goals that they needed to achieve. Negotiating the scope, the time, and the deliverables (without mentioning the price), I stated clearly the prerequisites for a successful start-up of the PMO but there were two items that I wanted to be sure of before making any decision to accept this mission:

◆ I wanted the PMO sponsor to be the CEO of the organization, the person who has clear power to decide and to enroll the work. Any less authoritative position as the sponsor of the PMO might lead to priority conflicts for the activities undertaken by the PMO and the ongoing project manager's activities.

◆ What was to be the role of the consultant? Remaining an external consultant, it is important to participate in the implementation of any process developed by the PMO. This participation means that an executive and formal position, as part of the PARTNER organization structure, must be occupied by the external consultant to develop the PMO and implement its projects and plans. This person must have the power and the eligibility to participate, not only on the planning and controlling activities, but also in the direction and execution of what the PMO would like to achieve at the end, having all the identified stakeholders as the PMO performance team.

Any PMO establishment and integration within the organization generates changes that can be rejected or difficult to accept by the rest of the team in the organization; so get the highest sponsorship possible to give the authority and implementation opportunity for all these changes to materialize.

When you are an external consultant, be sure to participate in the daily performance of the PMO with the team that you elect to act.

The Start-Up (Building the Castle)

Let's go back to the story of George and his Big 5 consultant. George started his activities by assessing the knowledge and the practice of the project managers on his client's team. Although it is a normal and logical step at the start of consulting activities, it also has its advantages and disadvantages and one must deal with both. Two constraints in such a process are the time and the cost. Having said that, it is clear that the first part of the message of our PMO guru friend mentioned earlier wouldn't be possible; this option takes longer than six months to bring results and costs time and money to understand and document what the client team knows and has as policies and standards currently applicable (the as-is findings).

Actually, I always wonder when organizations seek to implement changes or new improvement investments using external consultants, why they do not assess and document their as-is state with the current knowledge and practice of the corporation and have it ready for those consultants assigned to improve the current-state to the desired-state. Being internal and having the everyday knowledge of who is doing what would be the best fit for such activities and would save money, time, and ambiguity. We all say about consultants, you pay them to tell you what you already know. So why are the organizations paying them? They are just documenting the practice that could be done cheaper by internal resources.

Before calling for external consultants or even before investing on any asset, do your homework thoroughly and document your current state in details and make that part of the improvement investment process.

Additionally, document your current ongoing or approved development plans for all of the improvement investments that might directly or indirectly depend or have an interrelation with the required to-be improvement; the consultants need that to understand and plan the future big picture more effectively.

PMO Start-Up Path

It was my misfortune that I was unable to get the clear as-is documentation from my PARTNER to help create the new PMO, but this did not stop me from following the correct path; a short and fast understanding of the as-is and to-be big pictures. The following steps are the beginning of the path for any PMO start-up:

♦ Build a quick and high-level understanding of the as-is and to-be states of the organization
♦ Develop the PMO charter with clear vision and enough information, identifying the goals and the authority
♦ Get the buy-in of the CEO
♦ Define the measurable deliverables based on the objectives defined in this book
♦ Detail the to-be state using international best practices in the short-, medium- and long-term with relation to the maturity of the PMO and the maturity of the project management in the PARTNER organization
♦ Develop an awareness plan for the management
♦ Train the end-users
♦ Implement the change

Knowing the organizational structure and culture of the PARTNER, I started from my first day acting as project management office director by identifying (listing) the PARTNER's written policies, processes, guidelines, rules, and regulations. It was important to know their existence without spending the time reading them (I did not think entering and reading their details at that moment would bring any added value to my activities).

To develop your PMO charter, it is important to have interviews with the appropriate key stakeholders and the selection of these key stakeholders can be different for different cases. Some of these individuals who can give you the big picture of your PMO mission are:

♦ From the top management, get the CEO to identify his vision and expectations from the PMO and confirm his commitment
♦ From the strategy department, get the director (if he exists or anyone acting in the capacity of developing the organizational strategy for the coming years) to confirm the strategic objectives and the incorporation of the PMO and its role as part of company strategy

◆ From the operation division, get the chief operating officer (if she exists or anyone managing the organization operations and operational teams) to confirm the operational capability, current problems, and future needs and plans

◆ From the quality management department, get the director (if he exists or anyone developing the organization quality system as well as processes, procedures, rules, and regulations) to understand the domain of the current implemented processes and the level of their compliance

◆ From the finance department, get the director to give full confirmation and commitment for the PMO funding and allocated budgets for the new changes and implementations investments

◆ From the functional business units, get the director of one functional business unit to learn how the business units are managing the projects, the dedicated and shared resources, and the current ground rules

◆ From the project management teams, get the project manager of one ongoing complex project to define the practices used in running projects, to explain the approaches used in allocating/releasing of the project resources, to offer the current control processes, and to identify the unwritten policies

Each of these interviews lasted two hours and was enough for me to have the overall (and sometimes deep) picture of the current state. I then developed the PMO charter that was approved within the first two months of the work. In the charter it was important to identify the type of services the PMO expected to deliver, the level of its integration within the PARTNER organization, the SMART objectives, and the process of rolling out the deliverables. Figure 10.16 shows the table of contents for the project charter for the PMO that was developed based upon the interviews with the participants.

During your quick scanning of your client organization, do not forget to look carefully at the following three elements. If overlooked, they might open vulnerabilities in your PMO development:

1. The current politics operating in the organization
2. The mindset of the entire management and its readiness for the change
3. What the project managers need to improve their performances

The content of the PMO charter is, to some degree, detailed in this book and I will not detail further; however, I would like to clarify the three elements that I have mentioned, which must not be overlooked during any change preparation.

PMO charter
"Table of contents"

- Purpose
- Scope
- Executive summary
- Introduction
- PMO justification
- PMO vision
- PMO mission
- PMO goals
  - Success project delivery
  - Build project management professionalism
  - Keeping executive team and project management community informed
- Critical success factors
- PMO metrics
- PMO staffing
- PMO sponsor
- PMO organizational structure
- PMO stakeholders
- Expected benefits from the PMO
  - Executives
  - Business unit managers
  - Projects managers
  - External customers
  - Finance
  - Human resources

Figure 10.16   PMO project charter

Politics of the Organization

It is not enough to discuss the changes that the PMO implements and the benefits that it brings; you must do a systematic stakeholder's analysis that helps to identify the stakeholder's expectations and concerns. The possible existence of the power/politics struggle within your client's upper and middle management must also be identified and plans implemented to keep the PMO as neutral as possible within the organization. In real life, managers are in different camps and barely talk and listen to each other. Failure to identify the impact of such power and survival needs from the start, even at the management level, creates stronger resistance than the ones coming from the end users, the project managers. Actually, once implemented, the PMO withdraws many cards from the hands of many units and individuals involved in this environment. Instead of understanding and accepting the change and being part of it and moving with it to the next maturity level with different cards to play, these individuals view the PMO as a threat to their authority over what is happening in the organization.

Mindset of Management

Although the PMO initiator is the CEO of the organization (it was in my case), the PMO mission is a long path and as it is often said there is a huge difference between knowing the path and walking the path. If the other members of management are not committed to such change, knowing a clear path for such a mission (the conflict and the consequences) becomes impossible unless the results are defined and known in advance.

Needs of the Project Managers

Knowing how important the decision to create the PMO is, such a decision is still based on more effecively controlling projects to improve their success rates. You must check the real needs of the project managers who are involved in delivering the projects. Do they really need a new set of rules and policies because the current ones (even informal or unwritten) did not give them the satisfaction required? Do they need training? Do they need more resources? Do they need more funding? Do they need more time? These are all reasons for poor performance; the PMO might not be the only solution needed.

By failing to identify the potential risks coming from these three elements, you actually allow vulnerable holes to develop in the protection that is needed by the PMO to secure its success. In fact one major and recurring activity is change management. Change management is a necessity and as important as any other project performed by the PMO.

To understand the magnitude of such risks and why many PMOs do not deliver what they were built for or to ascertain why they were blocked from further progress in their maturity, PMOs have to play major roles in the organization that were played successfully or not, directly or not, formally or not, by other units, departments, and even individuals. The switch of roles within the organization definitely creates conflicts among the different parts of the organization, and when these parts are located within different camps built before and even during PMO establishment, one can imagine the territorial wars for survival that inevitably arise and claim many victims. Among the casualties are members of the PMO team, the PMO director who dares to touch the properties of the others, and last but not least, the entire PMO and the whole castle falls down.

To understand this tragedy let us have a look at some of the main roles that, once effectively established, the PMO has to fully or partially centralize. Figure 10.17 shows these roles and, to build its success, the PMO absorbs its

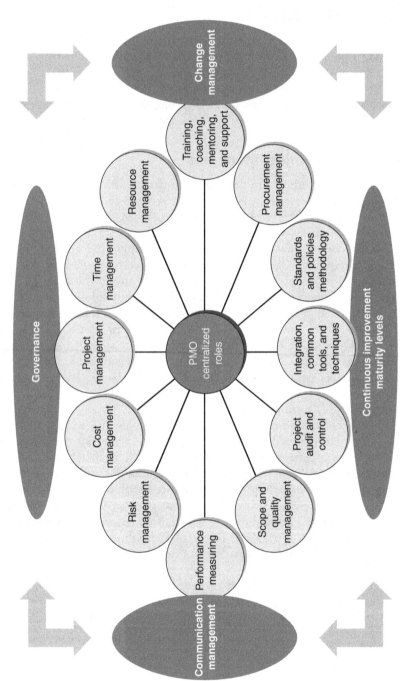

Figure 10.17 PMO partially or fully centralized roles

power from those who were occupying these roles (partially or totally, correctly or incorrectly) within the organization:

> *What happens when the PMO becomes the centralized authority for standards, best practices, and the policy maker on project management? Of course things might look differently depending on the goals defined and approved for the PMO. Would you want a PMO that is an active supporter, advisor, and coach? Or a passive source of information? Should the PMO be a laissez-faire source of information to use as you will or an active influencer in ensuring projects will be successful? In all cases the project managers must weigh-in and provide their perspectives while developing the PMO; they must contribute to the design of the perfect PMO.*

Summary

The creation of the PMO is not an objective by itself, but rather it is the way to develop and implement the changes in the organization required for solving many related problems. The PMO is the start of the journey, but the focus should be on the changes and the benefits after each change. The PMO is not only a simple project organization, but rather a program organization composed of several projects (projects that can exchange inputs and outputs and benefit from other activities outside their scope, including production periods and recurring activities).

Change management is a recurring activity that has to function in order to prepare, support, and protect the changes once developed and implemented by the PMO. Resistance for the change in an organization might come from many different parties, including upper management, especially if the change is seen as a threat to the power and property of the individuals and business units.

The PMO has to centralize many of the de-centralized activities within the business units that developed the problems for which the PMO is created to solve.

An external subject matter expert is essential to remain as neutral as possible while different existing power struggles are prepared to keep the current processes and authorities.

Even if for some reason one project of the PMO fails to deliver on time and as per the budget, remember that the PMO is a program and must capitalize on this concept. Expect execution difficulties and learn by them to improve the process or processes that resulted in the difficulty. Be committed to continuous improvement and delivering value. . . . And, the PMO must not be dissolved two years after its creation.

11

Line of Business PMOs:
The Ubiquitous Nature of
Project Management

Far too often many project management offices (PMOs) and those in the project management community take an inward view of project management. They view project management as a professional practice limited to those who have been formally trained and work in a formal project management organization. The cartoon in Figure 11.1 sheds light on a common PMO oversight; the ubiquitous nature of project management. It is everywhere. To assume that projects outside of the parameters of the strategic project office or formal PMO are simply informal and unimportant endeavors is a gross oversight and misunderstanding of the value to the organization of such efforts.

Staffer to Project Manager

Not long ago, except for project-based companies, most companies did not have many project managers or PMOs. Back in the days of large and burgeoning corporate bureaucracies, workplace professionals who were not on the front line marketing, selling, and delivering or not in the back office innovating, developing, and supporting were simply called staff. What did staff do? Mostly the staff managed projects or were members of project teams. What was their job title? For most organizations, the job title of a staff person was simply *staff* and it was a title for which to be proud.

I can remember vividly the feeling of pride that I had when well over twenty-five years ago I was promoted from the IBM field branch office to the

Figure 11.1   PMO comics—formal and informal

IBM region staff. My actual role and job duties were that of a DB2 project manager and I managed a variety of marketing and technical support projects. Nonetheless my business card simply read 'IBM Region Staff.' Being a member of the staff of a corporation back then was like having a double chevron on your sleeve. You were higher in rank than others were and on your way up the corporate ladder.

In the mid-1980s there was a confluence of two significant events, however, that forever changed the way corporate staffs would be viewed. One of those events was the paradigm shift occurring throughout businesses all over the world—especially in the United States—away from large corporate bureaucracies. Once companies bragged about their size in terms of the sheer number of employees, but they were now facing economic pressures to downsize, especially nonessential jobs. Large corporate staffs were no longer enviable or the sign of a great company; rather large staffs were indicative of organizations that had allowed themselves to grow too large without any kind of periodic pruning of nonperforming assets, including departments and people who weren't pulling their weight.

For many firms the new mantra was, 'If you don't make the product, sell the product, or fix the product, then you're expendable.' This new mindset, driven by competitive pressures and endorsed by Wall Street analysts, sent shivers up and down the spines of companies of all sizes. When asked about the health and long-term viability of the IBM Corporation, one such analyst responded that IBM was a sound company in a stable industry and its only problem was that it employed 465,000 people when it really only needed 250,000. Needless to say, of all those worried about their jobs, those on corporate and regional staffs had the most to worry about.

The other event of that time period was the recognition and acceptance of project management as a profession. The Project Management Institute

(PMI), founded in 1969, greatly contributed to the advancement of project management as not only a profession, but a valuable and strategic discipline that could benefit every company. By the mid-1980s companies were investing in project management, establishing project management job positions and career paths, providing training programs, setting goals for certifications and, more importantly, seeing the results firsthand that effective project management could produce. It did not take long for those at-risk corporate staffs to reinvent themselves and to align their roles and responsibilities to that of project management work and that of project and program management-oriented organizations.

By the end of the 1990s few, if any, corporations referred to internal organizations as corporate staff and, of course, there were no longer position titles or business cards that simply indicated staff as one's job. Currently, few workplace professionals under the age of thirty even know about or have a context for what large corporate staffs once were. Proudly and securely existing in a PMO or within what is now the emerging organizational construct called the *middle-office*, many in the project management community have developed an inwardly focused mindset for project management. Some of these people view project management as a formal discipline that should only be carried out by trained and certified professionals; a private practice if you will. Others view project management as an activity that is carried out by those in a formal project office such as an enterprise PMO or information technology (IT) PMO. Regrettably, whether out of protection of the profession, exaltation of one's livelihood, or just an unintended blind spot, far too few members of the project management community see project management for what it actually is; an activity that is ubiquitous.

Line-of-Business PMOs

There are many kinds of PMOs. Almost assuredly if you ask a member of the project management community about the different types of PMOs you are given descriptions of control towers, weather stations, and fighter squadrons, or perhaps a discussion of PMO placement. These perspectives are perfectly fine in the context of IT, enterprise, or strategic PMOs, and let's add Project Management Centers of Excellence; but regrettably they are confined and limited to an inside-the-box way of thinking about PMOs and the value of project management.

Consider the PMO as espoused by project management template provider, Method 123 (2006), "The role of a PMO is to improve the level of project management in an organization . . . The PMO is a cost center that does not directly generate revenue for the organization." This is a vivid example of the problem that many in the project management community have with respect to PMOs. This myopic point of view is simply wrong-headed and bad business thinking for two basic reasons.

First, organizations do not exist to improve the way they go about performing; they exist to meet the business objectives for which they were created. Can you imagine a vice president (VP) of sales espousing that the role of the sales organization is to get better at selling? Their role is to make their sales quota, to achieve their business objectives. No doubt improving the capabilities of the organization would be a supporting strategy and maybe even a critical success factor, but it would never be the role of the organization. In fact for many sales VPs, if they miss their sales objectives merely for one quarter, they find themselves out of a job, irrespective of whether or not the sales teams honed their sales skills.

Can you imagine a VP of marketing advocating that the role of the marketing organization is to get better at marketing? Not likely. Their role is to achieve their marketing goals and objectives, including measurable targets for market share, lead generation, and brand awareness and preference.

Can you imagine a VP of professional services having a mindset that the role of the professional services organization is to get better at what they do? Their role is to achieve their professional services business objectives. No doubt skills improvement would be part of the overall strategy of the organization, but the goals and measurable objectives of the professional services organization would be centered on such things as services revenue, resource utilization, and customer satisfaction.

Can you imagine a head of accounting advocating that the role of the accounting department is to get better at accounting? Of course getting better at the skills that are requisite to performing one's duty is, and always will be, important, but the head of accounting doesn't have a monthly business objective for getting good at things. They have monthly measurements for cash flow, accounts payable, accounts receivable, and days sales outstanding (DSO). When the head of accounting reviews performance with the head of finance and the chief executive office (CEO), there is no confusion about what the role of accounting is and what kinds of accounting objectives and measurements are expected to be achieved. Getting better at accounting is no doubt important, but it is not the raison d'être for the accounting organization.

We could go on and on and on from one organizational unit to the next in this manner and the inescapable conclusion is, of course, that any head of an organization or department who has a mindset that their role is to get better at what they do would likely enjoy a short tenure in their job. The PMO as an organizational entity and the PMO manager are not exempt from this basic business principle.

The second perspective of PMOs that is advocated by the project management vendor cited earlier is that PMOs are cost centers and do not generate revenue for the organization directly. Fortunately this view is not shared by everyone in the project management community and certainly it is not shared by those in the line-of-business units of the organization.

Leading PMO experts Gerald Kendall and Steve Rollins (2003, p. 28) provide a greatly expanded and enhanced view of the role of the modern PMO offering a new *throughput* PMO model that is value-driven and is focused on meeting organizational goals, a strategic balance of demand and market side projects, and the acceleration of benefits delivery. Their book, *Advanced Project Portfolio Management and the PMO*, is advocated by many, including Harold Kerzner, as a must read for business executives—not just project management executives, but C-level business executives.

In this book you do not find Kendall or Rollins referring to the PMO as a cost center, or an organization that does not generate revenue, or an organization whose role is to help the enterprise get better at project management. In addition to the leading PMO gurus, line-of-business organizations do not view project management or the PMO—their PMOs that is—as a cost center. On the contrary, they view their PMOs as a strategic enabler of their business objectives, a *war room* in which victory is declared when the objectives are achieved.

These line-of-business PMOs are the other PMO models that are tremendously valuable to organizations. For most business executives who comprise the leadership team of their organization, any discussion with their project management leaders about PMO models and types is much better served by illuminating where PMOs can fit and add value throughout the organization as opposed to simply describing the typical IT department PMO models and types as control towers, weather stations, and fighter squadrons.

So where are these PMO models called line-of-business PMOs and what do they do? As project management is ubiquitous, line-of-business PMOs can, and do, exist just about anywhere. They can exist in sales organizations, marketing departments, professional services organizations, product development departments, human resources (HR) organizations, training departments, engineering departments, research and development centers, finance departments, and merger and acquisition (M & A) units.

Sales PMO

Consider the value of the sales PMO. Many seasoned sales VPs advocate establishing a sales PMO, within the sales organization to be a critical enabler to achieving the sales objectives of the company. Of course, years back, these sales VPs had the luxury of a dedicated sales support staff headed by a sales operations manager, but organizational streamlining and cost-cutting eliminated such support staffs. However, unlike a support staff that could be viewed as, and often became over time, unneeded overhead in the form of bean counters, the sales PMO offers a much clearer and appreciated value proposition. Some of the many responsibilities that the sales PMO perform include:

1. Establishing a common methodology for the management of sales opportunities
2. Maintaining and updating the methodology to allow for improvements and additional best practices
3. Facilitating organizational and team communications by having a common process, deliverables, and terminology
4. Training internal and external team members to build and maintain core competencies
5. Mentoring and coaching teams to keep sales projects on track and out of trouble
6. Ensuring that sales projects at risk get the attention and resources they need to succeed
7. Ensuring that competitive threats are understood and that sales project risks are identified and mitigated
8. Participating in the planning and ongoing review of top sales opportunities critical to the success of the organization
9. Reporting organization results and expected achievements (forecasts) to support management review and decision making
10. Acting as the overall advocate to the sales organization for process adherence, on time delivery of results, and achievement of all of the goals, objectives, and measurements for the department

Collectively the roles, responsibilities, and duties carried out by the line-of-business sales PMO are not that dissimilar to what you expect to find in a traditional PMO.

Naturally, the variance of techniques is different, but the core value proposition of the PMO is the same. For example, whereas a traditional PMO naturally aligns its methodology and approaches to leading standards such as the PMI Project Management Body of Knowledge (PMBOK®) Guide or the Office of Government and Commerce standard known as PRINCE2, the sales PMO aligns its methodologies and approaches to accepted standards relevant to sales processes and best practices, including Miller Heiman's Strategic Selling®, the de facto standard sales process for complex, high-value sales. Such terms as initiating, planning, executing, monitoring and controlling, and closing provide distinct meaning and are found in the project management processes of the traditional PMO, whereas in the sales PMO the processes for managing complex sales initiatives have different terms such as identifying, qualifying, selling, and implementing.

In addition to processes, the tools of the PMO are different. A traditional PMO might use desktop tools for managing projects like Microsoft Project Professional and server-based applications like Microsoft Project Server, whereas the sales PMO might use desktop tools like Miller Heiman's Sales Access Manager that enables sales professionals to plan and execute sales process activities and tasks and to integrate data into the organization's customer relationship management (CRM) system.

Furthermore, the project mix of the PMO is different. The traditional PMO reports to the IT department, or is a peer to it, and has a project mix of mainly technology and application development projects of some kind, whereas the sales PMO performs a mix of sales projects that typically do not even have a technology or application development component. Examples of sales PMO projects include:

- Sell a complex, high-value solution to a large strategic account with many buyer types and participants
- Expand or open a new sales region
- Analyze and benchmark leading competitors
- Develop or refine the sales process
- Develop or update the total cost of ownership (TCO) or return on investment (ROI) sales tools and techniques
- Plan and manage an executive roadshow
- Coordinate customer invitations and attendance at the annual customer conference
- Refine generic marketing brochures into industry specific sales collaterals
- Build a knowledge base of example proposals, benefits analysis, and objection handling techniques
- Build a customer reference database by industry and by strategic selling decision-maker type (economic buyer, technology buyer, user buyer, and champion)

The projects of the sales PMO and of the various sales professionals who the sales PMO supports provide tremendous value to the organization. Of course they are all but invisible to those in the formal PMO. Are the people who are managing these projects well versed in the language of the project management community? Do they know what the PMBOK® Guide is or that there is such an organization as the Project Management Institute? Has anyone from the traditional PMO reached out to these sales professionals to offer any kind of project management guidance, support, or tools? The answer to these questions is likely to be no.

Sales professionals are probably no more familiar with the processes of the PMBOK® Guide than their project manager counterparts in the traditional PMO are familiar with the processes of strategic selling. Whereas project managers in the traditional PMO might not have a business need to be exposed to processes of strategic selling, sales professionals do have a business need to be exposed to the processes of project management. For those who manage smaller sales projects, a basic exposure to project management concepts might be all that is required. For those who manage complex sales projects that take up to a year or more to complete, formal training in project management is of significant value in helping sales professionals and members of the sales PMO to plan, manage, and successfully deliver their projects.

One last point of comparison and contrast between traditional PMOs and sales PMOs is in the area of metrics. Many traditional PMOs struggle with the concept of PMO metrics. While there is no shortage of excellent techniques and approaches for applying metrics to aid in the measurement of the progress of the project, when it comes to measuring the achievements of the PMO some organizations simply don't try to do it. As project management and IT veteran Tom Mochal (2002) observes, "Many companies [PMOs] don't know much about defining and capturing a good set of metrics."

Sales PMOs, on the other hand, have no difficulty in establishing metrics. In addition to the sales objective for the organization, an obvious measurement, sales PMOs track and report on other key measurements, including competitive wins and losses, new account signings, sales of strategic products, sales by industry/region, and cost per sale. Most sales PMOs inherently abide by the guiding principle of management and measurement by objective—that which is expected should be inspected—and its corollary—that which is not inspected is not achieved.

Sales Project Case Study—The Value of Informal Projects

Why bother about the informal projects of the business units? Doesn't the project management community have enough to do without having to support accidental project managers and their informal projects? These accidental projects aren't part of the project portfolio of the formal PMO and, in the broader scheme of the organization, they are just not that important; or are they?

If you recall, numerous examples of the value of informal projects were cited in the preface of this book. Let's revisit just one of those. Scott, an enterprise software sales representative, was managing a large sales opportunity. The sales effort, which Scott refers to as a project and Scott's manager refers to as a project, was a temporary endeavor that spanned nine months, utilized numerous resources, was guided by a documented and frequently updated project plan, that sought to achieve a unique outcome; in this case a decision by the customer to purchase and implement a $2M security software solution for identity and access management.

Scott's company, an $80M publicly traded firm with a market capitalization of $3B, was forecasting a $20M revenue performance for the quarter, which included Scott's $2M sale as it had been forecasted by management and committed to investors. Regrettably, Scott's project schedule for the sales opportunity lacked integrity. He did not allow sufficient time for the customer legal team to review the software contract, to examine the services statement of work, and to negotiate contract terms and conditions.

Furthermore, Scott's project plan lacked any kind of risk management. There was no risk management plan to anticipate likely risk events and plan mitigation strategies to keep the project on track. As a result each risk event incurred delayed the project for days, if not weeks.

As a result of poor project management the project would not complete on time. Hence, the $2M sale of the solution, and thus revenue recognition for the firm, would not happen as forecasted. When Scott's firm posted the revenue results for the quarter, which fell short of the company's prior forecast to investors by the $2M of Scott's slipped sale, the stock price plummeted from $84 per share to $42 per share in just one day. Scott's project management skills, or lack thereof, cost the firm over $1.5B in market capitalization.

Scott did eventually make his $2M sale, albeit six weeks late. Had Scott applied the barest amount of project management discipline, as opposed to hope and prayer, he could have avoided this project and business disaster. Scott's company did have an IT PMO and, importantly, the collective value of all of the formal project efforts performed by the IT PMO since its inception come nowhere near the $1.5B loss in market capital directly attributable by Scott's informal project effort.

Engineering PMO

Another example of a line-of-business PMO is the engineering PMO. Imagine the number, scale, and impact of projects in an engineering department. Engineering departments exist in a wide variety of organizations from small specialty firms to large corporations to public service providers such as water utilities. Take the case of the Orange County Sanitation District (OCSD) in Fountain Valley, California. OCSD is one of the largest water treatment organizations in the United States serving nearly three million residents. Their infrastructure consists of two hundred miles of sewers, over twenty pump stations, and two large treatment plants. With the environment and public safety at stake, the value of a PMO to the engineering organization could not be more essential.

That is why the director of engineering, David Ludwin, sought to improve the way his organization managed projects. After all, the primary purpose of the department was to do projects. Ludwin observed that engineers were doing double duty, working both on developing and controlling technical designs while at the same time managing project work. While there were some good project results, he felt that better results could be achieved by establishing a

PMO and separating the management of projects from the discipline of engineering. Working with his PMO manager, Matt Smith, the two men planned and established the PMO, which in the eyes of their engineering department, and OCSD in general, was viewed as a home for project managers, the repository of project management best practices, and the place to go to improve project management skills and to successfully deliver projects.

Commenting on the success of OCSD's engineering PMO, Janis Rizzuto (2004) quotes PMO manager Matt Smith, "There's more getting done, more visibility on projects, more professionalism, more respect for the project managers, and more management buy-in to the process." Engineering director, David Ludwin adds, "To try to manage that number of projects and those tight time schedules with our previous system would have been rough. We could have gotten the work done, but not as well."

Marketing PMO

Another example of a line-of-business PMO is the marketing PMO. Just what is marketing? It is an elusive and difficult term for many to describe. I can never forget a comment made by one of my college professors, an avid tennis player, during a lecture in his class. The topic of high-priced tennis shoes came up and the professor rhetorically commented, "Just think about how much less tennis shoes would actually cost if those companies didn't spend so much on marketing their product?" Of course, if no one knew about the shoes they wouldn't buy them. If there wasn't at least one superstar tennis player endorsing and wearing the tennis shoes, it is unlikely that admiring fans and tennis players would purchase them over competing and better-known alternatives and choices. To think that a highly educated professor at a distinguished university could be so adrift in his understanding of the value of marketing highlights the fact that marketing is one of those activities that not all people understand.

At its simplest form marketing is the execution of strategies and tactics used to identify, create, and maintain satisfying relationships with customers that result in a real, or perceived, value obtained by customers from the goods and services they purchase. As a practical example marketing is what compels a fourteen-year-old girl to beg her mother, offering the promise of good grades in return, for that special, must have, and absurdly expensive pair of designer blue jeans.

Commenting on marketing, Andrew Jacob (2008), founder of The Jacob Group, writes, "The absolute best marketing job on planet earth . . . Back in the day, blue jeans were never used as 'going out to impress' pants. Now they are. Why? Pure Marketing Genius from people who sell us the jeans. How genius? $350 to $450 a pair worth of genius."

Many people think of marketing as just tactics that companies employ to get customers to buy their product—advertising on television or radio, mailing out promotional pieces and coupons, or calling you at the dinner hour to offer you information on a new product or service and the opportunity to buy it. Tactics are important. Much like in a sporting contest, tactics are employed as part of the overall plan. For example, on a long par four with a generously wide fairway a golfer might choose to tee up a driver and give it a good wallop in order to have a decent chance to reach the green in two shots. Likewise, on a short par four with a punishingly narrow fairway featuring trouble on both sides, that same golfer might choose to tee up a three wood or even an iron just to keep the tee shot in the fairway. Hitting different clubs off the tee are merely tactics employed in the execution of the game plan to achieve the desired outcome.

And so it goes with marketing. Marketing is far more than tactics; it is the development and execution of a sound marketing strategy based on analysis, expert skill and knowledge, and proven best practices. What do people in the marketing department call the various things that they are working on? They call them projects.

There are many reasons to establish a marketing PMO. Marketing expert and PMO enthusiast Steve Miller (2007) advises, "Many people believe the rigor and discipline of project management mixes with the creative nature of marketing like oil and water. While it does take some getting used to, once the routines are established, the relationship not only works, but the marketing effectiveness actually improves." Traditional PMOs are typically established as a result of three fundamental factors: (1) there is a continued presence of projects; (2) there is a presence of people who manage projects; and (3) there is a presence of a desire by management to improve upon the degree to which projects are undertaken and managed. Of course there is a litany of other considerations, including tools, processes, and methodologies, skill required, and a wide variety of organizational and human resource considerations. However, the core value proposition of the PMO, whether an IT, enterprise, strategic, or line-of-business PMO such as a marketing PMO, is basically the same.

Marketing organizations abound with marketing projects and they are getting increasingly complex. Marketing organizations once went about developing products in somewhat of an opportunistic and ad hoc manner; however, more and more organizations have adopted leading marketing best practices for bringing products to market such as the go-to-market (GTM) process. The GTM process is a sequence of best practice steps for developing marketing plans and strategies. Collectively, the high-level processes of the GTM model include market segmentation, whole solution development, routes to market, financial planning, and performance review. Each of these processes reveals what is required in each marketing and channel program and how much is required to invest to achieve the business objectives for each target market segment. Naturally, outputs of the planning process include identification of the requisite projects to be performed as part of executing the marketing plan.

Many marketing heads view formal project management, as espoused by the project management community, as too rigid and bureaucratic for their needs. In most cases they are correct. Marketing PMOs that simply apply the full rigor of the project management discipline to their projects are likely to spend more time learning project management and project management tools than is actually required. It is far more important for marketing project managers to master and execute the fine details and nuances of the marketing processes, such as the GTM process, than it is to master the PMBOK® Guide.

Challenges of Marketing Project Managers

Most marketing project managers don't know or need to know the details of the PMBOK® Guide, much less be certified as a project management professional (PMP). From the outset it is important to realize that establishing a marketing PMO involves balancing a unique set of challenges. Six of these challenges are worth discussing.

First, the marketing PMO does not belong to, nor should it be merged with, the traditional PMO of the organization. Many people advocate that project management as a discipline is the same no matter what department is applying it. They think that one single, centralized PMO is all that an organization requires. In practical application, project management, and especially a PMO, needs to be tempered to the organization that it is serving.

In the article "Rebranding the PMO," David Hutchinson, chair of the PMI Marketing and Sales Special Interest Group, suggests that there is a public relations problem when it comes to the traditional PMO, "When marketing executives hear "project management" they're not hearing its strategic linkages . . . They're immediately envisioning guys in white short-sleeve shirts with pocket protectors applying slide rules with 40 page documents to complete temporary and unique projects, usually somewhere in the vicinity of the IT department." Hutchinson goes on to suggest that if the traditional project management PMO was rebranded as a performance marketing PMO, marketing executives would be inclined to work more effectively with the project managers of the traditional PMO. Soon after the project managers of the traditional PMO would evolve into high-level portfolio managers working side by side with chief marketing officers (CMOs) and CEOs.

While this might be one roadmap to the nirvana of the perfect, be all, PMO, for most organizations far more is achieved by having multiple PMOs; each with its own mission and set of goals. A strategic PMO at the CEO level is simply different from an IT PMO and that is different from a line-of-business PMO such as the marketing PMO. The projects are different. The magnitude of investment and resources are different. The process and tools are different. The mechanisms for project communication and collaboration are different as are the controlling mechanisms for management and review. While it is tempting to contemplate a theoretical world in which every project effort of the company is managed by just one PMO and captured in its project portfolio management (PPM) system, for most companies this is not a practical or particularly beneficial thing to do.

Second, the projects of the marketing PMO are different from those of the traditional PMO. Marketing projects are not informal projects or simply work efforts comprised of tasks that take on a *project-lite* form. Marketing projects might not have the same degree of technical complexity as IT projects, but they provide the same, and perhaps even greater, return of benefits to the organization. A marketing project to brand a product offering to best appeal to a target market segment might have minimal technology complexity, but it might be steeped in marketing process complexity. As advised by the Information Technology Services Marketing Association (2002), "While marketing projects are getting more complex, the margin of error is shrinking . . . An increasingly common response to these two pressures (complexity and need for project ROI) is the establishment of a project management office." The ITSMA suggests that the marketing PMO should be a relatively flat and agile team that fosters a project management way of thinking. It can then provide the level of rigor needed to ensure the success of marketing projects.

Third, those involved in managing marketing projects should not be cast as professionals in project management; they are professionals in marketing. Much like the university student who has majors in one subject, taking a number of classes to fulfill the requirement of the degree, and minors in another subject, taking a lesser number of classes to fulfill its requirement, marketing project managers should be majors in marketing. Marketing project managers should seek to master the marketing processes and best practices of the industry. Whether sponsored by their company or on their own, they should seek to join professional associations such as the American Marketing Association (AMA), consider becoming an AMA Professional Certified Marketer (PCM™), and continually increase their knowledge and hone their practical skills via ongoing professional development and networking with the community of professional marketers.

Project management should be viewed as a minor. This does not limit the amount of project management training that a marketing project manager should seek to obtain, rather it just places an important priority and understanding that, without the requisite marketing skill and knowledge, the marketing project manager will likely have difficulties being an effective member of the marketing PMO.

Fourth, those managing marketing projects should not be subjected to overly detailed project management methodologies (PMMs). There is no better way to dampen the enthusiasm of those developing a new skill than to inundate them with mountains of information that they do not need. Keep it simple. Marketing projects are inherently shorter in length than projects of the traditional PMO. They have fewer phases, activities, and tasks. To subject a marketing project manager to a PPM with each of the forty-two processes of the PMBOK® Guide is overkill to say the least.

Having said that, there are some useful techniques of formal project management that are rarely present in the management of line-of-business projects like those found in the marketing PMO. Aside from the project schedule and the project budget, many components of good project management are not well represented in the project management that is completed through the lines-of-business organizations. Communications management and risk management, in particular, offer significant help to marketing project managers in the management of their projects. The trick is to find the right balance of methodology and rigor while at the same time keeping the project management process as streamlined and simple as possible.

Fifth, those managing marketing projects should not be expected to learn and use advanced project management techniques such as earned value management (EVM) or detailed risk analysis or perhaps even dynamic scheduling. While it is technically true that simple methods of measuring project performance can be misleading, there needs to be a reasonable fit between the complexities of the project and the complexities of the analysis techniques.

For example, let's say that you have a one-year project and at the six-month mark you happen to ask your project manager how things are going and the response you get is, "The project is going great. We are half-way through the schedule and we have only spent half of the budget." Of course the fact that half of the planned project duration has come to pass and half of the project budget has been spent is of minimal value to know in terms of understanding the true status of the project. While EVM as a technique is far superior to simple time and budget comparisons for a year-long project, its practical value for simple, short-term projects is far less desirous. The same can be said for risk analysis, dynamic scheduling, and other advanced project management techniques. Don't expect, or hold accountable, marketing project managers to use these techniques unless they add value to the project effort.

Sixth, those managing marketing projects should not necessarily be expected to learn the tools of the traditional PMO like Microsoft Project unless those tools are a good fit for the needs of the project. If the project effort can be successfully managed using a simpler tool, then let the marketing project manager use it. If a tool like Microsoft Excel is all that is needed to plan and manage the tasks, resources, and budget of a project, then don't force the team to use a more complicated tool like Microsoft Project Professional. They likely would use the tool in a simplistic manner not taking advantage of the tool's many features and functions and project management tools are expensive. At over five hundred dollars per license, equipping even a small marketing PMO team with Microsoft Project Professional, along with a minimal amount of fee-based training, can be an expense equivalent to a new team member.

Additionally, other tools, while not as important to the traditional PMO, might be of greater value to the marketing PMO; tools for brainstorming, idea sharing, and collaboration.

Summary

Project management is all around us. It exists in nearly every aspect of our lives, both professional and personal. When an organization, any organization, reaches a certain critical mass with respect to projects and the number of people in the organization who are involved in managing projects, there might be a tremendous opportunity to improve project management and a good fit for a PMO.

For reasons too numerous to cite, most people have a preconceived idea of what project management is, what a PMO does, and to whom in the organization a PMO should report. Much of this stereotype is simply rooted in history. The project management that we take for granted today has been made possible by the tireless efforts of those in the project management community from the inception of the PMI in 1969 to the establishment and refinement of the PMBOK® Guide and other best practices and standards. To the individuals responsible for those works, the world owes extreme gratitude. However, standards for the application of project management, like any practice or endeavor, need to be improved over time and expanded to other realms of possibility. They need to meet the needs of both the most ardent of followers, seeking to master the craft, and the most casual of practitioner, perhaps even oblivious to the existence of the craft.

Enter the emergence of the line-of-business PMO. With a critical mass of people performing project management as a core part of their job duties, line-of-business PMOs help an organization to improve project management, utilize resources more efficiently, and achieve more beneficial results through improved processes. As always, it is critically important to understand the expectation of stakeholders. In line-of-business PMOs, unlike traditional PMOs, the primary concern of stakeholders is not beholden to the project management community. Their allegiance will always be, and should be, to their functional discipline and the achievement of the business objectives for which they exist to serve. A VP of sales no doubt appreciates the value that project management offers to the sales organization, but the first and foremost concern of each and every day is the achievement of sales objectives, rather than getting better at project management for project management's sake.

Rather than the traditional view of project management as a formal discipline to be practiced only by those in the official PMO of the organization, a new mindset for project management and the PMO is rapidly gaining popularity. This mindset is rooted in three simple and practical premises. First, project management is ubiquitous; it is everywhere. Second, efforts to introduce a right-sized level of project management rigor such as the establishment of a line-of-business PMO can help the organization achieve its functional goals and objectives. Third, though it is tempting to contemplate the existence of an uber-PMO, the practical reality that most organizations face calls for a simpler, easier to manage approach, the line-of-business PMO.

Questions

1. In what ways are project management and PMOs ubiquitous?
2. Is it an oversight to assume that projects outside of the traditional PMO are merely informal projects?
3. What two events of the 1980s changed the way in which large corporate staffs were viewed?
4. What is a line-of-business PMO?
5. What business drivers would lead to the establishment of a line-of-business PMO?
6. What are the benefits of a line-of-business PMO?
7. Should line-of-business PMOs conform to the processes of the traditional PMO?
8. Should line-of-business PMOs use the tools of the traditional PMO?
9. What is an example of the purpose of a sales PMO?
10. What kinds of projects are found in a sales PMO?
11. What is an example of the purpose of a marketing PMO?
12. What kinds of projects are found in a Marketing PMO?
13. To what extent do traditional PMOs provide support, guidance, and tools to those managing informal projects in the various lines of businesses?
14. Should line-of-business PMOs adopt the same processes and degree of rigor for managing projects that the traditional PMO of the organization has in place and uses?
15. What factors and attributes indicate that a line-of-business PMO is of value to the organization?
16. Should all the PMOs of an organization be consolidated into one overarching, large PMO?
17. Which is likely to be of more value to an organization, the formal projects of a traditional PMO or the collective (informal) projects that exist throughout the entire organization and outside the scope of the traditional PMO?

References

Hutchinson, David. 2008. "Rebranding the PMO." http://www.pmimssig.org. (Accessed June 16, 2008)

Jacob, Andrew 2008. "Designer Blue Jeans: The Absolute Best Marketing on the Planet." *The Jacob Report.*

Kendall, Gerald I. and Steven C. Rollins. 2003. *Advanced Project Portfolio Management and the PMO*, Florida: J. Ross Publishing.

Method 123 Project Office Methodology. 2006. "Role of a PMO." http://www.mpom.com/pmo.php. (Accessed June 16, 2008)

Miller, Steve. 2007. "Marketing Project Management Office Roadmap to Success." http://www.bizcovering.com. (Accessed June 16, 2008)

Miller, Steve. 2007. "Project Management Office Provides Better Marketing Results." http://www.ezinearticles.com. (Accessed June 16, 2008)

Mochal, Tom. 2002. "Leverage the PMO to Consolidate Project Status and Metrics." http://www.articles.techrepublic.com. (Accessed June 16, 2008)

Rizzuto, Janis. 2004. "Engineering PMO Success." http://www.projectsatwork.com. (Accessed June 16, 2008)

Executive Insights

Go-to-Market Project Management

Dave Larson

Marketing PMO Specialist, BOT International

In many companies one of the areas that project management has forgotten about is the marketing department. Project management can be of tremendous value to the marketing departments in companies of all shapes and sizes. I take this topic to heart because I have used it for many years throughout my career in one form or another. At BOT we use it and improve upon it incessantly. It is an integral part of our company culture and the way we do business, make decisions, manage projects, and fulfill our vision of what we seek to achieve and become as a company. It is called the go-to-market project management process, which we simply refer to as GTM.

In companies today the new and most important office is the PMO, and the most important team today are those that run the projects from start to finish. However, one fact that I have noticed is that many companies don't have a PMO team working on marketing projects nor helping the sales team with sales projects. I am not referring to the formal IT projects that support the end users of those departments such as implementing a CRM system like Salesforce.com or Siebel, rather I am referring to the departmental projects within marketing and sales such as a marketing event, a competitive analysis, or a complex sale.

Old Style Marketing

When I see a marketing project within a company, it is typically a push marketing project such as telemarketing, an email blitz, or some form of direct mail like a mass mailing of a letter or brochure. Push marketing is a numbers game. It is all about pushing material on a prospect in the hope that they respond to what they receive.

Here is the problem with a typical push campaign. On average 90 to 95 percent of the time the received item is tossed, pushed aside, or deleted from the email system, not even close to being opened. At a recent business partner event, which was sponsored by a large and well-known technology firm, the subject was helping small partners reach their business goals through marketing. I was attending this event as a guest of one of the reseller partners of this firm, a friend and CEO of a small systems integration company who I have known for years.

Most of the companies that attended were small firms, resellers of the partner, employing three to ten employees with a small or total lack of a marketing budget. They maintained a small sales team and a professional services staff that kept the firm afloat by providing billable installation and training services to its limited customer base. The amount of revenue, and in particular profit, derived from actually reselling products was not what kept these companies alive.

The speaker gave us a PowerPoint presentation on Marketing 101, which included:

◆ How to write a letter to a prospect
◆ How to put a marketing brochure together
◆ What color paper to use
◆ What color and size envelope to use so that a prospect opens and reads it (yeah, right)
◆ What kind of stamp to use on the envelope
◆ What day of the week to mail it
◆ How to fold the letter
◆ What color ink to use for your signature

WOW!! I couldn't believe my ears. Next in the Marketing 101 presentation was how to follow up on the letter sent previously. We learned how to call, what time to call, how to get past the administrative assistant, phrases to use, (Did you get my letter?) and other techniques for getting in the door. WOW again!! Marketing 101 for the 1960s and 1970s was being taught in 2008. The best part of the presentation was when someone asked what kinds of colored envelopes should be used and in what sizes so that they got past the gatekeeper and on to the decision maker. WOW again!! We spent over an hour on that question. It was almost as if this was somebody's idea of a joke. The presentation would have been funny if that were only the case.

New Style Marketing

I then started asking the presenter questions about newer, more contemporary approaches to marketing and the idea of executing a GTM strategy, rather than hope and prayer, using the current processes and tools that are working so well today. Since the presenter didn't know the concepts of web marketing, I gave her and the audience a short description of it. I mentioned such things as driving the target market to the company's website via search engine optimization, pay-per-click marketing, dynamic content like podcasts and blogs that provide a revisit value to prospects. I described the other side of the coin.

That is, the ability to monitor their visit in real time once the prospect has come to your business website and to interact with them by providing information, answering technical questions, offering a demonstration, or offering the visitor an opportunity to speak with a sales representative.

WOW! Current technology at work to drive leads, build a sales pipeline, establish a forecast, and achieve the marketing and sales objectives of the company. This is pull marketing. When I asked the presenter if she would be covering any of these marketing tactics, she said *no* and continued to stress that the traditional marketing (telemarketing and direct mail) works just fine when you're building a business, especially in a small shop environment in which customers need to see and have face-to-face contact with their small company suppliers.

I then asked the presenter this question, 'Would a prospect more likely open a letter, an email, or go to a website to learn more about my company?' The presenter answered back, 'A letter.' to which I replied, 'Wrong!' My next question was, 'If a prospect is evaluating my products and services, would it not be good to know they are in our website, browsing through our website pages, and then have the ability to communicate with them via live chat, to service their visit and to find out if they had any pressing questions?' Again I was told that traditional marketing in a small business environment works best. Again I replied, 'Wrong!'

My next question was on demand pull marketing via push marketing and between the two, what would her firm suggest we use to drive business? I already knew the answer I was going to get. It was push marketing. The rationale was the same old thing; it works just fine when you're building a business, especially in a small shop environment in which customers need to see and have face-to-face contact with their small company suppliers.

When the meeting ended a number of the attendees converged on me. They were all interested in how to get measurable results from the marketing efforts. By measurable results they were not referring to the number of telemarketing calls made or direct mail pieces sent, rather they were referring to such things as the number of new sales prospects, new qualified leads, and, of course, new sales. I can't recall anyone expressing much interest in the color or size of envelopes. That is not to say that there is not a place in the marketing mix for the traditional marketing approaches of yesteryear, only that they represent one small component of an overall marketing mix—a component that is increasingly costly and decreasingly effective.

Emergence of the Marketing PMO

Marketing departments as an organizational unit are nothing new. Large companies typically have a marketing organization of some kind. Smaller companies might have marketing and sales combined as a single organizational unit. Regardless of the size of the company and its organizational construct for marketing, all companies engage in some marketing.

Although it is generally understood that the marketing staff engages in planning and executing one marketing project after another, how best to support the project efforts of these people is far less understood. Project management and PMO enthusiasts might advocate training and using a project management tool to improve the project management abilities and results achieved by the team, but this would be an incorrect approach. The reason is simple; marketing people aren't in the business of becoming professional project managers, they are in the business of meeting their marketing goals and objectives.

Obviously the two go hand-in-hand, but the way to get there is different. The key is not to focus on project management for project management's sake, but rather to focus on the needs that the marketing organization has that can best be met by applying project management techniques and by establishing a marketing PMO to drive the efforts and achievements of the marketing staff.

Let's take a look at how your marketing PMO can help you do this. The first thing to understand is that traditional push marketing, such as telemarketing and direct mail, is task-oriented; pull marketing is project-oriented. The second thing to understand is that before we talk about the many kinds of pull projects a marketing PMO can pursue, there needs to be a clear view on why pull marketing is of any importance to the organization. In particular the sales team in a marketing role must at least enable, if not drive, success in sales.

Benefits of Pull Marketing

Pull marketing, often referred to as demand pull, is all about pulling your target marketing customers to you as opposed to pushing yourself on them. Who is likely to be a better prospect for your next sale? Someone who comes to you and visits your website after doing a Google search to find a particular product or someone that you go to perhaps telemarketing them and interrupting them in their busy day (assuming your call was even answered). I think you would all agree that someone who comes to you and who already has an interest would be a better prospect. Consider the following marketing and sales universal truths:

- ◆ Most sales VPs need more qualified leads, not more salesmen
- ◆ The sales organization is responsible for revenue attainment
- ◆ The marketing organization is responsible for generating qualified leads
- ◆ For every dollar of sales quota, marketing must produce a GTM plan to achieve four dollars of qualified leads—no exceptions, no excuses

- ◆ All sales VPs have a revenue quota
- ◆ Few marketing VPs have a quota for lead generation
- ◆ Deming, an intelligent man, once said, "Fix the process, and you fix the problem."

Hence, before talking about a marketing PMO, it is actually quite important to address what marketing should do and what marketing should be held accountable for. Figure 11.2 illustrates the significant benefits of pull marketing.

A driver and fundamental principle of GTM planning is the accountability of marketing. First, they must have quotas just like their sales counterparts. For example, let's say that the revenue objective (sales quota) for the sales organization is $50M. If it takes four dollars of qualified leads to produce one dollar of sales, then marketing must have a lead generation quota of $200M—the requisite amount per the qualified leads to sales multiplier.

Now this doesn't mean that marketing directly performs all of the work to achieve the needed qualified leads. However, marketing is on the hook for the GTM plan and how all of the various components of the plan, including direct sales, business partners, and marketing, contribute to the overall plan requirement for qualified leads. As an example it is customary that the sales team does some prospecting, cold calling, and business development. However, if the sales teams are the only people in the organization doing lead generation, then that is an expensive lead generation channel, not to mention a clear

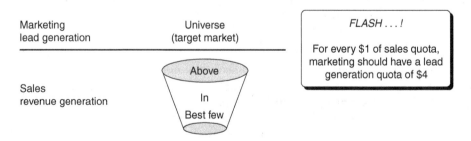

Benefits of pull marketing

1. Customers that come to you are 4 times more likely to buy than customers that you have to find

2. The sales cycle is significantly shorter when customers come to you

3. The need to price discount is significantly less and often not required when customers initiate the purchase

Marketing lead generation	Universe (target market)	
	Above	FLASH . . . !
Sales revenue generation	In	For every $1 of sales quota, marketing should have a lead generation quota of $4
	Best few	

Figure 11.2 Benefits of pull marketing

sign that the head of marketing is not doing much of anything for the sales organization.

Marketing tasks such as creating a logo, designing business cards, developing and maintaining presentations are just work tasks. These things are not a marketing plan, nor the achievement of any kind of marketing plan objective. The sooner the executive team realizes that marketing too should have a quota and it should be based on, and directly related to, the quota of the sales team, the sooner marketing develops a GTM plan and engages in GTM projects to achieve that quota.

Case Study

I recently met with the VP of marketing and VP of sales of a company trying to change their marketing and sales direction. This company had gained all their business from U.S. government contracts and wanted to start penetrating the commercial marketplace, so they decided to change their product marketing strategy—sales-pitch—to meet the needs of this new target market.

Before my visit I started doing my homework on this company to see what story they had in the wonderful world of the internet and what kind of awareness they had achieved on the internet. On my first Google search, the first article that came up was on a lawsuit that was filed against them, and the second item was a negative article about them, and finally moving down the Google page, the company website showed up in position 7. WOW!!

I asked the VP of marketing and sales when they planned on fixing the search engine mess, changing their search engine key words, and contacting Google to get the first position negative item removed. I also asked if they had started working on their GTM strategy for the commercial marketplace and what their plan was to build a sales pipeline of qualified leads rapidly for this new market segment.

Here is the answer, 'We are creating a new brochure' and 'all that other stuff we haven't really thought about.' WOW again!!!

They asked me to explain further the GTM process in terms of plans, strategies, and projects. The company realized that despite their high hopes for entering the new commercial market segment, all they really had to show for their time, thoughts, and efforts was a dressed up, made over brochure. This wasn't a plan; it was just a hope and not even a good one at that. Here was a company that had no marketing PMO to help them, had no GTM plans and projects, and was not sure what to do next. Here was a company destined to fail, if not, at least be outcompeted, in its effort to enter a new market.

Requirements for Pull Marketing

There are three components that are required to successfully engage in GTM pull marketing; GTM planning, GTM traffic building, and GTM pipeline building. GTM planning involves the ability to skillfully segment and select the target market, provide solutions that meet a minimum set of unmet needs required to satisfy the target market customer, execute the best possible routes-to-market mix, and align the specific objectives for the functional units such as sales, marketing, business development, services and support to the revenue commitments of the company's business plan.

GTM traffic building consists of web marketing techniques such as search engine optimization to enable the target market customers to find your business website. This involves developing good webpage content and good webpage coding of the various HTML tags that search engines use to index your website. Additionally, web marketing techniques such as pay-per-click ads and banners along with directory listings all contribute to enabling the target market customer to find you.

GTM pipeline building refers to the building of a sales pipeline of qualified customer prospects in the target market. Once you have pulled the target market to your business website, you must say hello. This involves monitoring your business website and engaging with your customers in real time.

Some old style marketers use such techniques as providing a website form for a customer to fill out so that they get a white paper, but these are yesterday's tricks and they rarely ever work. Most customers are reluctant to give out their contact information too early in their information gathering process. Hence, most so-called leads from white papers are nothing more than consultants and competitors surfing the web for information and insights.

Driving the target market to your website and servicing them once they are there is a far better approach. Think about it: if you were the owner of a shoe store and a customer prospect entered your place of business, wouldn't you say hello and offer to be of assistance. Not to do so would be bad business, and, to some, customer insensitive. Additionally, you need to think about the high cost of participating in an event or industry conference and the time or cost involved with planning for it, doing it, not to mention all of the follow up. You might budget and pay $25K to participate in such a conference attended by a few hundred customers, maybe less. At the same time, every day at your website are hundreds, maybe thousands, of customer prospects. They are already in your shoe store and you aren't even saying hello. WOW!!

Why We Have a Marketing PMO

Our company created a marketing PMO, not to learn project management, but to drive the strategic vision of our company and to achieve the aggressive sales and marketing goals and objectives that we felt were needed to become the kind of company that our target market customers would seek out. As the head of the marketing PMO, I can tell you that it was not about project management; it was all about the customer. How to know what they want? How to service them? How to engage in forward going business discussions in the manner that is customer-oriented? How to save the customer time and money in their evaluation, selection, and implementation process? How to anticipate all that the customer needs and to best position ourselves where we can help and where we cannot help in their *big* picture, not just our view. The answers to all of these questions are driven by the strategies and projects of the marketing PMO. Everyone else in the organization (I like to say) is a gear-box, a high-performing well-oiled machine that follows and continuously improves upon their work processes. But the marketing PMO plans and executes the GTM projects.

How We Did It

Any company can have a marketing PMO and do what we did and here is how. To get started, name your marketing PMO manager. For a larger company this is a full time role, but for a smaller company it can be an assigned duty and a virtual PMO office-style organization. It is not important that the marketing PMO manager be a certified PMP; I wasn't one. But it is important that the marketing PMO manager have domain knowledge in the processes and best practices of sales and marketing, and it helps greatly if the marketing PMO manager has had experience in some kind of quota-based position such as a sales rep, sales manager, or business unit manager. It has been my experience and the experience of others that it is difficult for those who have never been on a quota to step into an objective-rich environment in which people are actually held accountable for their results.

Go-to-Market Planning

After naming the marketing PMO manager, the next step is to develop the GTM plan. This is a project all on its own. Domain knowledge in sales and marketing best practices is far more important than knowledge of the PMBOK®. Having said that, it is quite important to treat the GTM plan development as a project effort; otherwise there is a natural tendency to plan, and plan, and plan, and never execute the plan. There are countless changes in scope that are inherent to the project. These scope additions (opportunities) need to be managed via good project management techniques. If not, the GTM plan is subject to continual re-planning.

Phases of the GTM project plan are (1) market segmentation, (2) whole solution development, (3) routes to market, (4) financial planning, and (5) ongoing management review of the performance of the GTM plan and the GTM projects (see Figure 11.3).

Going into the details of each of these GTM project phases would be a chapter in itself, therefore we simply offer a few comments. What is most important to realize is that GTM project management process offers an organization the opportunity to plan, execute, and achieve business sales and marketing objectives as a matter of process and project management as opposed to hope and prayer. Naturally the output of the GTM plan is a list of the specific, prioritized GTM projects for the marketing PMO to perform as well as a sales and marketing balanced scorecard measurement model that aligns both the marketing goals in the form of quotas to the strategic business plan measurements such as revenue, profit, market share, and customer satisfaction. It is important to note that for most organizations none of these projects are found among the formal projects of the formal PMO. These are line-of-business, end user projects.

GTM Traffic Building

The next step in the GTM project management process, in support of the GTM plan and GTM projects, is GTM traffic building. As mentioned earlier, this is all about getting the target market to your business website. We looked at hiring a web marketing firm that specializes in search engine optimization to do this work for us, but we felt it was too important to outsource. We needed to acquire the skills and knowledge ourselves to sustain our efforts. We were concerned that reliance on a third party for this work might result in this important element of our GTM strategy being rendered to a one-time effort as opposed to a continuing priority.

We purchased a tool from Webtrends called Web Position 4 and began the process of optimizing our business website. A key consideration in optimizing our website was the desire not just to increase the traffic to our website, but rather the traffic of our target market to our website. These are two different things and were important concepts for us to grasp, especially when it comes to paying for our traffic. Search engine optimization of our business website enabled our target market to find us (see Figure 11.4).

After a few months of effort we could be found on the World Wide Web. For many keywords that were important and relevant to our product, we were able to achieve a prominent first page position from the search results

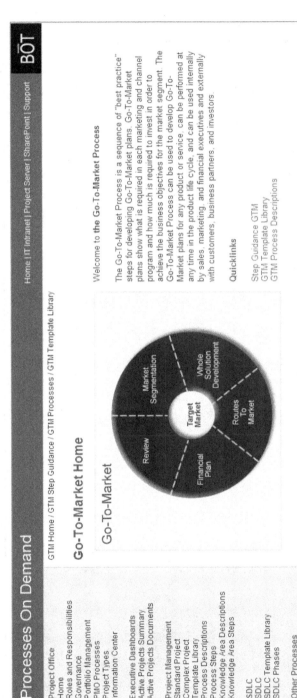

Figure 11.3 Go-to-market project management

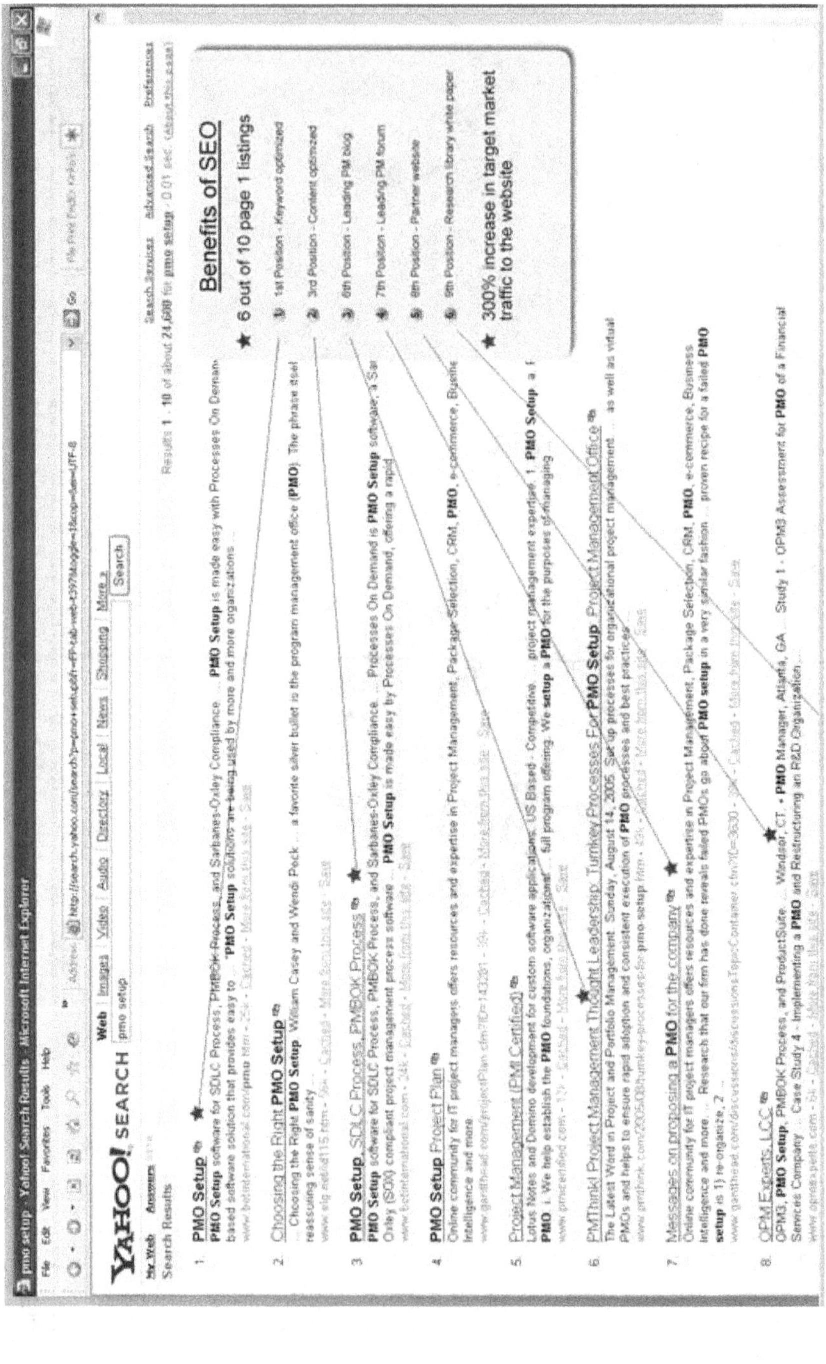

Figure 11.4 Search engine optimization

of Yahoo and Google. In some cases, of the ten listings on the first page (see Figure 11.4), we would occupy several of those coveted spots. As a result our business website traffic increased 300 percent in six months.

In addition to search engine optimization, we also used Pay-Per-Click web marketing to enable our target market to find us. Again, these efforts were managed as GTM projects; not just marketing campaigns or spends. Our Pay-Per-Click GTM projects were extremely important to us because they enabled us to be found by our target marketing customer when they used certain keyword searches that, due to circumstances beyond our control, would not list us in the natural search return results (see Figure 11.5).

Pay-Per-Click marketing enabled us to target ads to specific keywords. This ensured visibility to our target market and it increased our website traffic another 100 percent. Again, our Pay-Per-Click GTM projects were managed as projects. As we had over 100 various ads, it was important from both a cost and effectiveness perspective to manage these ads in parallel to our other marketing mix investments and in parallel to the activities and priorities of the sales team. For example, if we were introducing a new product capability or entering a new country, the GTM project plan was updated to reflect and support that strategy. Also important to note, we took pains not to be found and not to increase web traffic outside of our target market as this would result in both higher costs of marketing and potentially time-consuming activities with organizations that would be unprofitable for us to serve.

GTM Pipeline Building

The next step in the GTM project management process, in support of the GTM plan and GTM projects, is GTM pipeline building. This offers the marketing PMO the chance to truly be a hero to the sales organization. In our marketing PMO, GTM pipeline building is performed as a GTM project. At a high level, GTM pipeline building involves three things; monitoring the website, servicing target market customers who are visiting the website, and achievement of the GTM pipeline building project objectives.

We looked at building our own monitoring system but quickly discovered that there are numerous Software-as-a-Service (SaaS) tools out there with great functionality that we could never develop internally as well or at an equivalent cost. They come with knowledgeable customer service people too! Besides, we are not in the business of building website monitoring and communication systems. Our website monitoring tool enables us to see who is in our business website, what pages they are looking at, and how they found us—a Google search or from a URL link of another site (see Figure 11.6).

Of course the greatest value of the tool is that it enables us to immediately and in real time communicate with our website visitor. Over the years we have learned some interesting facts for GTM pipeline building. Did you know

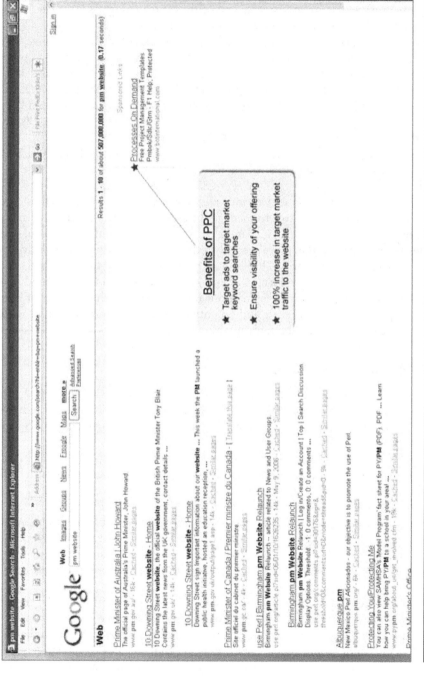

Figure 11.5   Pay-per-click

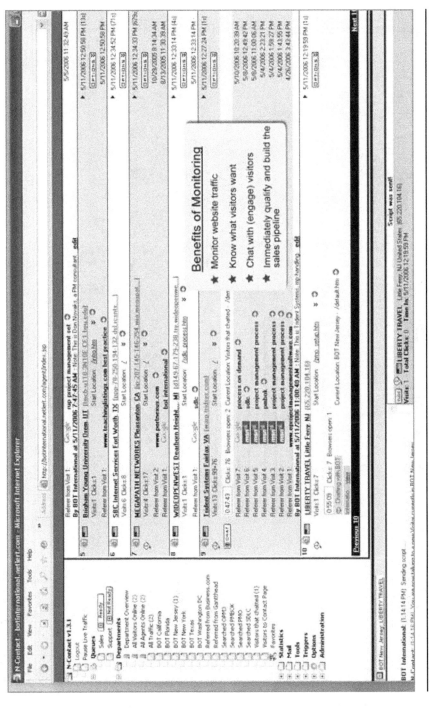

Figure 11.6   Website monitoring

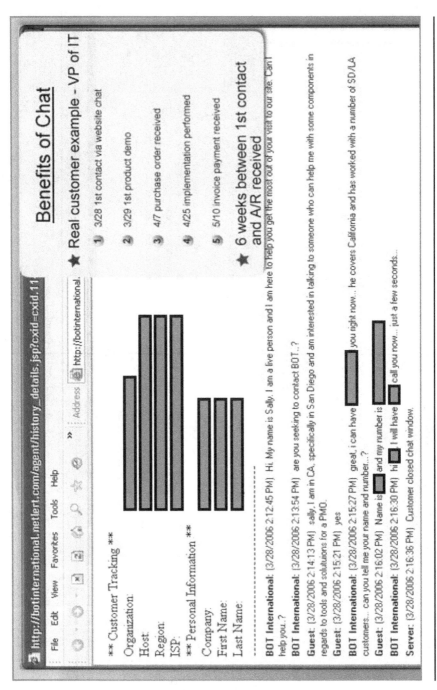

Figure 11.7 Website chat

that only two percent of website visitors fill in a contact form? Decision makers do not want to provide their contact information or talk to a sales rep too early in their information gathering process. Often this is pre-evaluation.

Did you know that only four percent of website visitors call a toll-free number? Again, many decision makers do not want to provide their contact information or talk to a sales rep too early in their information gathering process.

Did you know that nine percent of website visitors click on an email link? When offered, decision makers click on an email link and prefer it over entering the contact information into a website form. Even with the auto-fill feature of most browsers, decision makers are reluctant to have their contact information residing in a vendor's marketing database.

Did you know that 38 percent of website visitors respond to a website's live chat? Some visitors no doubt close a chat invitation or might not even recognize it as a live person, thinking it to be an automatic popup. However, when offered, most website visitors interested in the product interact with a knowledgeable and helpful live chat agent. This can greatly improve their website experience, provide them the information that they need, and, most importantly, it is all conducted at the time and convenience of the website visitor. Figure 11.7 depicts the effectiveness of website monitoring and chat.

From the initial website visit of the target marketing customer to not only closing this business opportunity, but performing the implementation and receiving customer payment, the entire sales cycle took a mere six weeks. This is how the marketing PMO makes the VP of sales, and the CEO of the company for that matter, happy.

As part of the GTM strategy and GTM projects, we continually review the performance of the GTM projects. Metrics are part and parcel to the success. From the initial contact to the receipt of payment, we track just over ten key measurements that inform us and provide insight into how well we are doing. Well before the end of the quarter, the marketing PMO has a view (and provides it to management) of the quality of the sales pipeline and veracity of the quarterly revenue forecast.

Summary

I hope you find this discussion of GTM project management and the value of the marketing PMO to be informative and enjoyable. I started my career over three decades ago as a controller for U.S. Steel. I like to think that I am an outgoing, personable individual, but deep down at heart I am a numbers guy. When the numbers don't add up or the plan doesn't make sense, I am not one who can sit idly by and hope for the best. When it comes to managing a business, if given a choice between immaculate hope and prayer or sensible processes and projects, I always choose the latter.

The traditional marketing organizations that are found in today's businesses are slowly adapting to the possibilities of today. Nonetheless, I am continually dumbfounded with some of those old style marketing types who really believe in those colored and oversized envelopes as the method to reach new customers. All I can say is that if it works for you, keep at it. But what I am seeing more and more, and find much more interesting, is the emergence of line-of-business PMOs in the various divisions and operating units of a company. Of all of those potential places for a line-of-business PMO to land, I can't think of a more strategic place for the company than the marketing department.

There are some who advocate the concept of the Uber PMO, but I am not one of them. The formal projects of a strategic PMO are vastly different from the informal projects of the lines of business as are the processes, tools, and staff. Although I don't like the terms informal projects or accidental project managers—they tend to diminish the value and importance to the organization of such projects and people—I would rather have those terms than to mash everyone up into one PMO and one view of how projects and PMOs are to be managed.

The marketing PMO is all about accountability; not doing projects for project's sake. For far too long those in marketing have had no real skin in the game. Whereas the sales VP is on the hook for meeting a quarterly revenue objective, the marketing guy is tending to marketing brochures, website logos, and business cards. For those organizations that understand the value of setting concrete and specific marketing goals and objectives, aligned to the objectives of the sales team, and driven by the overall business plan, they find that a key strategic enabler to achieving those objectives is the marketing PMO. Business plan aligned marketing projects or colored envelopes. The choice is yours!

12

Advancing Organizational Project Management:
From Theory to Practice

For many enthusiasts of project management maturity, the cartoon in Figure 12.1 hits close to home. Maturity, in any discipline, has at its roots a passion for getting things correct and, arguably, the Organizational Project Management Maturity Model (PMMM) referred to as OPM3® is the leading standard and crème de la crème of maturity models for organizational project management, bar none.

OPM3® was developed by the Project Management Institute (PMI) to help organizations improve on their project management capabilities. It is but one of many PMMMs. What makes it particularly unique is that it was developed with the participation and input of thousands of project management professionals (PMPs) all over the world, using a consensus building process and approach to enable OPM3® to be recognized as an official standard for assessing, developing, and improving project, program, and portfolio management capabilities. OPM3® seeks to deliver its value promise of helping organizations execute their strategies through projects, the key to organizational project management, by providing three interlocking elements: (1) knowledge; (2) assessment; and (3) improvement.

The knowledge element refers to foundational concepts. OPM3® can be viewed as a body of knowledge for organizational project management and, in essence, it extends the PMI Project Management Body of Knowledge (PMBOK®) into the additional domains of program management and portfolio management. PMI's *PMBOK® Guide* is integral to any maturity assessment for an organization, and the assessor's detailed familiarity with this standard is

Figure 12.1   PMO comics—improvement

required. The assessment element refers to the evaluation of the organization. This is completed via the OPM3® Self Assessment (OPM3® Online) or via the OPM3® ProductSuite Assessment® administered by a PMI certified OPM3® Assessor/Consultant. The improvement element refers to roadmaps that can take the organization from its current state of capabilities to its desired state.

Conceptually, the big picture of OPM3® is that it helps organizations to bridge the chasm that exists between their strategy (on one side) and their ability to successfully, consistently, and predictably deliver projects that affect the organization's strategy (on the other side). In terms of project management speak, OPM3® spans the domains of projects, programs, and portfolios. Projects are temporary endeavors undertaken to create a unique outcome. Programs are groups of related projects managed in a coordinated way. And portfolios are collections of projects and programs grouped together enabling management to meet strategic business objectives. Similar to other process improvement methodologies and approaches, including Six Sigma, OPM3® provides sequential stages of process improvement. In OPM3®'s case, four stages of process improvement—(1) standardize, (2) measure, (3) control, and (4) continuously improve—referred to as SMCI, are provided.

Caveats of OPM3®

Theoretically, the benefits of OPM3® are that it enables an organization to understand its current level of maturity, identify areas for improvement, and implement improvements that enable the organization to advance its strategies through the successful management of projects. However, before making a commitment to go forward with an OPM3® initiative and to realize the promise of OPM3® and reap practical value from its theoretical construct, there are a few caveats to consider.

First, OPM3® is not the only approach to organizational project management maturity. Nearly every firm that provides project management solutions, consulting, and training has their own version of what is referred to as a PMMM for the organization. Some organizations get clever with their acronyms naming their PMMMs in a variety of ways such as P3M, PM³, and P2MM. The point is that long before there ever was an OPM3®, there were, and still are, other maturity models provided by project management firms and used by hundreds of organizations, at least for now. In fact the team that developed OPM3 studied twenty-seven different maturity models that were in the market at the time of OPM3's original development.

Additionally, many of these other models and approaches have been vetted through numerous project management maturity engagements. The accumulated skills and experiences of the consulting professionals that do this work bring tremendous value to organizations seeking to improve their project management capabilities via a fee-based consulting engagement of some kind. Perhaps the most important point of consideration is that firms that specialize in doing this work go about it with their eye solely on their client. With no other distraction such as developing and improving upon a worldwide standard, these various consulting firms and consultants can develop and continuously refine their practice and their target marketing and engagement techniques.

Unbridled with all that developing and managing that a worldwide standard of excellence entails, consulting firms and consultants can remain loyal and committed, if they choose to do so, to their own homegrown PMMM and organizational project management consulting practice. They can streamline their offerings to actionable and sellable services engagements that they can successfully deliver within the knowledge, skill sets, and practical experiences of their teams. These firms are not concerned with, nor held highly accountable for, conforming to a standard from which a certification can be administered. Additionally, they are not concerned with ensuring adherence to other prior works and domains into a common structure. While the plurality of the benefit of OPM3® serves the project management community at large satisfactorily, it is sorely needed and has been greeted with nothing short of fanfare. That doesn't necessarily mean that it is the only show in town. As a practical matter there is, and probably always will be, more than one way to skin a cat.

As a second caveat, OPM3® incorporates the PMBOK®. As an asset to the project management community, the PMBOK® provides tremendous value as the standard from which the most widely recognized certification for project management can be administered. As an asset to project management training firms and the PMI, the PMBOK® has created a certification and training industry and a steady-state revenue stream. As an asset to organizations that manage projects, the PMBOK® describes the *what* in terms of project management knowledge that many project managers need to possess and there is a degree of value in this. However, the PMBOK® does not provide any kind of *how to* context for actually managing a project. It is not a project management methodology (PMM) or project life cycle or project life span. OPM3® helps organizations do the work of creating the governance structures, policies, processes, metrics, control systems, and other culture-changing elements that are unique to each organization.

It is up to the organization to develop such things using the PMBOK®, where useful, as a helpful foundation along with other content assets. OPM3® has already proven its value as a standard from which a certification can be administered and as a revenue stream enjoyed by the usual parties, but its value to project management offices (PMOs) still needs to be earned each and every day. Would a newly certified OPM3® consultant do a better job with a client than a seasoned consultant with years of practical experience and a track record of success using their own approaches?

In fairness this is actually a partial caveat. While the seasoned practice team with their own model might perform a stellar engagement to the delight of the client, what is the long term vitality of that team and their model? Would that firm have the resources to develop and extend upon their working model to include the leading thoughts and experiences of experts all over the world? Of course they would not.

Thirdly, to the skeptical consultant with his/her own model, OPM3® is a competing product. It might have started out as a work effort to produce a worldwide standard and it no doubt has PMI origins, but it is a product offering nonetheless and is intended to achieve success by measure of mindshare, market share, revenue, an obliteration of other alternatives, and granted successful outcomes. Though it has been *anointed* by the upper levels, like any other product offering, OPM3® is not immune to shortcomings and difficulties in execution. It must earn its keep and continually improve not only to fulfill its initial value promise to its customers but to be a pertinent offering over the long haul worthy of continued attention. These are the caveats of OPM3® or are they?

In voicing concerns over OPM3®, Craig Curran-Morton (2004) who offers a maturity model that competes with OPM3 writes, "An initial concern with the OPM3® involves the survey methodology. It is based on Yes/No answers that are perplexing when you're trying to conduct a comprehensive assessment of an organization's project management practices." He goes on to cite the example of a woman being either pregnant or not. Such binary assessments of condition are almost always problematic when assessing a capability and they rarely allow for degrees of quality and attainment.

For example, consider the first question in the PMI OPM3® Self Assessment (2003), "Are the sponsor and other stakeholders involved in setting a direction for the project that is in the best interests of all stakeholders?" In terms of understanding and answering this assessment question, there are a few problems. The *sponsor* is an unambiguous term, but *other stakeholders* leaves quite a bit of room for interpretation. Likewise, *setting a direction for the project* and *best interests of all stakeholders* can be ambiguous and mean quite different things to different people. What kind of direction and how good of a direction are we talking about? Best interests by its nature are subjective. To what degree of consideration are we truly assessing? Is this consideration in the form of a roll call, a vote, an assumption, or a guess? Do we really mean all stakeholders or just the important stakeholders. It is easy to agree with the critics that a yes/ no answer to these kinds of qualitative assessment questions, as opposed to a scale, makes for inaccurate answers and an inaccurate model.

Let's take a look at question two of the assessment, "Does your organization consider risk during project selection?" Once again, to what degree are we talking about? Are we talking about a detailed consideration of all risks or merely a glance and a wink? Are we talking about all projects or just the ones that have a risk component requiring consideration?

Additionally, while high-level risks are addressed in any project selection process worth its weight in salt via standard documentation, what about the projects that the executives approve and tee up for project initiation without going through the project selection process? Some projects are obvious to the organization and to the executives and do not require any kind of formal pre-initiation work. If the organization behaves in this manner from time to time, how does an assessor answer this question? One could evaluate each and every question of the OPM3® Self Assessment in this manner, but they would never finish. After about the fifth question, it becomes obvious that a binary Yes/No answer is not only difficult to give, but it is inherently inaccurate as well.

Fortunately these shortcomings of the OPM3® Self-Assessment Online tool were addressed in OPM3® ProductSuite with additional guidance regarding each question and more detailed scoring options including ranges instead of binary terms. Nonetheless the OPM3® Self-Assessment remains available in its current form without this additional guidance on questions and detailed scoring options, and those who use the OPM3® Self-Assessment instead of OPM3® ProductSuite face the difficulties and inaccuracies inherent to the tool.

In his critique of OPM3®, Abhay Padgaonker (2007) writes, "Standards such as OPM3® also can seem overly bureaucratic. OPM3® is heavily theoretical . . . Application of standards in a vacuum without properly understanding the logic, culture, or context under which they might work, often leads to a superficial bandage." Like Padgaonker, many critics contend that too much focus on theory over practice can lead to *the surgery was successful, but the patient died* syndrome. One assumes that a body of knowledge is an execution framework. This is a false assumption. The body of knowledge provides the theoretic construct from which to build an execution framework. For many organizations, a discussion not to mention an obsession over maturity can be grossly premature if some tangible degree of process birthing has not yet truly taken place.

Also commenting is Ralf Friedrich (2007), a member of the volunteer OPM3® Program, "The standard self-assessment is too superficial to be effective . . . It [OPM3®] is part of the business of all managers within an organization and in particular the C-level. They should be the primary users of OPM3®. However, for this user group, OPM3® needs a functional packaging." Friedrich acknowledges that as a product offering, OPM3® has ample room for further development and improvement.

The self assessment is problematic. In fact, the OPM3® Self Assessment should not even be called an assessment. John Schlichter (2004) who directed the original development of OPM3® on PMI's behalf perhaps positions the self assessment most correctly, "The High Level Assessment does deserve criticism. The High Level Assessment (151 Yes/No questions) is a sociological exercise, merely a survey of people's perceptions. It results in an inference, which is not the same thing as an assessment of fact or evidence." For this reason, Schlichter recommends the OPM3® ProductSuite, but not the OPM3 Self-Assessment (OPM3® Online) tool.

In addition to improving the self assessment, improving OPM3® in terms of functional packaging is much needed, and until that occurs, prospective users of OPM3® might defer to OPM3® ProductSuite as the preferred alternative for using OPM3®. Management could greatly benefit by extending OPM3® from a knowledge-oriented assessment offering to an execution framework complete with processes, metrics, and dashboards in a language that executives speak for actually doing organizational project management. Kim Sienkiewicz (2007) explains the requirements to sell the executive team, ". . . delivering a value proposition structured the way they [executives] like to see it, and preparing to become an effective observer combine to significantly increase the probability of mobilizing your 'C' Level [executives] to understand and actively commit to increasing project management maturity using OPM3®." OPM3® ProductSuite is a program administered by PMI that certifies professional assessors and consultants in robust assessment software that allows users to ascertain the bona fide capabilities of organizations in details, creating a picture of an organization's current state, and framing improvement options in terms of the parameters that resonate with executives, that is, strategic priorities, benefits, costs, and technical prerequisites for orchestrating sustainable solutions.

Such functional packaging is a logical next step for two reasons. First, it is a logical outgrowth. The maturity model and assessment process leads to establishing capabilities and improving on them. All of the various tools and point products for project management are well understood. Why leave this work undone? It is not too different from the high-priced management consultant who provides advice to the client but when asked if he accepts a job to actually do the work responds, "We just provide advice on how to do it; we don't actually do any of this stuff." Second, such packaging is needed. It is beyond the scope of project portfolio management (PPM) vendors to provide this and even if they wanted to, the permissions, rights to use, and licensing fees of OPM3® content are difficult obstacles to overcome.

Levels of Maturity in Project Management

As a first step to realize the value proposition of OPM3® and reap practical benefits, it is imperative to understand and acknowledge the starting point for the journey completely and to commit to an honest assessment, appraisal, and go of it. Both of these areas warrant further discussion.

When identifying a starting point for organizational project management maturity, most people intuitively think of the five levels of maturity commonly associated with the capability maturity model (CMM) and the various PMMMs. In many of these models the five levels of maturity are described as:

♦ Level 1: Ad hoc. There are no formal processes, methods, or procedures.
♦ Level 2: Planned. Processes, methods, and procedures do exist within areas of the organization, but they are not considered an organizational standard.
♦ Level 3: Managed. Processes, methods, and procedures exist throughout the organization and they are backed by formal documentation and management support.
♦ Level 4: Integrated. Processes, methods, and procedure are refined along with formal documentation and management support. Metrics are developed and used to collect performance data in support of project performance and proposed refinements.
♦ Level 5: Sustained. Lessons learned, best practices, and improvements are continuously applied. Metrics are used to enable the organization to evaluate capability improvement opportunities.

OPM3® speaks a slightly different language with respect to maturity levels and discusses this in terms of the four stages of process improvement; SMCI. But for some organizations, far more important than two different approaches for describing a common sense positive progression of process improvement stages or capability levels, is the recognition that negative levels of maturity do exist and need to be addressed in order to start the journey and achieve any kind of lasting organizational improvement. Non-positive and negative maturity levels important to recognize might include:

♦ Level 0: Apathetic. There are no formal processes, methods, or procedures and there is no cognitive recognition or appreciation within the organization for what these things are. An apathetic (don't know, don't care) mindset regarding project management processes, methods, and procedures is prevalent.

◆ Level −1: Conscientious objector. There are no formal processes, methods, or procedures and there are individual and organizational entities that stand in the way of any attempt to change the way they work. The resistance to change is seemingly passive and sometimes not apparent, but, in fact, the conscientious objectors can thwart even the best of organizational improvement plans. The conscientious objector has no real preference or *horse in the game*, rather they object to whatever ideas and proposals are brought forward, typically by making snide comments or suggesting there could be a better way although they never offer one.

◆ Level −2: Misfit. There are no formal processes, methods, or procedures and there is the presence of one or more misfits. Misfits are individuals and organizational entities that are unable to adapt to even the simplest of circumstances. Far worse than conscientious objectors, misfits set organizational improvement tactics back simply by not getting things correct. Misfits are difficult to work with and are often highly valued contributors and brilliant executives who vacillate from genius to a much lower form of intelligence.

◆ Level −3: Saboteur. There are no formal processes, methods, or procedures and there is the presence of one or more saboteurs. Saboteurs take deliberate action to foil the plan. As there is nothing easier to derail than an effort to improve the project management capabilities of an organization, saboteurs must be recognized for what they are and summarily dealt with. Regrettably they are difficult to identify. Saboteurs are much like professional, highly skilled, conscientious objectors who take the art form of derailing organizational maturity to the highest of levels.

◆ Level −4: Deviant. There are no formal processes, methods, or procedures and one or more deviants are present. Deviants are usually individuals, not organizational entities, that are conditioned to diverge from the accepted standard, attaining immense pleasure from doing so. Deviants can be treated, cured, and converted into organizational project management protagonists heroically supporting the improvement efforts of the organization. It is widely believed that most process improvement gurus were once deviants who, upon seeing the light, found their true calling.

◆ Level −5: Terrorist. There are no formal processes, methods, or procedures. There is the presence of one or more terrorists. In the context of organizational project management, terrorists are not the gun-toting, suicide bombers who we hear about on the news, rather they are ultra-early adopters of technology. They are the ones who seek to implement a technology solution for every problem without first understanding the processes, or lack thereof, that led to the problem in the first place. Terrorists implement complex PPM applications never having the time to plan for it, but always having the time to do it over and over again. Obsessed with technology for technology's sake, terrorists no longer understand or care about the business that the company conducts and the customers who they serve. The resulting problems they cause goes beyond frustration for the company; they institutionally terrorize it at all levels—employee, manager, executive. Whereas Deming lived by the motto, "Fix the process, fix the problem," these technology terrorists live by the motto, "Use enough technology, and the problem should go away." The terrorist level of maturity is the most dangerous level.

Learning the true starting point of the organization is the purpose of a maturity assessment and requires both quantitative and qualitative inspection. Additionally, when referring to the organization it is helpful to encapsulate the specific group who is being referred to. Is the organization the company at large, the division, the group? It is not only possible, but probable that different parts within the organization exhibit different levels of maturity and it is incorrect to assume that a common level of maturity exists organization-wide. This needs to be taken into consideration for any organization-wide improvement program to be effective.

Perhaps the most important caveat to consider is the true intent behind the decision to use an organizational project management maturity model. In an altruistic world the intent is to best serve the needs of the organization. Regrettably, according to some experts who wish to remain anonymous, many OPM3® engagements are undertaken for other reasons. Often cited are cases where OPM3® is used to benchmark and to show favorably high levels of project management maturity of the organization as compared to peer companies and other organizations. In such a case the intent is to use the tool to produce a score that can lead to some form of recognition, rather than using the tool to produce findings that can lead to improvement. This is where using a PMI-certified OPM3® ProductSuite Assessor—who is beholden to a code of ethics and loses his or her certification and license by transgressing that code—can be helpful for ensuring integrity and transparency.

Other cases involve the introduction of OPM3® to the organization by internal staff for the primary purpose of advancing a personal agenda such as acquiring knowledge and gaining experience with the tool, rather than being needed and a good fit for the organization relative to other alternatives and priorities. Most project management professionals thoroughly enjoy performing a maturity assessment and developing or revitalizing a PMM. They like to get their hands dirty and do the actual work; especially if they are given dedicated and undivided time to do it. Hence, in many cases, recommendations from internal staff to management to perform an OPM3® assessment need to be taken with a grain of salt.

The use of OPM3® cited in these cases as a means to an end involve the community of project management consultants for whom OPM3® represents not just a lengthy billable services engagement with a client, but an opportunity to establish an entire consulting practice. It doesn't take an opportunistic consultant long to realize that OPM3®, by its nature, presents an endless roadmap of consulting services engagements that can be started and stretched out to eternity with a minimal amount of client management skills. While this caveat is true of all consulting, it might be a caveat that prospective clients consider using a firm that is dedicated to OPM3® implementation exclusively over those *also-rans* who tack OPM3® consulting onto a menu of *everything under the sun* services.

These are things that are all made possible and do happen when you have a standard; any standard. This is in spite of, not because of, such standards. Amid the value and fitness for use, there is always misadventures; some because of honest efforts gone awry, others because of organizational mischief. One has to look no further than to all of the misapplied and misguided efforts at TQM, Baldrige, and Six Sigma to find examples of consultants, internal or external, gone wild. Standards in fact exist to alleviate such exploitations. As the saying goes, a fool with a tool is still a fool. Learning how to translate theory into practice while avoiding common pitfalls is wise.

Taking Theory to Practice

In going forward with OPM3®, these three tips are helpful. First, recognize that OPM3® is a standard. Second, bring in an outside consultant who is an OPM3® expert. Third, staff and develop your own internal OPM3® expert.

Recognizing that OPM3® is a standard is quite easy for some, yet difficult for others. Why? Project management vendors and consulting firms that were helping organizations advance their project management capabilities prior to OPM3® via their own practices, maturity models, and toolkits have found out that someone has moved their cheese. Despite extensive expertise, effective maturity models, and a long list of satisfied customers, these firms and individuals have suffered a huge competitive blow. For most of them the only viable recourse is to abandon their models and hop on the OPM3® bandwagon.

Commenting on the hype of OPM3® and its claim of being widely endorsed, Craig Curran-Morton (2004) writes, "Those marketing the benefits of the OPM3, from consultants to the original developers, seem to believe that the title of 'standard' has already been granted to it. . . . PMI should be waiting for the project management community to endorse the product as a standard through use, feedback and, ultimately, acceptance." Just because PMI says

OPM3® is a standard, that doesn't mean it is a standard. Or does it? As John Schlichter, the original PMI OPM3® program manager and chief executive officer (CEO) of OPM Experts, points out, "Actually, if you are an accredited standards developer like PMI, then something is a 'PMI standard' precisely because PMI says it is . . ." Those seriously considering OPM3® must dig a little deeper than critics who compete with OPM3® and have the obvious axes to grind, evaluating the merits of PMI's role as a standards developer, accredited by the American National Standards Institute (ANSI), which is a counterpart to the International Standards Organization (ISO).

Most consulting firms and independent consultants quickly accept OPM3® as the standard for organizational project management maturity if for no other reason than the fact that their clients have already done so. For those who are reluctant to do so or for those who go about accepting OPM3® as the standard in a begrudgingly half-hearted way, the following five phases of acceptance can serve as a roadmap for accelerating the inevitable adoption of OPM3® as the premiere standard for assessing and developing organizational project management capabilities:

◆ Phase I: Doubting the merits of OPM3®. In this phase the merits of OPM3® are questioned. Is this a body of knowledge to promote the latest certification and the cottage industry that benefits therein? Or is this actually something that can be effectively used, as advertised, to bridge the chasm that separates business strategy from project delivery? The high-level self-assessment is criticized as too superficial and the knowledge behind OPM3® is deemed too self-serving and overly detailed. As OPM3® represents the collective work of hundreds of brilliant participants, it is best to accept the merit of the work rather than doubt it.

◆ Phase II: Denying that OPM3® is a standard. Some argue the case that OPM3® is not a standard, rather it is a product. These nay-sayers argue the merits of experts affiliated with various commercial products over the merits of an industry standard developed under the auspices of the global project management advocate and, subsequently, commercialized with assessment products that can be used only by PMI-certified assessors and consultants. It can even be argued, though not as effectively, that PMI is no longer a standards organization; rather it is a fee-based, revenue-driven provider of memberships, products, and services. On the other hand, the incredible contribution that PMI has made to the world in advancing project management cannot be doubted; such an undertaking and record of achievements over these last four decades could only be envisioned and carried out by them.

◆ Phase III: Explaining why your model is better than OPM3®. For project management consulting firms and consultants with their own models and approaches to organization project management maturity and years of experience successfully helping their clients, defending their turf is a natural and expected reaction. It can be shocking to discover, and it might seem unfair, that a proven approach and years of experience can be dismissed as irrelevant. To add insult to injury, what was once a nonprofit standards body (in the eyes of many) that everyone stood to benefit from is now a heavy-handed direct competitor with unlimited marketing and influence. OPM3® claims of success such as widely endorsed, widely accepted, and proven successful, etc. cannot be contested. There is no balanced playing field to be found for an alternative model, therefore, there is little point in defending one.

♦ Phase IV: Getting to know OPM3®. For many project management consulting firms or consultants who have sweat-equity in their own models and approaches for organizational project management, getting to know OPM3® can be like eating *green eggs and ham*. Though there can be a strong resistance to giving it a try, even the most critically minded people can discover significant benefit in OPM3® from which to find favor. In the children's book alluded to previously, once they try it, they might be surprised to find that they actually like it.

♦ Phase V: Embracing OPM3®. The final phase of acceptance is simply embracing OPM3®. If you are in the business to provide organizational project management consulting, sooner or later you will invest your time, energy, and passion into OPM3® and become a certified OPM3® assessor or consultant or, perhaps, work for one.

After recognizing OPM3® as the standard of excellence in organizational project management, for many organizations a good next step is to bring in an outside expert consultant to help you achieve measurable business improvement. Perhaps the best way to do this is to engage an expert to discuss the best ways to advance your organization's strategic intent with OPM3®, focusing on ways to build momentum. This usually begins with the identification of strategic priorities and the decisions concerning the scope of the OPM3® standard to use and the scope of the organization in which to use it. The outside expert can also provide insights and advice on how long an assessment takes for the company, who is involved, and procedures. The actual length of an assessment can vary from weeks to months, depending on the organization being assessed and the scope of the assessment as well as the strategy for assessment. As an example of strategy for an assessment, many organizations can benefit by an assessment approach that facilitates quick wins, positive visibility, and a momentum that can be sustained as opposed to an all encompassing assessment that might take too long to finish or show progress, which might in turn result in disenfranchisement with OPM3®.

As part of working with outside experts, or in preparing to work with them, any organization seriously considering using OPM3® is advised to identify and staff their own internal expert. Internal staff members (assessors), unlike external consultants, have the benefit of possessing knowledge about the organization. Furthermore, they can quickly confirm the veracity of claims and assertions regarding existing capabilities. More importantly they can support improvement activities. An assessment is just a step within the life cycle of implementing OPM3®. One way to cultivate an internal expert is to require the external expert to coach such a person within your organization as part of the OPM3® implementation engagement. Internal staff can be cultivated to guide the assessment-based improvements recommended by an expert between intermittent third-party assessments. It is important to emphasize that an improvement program, especially for organizational project management, must be an ongoing commitment and not just a one-time endeavor. Referring to improving project management, project management guru George Pitagorsky (2007) writes, "Managing project management improvement means managing an ongoing program in which people, processes and tools are integrated to ensure that there is a practical and flexible standardized process, measurement, control and continuous improvement targeted at meaningful performance improvement." This takes earnest commitment and work and is especially true for OPM3®.

In helping the organization view improvement as an ongoing program, not a point-in-time endeavor, OPM3® provides a straightforward and common sense approach called the OPM3® cycle, which consists of five steps. The first step in the cycle is to prepare for the assessment. As mentioned before, an OPM3® assessment facilitated by a certified assessor or consultant is an excellent way to start.

To successfully apply OPM3®, an expert needs to explain to key participants the model and concepts. Just as an OPM3® assessment does not ask everyone throughout the organization all of the same questions, it is unnecessary for everyone to understand everything about the model, but critical for key change agents to know the few things that are essential. The underlining basics are not complicated, but OPM3® is voluminous and it takes some time to absorb all of the material, text, and directories as well as to determine how best to utilize them. Adequate planning for the assessment requires key participants to learn and ultimately to have a firm grasp of the best practices associated with project management maturity of the organization. The directories outline and clarify how capabilities sequentially aggregate to make up each best practice.

As this information represents a well-thought-out theoretical model or desired state, it is tremendously important to recognize that few organizations are currently any place close to the model. Wide gaps should not be viewed as something to question or to be overly defensive about, rather they should be viewed as an opportunity for improvement. A seasoned user of OPM3® can frame low-maturity scores in ways that accurately depict the status while offering a practical basis for building on any beneficial work the organization has completed. Experts in OPM3® know that the assessment is the ante to the game, and the improvement is the prize. For this reason, maturity assessments should never be indictments. Instead they are inputs to planning.

The second step of the OPM3® cycle is the performance of the assessment. This is an insightful and enjoyable step that involves comparing the current state of maturity of the organization with the model. First, the best practices that are in the standard that are not exhibited by the organization are identified. If the organization is using the OPM3® Self-Assessment (OPM3® Online), much hidden work should be expected in terms of identifying what each self-assessment question means. Each self-assessment question might correspond to multiple best practices in the model. Each best practice has multiple capability-outcome questions. Therefore each self-assessment question actually corresponds to many more questions than apparent. Most people do not know this, but now that you do, you can plan for the hidden work of mapping questions to best practices, best practices to capability-outcome questions, and collecting answers to the myriad of hidden questions implied by each OPM3® Self-assessment (OPM3® Online) question. Assuming you can accomplish this mapping, and assuming you know what each of the implied questions really means, you can get a result that is useful for the purpose of planning improvements. But because these assumptions might hang an albatross around your neck, you might be better served by engaging a certified OPM3® ProductSuite Assessor to perform your assessment for you; in which case you must decide between a desk assessment and a rigorous assessment.

In a desk assessment, a certified assessor interviews a representative who speaks on behalf of the entire organization. This person's assertions regarding the maturity of the organization is taken at face value, sitting at their desk so to speak, without walking around the organization or talking to others to validate those assertions. By comparison, in a rigorous assessment, a certified assessor interviews both process owners and practitioners, examines artifacts, and determines the bona fide capabilities of the organization. Because the more accurate an assessment is the more useful it is for planning improvements, a rigorous assessment is usually the preferred option.

Step three of the OPM3® cycle is planning for improvements. The results of the assessment provide the documentation of outcomes not observed, indicating the best practice capabilities that are lacking. These are opportunities for improvement. These opportunities are ranked according to the timings, needs, and priorities of the organization. The list of best practices requiring attention is nearly always too long to effectively address; therefore the organization needs to prioritize and shorten the list based on domain (project, program, and portfolio) and process improvement stage SMCI. OPM3® ProductSuite consultants are trained to facilitate decisions regarding which improvements to make in terms of their strategic priority, cost, benefit, and technical prerequisites.

For such decisions to be actionable, the evaluation of capabilities must be quite analytical and rigorous. It enables the organization to establish an objective view of maturity as opposed to subjective analysis and measures that can leave a wide margin of interpretation differences and errors. It can't be rushed and it can't be faked.

Additionally, the evaluation of capabilities provides the organization with a tangible construct from which they can decide whether or not to pursue improvement. An organization might feel that it is satisfied with its current state and that the level of maturity, while not the highest possible, is adequate. Other organizations might feel compelled to seek improvement and might pursue some or perhaps all of the identified capabilities.

Many organizations committed to OPM3® intending to perform assessments and to implement improvements on an ongoing basis might choose to first address capabilities that are easy to achieve. This enables the organization to gain familiarity with the cycle, demonstrate success, and build upon momentum and buy-in to OPM3®. Other organizations might be more aggressive, seeking to address capabilities that are strategically aligned to pressing business objectives and that provide the highest degree of tangible benefits. No two organizations are the same or face the same set of business pressures and constraints. Important to note, from the standpoint of the model a best practice is deemed to exist only when all of the associated capabilities exist. However, organizations can selectively decide for themselves which capabilities are most important to improve.

Any improvement in capabilities for a best practice, in fact, improves the maturity of the organization. Some of the capability dependencies for a best practice should not be viewed as an absolute prerequisite. For example, if an organization develops a process, it might help to have members participate in the appropriate professional organization providing the standard for that process. This obviously is not a requirement to developing an in-house process; rather it is a suggestion that is both beneficial and mutually self-serving. By contrast, some capability dependencies are indeed absolute prerequisites. For example, measurement of a project management process is a capability that must be developed before the capability of controlling that process can develop effectively.

In step four, improvements are implemented. The actual span of activities involved in planning and implementing organizational change are not within the scope of OPM3®. But the improvements, in essence, are projects themselves and the organization can benefit from adhering to the PMBOK® or their own in-house process for managing projects. Like any project a number of factors might impact the organization requiring changes to the project plan; a project to implement improvements per an OPM3® assessment is no exception.

The last step of the OPM3® cycle called *repeat the process* is really the first step of the new cycle. Having completed its first OPM3® cycle, the organization repeats the assessment step (step two of the cycle) to demonstrate its progress in the development of capabilities and to plan further improvements that increase maturity. While it is possible to achieve a great deal of improvement in a single cycle, for most organizations it is more likely that the first few cycles of improvement lay the foundation for much greater improvement achieved over multiple cycles. For example, an organization can hardly improve upon portfolio management best practices if project management best practices are not first in place. While the executive team might yearn for improvement in portfolio management capabilities, if the core project management processes are not in place or are lacking, then the integrity of the portfolio is suspect. No amount of portfolio management improvement effectively benefits the organization until such time that projects are managed with a degree of project management maturity and integrity.

Summary

Advancing organizational project management is not easy. There is no quick fix for the organization that wants to improve upon its current state of maturity and capabilities in pursuit of a higher state. It takes time, commitment, and a certain presence of passion and dedication to the organization and it is about getting things correct.

Some project management consulting firms with their own model and practice teams no doubt have more than a few reasons to feel threatened and perhaps be perturbed by the manner in which OPM3® came onto the scene, anointed itself as the worldwide standard, and declared widespread acceptance without having first achieved years of practical experience and engagement success. However, OPM3® has been on the scene for a decade now, and there are far more reasons to embrace OPM3® enthusiastically. Is it competitive and a threat to other approaches? Of course it is. Do consulting firms and consultants have to put their own approaches on the back shelf and jump on the OPM3® bandwagon to get work? In a word, yes, whether embraced enthusiastically or out of a real sense of survival.

OPM3® provides a wide range of benefits to a wide range of people in an organization, including project managers, business analysts, project team members, developers, functional managers, business executives, senior management, and the leadership team. More than just a theoretical model, it provides a practical and effective way to address some of the most complicated organizational issues surrounding best practices, capabilities, and outcomes. Prospective users of OPM3® undertake a process of knowing excellence, assessing oneself rigorously, creating accountability, and distinguishing action for achieving higher levels of maturity. OPM3® offers the value proposition of crossing the chasm and strengthening the link between strategic planning and the execution of the projects, programs, and portfolios. It's the real thing. And yes, it is that good.

Questions

1. What is the business value proposition of OPM3®?
2. How was OPM3® developed?
3. How do you defend the claim that OPM3® is a worldwide standard?
4. How do you defend the assertion that OPM3® is a product offering?
5. What are the three interlocking elements of OPM3®?
6. What are the components of the OPM3® knowledge element?
7. What does the OPM3® knowledge element refer to?
8. What does the OPM3® assessment element refer to?
9. What does the OPM3® improvement element refer to?
10. For organizations seeking to improve project management capabilities and maturity, what are some of the OPM3® caveats to consider?
11. Why is an OPM3 ProductSuite assessment performed by a certified assessor superior to an assessment using the OPM3 Self-Assessment (OPM3 Online) tool?
12. Describe the levels of project management maturity?
13. In OPM3®, what are the four stages of process improvement?
14. What are examples of negative levels of maturity?
15. What are the typical objectives of an OPM3® assessment?
16. What are the benefits of using external consultants in performing OPM3® assessments?
17. What are the benefits of using trained, internal staff to support OPM3® assessments?

References

Curran-Morton, Craig. 2004. "Beyond the OPM3 Hype, A Reality Check." http://www.pmforum.com. (Accessed on June 19, 2008)

Friedrich, Ralf. 2007. "The Essence of OPM3®." http://www.allpm.com. (Accessed on June 19, 2008)

Padgaonkar, Abhay. 2007. "Assessing OPM3." http://www.projectsatwork.com. (Accessed on June 19, 2008)

Pitagorsky, George. 2007. "The Business Value of Maturity Assessment: Performance Improvement." http://www.allpm.com. (Accessed on June 19, 2008)

Project Management Institute. 2003. *Organizational Project Management Maturity Model (OPM3) Knowledge Foundation.* Pennsylvania: Project Management Institue.

Schlichter, John. 2004. "Beyond the OPM3 Hype Article—A Reply by John Schlichter." http://www.pmforum.com. (Accessed on June 19, 2008)

Sienkiewicz, Kim. 2007. "OPM3® and Your "C" Level." http://www.allpm.com. (Accessed on June 19, 2008)

Executive Insights

Transforming the Culture with Your PMO

John Schlichter

CEO of OPM Experts

Ask yourself what culture means and you might find it difficult to state a clear and succinct definition, but it is likely that you can recall an organization in which you have worked that had a healthy culture; and it is just as likely that you might recall an organization that you characterize as having an unhealthy culture. Why is that? Although culture is a many-faceted thing that might seem difficult to boil down into a sound bite, it is something that impacts everyone. The culture determines how people define themselves and their relationships with others and greatly influences a person's sense of self.

In organizations that thrive on projects, a healthy culture is a prerequisite to high performance because *teams* are the lifeblood of projects; teams of *people* who must repeatedly mobilize into temporary endeavors that deliver change in the midst of business environments that are always changing. In such organizations the culture (people) is often the thing that prevents complexity from degrading into chaos. It is nearly always the case that high-performing organizations have highly developed cultures, and it is nearly always the case that low-performing organizations suffer from problems associated with how the people work together, how they define themselves and their relationships with others, and the experiences and views that individuals have regarding their sense of self within the organization. So why don't we see more organizations carrying out specific, measurable, and effective programs to transform their cultures?

Understanding Culture as the Key to Execution

One would think that transforming the culture is a primary focus for any PMO implemented to help organizations deliver projects successfully, consistently, and predictably, but too often this is not the case. Too often the culture is not understood as the key to execution that it is, and those leaders who do give priority to transforming the culture might not know how to translate that priority into action with a PMO. We can summarize four main reasons as to why:

1. The organization's leaders might not have a clear sense of what a healthy project management culture is according to industry best practice. This is about *knowing excellence*.
2. The leaders might not have assessed the organization methodically to see the current state-of-affairs according to the views of people throughout the organization. This is about *assessing oneself rigorously*.
3. The organization might not have created clear ownership for transforming the culture. This is about *creating accountability*.
4. The organization might not have created a realistic and measurable plan for transforming the culture. This is about *distinguishing action*.

These reasons are cumulative in their effects just as the steps for transformation of your culture are hierarchical (see Figure 12.2).

If an organization does not have a realistic and measurable plan for transforming the culture, it is often because they have not created clear accountability for developing and executing such a plan. If they have not created that accountability, it might be precisely because they have not assessed the orga-

Hierarchical steps of culture transformation

Distinguishing action

Creating accountability

Assessing rigorously

Knowing excellence

Figure 12.2   Hierarchical steps of culture transformation

nization in actionable ways that give them the information needed to effect change. Leaders are unable to develop effective strategies and tactics to transform the project management culture without an actionable assessment of the organization, and even though people might want to change, they might not know what to do without that information to help them. An actionable assessment is difficult to achieve without a clear standard for excellence, describing the many elements that comprise a healthy project management culture.

People focus on what they know. Many organizations that have implemented a PMO or are considering implementing a PMO focus their attention on the project management processes. They focus on defining the processes for managing projects and making them capable through process management. As the saying goes, this is *wise as far as the beard*, or wise in appearance, but only truly wise if the culture is addressed also. It is the job of the PMO to create a virtuous cycle between the transformation of the project management culture and development of capable project management processes (see Figure 12.3).

Management processes are performed by people, and the culture defines the norms for how people work together. One must cultivate both the management processes and the environment in which those processes operate; more specifically, the culture that makes the environment conducive to successful projects. Because the science and art of making processes capable has been developed and implemented with demonstrable success across the globe and throughout industry, many organizations know about the four stages of process management, i.e., standardizing processes, measuring processes, controlling processes, and continuously improving processes.

By comparison, the agenda for transforming one's culture might seem less clear cut. Ironically once practitioners learn key elements of transforming the project management culture, some find it easier to address the culture than to do the things necessary to make processes capable. This is probably because

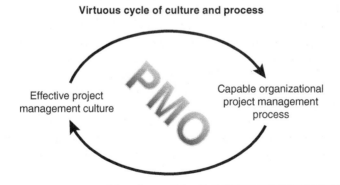

Virtuous cycle of culture and process

Effective project management culture

Capable organizational project management process

PMO

Figure 12.3   Virtuous cycle of culture and process

the hands-on application of process management techniques to management processes, as opposed to manufacturing processes, remains the domain of specialists. No matter what one's level of knowledge is regarding process management versus culture transformation, and whether one or the other seems easier to address, the bottom line is that the building of capable project management processes and the transformation of the project management culture go hand in hand. It is necessary to understand what each is in relation to the other, and to cultivate both.

Organizational Project Management Maturity (OPM3®)

Process management standards have been gaining popularity for nearly a century; whereas the standards for transforming the project management culture have catapulted to center stage only within the past decade. In 1998, PMI chartered a program to create an international standard for assessing and developing the ability of organizations to achieve their corporate strategies through projects. The resulting standard, OPM3®, focuses equally on both process capability and transforming the culture.

The agenda for building the organization's process capability starts with effective governance and policies, documenting processes, and standardizing to achieve consistent implementation of work methods. This process management agenda is advanced further through metrics that make the processes measurable, which generates the data necessary to control process performance and variability. Internal systems are created to manage the performance of processes with data, and the resulting infrastructure enables the organization to create widespread participation in sustainable process improvements in ways that can benefit the top and bottom lines. This process management agenda has been elevated to the status of gospel over the years through the works of Shewart, Demming, Dewey, Ishikawa, Juran, Crosby, Taguchi, and many others.

Thanks to these icons, I knew of the rich body of knowledge developed over the past century in the domain of process management when I accepted the role of program manager of the original OPM3® Program on PMI's behalf in 1998, and wrote the PMI OPM3® Program's charter. But I also knew that every person we recruited to the OPM3® Program had their own ideas about what contributes to organizational environments in which projects are successful. PMI agreed to the incorporation of both primary and secondary research into our charter, i.e., secondary research involving the summary of existing research and primary research involving the collection of data that does not already exist.

We mobilized a research team within the OPM3® Program to solicit ideas methodically. Secondary research included a review of process management standards and maturity models and primary research included surveys that were deployed repeatedly to over 30,000 practitioners. Bridging the gap between theory and practice, this research assimilated input from real practitioners sharing their own experiences in real organizations of all shapes and sizes across industries in 35 countries.

Over time I began to understand many of the inputs we received from a cast of thousands as elements we might characterize in terms of culture. Together those elements determine how people work together and how people define themselves and their relationships with others. The more widely known stages of process management, from governance and standardization through continuous improvement, were integrated with the agenda for transforming the project management culture, which was delineated in terms of so-called *organizational enablers* that enable the environment in which project management processes occur. Today, leaders are leveraging the legacy of standards for making processes capable in tandem with these standards for transforming the project management culture. These organizational enablers are divided into seventeen categories:

1. Organizational project management policy and vision
2. Strategic alignment
3. Resource allocation
4. Management systems
5. Sponsorship
6. Organizational structures
7. Competency management
8. Individual frequent performance appraisals
9. Project management training
10. Organizational project management communities
11. Organizational project management practices
12. Organizational project management methodology
13. Organizational project management techniques
14. Project management metrics
15. Project success criteria
16. Benchmarking
17. Knowledge management and project management information system (PMIS)

Even the titles of these organizational enablers—categories of cultural capability—suggest various kinds of processes, which underscores the truth that building process capability goes hand-in-hand with transforming the culture.

Whereas the process management stages of OPM3® describe process management in detail, the organizational enablers help us to discern a clear agenda for cultivating the *environment* in which those processes operate. The environment is comprised of people who require a vision, policies, systems, training, methodologies, and communities in order to gel into a cohesive whole that brings order to chaos in the midst of change. Together these many elements determine how people work together and define how people see themselves and their relationships with others. They address the aspect of executives communicating the importance of project management to the organization. They address the strategic alignment of project managers to the organization's strategies. They address the definition of required management roles and the need to provide the management support necessary for project managers to fulfill their roles. They address the management of a competent resource pool, the cataloguing of skills relevant to key roles and the evaluation of activities to raise visibility of the competency-building process and progressive career paths. They address the implementation of policies for performance reviews and training, learning from others, and the management of knowledge. The list of examples of elements in OPM3® that address how people work together and how people see themselves and their relationships with others goes on and on.

Through implementation of OPM3®, organizations can design their PMOs to fit the organizations those PMOs serve, focusing on the integrated agenda of building process capability while orchestrating a transformation of the culture. OPM3 is a foil for clarifying what the project management culture is and enabling leaders to assess the organization from a variety of perspectives in the organization in actionable ways that predicate the creation of accountability for specific and measurable steps to build the organization's project delivery capability.

OPM3® Implementation Examples

Two organizations that OPM Experts has helped to implement OPM3® to advance their respective PMOs exemplify the ways in which building capable project management processes and transforming the project management culture go hand-in-hand and demonstrate impacts that each might have on the other, i.e., processes on culture and culture on processes. The first of these clients is Harris Corporation's RF Communications Division (RFCD), an international communications and IT company. The second is the National Information Center (NIC) of the Ministry of Interior in the Kingdom of Saudi Arabia. OPM experts has helped each of these organizations to advance their strategic intents with OPM3®.

Harris RFCD demonstrates the impact of *process on culture*. Harris is a multi-model environment, which includes the CMMI, ISO, and OPM3®. Process requirements are the focus of change. The process-oriented culture within RFCD has driven the cultivation of many aspects of the environment pertaining to the project management culture. By contrast, the Saudi NIC demonstrates the impact of *culture on process*. The culture within the Saudi government and the NIC in particular, draws heavily upon a rich legacy of leaders who have imbued the organization with a tradition of deference to the vertical management hierarchy. As the NIC has evolved, it has matured its PMO to transform this inward-focus on the management hierarchy into one that faces outward to the customer of the PMO, which requires a different perspective.

Both Harris Corporation and the NIC offer compelling insights into the impacts that process can have on culture and vice versa. Each of these organizations understood the four reasons why many organizations fail to transform their project management cultures, and they avoided these pitfalls with their PMOs. Both of these organizations understood the need for recognizing excellence, the need for assessing oneself rigorously, the need for creating accountability, and the need for distinguishing action. Each organization addressed these needs by combining the PMO and OPM3® to transform their project management cultures.

Transforming the Project Management Culture at Harris

Mark Scott

PMP, Sr. Engineering Manager, Harris
Corporation, RF Communications Division

There is a reason why Harris Corporation's RFCD is number one in the global tactical radio market. Harris delivers technology that makes battlefield communications reliable, secure, and simple. Harris's comprehensive line of software-defined radio products and systems supports critical missions around the world. The company is known for delivering reliable communications products, systems integration, and IT to government and commercial customers. The need to bring these solutions to market fastest throws the importance of project management into sharp relief. Process excellence is not just good business, it can make a difference in the delivery of solutions that impact lives. Being the best-in-class global provider of mission-critical systems and services to its customers, combining advanced technology and application knowledge, requires a commitment to excellence in the project management culture, its processes, and the project management delivery system.

The solutions offered by RFCD are the products of many dedicated cross-functional project teams that translate process excellence into the culture. RFCD focuses on some of the most specialized areas of technological expertise. Project teams are comprised of highly educated, skilled engineers and research scientists in electrical, mechanical, test components, hardware, software, systems, and advanced materials. Processes apply these skills to communications and IT applications. The building of capable project management processes used by RFCD project teams and the transformation of the project management culture that enables these processes go hand-in-hand. In today's troubled economy, project management is the competitive advantage. As John Schlichter of OPM experts points out, the RFCD agenda for advanced project management capabilities is about knowing excellence, assessing oneself rigorously, creating accountability, and distinguishing action.

Knowing Excellence

RFCD's pursuit of product and process quality is viewed as a journey, not a destination. Since early 2000, RFCD has established, maintained, and implemented a continuous improvement roadmap for the pursuit of higher process and product development capabilities. The roadmap helps the RFCD community understand the historical, current, and future state of process management and improvement

RFCD's early implementation of the process standards gave rise to self-optimizing teams in engineering and among RFCD functional organizations and business groups. A by-product of the earlier approaches was the creation of multiple product development engines each having its own unique set of project phases and project management processes. Project management processes overlapped and were duplicated among the engines (see Figure 12.4).

In 2007, engineering launched a lean product development initiative to achieve greater efficiencies in functional and cross-functional process performance. This ongoing effort has sought to eliminate waste and increase sub-process cycle time within and among the development engines.

The introduction of OPM3® has its origins in the lean product development initiative with the intent to pilot the standard and later spread the standard throughout the engineering community. RFCD's Divisional Process Group (DPG) initially used OPM3® to provide project management best practice support to improvement projects within the standard's project management domain. The DPG stewards and facilitates the achievement of engineering process improvement goals and objectives. It is the operational arm of the Engineering Continuous Improvement Program and champions the program's creation and maintenance. The approach allowed the DPG time to develop OPM3® expertise and deployment competencies before a more widespread use of the standard within the organization.

Figure 12.5 illustrates the three phases of the lean product development initiative. Phase 1 is characterized by best practice introductions and demonstrated compliance to key process standards. Phase 2 shifts from process improvement to process performance, more specifically, process interfaces between engineering disciplines and other RFCD functions. Process reengineering is Phase 3, the final phase. The product development capability is viewed as a key component of the overall business process system.

Each bubble contains a portfolio of improvement projects. The vertical axis shows the types of process notations used to characterize and measure RFCD processes. The horizontal axis identifies the focus of process-related evaluations. The center arrow identifies measures of interest. The large lean product development bubble indicates the primary area of improvement emphasis. Improvement projects might overlap these phases, depending on their scope. The DPG executes improvement projects in accordance with OPM3® recommended guidelines.

Having achieved success with the pilot of OPM3® in lean product development, the DPG made plans to extend the OPM3® methodology throughout engineering. RFCD operates in a multi-standard, multi-model process improvement environment. The division has a Quality Management System (QMS)

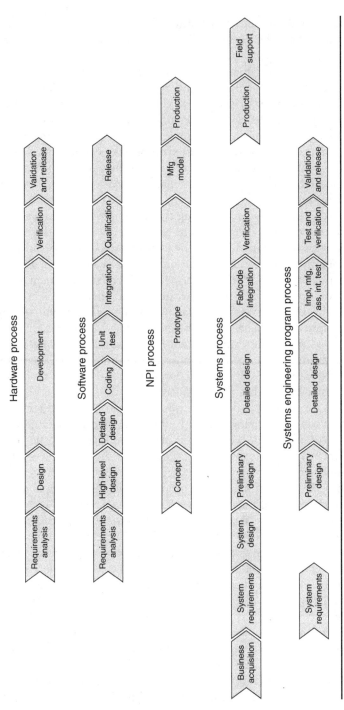

Figure 12.4   Multiple product development engines

RFCD's lean product development initiative

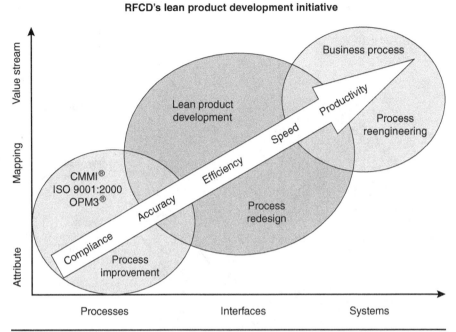

Figure 12.5   RFCD's lean product development initiative

that includes best practice requirements associated with ISO 9001:2000, CMMI®, and other process standards. The QMS embodies the core process requirements of the organization.

Practices from various process standards, like OPM3®, are mapped and evaluated for best-of-fit before being introduced into the QMS (see Figure 12.6). Process requirements are the focus of change, not the standard.

The DPG codified OPM3®'s introduction into the QMS using engineering's yearly process improvement plan. The plan includes provisions for:

◆ Sponsoring and oversight of senior management
◆ Aligning OPM3® with the division's strategic growth plan (SGP)
◆ Linking OPM3® to various other process initiatives (e.g., lean product development)
◆ Mapping OPM3® best practices into the QMS
◆ Establishing a PMO
◆ Identifying and involving partner RFCD functions and projects

Special care was taken to bill OPM3® as a complementary standard and not a competing standard to other process standards and improvement initiatives. For RFCD engineering, knowing excellence is all about knowing the current

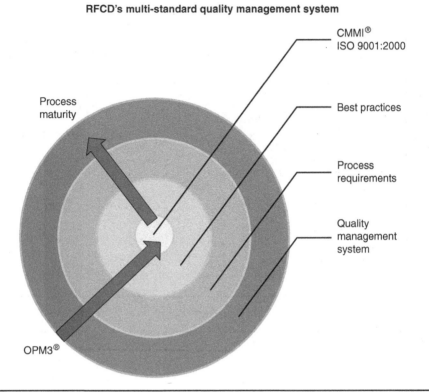

RFCD's multi-standard quality management system

Figure 12.6   RFCD's multi-standard quality management system

process context of the organization and how a new process standard can modify that context to successfully promote and advance a culture of excellence responsive to the strategic imperatives of the organization.

Assessing Rigorously

Entry into the OPM3® via an assessment is an attractive feature of the model. While other standards might require process build-ups before appraising the organization, OPM3® begins with an assessment. RFCD engineering values assessments as a means to measure process maturity and to identify improvement opportunities. The division is registered as an ISO 9001:2000 company and its systems and software engineering groups have been successfully appraised to CMMI® Maturity Level Three. Engineering supplemented its internal OPM3® pursuits by contracting OPM Experts to perform a rigorous assessment. The third party rigorous assessment focused on project management capabilities associated with the systems, software, and hardware engineering disciplines.

Multiple project management policies and processes were embedded in these disciplines. Although the engineering development life cycles differ to some degree, the overlaying of OPM3® standards by the assessment tool helped distinguish how the project management processes can be the same, tailorable when appropriate, and applicable to most projects most of the time.

The OPM3® value-added insight inspired the DPG to seek greater maturity in product development by transforming multiple product development engines into a single, unified product development framework. To support this concept the DPG has sought to institutionalize a standard set of lean project management processes that engineering project managers can use to deliver their solutions faster and cheaper through the framework.

The OPM3® rigorous assessment revealed how the various project management processes within engineering could be consolidated, thus reducing the costs and complexity of maintaining multiple sets of project management processes for each product development engine. By establishing a unified set of lean project management procedures, the process asset links among the product development engines could be reduced by more than two to one. The DPG used the PMBOK® to steer this reduction effort.

Creating Accountability

The building of capable project management processes and the transformation of the project management culture go hand-in-hand. For engineering, these two concepts converge in two RFCD strategic imperatives: time-to-market (TTM) and cost reduction. For the kinds of applications that RFCD develops, only the best will do, and getting these solutions to market fastest can make a life saving difference.

The DPG uses OPM3® to continually improve the RFCD brand of lean project management processes and to establish a common lexicon in support of the unified product development approach. Such a process involves accountability, especially in the establishment and maintenance of key organizational enablers, such as a PMO, to help steer the development and institutionalization of processes supporting a unified product development system.

The DPG launched a PMO to advance the unified product development agenda by increasing RFCD engineering capabilities in the OPM3® specified project, program, and portfolio management domains. PMPs, Six Sigma Black Belts, and a PMI-licensed OPM3® assessor staff the PMO. The PMO has a three-fold mission:

1. To establish and maintain a standard set of lean project, program, and portfolio management processes
2. To develop competencies in lean project, program, and portfolio management

3. To measure the benefits of increased project management maturity in both engineering product development and internal improvement projects

The chief duty of the PMO is to oversee the creation and deployment of lean project, program, and portfolio management processes that enable a lean project management culture responsive to RFCD strategic-growth imperatives. It works hand-in-hand with the engineering community to reduce duplication in project management processes, where appropriate, and to develop *vanilla* project management processes (i.e., processes that are not hardwired to a specific engineering discipline).

Engineering has established tailoring guidelines to ensure that the correct amount of process is applied to product development efforts. Lean project management processes are nonprescriptive and cover the full product development life cycle. Smart process selection and tailoring empowers engineering project managers to achieve their schedule, cost, and quality objectives.

Distinguishing Action

OPM3® serves as a foil reinforcing the PMOs accountability and fidelity toward its mission. Although the PMO is in its early stages of development, PMO activists have contributed to the establishment and maintenance of RFCD engineering's policies, procedures, tools, training, and performance management systems. The PMO created a web-based project management process asset library for use by the engineering project management community. It has a project scheduling function that provides scheduling expertise to all RFCD project managers when requested. The PMO is sponsoring a collaborative environment for the sharing of best practices and lessons learned. It actively manages engineering's portfolio of improvement projects, and it supports RFCD leadership in its strategic-growth imperatives in functional, cross-functional, and project environments.

The PMO publishes a lean product development dashboard that explicitly links its value proposition to RFCD TTM and cost reduction pursuits (see Figure 12.7). The purpose of the dashboard is to enable a lean project management culture through the use of measureable indicators. This dashboard only identifies support process improvement projects. Support processes are generic processes available for use by all engineering projects. Project specific improvements are not shown due to proprietary restrictions. Not all PMO improvement efforts are included on the dashboard. Some improvement projects are categorized as simply *go do it* projects. Other improvement efforts require a more disciplined project management approach. RFCD leadership requires an understanding of the benefits of significant improvement efforts. Hence, an aggregated return on investment (ROI) is calculated for these types

Improvement dashboard

Work code	Sponsoring team	Project name	Cost reduction/ TTM/both	D	M	A	I	C	Target parameters	Lead time baseline	Lead time current	Cost avoidance opportunity	Cost of delay	Work code labor cost (JTD)	Total cost avoidance
CMMI-HWE	Hardware	Parts number request	Both						< 48 hours	21 days	5 days	$ 299,000	$ 257,889		
CMMI-HWE	Hardware	Printed writing board	Both						< 20 days	32 days	27 days	NA	$ 229,618	($105,854)	
CMMI-HWE	Hardware	Parts order	Both							22 days	10 days	NA	$ 296,247		
CMMI-POP	Sustained engineering	Obsolete parts track	CR							4 days	1 day	$ 16,640	$ 74,062	($492)	
LSS-SWW	Software	Integration and wringout	CR									$ 739,936		($18,268)	
CMMI-CLAB	Calibration lab	Process improvement	CR						3 days	6 days				($2,072)	
LSS-HWPO	Hardware	Proto parts ordering—Phase 1	Both						0 days	4.5 days				($17,189)	
LSS-WLP01	South engineering	Defect reduction	CR												
Total												$ 1,055,576	$ 857,816	($143,875)	$ 1,769,517

Complete
Current effort
Limited effort

ROI = (Total cost avoidance − labor costs)/labor cost
ROI = 1230%

Figure 12.7 Improvement dashboard

of projects. The dashboard also serves as a key indicator of where lean project management culture, and its thinking, is being deployed in the organization.

Conclusion

Successful product development groups reinvent themselves with the aid of best-in-class process standards that drive increases in process maturity. They also link the use of these standards to strategic imperatives that challenge project delivery systems to increased levels of efficiency and productivity. Process maturity is linked to business value. Through its use of OPM3®, RFCD engineering is focusing on the integrated agenda of building process capability while orchestrating a transformation of the engineering project management culture. OPM3® is a foil for clarifying what the project management culture is and how this culture can contribute to the business bottom-line. It has been especially helpful for clarifying the impacts that processes have on the RFCD engineering project management culture and the cultural impact on engineering project management processes.

Transforming the Project Management Culture Within the Ministry of Interior, Kingdom of Saudi Arabia

Abdullah Tamimi

Assistant Planning Manager, Saudi Arabian
Ministry of Interior's National Information Center

The Kingdom of Saudi Arabia (KSA) is the largest country of the Arabian Peninsula and its stability, security, and tranquility is the responsibility of the Ministry of Interior (MOI), which is comprised of 30 main sectors and emirates. A sector is an MOI organization with responsibility for administering the national policies of the Kingdom in specific functional areas through its branch offices and, within the sector complex, functional responsibilities might be further subdivided into departments. An emirate is an MOI organization, which provides civil administration for a region of the Kingdom (Province) and there are thirteen emirates in the Kingdom (see Figure 12.8).

The NIC provides services to sectors of the MOI, utilizing the most advanced and powerful computer systems in addition to a vast information network that covers all areas of the Kingdom.

The Ministry has a rich culture, taking pride in a lineage of leaders dating from 1344H/1925 Gregorian. From a management science perspective, a tradition of deference to one's leaders has prevailed within the government, and this is no less true within the NIC. However, in keeping with its mission to serve the sectors, the NIC has evolved into a professional services organization, which treats the sectors as its customers or as the beneficiaries of many of its project management processes. This has posed unique challenges to the PMO, especially in terms of the impact of the project management culture on the project management processes. Committed to excellence in the delivery of its projects, the NIC has worked with OPM Experts to develop its knowledge of excellence in organizational project management, to assess itself rigorously, to create accountability for improving project management, and to distinguish actions that mature the PMO in strategic directions.

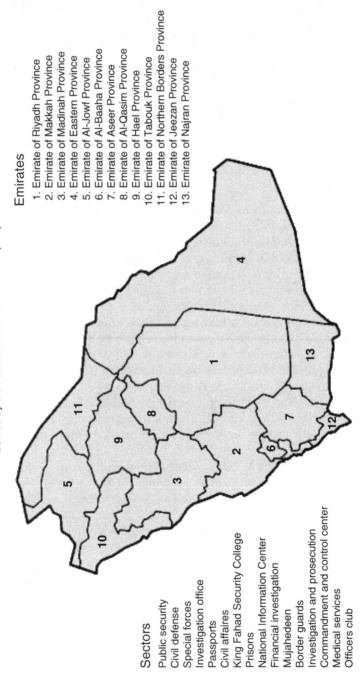

Ministry of Interior (MOI)
Sectors and Emirates
Served by the National Information Center (NIC)

Sectors

Public security
Civil defense
Special forces
Investigation office
Passports
Civil affaires
King Fahad Security College
Prisons
National Information Center
Financial investigation
Mujahedeen
Border guards
Investigation and prosecution
Commandment and control center
Medical services
Officers club

Emirates

1. Emirate of Riyadh Province
2. Emirate of Makkah Province
3. Emirate of Madinah Province
4. Emirate of Eastern Province
5. Emirate of Al-Jowf Province
6. Emirate of Al-Baaha Province
7. Emirate of Aseer Province
8. Emirate of Al-Qasim Province
9. Emirate of Hael Province
10. Emirate of Tabouk Province
11. Emirate of Northern Borders Province
12. Emirate of Jeezan Province
13. Emirate of Najran Province

Figure 12.8 Ministry of interior, sectors, and emirates

The Ministry's development started when the Prosecution was formed in 1925 to monitor the Al-Hijaz region administratively. The Prosecution was divided into two divisions:

- First Division: Ministry of Interior, including health, education, telegraph and post, legal courts, general police, municipalities, and endowments
- Second Division: Deputies Councils consisting of chairman and deputies from the Ministry of Foreign Affairs, Ministry of Finance, and Al-Shura

Responsibilities of those two divisions at that time were assigned to the Attorney General HRH Prince Faisal Bin Abdulaziz (may Allah have mercy upon his soul). As the Ministry evolved, it gradually became responsible for the local administration represented by the Region Emirates and Security Sectors in all the Kingdom's regions. Responsibilities were assigned to a series of qualified ministers, and currently, HRH Prince Naif Bin Abdulaziz Al-Saud is the Minster, and the Deputy Minister of Interior is HRH Prince Ahmad Bin Abdulaziz Al-Saud. Ministers of the MOI have delegated responsibilities vertically through the management hierarchies. Within the NIC, the PMO currently has oversight of all NIC projects, providing computer and telecommunication systems, secured communication networks, public services and administration, and a full range of ITs that are essential to daily life in the Kingdom.

In Saudi Arabia large power distance and uncertainty avoidance are the predominant characteristics of the culture. It is expected and accepted that leaders separate themselves from the group and issue complete and specific directives. Historically, deference to the vertical line has been the rule within the NIC PMO. As such, the PMO manager deferred to the planning manager, who deferred to the director general, as depicted in the organization chart in Figure 12.9.

Basic NIC organization chart

Figure 12.9 Basic NIC organization chart

In his wisdom, the director general of the NIC Dr. Khalid Al-Tawil has sought to develop the capabilities of the PMO in keeping with the needs of the Kingdom. As such, NIC leaders have committed themselves to knowing excellence, assessing the organization rigorously, creating accountability, and distinguishing action for improving the PMO, the project management process, and the project management culture. This has involved maturing the PMO to face outward instead of inward.

Knowing Excellence

The standard of excellence in organizational project management is PMI's Organizational Project Management Maturity Model (OPM3®). The most widely adopted standard of excellence for managing individual projects is PMI's *PMBOK® Guide*. OPM3® incorporates the PMBOK® and expands it into the domains of program management and portfolio management. The preferred method for implementing OPM3® is through assessors and consultants who are certified in an advanced toolset called OPM3® ProductSuite. To evaluate the NIC's OPM3® efforts to date, the NIC hired John Schlichter of OPM Experts, who led the development of OPM3® on PMI's behalf and supported the creation of OPM3® ProductSuite. The purpose of the OPM3® assessment by OPM Experts was to advance the PMOs implementation in keeping with the director's commitment to develop the capabilities of the PMO to address the needs of the Kingdom.

Assessing Rigorously

The NIC undertook a series of OPM3® assessments. Each assessment involved the evaluation of process governance, policies, processes, training, compliance, metrics, control systems, as well as myriad elements of the project management culture. The first assessment had been contracted as a so-called desk assessment. In a desk assessment, the assessor sits across the desk from a representative of the organization and takes that person's assertions regarding the organization's maturity at face value without validating those assertions. Having completed the first assessment, the NIC then engaged OPM Experts to evaluate the first assessment and to perform a follow up assessment. Committed to assessing rigorously, the PMO directed OPM Experts to expand the second assessment beyond the previous assessment, and to include process owners, practitioners, NIC leadership, and key vendors. As a result, OPM Experts interviewed the NIC assistant director general, sponsors, planning director, PMO director, program managers, project owners, PMO officers, vendor managers, vendor PMO manager, and vendor project managers. A detailed organizational chart describing the relationships between these roles is shown in Figure 12.10.

Detailed NIC organization chart

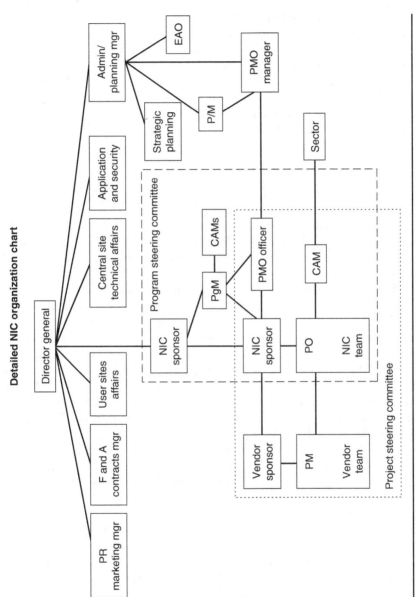

Figure 12.10 Detailed NIC organization chart

The first assessment had aligned to the cultural precedent within the MOI to focus on the needs of the leaders of one's organization. During the initial desk assessment the assessor took at face value the assertion that effective process governance had been established as a body comprised of the appropriate people. These people, the assessor assumed, met on a regular basis to identify and decide improvements to the project management processes. The assessor took at face value the assertion that project management policies had been established and also judged that the beneficiary or customer of all project management processes was the PMO director. In turn, OPM3® required the organization to collect metrics, which ensure the project management processes perform in the manner required by the customers of those processes. The desk assessment determined that all project management metrics did address the needs of the planning manager.

By contrast, the second assessment was rigorous, included more people than the desk assessment, and aligned to the strategic priority that the director placed on building the capability of the PMO to serve the sectors (facing outward instead of inward). The rigorous assessment determined that a process governing body responsible for institutionalizing project management standards across the sectors needed to be comprised of more than the PMO director alone. Additional people would need to be included in process governance to standardize, measure, control, and continuously improve the project management processes in service to the sectors. The process governing body needed to include authorized representatives of the director general, PMO, planning function, portfolio management function, and resource managers at a minimum. Other functions also needed to be included from time to time, particularly during discussions of particular process changes, e.g., the contracts department in the case of the contract administration process.

Additionally, during the rigorous assessment we agreed that those involved in the previous desk assessment had viewed the decisions of the PMO director, captured informally, as the organization's project management policies (as opposed to formal policy artifacts, which could be shared with those expected to carry out the processes governed by those policies). Likewise the NIC PMO had assimilated a large number of metrics as part of its project management processes. In the more rigorous assessment, we agreed that we needed to ensure that the organization measures the appropriate things and does not measure more things than necessary. For this reason the NIC PMO needed to develop policies that focused the NIC on the critical characteristics of each process, kept the processes lean, and ensured customer needs were met. It was agreed that to mature the PMO in service to the sectors, the customers of the project management processes are rightly the sectors (not only the PMO director). As such the sectors needed to be engaged to incorporate performance requirements into the project management metrics collected by the PMO.

Assessment one vs. assessment two

Desk assessment (1) Performed previously	Rigorous assessment (2) Performed by OPM Experts
Relied on views of PMO manager who views his supervisor as the PMO customer Viewed the planning manager as a unilateral process governing body Viewed the planning manager's informal decisions as policies Viewed the planning manager as the customer of project management processes Identified metrics the PMO had implemented to serve the information processing needs of the planning manager	Incorporated interviews of the full management hierarchy and all functions horizontally Judged that a cross-functional governing body was necessary to institution-alize processes throughout the ministry Judged that formal policy statements from the process governing body were necessary to achieve the NIC's strategic intent Judged that the sectors and key vendors were beneficiaries of project management processes, in addition to the planning manager Judged that metrics should focus on modifying the behavior of the sectors and key vendors

Figure 12.11   Assessment one vs assessment two

As a result of the contrasts between this more rigorous approach and the previous approach, which was restricted to fewer interviews and which took assertions at face value (see Figure 12.11), the second assessment revealed that the PMO had matured significantly even though the initial assessment had inflated scores in certain areas, as dictated by the charter of the original assessment to be conducted as a desk assessment and to rely on the views of a proxy within the organization who was subject to the culture shaping his views.

The first assessment was characterized by a culture of power distance and uncertainty avoidance, which was embodied in the many ways in which the planning manager was the focus of efforts to increase the maturity of the PMO (see Figure 12.9), whereas the second assessment aligned to the director's intentions for developing the PMO in keeping with the needs of the Kingdom by institutionalizing capabilities across the sectors (see Figure 12.10). The rigorous assessment laid the foundation for developing the PMO to serve the sectors and to take the PMO in new strategic directions. While scores pertaining to the project management process were lower in the second assessment, scores were especially high in the areas of OPM3® pertaining to the culture, i.e., organizational enablers. These enablers corresponded to the project management culture, which scored nearly four times as high as the project management process elements described.

As John Schlichter indicated previously, it was the culture that drove development of the project management process within the NIC. The conclusions of the first assessment demonstrated deference to the vertical management hierarchy and were indicative of the wider culture within the NIC and within the MOI at large. In turn the conclusions of the second assessment aligned to the director's vision of maturing the PMO to serve the sectors. It showed that elements of OPM3® that pertain to culture offered the most leverage for increasing the capability of project management within the organization.

Creating Accountability and Distinguishing Action

Just as knowing excellence enabled a rigorous assessment, the rigorous assessment in turn enabled the creation of accountability for improving the project management process and project management culture in keeping with the director's vision for the PMO. I was promoted from planning manager to a new position and given the mission to expand the capabilities of the organization into the domain of portfolio management and other strategic directions. My successor in the PMO picked up where we left off and refocused the organization on key elements of standardizing and measuring the project management process while cultivating the project management culture, increasing the capability and scalability of processes within the sectors' projects.

Conclusion

Through implementation of OPM3®, the NIC is focusing on the integrated agenda of building process capability while orchestrating a transformation of the culture. OPM3® is a useful tool for clarifying what the project management culture is and enabling leaders to assess the organization from a variety of perspectives in the organization in actionable ways that predicate the creation of accountability for specific and measurable steps to build the organization's project delivery capability. Within the NIC, OPM3® has been especially helpful for clarifying the impacts that processes have on culture and the impacts that culture has on processes.

The NIC has understood the reasons why many organizations fail to transform their project management cultures and has avoided these pitfalls with our improvement initiatives. Working with OPM Experts, our leaders have understood the need for knowing excellence, assessing oneself rigorously, creating accountability, and distinguishing action. This straightforward approach has helped to advance the organization's mission to ensure projects across the sectors are successful, promoting the stability, security, and tranquility of the Kingdom.

13

Project Management Office Passion:
Where Does It Come From?

The cartoon shown in Figure 13.1 brings to mind the famous expression and its many incantations, "one man's pleasure is another man's pain." It is not so much the concept of Schadenfreude or Roman holiday in which delight is derived from the suffering of others that is intriguing, rather the simple premise that two people of relatively similar backgrounds in terms of education, job position, and skills can view the same task as enjoyable or as a chore. In the context of today's businesses, the passion for the project management office (PMO) is an excellent example of one of those things that elicits varying responses that differ greatly from one business professional to the next.

What makes us passionate about what we do and to what degree is passion an acceptable emotion to display in the workplace? My first experience with passion in the workplace occurred over twenty-five years ago. It was a negative experience that I remember vividly. I was a young IBMer in 1983, a part of the regional staff in Dallas, Texas, and recently promoted from the field. I was part of a special team of people, hand selected, to lead in the field marketing of a soon-to-be-announced, revolutionary and controversial product called DB2.

As part of our training and readiness for the DB2 announcement, the DB2 regional team members all over the United States were flown to Silicon Valley for a week of presentations and hands-on workshops at the IBM Santa Teresa labs. It was there that I learned the history behind DB2 and the incredible story of the birth of what is now taken for granted as the relational database. I heard all about Ted Codd who, while working for IBM, invented the relational model for database management and IBM's initial refusal to implement it to

Figure 13.1   PMO comics—passion

preserve and protect the market share and revenues from its then highly successful hierarchical database model called IMS. Codd then showed his relational model directly to some of IBM's largest, most sophisticated customers and they in turn pressured IBM to develop it. While the IBM relational database advocates and IMS hierarchical database protectors were cat fighting internally, Larry Ellison, a crafty businessman inspired by Codd's work, came to believe in the promise of the relational model and set his sights on developing his own relational database, now simply known as Oracle. The week of training and indoctrination was intense and it ended with a dinner meeting and presentation by none other than Ted Codd himself, the inventor and father of the relational database.

The following week I was back in Dallas for a regional review of the DB2 launch. As part of this review with the regional IBM executive team, my technical colleague gave a detailed presentation on DB2, and I followed him with a live demonstration of the product in action. We practiced our presentations and demonstrations and looked forward to updating the regional IBM executive team on the importance of DB2 and the opportunity that it presented for our customers, many of whom anxiously awaited product availability.

My colleague's technical presentation was informative and insightful, and I thought I did an acceptable job demonstrating DB2. I described a handful of technical challenges that our customers faced and demonstrated how DB2 met these challenges. It was difficult not to be enthusiastic over the capabilities of DB2 and ease of use of the SQL language in querying the database and manipulating the data. I earnestly believed in the power of the relational database and was passionate when talking about it and considered it a joy to show it off in action.

After the review with the regional IBM executive team, my manager called me into his office. He proceeded to tell me that he had feedback from one of the executives in attendance that my demonstration was over the top. When I asked what that meant he told me that it meant that I was too enthusiastic and that I needed to talk more like a database specialist and less like a personal computer sales rep. The presentation and demonstration techniques that I learned and practiced at the IBM Santa Teresa labs that received high marks from my expert instructors were not met with favor by my regional executive team and I was told to tone it down. After all, DB2 was just a database. In the scheme of IBM's water-cooled mainframe computer processing systems, it was not like DB2 was that important to the executive team or our customers.

All of the enthusiasm and passion that I had for both my product and my job came to a screeching halt. How could you be an IBMer, much less an IBM executive, and not be proud, excited, and enthusiastic with the announcement and much awaited and anticipated availability of DB2? Not to mention the fact that our customers wanted it, and our competitors were rapidly trying to catch up to us and edge us out with their own relational database products. Did working for IBM mean that you needed to check your passion at the door? Is passion in the workplace considered to be a bad thing? According to my manager at IBM, passion was considered unprofessional.

Importance of Passion

Years later I had come to appreciate the value and business necessity of passion. Consider the following perspectives:

♦ Michael Sheffield (2008) writes, "It is curious how passion is usually positioned opposite of reason as if the two were mutually exclusive emotions. While facts and figures are important to how products are prepared and companies are created, it is emotion that determines the actions of customers, distributors, and employees."

♦ Richard Chang (2001) suggests that passion is a right and a competitive advantage that all organizations can leverage. In speaking about the importance of passion Chang asks, "Are your clients and customers excited about and loyal to your products and services? Does it attract and retain high-performing employees and strategic partners? If not, then it may be missing out on the greatest competitive advantage an organization can claim: passion."

♦ In discussing processes and passion in a Six Sigma context Edoardo Monopoli (2006) writes, "To see a new idea become a reality, an individual or company has to have enough passion to overcome the obstacles. In fact, if an idea does not kick up serious resistance, it probably is not very innovative."

♦ Also emphasizing the importance of passion in a Six Sigma context is Gianna Clark (2007) who states, "Changed processes, changed skill sets, changed thinking and changed performance. Six Sigma is all about change. Passion, defined as 'boundless enthusiasm', is the seed of change. With it, Six Sigma flourishes. Without it, project implementation is a constant struggle."

◆ Commenting on the importance of passion and advanced project management Alan Orr (2004, p. 149) writes, "Passion is a culture within an organization and it should be build into the fabric of how the advanced project operates. Those in the project should be striving to achieve their best work at all times. You must lead this passionate charge from within the project."

◆ And Carmine Gallo (2006), writing about Donald Trump's perspectives on passion writes, "Passion generates energy, enthusiasm, and excitement, all the qualities that make you likeable. And if people like you, they are more likely to do business with you."

It is difficult to argue that passion is not important in today's business environment, especially in businesses and workplace settings that involve a high degree of human contact and interaction. Next to sales, perhaps the most collaborative work environment is the environment in which project managers and project teams find themselves on a daily basis. So if you are a project management professional (PMP), a PMO manager, a director or manager of a project-based organization, how do you recognize and find your passion?

How to Find Your Passion

For some PMO professionals, passion is a natural quality. The enthusiasm that comes with being helpful, knowledgeable, solving organizational problems, and delivering projects to the delight of stakeholders is a common trait among project managers and PMO managers. But if passion does not come naturally, or if it is here today and gone tomorrow, how do you achieve a natural state of passion rather than one that is artificially manufactured? Figure 13.2 illustrates that passion exists and is driven by four critical aspects: purpose, pleasure, problematic, and personal.

To be passionate one must first have a strong sense of purpose. People are driven by their sense of purpose and this is especially true in a PMO. Unlike other organizational functions, such as sales, that are driven and rewarded based on monthly or quarterly performance, project management professionals are driven from within. In fact, much of what great project managers do goes unnoticed. Certainly the progress of the project, issues, status reports, and the completion of the project, on time, on budget, and within the agreed to specifications, are visible for all to see, but most of the work effort expended by the PMO manager, project manager, and team members is not. Without an inner sense of purpose, passion cannot exist.

The 4 Ps of passion

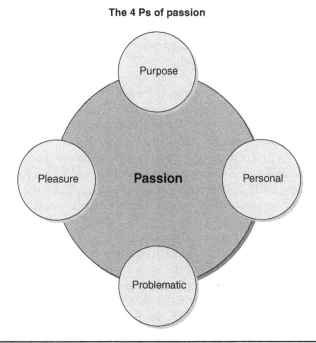

Figure 13.2 The 4 Ps of passion

Passion and pleasure aspects are closely related. It is crucially important to enjoy one's passion. This doesn't necessarily mean that the object of one's passion must be fun, but it does mean that there is an ability to make it fun. For example, my dear friend and colleague, Russ, loves to run, and he can be found running five miles every morning. One day Russ admitted to me that he actually loathed running; he abhors it as much as I do. However, he thoroughly enjoys the way he feels after a run. It keeps him in superb shape and carries him through the day.

In a similar fashion I have never met a better sales person at cold calls than John, a sales professional I met years ago. John was the best cold-call salesman in his company. He loved sales, he loved cold calling, and he really loved commissions and bonuses. Where John was different than most sales professionals is that he expected a high degree of rejection. In fact he planned and thrived on it. He tracked and measured his cold calling activities. Out of one hundred calls, he would know in advance how many prospects would have no interest, a passing interest, or a degree of actionable interest in his products. Whereas John's colleagues would get dejected with cold calling because ninety out of one hundred prospects showed no interest in what they were selling, John would be enthusiastic in anticipation that ten out of one hundred would likely have some degree of interest. Of those ten, three would in turn likely be a good fit for the company's product offering; and of those three, one would predictably become John's next sale.

John didn't like being rejected ninety times out of hundred any more than his sales colleagues were, but he developed his cold calling system complete with process and metrics and thoroughly enjoyed following it and the results it produced. His sales colleagues would bemoan the monthly cold calling aspect of the job, but John thoroughly enjoyed it.

There is also a problematic aspect to having a passion. It is not enough to have a purpose and enjoy what you do. More is needed for passion to sustain itself and solving a difficult problem is a key aspect of passion. Many people can relate to golf as a passion. One can spend a lifetime pursuing ways to become a better golfer. If it was easy everyone would be mastering it, not just Tiger Woods, and it wouldn't be a passion. Can you imagine a Tiger Woods of Tic-Tac-Toe? It takes little time and effort to master the nuances of the game even for a novice. Hence, it is doubtful that there will ever be a person, beyond kindergarten age, who is truly passionate about Tic-Tac-Toe.

Much like golf, project management presents its fair share of problems and obstacles. Great project managers thrive in project environments that call on and test their skills. To the passionate project manager a difficult project is much more rewarding to manage and successfully deliver than a trivial project. It is the problematic aspect of things that fuels the passion of a project manager who truly enjoys managing projects. Some even call project management an art; a work of beauty when done well.

The personal aspect of our passion is what confirms and reminds us who we are and what our business is. Those who are passionate know who they are and what their business is and that for any work, job, or task that must be done, there is pride in that effort and pride in a job well done. I can think of no better example of the personal aspect of passion than Tomima Edmark.

Most people know Tomima through her incredible success story as the inventor of Topsy Tail and the founder of the company by the same name. Tomima, a beautiful woman with long blond hair, always had difficulty styling her locks. Making herself elegant more than inventing, she came up with a hair-styling contraption that could flip ponytails inside out and make intricate hair designs. She refined her product, patented it, and brought it to market. The Topsy Tail was an instant success, becoming the rave of teenage girls and achieving sales of more than one million units.

Tomima didn't stop there. She went on to write an insightful little book about kissing and all of the ways around the world that people go about it. She also founded and manages an online company called HerRoom that sells lingerie of every style and type imaginable. Through her success Tomima has become the leading undergarment expert, providing advice to women all over the world on the nuances and possibilities that lingerie can offer today's woman.

Of course I knew Tomima Edmark long before she had become a successful entrepreneur and millionaire. Over twenty years ago we had both worked together at IBM in Dallas. We were on the same team that sold IBM's data processing equipment, including mainframe computers, system software, direct access storage devices (DASD), network equipment, and a wide range of input/output devices to the EDS Corporation. Tomima exhibited style and brilliance in everything she did. She always made her performance objectives and she was well liked by all of the customer personnel with whom she worked. That alone was a feat of extraordinary measure because back then EDSers and IBMers mixed like oil and water.

Tomima always had an incredibly positive attitude and outlook. There was no limit to her potential and to what she could achieve at IBM. Then, one day, IBM announced that it was planning its first layoff ever. Up until that time IBM had a full employment policy and scoffed at the notion of employee layoffs. The workforce reduction had a benevolent name, the Voluntary Transition Program, which IBM soon referred to as VTP. Tomima was one of several IBMers that was offered the voluntary separation package, a package that really wasn't that voluntary. Where others who were offered the program felt devastated, Tomima didn't even bat an eye. She left IBM without regret, turned her passion elsewhere, and quickly became a successful and wealthy woman. Tomima possessed all aspects of passion, particularly the personal aspect. With all of the difficulties that IBM faced in the mid- to late-1980s, it is a pity that they let such a talented individual go. The loss was clearly theirs, not hers.

When passion has taken over it can be much like holding the tail of a race horse. You know you are going somewhere, often at a spirited pace, but you are never quite sure how long the adventure will last or where it finally ends. Consider the following people, such as Tomima Edmark, who possessed the four Ps of passion and held on for the ride.

George de Mestral, a Swiss engineer, took a walk one day in 1948 and returned home with his cloth jacket covered in cockleburs. He loosened them and examined one under a microscope. He discovered a simple principle. The cocklebur was simply a maze of thin strands with hooks that would cling to just about any kind of fabric or fur. George de Mestral recognized the potential for a practical new fastener. It took eight purposeful years to perfect his invention, which consisted of two strips of nylon fabric; one containing thousands of small hooks and the other containing small loops. When pressed together the two strips make a strong bond useful for a wide variety of purposes. Velcro, the name he gave to his invention, was created and has been used by people all over the world.

Ole Evinrude, a motor shop owner at the turn of the century, was already passionate. He was in love and while enjoying a picnic on a small island with his future wife, Bess Cary, she mentioned that she'd like some ice cream. Ole volunteered, as one in love would do, to go get it even though it meant rowing quite some distance to another island. By the time Ole returned with the gallon of ice cream it had melted away. However, this arduous and amorous day inspired Evinrude to create a lightweight, detachable motor that could power small boats.

Earle Dickson, a cotton buyer for the Johnson & Johnson Company, had a lovely wife whose kitchen knives were as sharp as her wit. While in the kitchen preparing food, she was always cutting her fingers. At that time there were no band-aids; a bandage consisted of separate gauze and adhesive tape that you had to cut to size and apply yourself. Dickson noticed that the gauze and adhesive tape his wife used soon fell off her active fingers. He decided to invent something that stayed in place and protected those small finger wounds much better. Dickson took a piece of gauze and attached it to the center of a piece of tape, and then covered the product with crinoline to keep it sterile. His boss, James Johnson, saw Earle Dickson's invention and decided to manufacture band-aids to the public and make Earle Dickson vice-president of Johnson & Johnson.

All three of these gentlemen are examples of ordinary people, like so many others, who came across a problem and were inspired with an idea. They enthusiastically toiled with their efforts as if on a personal mission and never gave up. It was their passion that turned their fanciful ideas of what could be into tangible realities that were.

In addition to being aware of the four aspects of passion (purpose, pleasure, problematic, and personal), finding your passion can sometimes be like solving a mystery. Nancy Anderson (2004) advises that you need to know how to interpret the clues of your passion to stay on track. In her book, *Work With Passion*, Anderson provides a list of ten clues; of which five she calls passion clues and five she calls off track signals:

◆ Passion clues:
 1. You would do the work for little or no pay
 2. You seek to master your work, not just achieve the expected results
 3. You become a better person as you do better work
 4. You are not aware and do not care that time is passing
 5. You receive your salary because of who you are, not because of the position you hold
◆ Off track signals:
 1. You are only in it for the money
 2. You are more focused on your reputation than what you actually can do
 3. You only care about getting the job done, not the process or how well you do it

4. You look for shortcuts to finish your work so you can turn your attention to something else
5. You are too busy running around therefore you don't take care of yourself physically or mentally

Interpreting passion clues is critical to finding your passion. When you are passionate about your work you seek to master it. Rather than wishing time to pass, you are not even aware that time is going by. You view your salary as compensation for who you are to the organization, not for the number of hours that you put in that week.

Whereas passion clues help you find your passion, off track signals help you keep your passion by letting you know when you are no longer on the right track. Those passionate about what they do are concerned about how they go about it, the process. Maintaining one's professional passion is much like career planning and development. It is not enough to just pursue advancement, fame, and money. Those things are no doubt important, but they do not satisfy a professional for long. Workplace professionals, especially those managing projects, are likely most fulfilled and passionate over mastering their craft and being of value to others.

Commenting on the importance of passion Vera Raposo (2008) advises, "Having passion for your business is critical to your success. Why? Without passion and enjoyment for your business you won't be motivated to make it the best company it can be." And for those who need to find a way to put the passion back into their work, Raposo offers a five-step approach:

1. Eliminate the tasks that drive you mad. Make a list of the activities that you like to do and then make a list of the activities that you don't like to do. What can you do to compartmentalize and minimize the tasks that you don't like to do? In many cases the answer is simply to do the tasks you don't like as quickly as possible rather than procrastinate and have them hang over your head longer than they should.
2. Refresh your memory and take time to reacquaint yourself with the reasons why you have chosen to do what you are doing. What were your initial goals and motivations? Write down all that you have achieved and compare that progress to your goals. You might be surprised to see how far you have come. Revisiting your goals rekindles your passion.
3. Be grateful. It is far too easy to overlook and take for granted that which we should be grateful for. Few people can achieve extraordinary success solely on their own accord. I can think of no better example of a grateful professional than one of my early career mentors, Paul Hollrah, a senior sales representative with IBM. On receiving the prestigious Salesman of the Year Award for the second time in his ca-

reer, a feat never before or since achieved, Paul spent a portion of his Christmas holidays that year writing thank you letters to all those who played a role in his success. By the time Paul had finished he had written over 250 letters of thanks and appreciation. Not only were the recipients happy to receive a heartfelt letter from the salesman of the year, but Paul found that his enthusiasm and passion for the up-and-coming new year had been reinvigorated as well.

4. Work with and surround yourself by passionate and motivated people. Just as a positive attitude is contagious, a negative attitude can be like a deadly workplace virus. Recognize the importance of having a positive mental attitude and nurturing it by recognizing your successes, both large and small. There is no quicker way to lose one's passion that to exhibit a negative attitude or even to be in the presence of those who exhibit a negative attitude.

5. Recognize that you have many passions and seek ways to integrate them into your work. Some people are passionate about technology and are the first in line to find ways to adopt new technology products in the workplace. Others are passionate about sports, the arts, or travel. There is no better way to enhance relationships in the workplace, with partners, and with customers than to find and enjoy common passions with one another.

How to Keep Your Passion Alive

Now that you have found your passion how do you keep it alive? Recently I had dinner with Leslie, a retired information technology veteran who I have known for many years. During our dinner I asked Leslie how he managed to keep his passion and attitude so vibrant and positive throughout the life of his career. Expecting to hear wise words of wisdom I was quite surprised and amused to hear his simple answer, "Don't ever let the bastards get you down." Leslie went on to add that there are always going to be people who deny you a promotion, cheat you out of an award or bonus, hold back on a pay raise, or worse, much worse. You might even have a new boss arrive and try to fire you before even meeting you so that he can hire a friend. It happens. The trick is to not let the behaviors of bad, manipulative, unscrupulous people bring you down to their level. You must keep your passion alive and your perspective in check.

Michelle LaBrosse (2008), the charismatic chief executive officer (CEO) of Cheetah Learning, offers her advice on how to keep passion alive. She offers five tips that can help any project manager and project team keep the passion alive when the enthusiasm begins to wane and the project team finds itself in the tight grip of project fatigue:

◆ Tip 1: Acknowledge the elephant. There is nothing worse than empty platitudes and half-hearted cheerleading when everyone knows the ship is sinking. This is when humor can be effective. Consider making light of the situation and go ahead and say what everyone in the room is thinking. Turn the malaise into laughter with the simple truth. Try saying something like 'We all know this project is in the ditch and no one thinks we can pull it out, so how can we prove them all wrong.'

◆ Tip 2: Ask 'why do we care'? The greatest problem with projects that take too long and seem to go on forever is that it is easy to lose sight amid the day-to-day project problems of the purpose, value, and importance of the project. Paint the big picture and ensure that it is kept in view for all to see. Reinforce small project victories along the way with incentives and recognition. Surprise the team with appreciation.

◆ Tip 3: Revisit expectations and goals. Over the course of a complex, long-lasting project, expect plans to change. In addition to the normal kinds of changes that all projects have, longer-term projects are especially prone to experiencing people changes. Continually recharge your team and bring out their passion to achieve by revisiting the expectations for the project and ensuring that they are realistic. There is no quicker way to reset a positive attitude than to replace objectives that are unachievable with ones that are achievable.

◆ Tip 4: Find ways to inspire your project team. Consider having a member of the executive team hold a roundtable. Invite an inspirational speaker to come in for a short meeting. Even on a limited budget you can take a break from a weekly meeting and do a number of creative and participatory team-building exercises.

◆ Tip 5: Visualize the end. One technique that works well for long-lasting, complex projects is to lead a visualization exercise in which all members of the team spend a few minutes visualizing the end of the project. What does the end look like? How does the team get there? Does the team know when they do get there? Anticipate that the project team gets stuck in the mud and loses their passion. As their leader be prepared to help them find a way out.

In keeping the passion of the project team alive, it is important to walk the talk. As John Rey (2008) advises, "The trick is not just to feel passionately about your job, but to act passionately too. Use your passion to move projects ahead, to find innovative solutions to perplexing problems, to work through the interpersonal conflicts." In keeping the passion alive it is also important to realize that your professional needs and wants change. Your passion also has to change.

In "Find Passion for Your Work," Bill Dueease (2004) writes, "Many people think that because they finally found the position they are passionate about, that they will want to stay in it forever. The position that is ideal today will probably not be ideal in a couple of years." This is especially true of PMOs. In many organizations a PMO is initially started to achieve one set of objectives and with time might mature to a new set of objectives or be disbanded altogether. It is important to realize that no matter how passionate you are about your current profession, job, or assignment, it is highly unlikely that you will have it forever. Embracing change, or at least anticipating it, helps keep you alive and on the right track.

Summary

For nearly all organizations and businesses today, passion is an important ingredient for success. When people are passionate about their work, they have a TGIM—Thank God It's Monday attitude. They are eager to go about their work and strive to meet, and usually exceed, their objectives.

What makes us passionate? The answer to this simple question is not easy at all to give and is different for each of us. It can be easy to follow in the footsteps of others or to pursue the standard career path as outlined in the company manager manual. But as individuals each of us have our own unique skills, capabilities, and desires that have more differences than similarities.

PMO managers and project managers are typically service-oriented professionals. They are high-value employees with a wide range of useful skills from technology to project management skills, and a wide variety of professional soft skills, including communications, negotiations, mentoring, and leadership. For most professionals who are in the service of others, their enthusiasm, motivation, and passion come from within. While monetary motivation comes into play to an extent, if a professional had the sole ambition to become a millionaire they probably wouldn't pursue a career in project management. Service with a smile is more than a hospitality industry slogan; it is a vivid reminder that providing service, any service, is inherently a line of work that is well-served by a high level of caring and passion. This is especially true and applicable in today's PMOs.

For even the best of positive mental attitude practitioners, it is not too difficult to find challenging situations and difficult people who can, and often seek to, put a damper on the enthusiasm and passion that we have. Because of such events and people, it is all the more important to acknowledge the importance of passion, develop ways to discover what makes you passionate, and once you have it, take aim and care to keep it. Much like a warm fire on a cold winter's night, if not tended to it goes out.

Questions

1. What role does passion play in today's workplace?
2. What are the four Ps of passion?
3. What are passion clues and off track signals?
4. What approaches can be taken to find one's passion?
5. To what degree can a PMP that is currently passionate about their project, their job, and their company expect that passion to last?
6. What approaches can be taken to keep one's passion alive?
7. As a provider of service, why is it important for PMPs to be passionate about their work?
8. In what ways are PMPs likely to be more driven and motivated by providing a service than making money?
9. To what extent do monetary rewards such as pay increases and bonuses motivate and impassion PMPs?
10. What role does a project manager have in instilling passion into the project team?
11. What factors result in the project team losing their passion for the project?
12. Describe approaches and techniques that PMPs can use to rekindle the passion of the project team?

References

Anderson, Nancy. 2004. "Work with Passion—10 Clues to Keep You on Track." http://www.newconnexion.com. (Accessed June 19, 2008)

Chang, Richard. 2001. "Turning Into Organizational Performance—The Role of Passion in Business Management and Leadership." http://www.findarticles.com. (Accessed June 19, 2008)

Clark, Gianna. 2007. "Passion is the Seed of Change." http://www.blog.isixsigma.com. (Accessed June 19, 2008)

Dueease, Bill. 2004. "Find Passion for your Work." http://www.findyourcoach.com. (Accessed June 19, 2008)

Gallo, Carmine. 2006. "Talk About the Passion." http://www.businessweek.com. (Accessed June 19, 2008)

LaBrosse, Michelle. 2008. "Top Five Ways to Keep Project Passion Alive." http://www.cheetahlearning.com. (Accessed June 19, 2008)

Monopoli, Edoardo.2006. "Six Sigma and Business Innovation: Process or Passion?" http://www.realinnovations.com. (Accessed June 19, 2008)

Orr, Alan. 2004. *Advanced Project Management.* London: Kogan Page Publishers.

Raposos, Vera. 2008. "5 Effective Ways to put Passion Back into Your Business." http://www.smallbusiness branding.com. (Accessed June 19, 2008)

Rey, F. John. 2008. "Passion Pays." http://www.management.about.com. (Accessed June 19, 2008)

Sheffield, Michael. 2008. "Passion for Your Business." http://www.mlmlegal .com. (Accessed June 19, 2008)

Executive Insights

Project Management Office Passion

Cornelius Fichtner

Host of "The Project Management Podcast"

Have you ever been to the Sistine Chapel? It is a beautiful building. The architecture itself is breathtaking, but it is the frescos by renaissance artists including Michelangelo, Raphael, Bernini, and Sandro Botticelli that make it extraordinary. Michelangelo painted 1100 square meters of the chapel ceiling between 1508 and 1512. It is these frescos that evoke the passion in visitors like you or me. In this case the building is merely the canvas for the artist's passion. In a PMO, on the other hand, I have never come across any breathtaking frescos. Instead I have come to appreciate the beauty of the architecture and the framework, and that is where the focus of my passion lies. But let's start at the beginning and ask the most important question. Why am I passionate and why should you be?

In the 1990s I was a junior project manager in Switzerland's second largest supermarket chain. The CEO of the company realized that to turn his vision of a revamped company into reality, several medium and large projects were required. They needed to be managed effectively. He entrusted our department with setting up what he called the Project Management Center of Excellence. In today's terms this would be considered a basic PMO with limited oversight that provides a PM standard to be used across all projects. We were asked to define, document, and roll out a project management methodology (PMM) that was easy enough to follow, such that individual subject matter experts in the various departments without PM experience could manage the many projects that were coming their way.

There were no standardized methodologies available at the time, so we couldn't just go out and purchase one for customization. Instead we brought in a project management consultant with the appropriate expertise. Four of us worked closely with this consultant in developing our custom-made internal framework that fit our needs. The result we produced was appropriate. It fit our organization like a glove. It worked. It was beautiful. I loved it.

The framework we built brought many people from several different departments onto the same page. Suddenly they all used the same language.

They all followed the same methodology. We gave them a process to manage their projects regardless of project type, subject, or application area.

In my view all the work that I had been assigned in setting up this PMO was extremely creative. There were no rules because this had never been done before. I was asked to create something new that would fundamentally change how people approached their assigned projects. We were able to mix the consultant's methodology with our project management expertise and subject matter expertise to create a methodology that fit. In my head I saw the picture of how people managed projects today and envisioned where we needed to go, and it was my task to create the processes of how they would do it in the future. This work was so attractive to me that it felt as if I had died and gone to heaven except that I still needed the healthcare benefits.

I also participated in training the subject matter experts in how to use our PMM. Being a bit of a ham, I have always enjoyed teaching adults, but this was different. I was able to teach about our own creation and educate our colleagues who, let's face it, were only there because the CEO had told them to attend. Seeing the students transform from 'I'm bored' to 'This makes sense' was even more gratifying than usual. It also felt rewarding when, a few months later, I saw that our methodology was being used successfully in everyday projects by all of our *accidental* project managers.

Then it began to dawn on me that there were also significant business results that our work produced. At a supermarket chain the goal is to have customers put products into their shopping cart and pay for them at the checkout. The methodology and processes we defined and laid out in our center of excellence enabled our subject matter experts to manage projects that significantly improved the company's ability to reduce the cost involved in both the logistics of getting the products to the store as well as the overall product life cycle. Our work had an evident effect on the bottom line. What's there not to be passionate about?

And that is how I first got involved with PMOs, and it kindled my excitement for them. It is this kind of energy that we want to harness in ourselves or others as we are working in our own PMOs. Let's take a look at what it does for the individual.

Passion is an excellent motivator. Being enthusiastic about PMOs enables you to envision the result of what you are creating today. You bring order from chaos and you bring clarity to project processes that affect many people and organizations as a whole. Passion enables you to see a vision in your mind that drives you and makes you want to go beyond simply doing your job. In fact going to work becomes a joy. You identify with the work results and you want to make sure that what you produce is indeed what your organization needs. You might not see your name in lights, but make no mistake about it, the work you create in a PMO is your legacy.

Knowing that my creative work would live on long beyond the end of my career with the company was a thrill. I spoke to my former boss about five years after I had left. I learned that, while the PMO had evolved, some of the key results we had produced were still being used. It's an incredible confirmation of one's work and a boost to your morale.

In regard to your daily routine, passion gets you into *The Zone* where creativity flows. This affects your colleagues working next to you in the PMO and fosters a creative, collaborative environment throughout the organization. To the outsider a PMO too often seems to be a central node that consists only of rules and regulations. Your zeal adds the human touch. It makes your 200-page methodology seem a bit less daunting because your department now has a friendly, smiling face.

Passion also encourages humor, facilitating a good working environment in which everyone is more receptive. At least my kind of passion does. I always try and plant a harmless, unexpected surprise in my PMOs. At one point I created a standard operating procedure entitled *How to cross the desert on a horse without a name*. This SOP was loosely based on the song "Horse with No Name" by the group America. People loved it because after some initial confusion it gave them a moment of escape from the daily grind. In another PMO we had The Coffee Procedure in which someone detailed, in an absolute jumble of activities and regulations, how to use the coffee machine. It was hilariously funny and might even have produced something that could have resembled coffee. In my last PMO we inserted a secret, animated cartoon on our PMO intranet. If you clicked on a particular area in the methodology you saw our boss dance the Macarena. It got a lot of clicks.

At first glance you might think that these kinds of Easter eggs are a waste of time and have no place in a business environment. You couldn't be further from the truth. Go to any organization and ask what people think about their PMOs. More often than not you hear that people feel that PMOs add an additional burden on them by making them fill in all these additional forms. More often than not, the people who are most affected by a PMO do not understand that it is trying to help them succeed, not burden them or get in the way. PMO rules and regulations should not be seen as a burden but as a way to help manage projects consistently across the organization. Humor and play helps to lighten that first perception.

For me, my overall appreciation for PMOs came from within. I didn't need anyone to help me see how important my work was for the bottom line of the companies for which I worked. Others might need a little push. So how do you create and harness this kind of passion for the PMO in your own team members? Let me begin with a story about how Steve Jobs instilled passion in his engineers as told by Andy Hertzfeld (1983), who was a key member of the original Apple Macintosh development team during the 1980s.

According to Andy, the Apple development team always thought of the Macintosh as a fast computer. The Macintosh had a 68000 microprocessor that was ten times faster than the previous Apple computer. However, it took a long time to boot up, because of limited RAM, and this bothered Steve.

One afternoon Steve came up with an original way to challenge the team to make the Macintosh faster. Larry Kenyon, an engineer working on the file system, offered a few ideas for improving performance, but Steve was disinterested in minor adjustments here and there. Rather than frame the problem in terms of the technology, Steve framed it in terms of the tremendous impact that solving the problem would have. With over five million Macintosh users booting their system at least once a day, shaving ten seconds off of the time it took to boot the computer was the equivalent of fifty million seconds every day. Steve went on to add that over the course of the year the amount of time saved was the equivalent of a dozen lifetimes. Hence, if you can solve this problem and make the Macintosh boot ten seconds faster, then you will have saved a dozen lives. Wouldn't that be a feat?

Needless to say the Macintosh development team felt motivated and up to their new challenge. Within the next few months, they managed to save more than ten seconds off of the Macintosh boot time. Whether or not Steve Job's motivation technique was the cause of their success only the Apple development team knows. But what we do know is that Steve's approach was an example of his relentless passion. He took his vision of a faster booting computer and turned it into a challenge to his engineers. He called on their professional pride of building a great computer, showed them what an incredible result just an incremental improvement can be, and was able to not only instill but also harness their passion for the good of the company.

You Can Do the Same!

Your PMO might not have the ability to save lives unless your company produces components that are life sustaining like airplane wings, medication, or hamburgers, but your PMO no doubt helps improve productivity and decrease waste. Just like in the story with Steve Jobs, these improvements multiply their effect throughout the company: software testers spend fewer frustrating hours with bugs because quality is built in; everyone understands the project better because of the clearly defined processes; and customers get consistent project delivery. These factors can be turned into concrete numbers and you can use them to motivate yourself and your team.

Did you notice that at the end of the Macintosh story the team managed to shave off more than ten seconds? This is another result of you harnessing the passion of everyone working in your PMO. Passionate people go beyond what you expect them to do. Because we are passionate about our work we tend to raise our bar higher and achieve better results.

This is best shown in the methodology I put into place for the local division of a worldwide financial institution. My task was to implement the 500-page corporate PMM at the IT department of this division. At the time we started there was little defined around the software development and maintenance processes. There were no standards to follow and there was no default way of documenting any parts of the project. So it made sense to move toward a more formalized approach. Unfortunately, due to bank internal regulations, the term software maintenance did not exist. Everything was considered a project, requiring the full-blown methodology even though we knew that our average project effort was less than twenty hours.

Use a 500-page methodology on every twenty hour long project? I had just been handed my challenge on a silver platter. Let us first think about what happens if you hand this kind of an assignment to a project manager who does not share our passion for PMOs. Very likely what you receive is a methodology that is reduced in size and complexity so as to make it fit the needs. It works in the environment of this development organization. It is what we call a normal methodology. However, during and after the rollout there would be a lot of pushback from the teams because 'we really don't need all these templates to deliver our software.' Nobody would have used it.

But I had passion. I wanted to shave *more than ten seconds* off this methodology. I wanted to go beyond what was considered an appropriate solution. It had to be perfect. After about a week of methodology and environment analysis I had created my vision: we are going to reduce this 500-page methodology down to a single page.

It took around six weeks of talking, convincing, and developing. The greatest portion of this time was spent analyzing and documenting why each section that we wanted to cut out of the methodology was not needed in our environment. If I hadn't been passionate about it, I would never have been successful in convincing the powers that be that I could succeed in making this enormous reduction. But in the end we received the approval from headquarters. Our final methodology template fit onto one page and we rolled it out to the project teams. Unfortunately, nobody used it. We'll get back to that in just a moment.

Of course the point here isn't that passion drives you to shave off parts of your PMO. The point is that it makes you want to go beyond what it expected. You want to look beyond the obvious assignment and deliver outstanding results. It is the kind of passion that you want to instill and harness in your PMO team. You want them to deliver an outstanding PMO portal, exceptional methodology, and terrific templates. You want them to be dazzling during user training and anyone calling for assistance will get superior support in applying the PMO processes. Your ability to instill this almost fanatical mindset in your PMO team can make an enormous difference in successfully rolling out and sustaining a PMO.

This starts with you. If you are not passionate about your own involvement with the PMO, if you cannot communicate the enormous trickle-down effect that the PMO will have company wide, then your results will only go so far. However, if you deliver your arguments with the appropriate level of intensity and zest then you not only capture the interest of management and team members, you might even see the spark jump over.

But sometimes that spark just doesn't jump. No matter how great and fabulous your PMO might be, people are too wrapped up in their current ways to see the future business benefit in becoming a more mature organization. This was one of three reasons why the remarkable one-page methodology did not get adopted no matter what we tried. The other two reasons were that we were lacking any formal authority to make people use it and that nobody in the senior management team was pushing the issue. There we were with a fabulous one-page methodology that nobody in our division wanted to use or support but which was mandated by the overall company. So I devised a cunning plan: I did absolutely nothing about it.

I knew that I was powerless to make anyone follow the recommendations of our divisional PMO because we were lacking authority. No matter how passionate I was there was no way that I could talk anyone into understanding that we needed this new maturity provided by the PMO in our division to move ahead. But I also knew that its usage was a corporate mandate and that the auditors would be at our doorstep in about six months. Therefore, for the next four months all I did is keep tally. The number of our small projects that did not follow the new processes quickly reached several hundred. We then presented this figure, combined with a few remarks about the impending arrival of the auditors, to senior management. Seventy-two hours later we had hired two technical writers and the teams in the division were instructed to work with them to create all required documentation. It was a rough time, but we managed to get the documentation ready for the audit even though the ink was sometimes not dry as we handed the documents to the auditors. Since then the one-page methodology has been used consistently.

This example nicely illustrates that passion without authority is useless. It also shows that passion combined with authority and an accelerator—such as auditors—is an excellent motivator. Therefore, the support of senior management is imperative for PMO success. This is nothing new because every author or consultant worth their money reminds you of it. The trouble is figuring out how to accomplish it.

So let's take everything that we have discussed so far and create a model for passion. While the specific approach differs from PMO to PMO, the following basic components apply (see Figure 13.3). Located at the center of the model we find the results for which we are all striving. Around these results we find the triple constraints of passion, which we have seen throughout the examples in this chapter: challenges, vision, and actions. If you analyze the making of

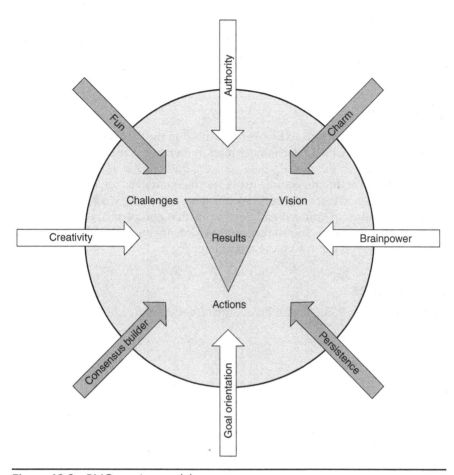

Figure 13.3 PMO passion model

any great invention, booming business, or successful PMO, you come to the conclusion that the men and women involved created the positive results by working with these three components. They are given a challenge and then develop a vision that is turned into reality through their actions.

Passion, however, is more than just these triple constraints. One could argue that any given task, assignment, or project revolves around this triangle; but to create passion several other essential elements are required. The first four of these elements, shown as the white arrows, are generic. Every passionate approach needs authority, creativity, brainpower, and goal orientation. Think of any passionate person around you and you find that they have all of these qualities. The second four, shown as the gray arrows, are personal. This is where PMO team members puts themselves into the equation. For myself, I found that fun, persistence, and consensus building with a dash of charm were the ingredients that completed my personal passion. Yours might be different. It is up to you to discover your own recipe for passion.

Summary

If you are on a journey to rediscover your passion for PMOs or are looking for a way to kindle the PMO passion in others, remember that passion is personal. As we have seen in the model, there are basic building blocks needed to create passion. However, the diagram is just a starting point. Passion does not follow a roadmap; it has to come from within. Use the model and personalize it. Find the qualities in yourself and your team that complete the model, ignite your passion, and allow you to realize the vision of your PMO. Once you have found the key, you can watch the magic happen.

References

Hertzfeld, Andy.1983. "Saving Lives." http://www.folklore.org.

Index